SO-BSB-282

THE WORKING PRINCIPLES
OF ARGUMENT

THE MACMILLAN COMPANY
NEW YORK · BOSTON · CHICAGO · DALLAS
ATLANTA · SAN FRANCISCO

MACMILLAN & CO., Limited
LONDON · BOMBAY · CALCUTTA
MELBOURNE

THE MACMILLAN COMPANY
OF CANADA, Limited
TORONTO

THE WORKING PRINCIPLES
OF ARGUMENT

BY

JAMES MILTON O'NEILL
HEAD OF THE DEPARTMENT OF SPEECH
UNIVERSITY OF MICHIGAN

AND

JAMES HOWARD McBURNEY
DEPARTMENT OF SPEECH
UNIVERSITY OF MICHIGAN

NEW YORK
THE MACMILLAN COMPANY
1932

Set up and electrotyped.   Published January, 1932.

SET UP AND ELECTROTYPED BY J. S. CUSHING CO.
PRINTED BY THE BERWICK & SMITH CO.

PREFACE

This book is an attempt to present a clear, carefully organized exposition of the fundamental working principles of argument in relation to the various situations in which argument plays a part. We have sought to treat the basic principles of all argument, from platform debate and public address to the informal arguments of everyday conversation. Our first effort at every point has been to achieve an accurate and thoroughly fundamental treatment consistent with acceptable principles and doctrines in such related fields as psychology, logic, and rhetoric. We have, moreover, kept constantly in mind the objective of promoting proficiency in the oral and written presentation of argument.

A new classification of propositions, including the overt-action proposition, a chapter on the audience, a complete analysis of argumentative types, and a consideration of the physiological factors in persuasion have been added to a discussion of issues, evidence, briefing, composition, delivery, and the fields of argument. A special chapter on debating, discussing objectives and methods in contest debating, has also been included. In chapters on Confirmation, Explanation, and Motivation are treated not only inductive and deductive argument or linear inference, but also the implicative system, and a methodology for arousing and associating desire with the propositions argued. This synthesis, we feel, has the merit of a greater unity and completeness than has been achieved in previous treatments of the subject.

While this volume is designed especially as a textbook for

college and university courses in argumentation, persuasion, and debate, it is hoped that it will prove stimulating and instructive to any mature reader who is interested in acquiring knowledge and proficiency in the field of argument.

We wish to express our obligation and appreciation to Professor Craven Laycock, Dean of the Academic Faculty and Professor of Public Speaking at Dartmouth College; to Professor Andrew T. Weaver, Professor of Speech at the University of Wisconsin; to Professor James A. Winans, Professor of Public Speaking at Dartmouth College; to Professor William E. Utterback, Professor of Public Speaking at Oberlin College; to Professor A. Craig Baird, Professor of Speech at the University of Iowa; to the late Robert L. Scales, Instructor in English in Dartmouth College; and to many others upon whose works we have drawn either consciously or unconsciously in preparing this text.

J. M. O'N.
J. H. McB.

THE UNIVERSITY OF MICHIGAN
December, 1931

CONTENTS

vii

THE WORKING PRINCIPLES
OF ARGUMENT

CHAPTER I

THE SCOPE OF ARGUMENT

CHAPTER OUTLINE

I. ARGUMENT DEFINED

Ever since the days of Corax, Aristotle, Quintillian, Cicero, and the other ancient rhetoricians, numerous attempts have been made to classify the objectives of discourse. Perhaps the most generally accepted and most useful classification lists five such objectives, to instruct, to convince, to actuate, to impress, and to entertain. Argument is concerned with two of these general speech purposes, to convince, and to actuate. It may be defined in terms of these objectives as the art of influencing others, through the medium of reasoned discourse, to *believe* or *act* as one wishes them to believe or act.

Some of the more recent writers in this field have been contending that in the final analysis there is but one objective of argument and that objective is *action*. This apparent disagreement is due largely, we feel, to a failure to agree on the meaning of the term *action* rather than to any very fundamental difference of opinion. If action is used in its broadest sense to mean response of all types, ranging from inward, neural activity to such overt acts as chopping wood and going to the theater, then action most certainly is the sole objective of discourse for the simple reason that the term has been defined to include every reaction that human beings are capable of making. On the other hand, if action is used in its narrower and more generally accepted meaning, it refers to overt movement, or those responses which involve the visible movement of the body through appreciable space. It is with this narrower meaning in mind that we define argument as the art of influencing the *belief* and *action* of others through the medium of reasoned discourse. While belief may constitute a form of activity (reverting to the broader meaning) in that it is reducible to so much neural and incipient muscular activity, we feel that it is profitable for our study nevertheless, to observe the distinction between this inner activity or belief, and overt action. In the words of Professor Winans, " If we say the only difference between believing and acting is one of extension, still we must recognize that difference." [1]

Another term in our definition which might require some interpretation is *reasoned discourse*. By reasoned discourse we mean that language which groups known truths and

[1] Winans, James A., *Public Speaking*, p. 186. The Century Company, 1923.

accepted premises in relationships which will cause readers or hearers to accept new truths or conclusions. These relationships may be such as to prove the conclusion, imply its truth, or merely motivate its acceptance. In any case it is a dynamic process which generates new ideas and conclusions from existing facts and beliefs. As such it is to be distinguished from pure narrative discourse, descriptive discourse, and other rhetorical forms which present more or less static pictures of existing facts and conditions. To the mere exhibiting of thought, argument adds the process of establishing or enforcing it as truth, or at least as accepted conclusions upon which conviction and conduct may be based.

II. The Importance of Argument

A. Importance to Society. — Having assigned to the field of argument that discourse which has as its objective the influencing of the belief and action of other people, we easily recognize its social significance. Wherever people live together countless adjustments in both their thinking and acting must be made if they are to get along. As society becomes more complex socially, economically, and politically, there is an ever increasing need for such adjustments. Certainly one of the most powerful agencies with which this need may be met is argument, as it appears in the press, over the radio, from the public platform, in legislative halls, in committee rooms, and what is probably more important, as it appears in the homes, the churches, and places of business and recreation of the various communities in which people live. As a means of effecting adjustments in the thinking and acting of other people, argument both written and spoken, fulfills a valuable social function which should be appreciated by every student of the subject.

B. Importance to the Individual. — Of equal interest is the importance of argument to the individual. Skill in argument must be looked upon as a great asset to any person and as a requisite to leadership in many fields of endeavor. Professional people such as lawyers, clergymen, salesmen, and most executives in business and commercial enterprises of all kinds, find proficiency in this art especially helpful. But one does not have to be interested in business, law, or any other particular profession in order to realize its benefits. As a means of influencing the thinking and acting of the people with whom we associate, it can contribute immeasurably to the happiness and well being of anyone who is proficient in its use. It is this factor which we would emphasize.

Aside from the advantages of being able to persuade others to think and act as you wish them to think and act, an intelligent conception of the principles of argument presents some rather definite defensive values. Regardless of one's own inclinations to participate in argument, it is certain that he must listen to the efforts of others. Salesmen, promoters, politicians, lawyers, advertisers, newspapermen, clergymen, and next door neighbors are going to argue with you. If fallacious and groundless argument prevails, it is because people are susceptible to that sort of thing. Certainly one effective way to combat the evils of sophistry and false propaganda is through careful instruction in the principles and methods of sound argument.

III. Educational Values

Our discussion of the importance of argument to society and to the individual has doubtless suggested many of its educational values. A brief summary of these values, however, may assist the student in realizing them more fully as he progresses in his study of the subject.

A. The first and foremost of these, as we have already said, is the cultivation of the ability to persuade others to think or act as you may wish them to think or act.

B. Closely related and of almost equal importance is the cultivation of the ability to size up problems and draw intelligent conclusions. Every day of their lives people are making hundreds of decisions varying from those affecting their whole careers to minor matters of passing importance. Surely the ability to see these problems concisely, to array the facts pro and con, to weigh the objections; in short, the ability to argue them through to a careful conclusion for their own benefit and satisfaction, is an ability of definite educational value. There is probably no course of study in the whole curriculum of the average college or university which can more rightfully lay claim to this value than a properly presented course in argument.

C. The study of argument also affords an excellent exercise in speech. There is a close relation between speech and argument. Argument is not persuasive unless it is effectively presented; and since most argument is delivered orally, the need for good speech is evident. It should be said also that even written argument is composed best in oral style, that is, in composition that delivers well. Whether the argument is oral or written, a student of argument benefits definitely by knowledge of speech composition and presentation.

It is equally true that the speaker benefits from a knowledge of the principles of argument. Much of our speech is argumentative in nature, and all utterance can profit by the clear, logical thinking which is essential to competence in argument.

IV. The Fields of Argument

In a later chapter we shall take up the fields of argument more fully.[1] We feel it important at this point, however, to correct some very common misconceptions concerning the scope of our study. Having defined argument as the art of

[1] See Chapters XVII and XVIII.

influencing the thinking or acting of others through reasoned discourse, we have indicated our field of study only in a general way. More specifically we are interested in argumentative speaking and writing of all kinds ranging from the most formal public address to the most informal arguments on the street corner and across the dinner table. We are interested in sales' arguments, legislative speeches, campaign speeches, debate, in public discussion, and in argumentative conversation. We do not wish students of this text to labor under the erroneous impression that the principles of argument set forth in these pages are applicable only to a few formal speeches delivered from the public platform. Nothing is further from the truth. This study is concerned with all argument, and since, as we have seen, every person must argue and be exposed to the argument of others, we feel that we are dealing with an activity with which every person is directly concerned.

A. Relation to Debate. — Another misconception concerning a course in argument arises from the failure to distinguish between argumentation and debate. College and university students frequently shy from such a course because they think they are not interested in debating. We wish to make it perfectly clear that argument is not synonymous with debate, nor should a course in argument be looked upon as a course in debate. Debate is one form of argument to be sure, and it is difficult to conceive of an individual making much progress in debate without a thorough competence in argument. The field of argument, however, is much more comprehensive than that of debate, and as students of argument we are concerned with this larger field.

Contest debating as practiced in colleges and universities offers excellent training in argument if properly conducted. No course in argument should overlook the opportunities for training presented by contests in debate within the class, or between classes, or even with other colleges and universities where the circumstances permit. To make skill in contest debating *the* objective of a course in argument, however, is a case of mistaking a means for an end.

V. RELATION TO OTHER FIELDS

Argument was defined earlier in the chapter as an art. It is an art which applies principles derived largely from other fields. These fields are principally psychology, biology, logic, rhetoric, law, and speech. Argument assembles certain principles from these fields and states them in a terminology suitable for their application to a highly important human activity. The student of argument needs to make no academic bow to his creditors, because it is he who is investing the capital where it will bring returns.

A. Psychology. — Since belief and action are the objectives of the persuader, we turn to psychology for information concerning the principles and mechanisms governing human reactions. If the speaker is to be effective in modifying the beliefs and actions of his audience, it is imperative that he know something about audience types and some of the more important factors determining their behavior. It is such knowledge that enables the arguer to adjust himself and his argument to the particular audience he has before him in such a way as to elicit the desired response.

B. Biology. — We derive similar assistance from biology. After all, the arguer is attempting to control the behavior of an organism whose thinking and acting is conditioned to no small extent by its own biological needs. Every human being is strongly motivated by the fundamental urges, to feed, to reproduce, to protect, and to conquer or excel. For that reason, many of the most persuasive argumentative appeals derive their force either directly or indirectly from their power to evoke these basic biological drives.

C. Logic. — Logic is another important contributor to argument. In every argument the persuader is endeavoring to lead an audience to think or act in some desired way. One of the most usual methods of achieving this desired belief or action is to present *proof* of the proposition under discussion. The requirements of proof are logical considerations. The logician is interested in these proof requirements from the standpoint of establishing the truth or falsity of propositions; the arguer is interested from the standpoint of influencing the thinking and acting of his fellow-men.

D. Rhetoric. — From rhetoric we derive principles necessary to the composition of good argument, methods and techniques to aid the persuader in stating his argument in good language.

E. Law. — Law gives us many of the forms in which argument appears. The brief or outline used in argument is a modified form of the typical legal brief. Many of the conventions, forms, and methods used in debating are borrowed from law. Perhaps the chief contributions, however, are in the study of evidence, analysis, and issues. Nowhere have these important phases of argument been given such a thorough treatment as in law.

F. Speech. — We have already observed the close relation between speech and argument. Oral argument is a form of communication which is conducted through speech symbols. In other words, it is a specialized type of speech. Thus, it is from speech that argument derives many of those principles which make its effective communication possible.

VI. SUMMARY

This chapter has explained the nature and importance of argument. We have shown it to be a universal human activity which plays a significant rôle in social adjustment and in individual well being. We have set up some definite educational values which the student can reasonably hope to achieve through a careful study and application of the principles of argument. We have allocated our subject in the curriculum and indicated its relations to the sciences whose principles it applies.

EXERCISES

1. Discuss the following quotation in relation to the distinction we have drawn between belief and action.

"There is very little, if any, qualitative difference between a thought and an overt action, subjectively considered. The behaviorists tell us that action involves movements of the muscles through appreciable space, while thought involves an increase in the tone or tension of the muscles, but that both are distinct activities. Nor did one need to wait for the behaviorists to point out this fact. Spinoza said the same thing years ago. *Belief* and *Action* as separate ends of composition are no longer accredited by progressive thinkers." — Collins and Morris, *Persuasion and Debate*, p. viii.

2. Discuss the following quotation in relation to the advisability of distinguishing between belief and action.

"Nothing would seem to be a plainer lesson of experience than that we mortals often leave undone those things we know we ought to do and do those things we know we ought not to do; yet this truth is constantly ignored by speakers, and with bad results. This truth is proverbial: 'The spirit is willing, but the flesh is weak'; *Video meliora proboque; deteriora sequor.* Certain knowledge that lack of exercise is undermining one's health does not necessarily drive one out of doors; yet one does not for a moment believe that one's work or pleasure is worth the cost. There must be, then, more than intellectual acceptance of truth to secure action." — J. A. Winans, *Public Speaking*, p. 187.

3. Discuss the following definitions and compare them with our definition of argument. What conclusion do you draw as to the three terms defined?

"*Argument* is the rhetorical process of influencing the belief and conduct of a hearer or reader by supplying him with reasons and motives for action." — A. Craig Baird, *Public Discussion and Debate*, p. 3.

"*Argumentation* is the art of influencing thought and conduct by an appeal addressed primarily to the understanding." — Winans and Utterback, *Argumentation*, p. 3.

"*Persuasion* is that form of instrumental composition which is used by a writer or speaker to influence a particular audience to shape its conduct (whether thought or action) in conformity with his desire." — Collins and Morris, *Persuasion and Debate*, p. 4.

4. A common distinction between argumentation and persuasion is that argumentation is primarily an intellectual appeal designed to secure belief or conviction while persuasion is primarily an emotional appeal for action.

Be prepared to give a three minute oral statement defending or opposing this distinction. Cite definite reasons for your position and cite authorities where possible.

CHAPTER II

THE PROPOSITION

11

I. THE NATURE OF PROPOSITIONS

A. The Proposition Defined. — The proposition may be defined as the expression of a judgment in language. The individual mind arrives at a judgment as a result of its own reasoning processes. This judgment is stated in a declarative sentence consisting of two terms and a copula. The subject of the sentence is one term; the verb is the copula or the connecting agent; and the object of the verb or some other predicative expression is the other term. When the judgment is so stated you have a proposition.

The following table divides several propositions into their two terms and copula:

First Term	Copula	Second Term
Sugar	is	sweet.
The United States	should	join the World Court.
Chain Stores	are	detrimental to the public.
Capital Punishment	should	be abolished.

B. The Proposition Distinguished from Other Topics for Discussion. — Every argumentative discussion should have a proposition as the topic for discussion. For instance, if a person were asked to speak or write on the topic *Woodrow Wilson*, he could narrate Wilson's life, or describe him as a man, but he could not argue any phase of this subject at all effectively without first phrasing a proposition. Usually, several propositions relating to any particular topic can be phrased. In the case of Woodrow Wilson it is conceivable that any of the following propositions might be argued: Wilson was the greatest President since Lincoln; Wilson's position on the League of Nations was sound; the Federal Government should appropriate money for a Wilson memorial.

A single term can constitute an adequate topic for many types of speaking and writing, but a proposition is the only adequate topic for argument.

C. The Forms in Which Propositions Are Stated. — In formal debate the proposition is usually stated in the form of a resolution as — *Resolved:* That a Federal Department of Education should be established, with a Secretary seated in the President's Cabinet. In less formal argument the proposition usually appears in the form of an expression of opinion such as, I think we ought to go to the theater tonight, or I believe the Federal Government ought to subsidize the farmer. The mistake should not be made of assuming that there is no proposition simply because it is not stated as a resolution.

Not infrequently the proposition may be announced in the form of a question or as a single term for the sake of convenience or more attractive statement. In advertising public debates, for instance, the proposition is often stated on posters or handbills in the form of a challenging interrogation, Shall Education Be Given a Place in the Federal Government? or, Shall the Farmer Be Protected? It is also a common practice to speak of a person as having argued the tariff, or prohibition, or some other single term. There is no harm in using these abbreviated forms so long as the student realizes that they are merely representative of the proposition which is basic to the argument.

II. The Functions of the Proposition

A. To Serve as the Basis of the Argument. — A proposition should be the basis of every argument. No intelligent argumentative discourse can take place in the absence of a proposition.   This is true no matter how formal or how informal the controversy may be.   It is not always necessary nor always wise for the persuader to express the proposition to the audience, but it should *always be phrased* for his own use.

In those cases where a single individual is presenting one side of an argument to an audience, a well phrased proposition is necessary if the persuader is to make an adequate analysis and an organized presentation of his subject; and a statement of the proposition will greatly assist the audience in following the argument and profiting by it, except of course in those cases where some preconceived prejudice, hostility toward the cause, or other reason, makes it seem best to withhold such a statement.

In arguments where two or more persons are engaged and both sides are being presented, a carefully phrased proposition is essential if the controversy is to be directed and kept within proper bounds.   Time after time people engage in long heated discussions only to find that they have been in perfect agreement from the outset.   Many such pointless and futile arguments could be avoided if at least one of the disputants would make it a rule to clarify the proposition before starting to argue.

Whether you are participating in argument as an auditor or as one of the disputants, always phrase the proposition for your own benefit; and wherever propriety and good taste permit, take such steps as will insure a clear discernment by the other participants of the proposition at issue.

B. To Name the Affirmative and the Negative. — There are two sides to every argument, the affirmative and the negative.   The side which affirms the proposition is known as the *affirmative* and the side which opposes the proposition is known as the *negative*.

In some arguments there may appear to be more than two sides. In fact, judging from the number of *positions* taken on certain propositions, it might seem that there were almost an infinite number of sides. This apparent multiplicity of sides, however, is due to the fact that people affirm or deny propositions for substantially different reasons. For example, you might oppose the proposition that Mary buy a new fur coat because you thought she didn't need one, and some one else might oppose the same proposition because he thought she would look better in a cloth garment. While the stands taken would be quite different *positions*, both would be negative on this proposition nevertheless.

We may say, then, that there can be as many *positions* on a given proposition as the occasion and the idiosyncracies of the disputants happen to provoke, but there can be only two *sides*, the affirmative and the negative.

C. To State the Action Demanded of the Audience. — We have already seen that thought and action are the universal objectives of the persuader. It is the proposition that states the thought or action demanded of the listener, and the adequacy of the argument is determined by the willingness or disposition of the listener to react as the proposition suggests. On the proposition that a certain audience endorse the entrance of the United States into the World Court, the argument must be evaluated on its effectiveness in securing such endorsement; and on the proposition that Mrs. Jones buy a new set of Fuller brushes, the merit of the argument must be measured in terms of its ability so to actuate Mrs. Jones. For our purposes the demands of the situation have been satisfied only in the degree that the reactor is led to think or act as the proposition suggests. Variable as this standard of achievement may be, any other test of the efficiency of argument must necessarily prove artificial and impractical. To set up an abstract, philosophical basis upon which to evaluate the success of argument, independent of the reaction tendencies of the audience, is a practice altogether too prevalent now and certainly one inimical to good argument.

D. To Place the Burden of Proof. — On every proposition that is argued, there is one side which will be dissatisfied if no action is taken. If a certain individual is anxious to have the street paved past his property, it is he who will be disappointed if no action is taken on the proposition that it be paved. Since he will be the party to lose if nothing is done, it devolves upon him to advance the proposition, or in other words, to go forward with the argument. This responsibility is known as the burden of proof. It can be defined as a burden, inherent in every proposition, which rests upon that party to an argument who will be dissatisfied if the action embodied in the proposition is not taken. O'Neill, Laycock, and Scales have the following to say regarding the burden of proof :

> "It is a concept used to represent the 'risk of the proposition,' the burden upon that party to the controversy who will lose if nothing is done. It is the burden of making good his claim which rests upon the one who starts an action, who demands a change from the existing situation." [1]

We have already defined the affirmative as the side which affirms the proposition and the negative as the side which opposes the proposition. It now becomes necessary to distinguish between the nominal affirmative and the actual affirmative, and the nominal negative and the actual negative. While the nominal affirmative is the side which affirms the proposition, the actual affirmative is always the side which has the burden of proof. Likewise, the nominal negative is always the side which opposes the proposition and the actual negative is the side which does not have the burden

[1] O'Neill, James M., Laycock, Craven, and Scales, R. L., *Argumentation and Debate*, p. 34. The Macmillan Company, 1917.

of proof, or the party who will be satisfied if the action stated in the proposition is not taken. *In a well phrased proposition both the actual and nominal affirmative and the actual and nominal negative will coincide.*

Consider the following propositions as examples:

> *Resolved:* That the United States should protect its investments in foreign countries.
>
> *Resolved:* That the United States should cease to protect its investments in foreign countries.

Since the United States now follows the policy of protecting its investments in foreign countries, the side which says " yes " to the first proposition (the nominal affirmative) will be satisfied if no action is taken, and is therefore the actual negative. On this same proposition the side which says " no " (the nominal negative) is the actual affirmative, because it is the side which will be dissatisfied if nothing is done. The second proposition is correctly reworded so that the nominal affirmative coincides with the actual affirmative, and the nominal negative coincides with the actual negative.

III. A CLASSIFICATION OF PROPOSITIONS

Propositions may be classified broadly as those of Policy and those of Fact. Propositions of policy are characterized by the fact that they always suggest a change in policy or a new policy, that is, some departure from the status quo. Every proposition of policy raises the question — Should this be done? The following are propositions of policy:

> *Resolved:* That capital punishment should be abolished.
>
> *Resolved:* That John Doe should buy a new Ford automobile.
>
> *Resolved:* That the regulation prohibiting the operation of motor vehicles by students of the University of Michigan should be abolished.
>
> *Resolved:* That you should vote for John Doe as mayor of Ann Arbor.

Propositions of fact, on the other hand, may be identified by the fact that they do not suggest any change from the status quo. They simply raise the question — Is this true? They state an alleged fact without any reference to action. The following are propositions of fact:

> *Resolved:* That installment buying is detrimental to the people of the United States.
>
> *Resolved:* That the next President will be a Democrat.
>
> *Resolved:* That term life insurance is a good investment.

A. Propositions of Policy. — In considering propositions of policy it will be discovered that there are two rather clearly defined types, both of which express changes in the status quo, and both of which raise the question — Should this be done?

1. OVERT-ACTION PROPOSITIONS. — First of all there are those propositions which call for personal, overt action. This is the type of proposition defended by the persuader who is seeking definite, overt action from his listeners. The salesman who is urging people to buy, the politician who is urging people to vote, the solicitor who is urging people to contribute, and countless others who are arguing for some change in the overt conduct of their associates are advocating matters of personal policy of this kind. We shall refer to propositions of policy of this type as overt-action propositions.

2. POLICY-ENDORSEMENT PROPOSITIONS. — A second kind of proposition of policy is that which calls simply for the endorsement or acceptance of a certain policy. These propositions are to be distinguished from overt-action propositions in that they call for the endorsement or approval of action to be taken by the federal government, the state, the county, the city, or by some other person or group of persons, rather than calling for direct personal action. Most of the propositions debated by colleges and universities in recent years have

been policy endorsement propositions. The following are illustrations:

> *Resolved:* That the United States should enter the World Court of International Justice.
>
> *Resolved:* That the several states should adopt a system of compulsory unemployment insurance.
>
> *Resolved:* That a Federal Department of Education should be established.

It is clear that a school debate on any of these propositions has endorsement of the policy under question as the objective rather than overt action of any kind; and so have countless other arguments which take place wherever people get together to discuss matters of public policy. In fact, in many cases of this kind the listeners are unable to act in the matter even though it is their inclination to do so. In many cases they do not have the necessary authority. United States senators may be able to take direct, personal action to effect the entrance of the United States into the World Court; likewise, state representatives may be able to adopt a system of unemployment insurance; but the average person is able to do little more than approve or disapprove of such policies. Nor does the fact that the average person can evidence his approval or disapproval by such overt acts as signing a petition, raising his hand in affirmation, etc., in-validate the fact that there are innumerable occasions on which mere endorsement with no overt accompaniment of any kind is the objective of the persuader.

In short, we are saying that there is a substantial and worthwhile distinction between propositions of policy which seek personal action from the audience, and those which seek the endorsement of certain action to be taken by someone else. We shall refer to the class of propositions discussed in this section as policy-endorsement propositions.

B. Propositions of Fact. — We also find it helpful to distinguish two types of factual propositions. A comparison of the proposition, *Resolved:* That the chain store is detrimental to the people of the United States, and the proposition, *Resolved:* That a straight line is the shortest distance between two points, will illustrate the distinction we have in mind.

1. PROPOSITIONS ADVOCATED AS THEORETICALLY SOUND. — While both of the above propositions are propositions of fact in that they suggest no change from the status quo and raise the question — Is this true?, the chain store proposition very apparently partakes of the nature of a proposition of policy as the other example does not. Baird refers to propositions of the nature of the chain store example as *propositions advocated as theoretically sound.* He has this to say regarding them :

> "A proposition of this type consists of an affirmation or denial that an alleged policy is theoretically desirable." [1]

Propositions advocated as theoretically sound differ from propositions of policy in that they do not suggest any change from the status quo ; they do not call for personal action, nor do they call for the endorsement of a policy change. The only question that is raised is the *desirability* of a given policy, entirely apart from the question of adopting or abolishing the policy. This distinction can be seen quite readily by comparing the two following propositions :

> *Resolved:* That the chain store should be abolished.
>
> *Resolved:* That the chain store is detrimental to the people of the United States.

The first of these propositions is one of policy calling for the endorsement of a specific policy change. The second is a proposition of fact calling for the indictment of a specific

[1] Baird, A. Craig, *Public Discussion and Debate,* p. 41. Ginn and Company, 1928.

institution without any implications as to the question of its abolition. We shall follow Baird in referring to the class of propositions discussed in this section as propositions advocated as theoretically sound.

2. PURE OR UNMIXED QUESTIONS OF FACT. — To complete our classification there remain to be discussed pure or unmixed questions of fact which are illustrated by the example already cited, *Resolved:* That a straight line is the shortest distance between two points. " Such propositions consist of statements that affirm or deny: (1) The existence of things; (2) The occurrence of acts; (3) The classification of objects; or (4) The connection of events." [1]

The following propositions are affirmations of the four classes of facts which are usually alleged by propositions of this kind:

Resolved: That there is gold in Sheldon's Canyon.

Resolved: That John Brown committed suicide.

Resolved: That (X) is an independent municipality.

Resolved: That the pistol was purchased before the murder.

IV. SELECTING THE PROPOSITION

A. Where It Is Imposed by the Circumstances. — Selecting the proposition does not always imply an independent choice. In fact, more often than not the exigencies of the occasion impose the proposition upon the disputants. When your chickens invade a neighbor's garden, he may make them the subject of argument without consulting your choice in the matter. When the automobile runs out of gasoline, if any argument takes place, it will doubtless center around the proposition as to how best to replenish the gasoline. In such cases the problem of selection is at least greatly limited, and becomes more a matter of careful discernment. See the

[1] Shaw, W. C., *The Art of Debate*, pp. 20–21. Allyn and Bacon, 1922.

issue imposed by the circumstances of the case and phrase the proposition accordingly.

B. Where a Deliberate Choice Is Made. — Selecting the proposition is quite a different problem when the persuader is making a deliberate choice of a subject for argument in public debate or in private conversation. Here the following suggestions may help to direct this choice.

1. SELECT A PROPOSITION WHICH CAN BE ARGUED PROFITABLY. — Many futile arguments take place on propositions which could be much better demonstrated by other means. Do not argue about the width of the street, the date of John's birthday, or any other subject which can be quickly and accurately determined by an investigation of the matter. Many propositions of fact are subjects of this nature, and for this reason the proposition of fact is usually less adapted to argument than the other types we have discussed. This is particularly true of the pure or unmixed questions of fact.

On the other hand there are many subjects which can be demonstrated in no better way than by good argument. The effectiveness of argument as a means of influencing the conduct of others from a purely utilitarian point of view has already been observed. Where instructive entertainment is the objective, propositions of policy involving national, state, and local affairs of social, economic, and political consequence are excellent subjects for argument.

2. SELECT A PROPOSITION ADAPTED TO THE PERSUADER. — Not all dull subjects are inherently dull, nor are all interesting subjects inherently interesting. Much of the dullness and much of the interestingness attaching to any argument must be attributed to the speaker or writer himself. Choose your proposition from those fields in which your study and experience enables you to say something of interest and profit. It is a strange fact that many persons seem most reluctant to speak about the very thing at which they spend most of

their time and about which they are most competent to speak. Yet it is axiomatic that your chances of interesting others will be greatly increased if you select subjects which are vital and interesting to you.

3. SELECT A PROPOSITION ADAPTED TO THE AUDIENCE. — The persuader should choose a subject which *he can make interesting to his audience.* This is in no way inconsistent with the previous suggestion that propositions of interest to the speaker should be chosen. It is difficult to conceive of any intelligent person, *competent in argument,* who could not find propositions of interest to himself, which could be persuasively presented to others, if the propositions were chosen with the interests of the various audiences in mind.

Not only should the proposition be of interest to the audience, or of such nature that the audience can be interested in it, but the action stated in the proposition should be such that it is clearly possible for those to whom the argument is addressed so to act. Time and again argument fails because the action sought is beyond the capabilities of the listeners. People most assuredly cannot be persuaded to think or do things that are beyond their abilities to comprehend or undertake.

4. THE PROPOSITION SHOULD BE ADAPTED TO THE OCCASION. — Subjects suitable for argument at one place and at one time are not necessarily suitable to all occasions or even to another occasion. The common rules of timeliness and propriety which are applicable to any other type of speaking or writing should be applied to argumentative discourse.

V. PHRASING THE PROPOSITION

We have already seen that the proposition should serve four important functions in an argument. It serves as the basis of the argument; it names the affirmative and the negative; it states the action demanded of the audience;

and it places the burden of proof. The application of the following rules will assist the student in phrasing a proposition which will adequately meet these demands.

A. The Action Demanded of the Audience Should Be Stated in a Single Declarative Sentence. — This should be a concise, accurate statement of the exact thing that you wish the audience to think or do.

B. The Burden of Proof Should Be on the Affirmative. — The proposition should always be so phrased as to place the burden of proof on the nominal affirmative; that is, to make the nominal affirmative coincide with the actual affirmative. Failure to do this will confuse the responsibilities of both the affirmative and the negative as we have seen earlier in this chapter.

Attention should be called to the fact that it is frequently necessary to state the proposition *negatively* in order to make the nominal affirmative and actual affirmative coincide. A proposition cited earlier in the chapter illustrates this point, *Resolved:* That the United States should *not* protect its investments in foreign countries. This proposition and many like it cannot be stated correctly without stating them negatively. The popular impression that it is incorrect to use a negative (not or no) in phrasing the proposition is erroneous.

C. The Proposition Should State the Specific Position of the Affirmative. — Not only should the proposition be so worded as to place the burden of proof on the side which affirms the proposition, but it should also state the specific position of the affirmative. The following proposition, for example, while placing the burden of proof on the affirmative, fails to state the specific position of the affirmative, and is therefore poorly worded, *Resolved:* That the petit jury should be abolished in Michigan. The affirmative position on this proposition as it is stated is vague and indefinite. No one is going to give serious consideration to a suggestion that the petit jury should be abolished unless the suggestion carries with it a plan which can take the place of the jury. Of course, this must be the implication of the above proposition, but it is our point that the proposed substitute should be specified in the proposition. The proposition, *Resolved:* That a judge or board of judges should be substituted for the petit jury in all the courts of Michigan, is a much better phraseology because it does state the exact position of the affirmative.

This rule, while applicable to all propositions, is particularly significant in those cases in which it is suggested that some institution serving a vital and necessary function should be abolished. In all such instances the substitute plan advocated by the affirmative should be definitely stated in the proposition as illustrated in the jury question. Failure to do this confronts the affirmative with an impossible situation.

D. The Proposition Should Embody One and Only One Central Idea. — It is impossible to argue two or more things at the same time and do it effectively. And yet this is a feat that we hear being attempted almost daily by persons untrained in argument. The cause is invariably to be found in a proposition which embodies more than one central idea. Such a multiplicity of central ideas confuses the argument and should be avoided.

The student needs to be cautioned in applying this rule, however, because many propositions which appear to be compound may in reality be simple. Not a few of the propositions introduced in Congress and other legislative bodies illustrate this point. A single bill may call for many activities and yet represent only one central, unitary measure. Take the Curtis-Reed Bill for example. This bill provides for the creation of a Federal Department of Education, a secretary seated in the President's cabinet, the appropriation of a sum of money to finance the activities of the department, and several other related changes. Since all these activities are germane to the central action demanded, namely, the creation of a department of education, the advocacy of this bill constitutes a single proposition and a very satisfactory subject for debate.

E. The Proposition Should Be Stated in Simple Language. — We have already stated that the persuader should select a proposition whose action-demand is capable of fulfillment by the audience. Not infrequently the language of the proposition plays an important part in the apparent difficulty of this demand. Simple things can be made to appear hard, and difficult things made to appear easy by the language in which they are stated. Needless to say, the barrier that you are asking your audience to surmount should be made as simple as possible. Phrase the proposition in the simplest language that will *accurately* express the judgment you desire to argue.

F. The Proposition Should Be Free of Ambiguous Terms. — An ambiguous term is one which can be correctly interpreted to have two or more meanings. The complications which arise in an argument from such phraseology are evident. Both sides will interpret the term to their own liking and insist that their definition is the correct one, with the result that there is no common basis for argument. It is true, of course, that the proposition is always the affirmative's proposition ; it is their proposal, and they have a perfect right to set up their own definitions as long as these definitions are permissible. It is not the negative's business to say what these terms mean unless they believe that the affirmative's definitions are incorrect and they are capable of demonstrating that fact. The unfortunate thing about an ambiguous term is that both sides *think* that their definition is correct, and as a matter of fact, both in all probability are correct ; but since any correct definition is a legitimate definition for the affirmative, the resulting discussion of definition must of necessity always be settled in favor of the affirmative.

There should be no misunderstanding on this point — the negative can and should, if it chooses, challenge any incorrect definition, but where two or more correct definitions are possible, the affirmative has a right to choose any one of them, and the negative must meet them on the definition they select. We might mention in passing that it is frequently possible, and certainly good argument where it is possible, for the negative to protest any questionable definition, give the reasons for its protest, and then proceed under protest to meet the affirmative on its own definition. There is an excellent illustration of this in the university debate recorded in Appendix A.

All terms are somewhat ambiguous and even the most accurate language is apt to permit of more than one interpretation. Certainly every precaution should be taken in phrasing a proposition to avoid needless ambiguity and the resulting confusion.

G. The Proposition Should Be Free of Question-Begging Terms. — A question-begging term is one which is prejudicial to one of the sides in the argument. For example, in the proposition, *Resolved:* That the much needed municipal auditorium should be constructed in Ann Arbor, the term *much-needed* is quite obviously prejudicial. It grants to the affirmative a part of the argument the truth of which that side should fairly be called upon to demonstrate.

VI. Summary

An understanding of the nature, functions, and classes of propositions, and the ability to select and phrase them correctly is an important part of the study of argument. In preparing an argument of any kind the determination of the proposition is the first step. It should be remembered that

this must be done carefully and intelligently before any subsequent steps in the process of preparation can be successfully undertaken.

EXERCISES

1. Phrase one proposition of each of the four types discussed in
this chapter on each of the following subjects :

    a. Unemployment insurance
    b. Football
    c. Capital punishment
    d. The Republican Party

2. Phrase twelve good propositions illustrating each of the four
types discussed in this chapter with three examples.

3. Criticize the following propositions :

    a. *Resolved :* That the paving on State Street should be improved.
    b. *Resolved :* That the jury system should be abolished and a judge
        or board of judges substituted for the jury in all the trial courts
        of the United States.
    c. *Resolved :* That the United States should protect the lives and
        property of its citizens in foreign countries.
    d. *Resolved :* That the jury system should be abolished.
    e. *Resolved :* That our present unjust immigration laws should be
        abolished.

4. Prepare propositions to illustrate each of the seven rules
governing the phrasing of propositions.   Make each proposition
correct in every respect except the point covered by the rule which
is illustrated.   Submit these propositions to the class and let the
members of the class invoke the rule which is violated in each case.

5. Discuss the following statement :

    A given statement of policy might properly be classified as an
overt-action proposition when argued before one audience and as a
policy-endorsement proposition when argued before another audience.
Read Section II of Chapter V in this connection.

6. List five school problems, five state problems, five national
problems, and five international problems which would make good
subjects for debate.

CHAPTER III

INVESTIGATING THE PROPOSITION

I. The Purpose of the Investigation

After the proposition has been phrased, the arguer is confronted with the task of investigating this proposition. Such an investigation may consist of a careful, critical survey of what has been written concerning the proposition, conferences with persons informed concerning the problem, and original studies and experiments relating to the proposition. It is the process of informing one's self regarding the proposition. While it might seem that most students should be more or less familiar with research and research methods, the facts of the case are that the great majority know very little about it and are very much at a loss as to just how to proceed.

II. Investigation and the Phrasing of the Proposition

While we are discussing the investigation of the proposition, as a step to be taken subsequent to the phrasing of the proposition, it should be kept in mind that not infrequently the information disclosed by this investigation will lead the arguer to revise the original wording of the proposition. It is often convenient and in some cases necessary that the investigator begin his study with only a tentative statement of the proposition and then check and revise this statement as his research progresses. This is especially true in those instances in which the arguer wishes the proposition to represent his conclusion regarding the phenomena under investigation.

There are, of course, many other cases in which the arguer is not at liberty to alter the wording of the proposition. In such cases, the investigation of the proposition is simply a matter of discovering the materials pro and con on the question as it is phrased.

III. TYPES OF INVESTIGATION

The types of investigation can be most helpfully classified for our purposes as original and unoriginal research.

A. Original Research. — By original research we mean a first-hand investigation as opposed to a study of the investigations of others. It consists of experimentation or studies, conceived, planned, and conducted by the person drawing the conclusions, or in our case the arguer himself. The writer recalls several original investigations made by university debating teams which will serve as illustrations. One team made a study of the comparative prices in chain stores and independent stores. A typical market basket of standard commodities was priced in a large number of chain stores and independent stores in several different communities, and the results recorded. Another debating team, preparing to discuss the adoption of the Ontario system of liquor control in the United States, availed themselves of the opportunity to visit this Canadian province and observe the operation of the system for themselves. High school debaters discussing the Michigan Jury System dispatched questionnaires to a large number of Michigan judges and recorded the results. In a recent debate between Michigan and Wisconsin, the Wisconsin team presented the conclusions drawn from a questionnaire which they had sent to various authorities on the subject. Wherever it is possible to conduct studies of this kind on a sufficiently comprehensive scale to permit of significant conclusions, the results are of real value both in analyzing the proposition and supporting it in argument. Students of argument should be encouraged to make original investigations.

B. Unoriginal Research. — Unoriginal research consists in studying the investigations of others as they are recorded in books, magazines, pamphlets, and other printed documents.

Wherever conditions are such that it is impossible for the persuader to investigate the phenomena related to the proposition for himself, as accurately and comprehensively as it has already been done by someone else, then he should rely upon the findings of others. Most of the research preparatory to argument is necessarily of the kind we have discussed in this section; *i.e.*, unoriginal.

IV. A PLAN TO DIRECT THE INVESTIGATION

When confronted with the task of investigating the proposition, the immediate question is how best to organize one's research. Since it is important that all phases of the proposition be carefully looked into if one is to be thoroughly prepared for argument, some approach which will insure the completeness of the investigation is much to be desired. We are suggesting a plan of study which with some modification should prove helpful in the investigation of most propositions, especially those of policy. It is not our purpose to imply that every proposition needs to be submitted to the elaborate plan of investigation set forth in this section, but rather to outline a method which may be applied as intensively as the occasion may demand.

A. Surveying the Background of the Proposition. — Certainly the investigation of any proposition should begin with a survey of its background. By that we mean: (1) Discovering the origin of the question; (2) Tracing the history of the question; and (3) Ascertaining the immediate cause for discussion. A knowledge of this background material will aid greatly in the definition and interpretation of the proposition and will assist in arriving at the issues in the question.

1. THE ORIGIN OF THE QUESTION. — The origin of the question is the first consideration in beginning the study of any proposition. Let us see just what is meant by this concept.

" On the one hand the origin does not often go back simply to the time when the question in its present form was first raised ; and on the other, it does not necessarily go back to the establishment of the institutions involved in the question. The origin of the question, in point of time, is when the seed of the controversy was sown; or we may say it lies in the cause for the first serious objection to the situation which the proposition proposes to alter.   For example, the question on government ownership of the railroads had its origin not in the establishment of railroads in this country, but in the first acts of the roads that gave rise to subsequent alleged evils in private ownership.   The origin of a question like that on limiting the power of the Supreme Court, however, is coincident with the establishment of the court, as its power was in the beginning seriously challenged and has been from time to time ever since." [1]

2. THE HISTORY OF THE QUESTION. — " The history of the question begins with the origin of the question, covers all subsequent events relative to it, and virtually terminates in the immediate cause for discussion.   The latter, we may say, is the particular turn in events that makes it important that the proposition be debated at the present moment." [2]   In surveying the history of the question, then, the important thing is to inform one's self regarding the significant events relating to the proposition, beginning with the acts or events which gave rise to the question and terminating in the last event of historical importance.

3. THE IMMEDIATE CAUSE FOR DISCUSSION. — As defined above, the immediate cause for discussion is " the particular turn in events that makes it important that the proposition

---

[1] Wells, Earl William, "A Study of the Technique of Argumentative Analysis as Treated by Ancient and Modern Writers," pp. 175–176. Master's thesis, University of Wisconsin, 1927.

[2] *Ibid.*, p. 176.

be debated at the present moment." In arguing the question
that a federal department of education be established, the
origin of the question might be found in the first efforts to
extend the powers of the federal government in this direction.
The history of the question would certainly involve the various attempts to establish such a department, the Bill of
1867 creating a Department of Education, the subsequent
reduction of this department to the status of a bureau in the
Department of Interior, and the more recent legislative
attempts to restore this bureau to a departmental level.
When this question was argued in 1926 and 1927, the immediate cause for discussion was the introduction into Congress
of the Curtis-Reed Bill proposing the creation of such a department. If the question were to be debated today, the
immediate cause for discussion might be the recent action of
the National Educational Association in going on record once
more in favor of such a department.

The immediate cause for discussion is simply the event or
events which precipitate the argument at any given time.
Sometimes this event may be tremendously important, and
in other instances it may be almost inconsequential. In any
case it should not be confused with the event or events giving
origin to the question.

B. Defining the Terms. — A proposition is valueless unless its meaning is absolutely clear. Any progress in an
investigation is impossible unless this condition is fulfilled.
Obviously, a question may be so simply stated that there can
be no doubt as to its meaning, in which case there is no need
for definition. This is not often the case, however. Accuracy of statement usually necessitates the use of language
which requires some definition. It is a good rule to check
carefully the meaning of each term in the proposition to be
certain that you are interpreting it correctly. Conduct this
study not to verify or corroborate your initial impressions,

but to find out the most accurate definition of the term in the context in which it is used.

In defining terms it is wise to consult the opinions of specialists and experts on the meaning of the terms under question. The best authority on the meaning of any term is the specialist in the field in which the term arises and in which it is most carefully and accurately used. Go to the economist for economic terms, to the chemist for chemical terms, and to the political scientist for terms relating to government and politics. The dictionary is helpful as a source of definition for general, non-technical terms, but on such terms as " property," " state," " amateur athletics," " World Court," " chain store," or any other term which has a technical usage, it is of little value.

The question frequently arises as to whether the definition of terms should not precede the survey of the background of the proposition in investigating the proposition. It is true, of course, that in many cases there must be at least a tentative definition of terms before any investigating can be done. The final definition of terms, however, should always be made in the light of the history of the question. Knowledge of the background of the question many times enables one to get a more appropriate and exact definition of the term in question than he would otherwise be able to obtain. The advantage of a definition drawn from the history of the question is that the definition arises from the question itself rather than being forced upon it and fitted to it.

There are various methods of definition. It has seemed best to discuss these in Chapter X in connection with supporting the proposition by Explanation. Knowledge of these methods is helpful in defining terms for purposes of investigation, and should be utilized in this connection. They are: (1) By classification; (2) By negation; (3) By context; and (4) By example.

step

C. Surveying the Materials for Proving the Proposition. —
After the background of the proposition has been investigated
and the terms carefully defined, the next step is to look into
the evidence and argument bearing on the question. This
survey should in all instances cover both sides of the question. No investigation is adequate preparation for argument which neglects one side of a question. A case drawn
from a one-sided survey will almost invariably be warped,
biased, and inconclusive.

While it is impossible to set up any type survey which will
profitably direct an investigation of the materials for proof
on all propositions, there is a group of questions relating to
all propositions of policy which is of great assistance in ap-
proaching a proposition of this kind. Since every proposition
of policy suggests some change from the status quo, it is
possible to work out certain type questions which will apply
to any proposed policy change. These questions constitute
a comparison of the status quo with the policy change proposed by the proposition and other possible changes. There
are ten such questions:

1. Are there existing evils?
2. Are these evils caused by that part of the status quo which
   the proposition proposes to modify?
3. Are these evils inherent in the present system?
4. Will the plan proposed by the proposition help to reduce
   these evils in some material way?
5. Will the proposed plan bring benefits other than the reduction of existing evils?
6. Will the proposed plan give rise to new and greater evils?
7. Are there other plans which would meet the present needs
   better than the plan proposed in the proposition?
8. Do these plans differ more or less from the status quo
   than the proposed plan?
9. Are these plans counter to the proposed plan?
10. Would such alternative plans give rise to new and greater
    evils to such an extent as to render them impractical?

1. THE PRESENT PLAN. — It will be noted that of these ten questions the first three relate to the desirability of the present system. A brief explanation of these points will make their meaning clear.

First of all, any proposal to do something that we are not now doing, or in other words a proposal to change an existing policy, has a basis only in so far as evils can be shown to exist in the present system. Not only must these evils be shown to exist, but their causation must be traced to the particular institution, practice, or policy which the proposition proposes to modify. Failure to do this, of course, makes it impossible subsequently to establish any causal relation between the diminution of these evils and the plan or remedy proposed in the proposition.

Not only must these evils be pointed out and their cause established, but it is necessary that it be shown that they are inherent in the present system. By that we mean that these evils are an inevitable and unavoidable consequence of the present plan or policy — that they cannot possibly be alleviated without materially changing the existing system. A failure to establish the inherency of the existing evils will very often make it difficult for the arguer to justify any plan abolishing or materially changing an existing institution, because the rejoinder will invariably be brought that these evils can be eradicated by reforming or patching up the present system, thereby removing the necessity for any further change.

An illustration from the proposition that a judge or board of judges be substituted for the jury, will clear up the points we have been discussing. Let us say that it is argued that the jury system causes a great delay in court procedure which it is alleged would be corrected by a judge or board of judges serving in the capacity of jurors. First of all, proof would need to be introduced to show that our trials are being delayed; then it would need to be shown that the jury is the cause of this delay; and further that this evil is the unavoidable result of the jury. Failure to establish this last step would make way for the negative to charge that improvements in the impaneling procedure, cutting down on the number of challenges, and other reforms could remove the evil without necessitating the adoption of the affirmative proposal. It must be made clear that such reforms will not remove the evil, or that they are impractical for other reasons. The inherency of the existing evils must be established.

2. THE PROPOSED PLAN. — It will be observed that of the ten points we have listed, questions 4, 5, and 6 pertain to the desirability of the plan proposed in the proposition. Once we have shown certain inherent evils to exist in the status quo, our investigation should lead us into a consideration of the ability of the proposed plan to reduce these evils. In making this study, the investigator should bear in mind that it is not necessary that a proposed policy be shown to be a panacea or cure-all for existing evils in order to justify its adoption; it is sufficient to show that this proposal will reduce these evils in some material way.

When one is considering the possibilities of the proposed plan in the way of meeting existing evils, it is also profitable to inquire into other positive benefits that might accrue. Many changes are justified not because there is anything outstandingly wrong with the institution they are to replace, but because they will usher in new advantages and new benefits not to be obtained under the old system.

A further consideration of vital importance concerning the desirability of the proposed plan is the possibility of this plan giving rise to new and greater evils. The investigator needs to consider this point very carefully. Will the new plan introduce evils greater than those which it is advocated to correct? Many strong negative arguments are made on this

basis.   In a debate on the advisability of the creation of a
Federal Department of Education, for instance, perhaps the
best negative argument is the charge that such a department
will result in a centralized bureaucracy and a dangerous
Federal control of education.

3. OTHER POSSIBLE PLANS. — Questions 7, 8, 9, and 10
relate to other possible means of meeting existing evils.   The
study of the proposition should be of such nature as to
familiarize the investigator with these plans.   An alternative
plan very frequently plays an important part in an argument
on a proposition of policy.

The first inquiry regarding any such alternative proposal
is its comparative ability to meet existing needs.   The comparison, of course, is made with the plan stated in the proposition.   The investigator should be thoroughly informed
regarding the relative merits of possible counter-plans and
the proposal under discussion.

It is important also to know whether a counter-plan differs
more or less from the status quo than the proposed plan.
For instance, it might be argued in opposition to a proposal
that Mary buy a new three-hundred dollar muskrat coat,
either that she buy a seventy-five dollar cloth garment or a
five-hundred dollar mink coat.   Both of these suggestions,
if properly argued, would constitute legitimate substitute
plans.   The proposal to buy a cloth coat differs less from the
status quo than the affirmative plan, and for that reason it
would need only to be shown that this coat would serve the
purpose *as well as* the muskrat coat in order to defeat the
affirmative plan.   On the other hand, in the case of the mink
coat, since it differs more from the status quo than does the
affirmative plan, it would need to be shown that it would
meet the needs *better* than would the muskrat coat.   This
difference frequently becomes a matter of some importance
in argument and should be thoroughly investigated.

Another point which needs to be looked into when considering possible alternative plans is whether or not these plans are actually counter to the affirmative proposal. Any legitimate substitute proposal must be one which meets the same situation which the affirmative plan is designed to meet, and at the same time is one which cannot possibly work along with the affirmative plan. It must either be totally inconsistent or contain within it certain vital features which are inconsistent with the affirmative proposal. Unless the negative plan really is counter in this way, the affirmative can simply thank the negative for presenting it, accept it bodily, and point out how the two proposals can work together.

The adoption of the negative alternative plan by the affirmative is illustrated by a recent debate on unemployment insurance in which the negative offered an elaborate plan to stimulate building and public works during periods of depression and thereby alleviate the unemployment situation. The affirmative responded by saying that as advocates of unemployment insurance, they had no objection to this scheme or any other plan which would tend to reduce unemployment. They went on to show that there would always be an irreducible minimum of men unemployed, regardless of stabilization plans, and that this was the group which demanded insurance. It was the affirmative position that the negative plan might work side by side with the plan they were offering without eliminating the necessity of their proposal.

The last point in our survey entails a consideration of the possible evils which might develop from a counter proposition. Just as the negative may attack the affirmative proposal by charging that it will create new and greater evils, so can the affirmative respond to a counter proposition with argument that it will create a situation worse than the one it is designed to correct.

This discussion of the survey of the background of the proposition, the definition of terms, and the survey of the materials for proving the proposition has been given primarily to assist the student in investigating the proposition and only secondarily to assist him in building a case. Later chapters will take up the various methods of supporting the proposition and constructing the case.

In presenting the plan for conducting an investigation of the proposition such as we have given in this section, there is always a danger that students will strait-jacket their research therein. Practically every proposition for argument offers helpful and interesting channels of investigation which are peculiar to it alone and therefore not included in any set of guiding questions which purport to be applicable to all propositions. Since this is true, we wish to make it perfectly clear that it is not our intention to so rigidly direct research as to deny the freedom necessary to originality in the investigation of different propositions. The plan we have given is suggestive only. We feel that in most instances it will be profitable, however, to investigate the several points we have raised, especially in studying a proposition of policy.

V. THE USE OF BIBLIOGRAPHY

Most of the investigation in preparation for argument whether the research is original or unoriginal consists in the study of library materials. For that reason we have considered it worth while to take up some of the more important aspects of library study.

A. The Nature and Purpose of Bibliography. — A bibliography is an organized list of references on any subject. Bibliographies are prepared on subjects of interest by librarians, publishers, and others, so that the materials available on a given subject may be found with a minimum amount of effort. In beginning a comprehensive study of any proposition, it is well for the arguer to prepare a bibliography for

his own use. A work of this kind will serve two purposes:
(1) To direct the investigator's own research; and (2) To
preserve the accumulation of references incident to his study
for future research. The preparation of an original bibliography is a much easier task where other bibliographies are
available on the same subject or some closely related subject.
Hence, the first step is to look for other bibliographies.

B. Sources of Bibliography. — Many libraries have bibliographies on file listing all the materials relating to various
subjects which can be found in the library. The Library of
Congress at Washington, D. C., has such bibliographies on
many questions which can be secured by writing to that
source. Text books, theses, and other scholarly treatises
frequently include valuable bibliography at the close of chapters, in footnotes, or in the appendices. The H. W. Wilson
Company, New York, among other publishers, makes a business of compiling bibliographies on questions of interest. The
company named also publishes a series of little books known
as the *Reference Shelf*, which contain some excellent bibli-
ographical data as well as briefs and considerable quoted
material related to the subject. They also have a series of
Debater's Annuals and *Debater's Handbooks* which include
bibliographies. The extension departments or divisions of
most colleges and universities are prepared to issue bibli-
ographical material on a great variety of subjects. The
same is true of many private organizations and commercial
houses. The *American Catalogue of Books*, the *English Catalogue of Books*, and the *Catalogue of the Library of Congress*
present exhaustive lists of books on practically every subject.
The Government Printing Office at Washington, D. C., will
supply indexes and price lists to government publications.
They have one such index prepared especially for debaters.[1]

---

[1] *A Bibliography for Debaters*, Superintendent of Documents, U. S.
Printing Office, Price List 74, September, 1929.

After all available bibliographies have been consulted, the investigator can then refer to the catalogues of his home library and complete his bibliography with such references as he may find there. Every library is equipped with a card catalogue which lists the books obtainable in the library. These catalogues list the books by the names of the authors, by the titles of the books, and also under numerous suggestive headings. There are also various indexes to current periodical literature which can be obtained in most libraries; *Poole's Index to Periodical Literature, The Reader's Guide to Periodical Literature, The Agricultural Index, The Engineering Index, The Industrial Arts Index,* and others. In using these indexes the reader should look under all the topics which relate to his proposition if the investigation is to be at all complete. For instance, in looking up references on the proposition that a Federal Department of Education be established, it would be profitable to consult such headings as Department of Education, Education, Federal Control of Education, Subsidy, Research, and any other topic that the proposition may suggest.

C. The Form of a Bibliography. — A bibliography should be divided into sections on the basis of the different types of publications cited. That is, place all the books in one section, magazines and current periodicals in another, government publications in a separate section, encyclopedias and yearbooks in another, etc. Within each section the references should be numbered and listed alphabetically as follows:

BOOKS

1. Bauer, John, *Effective Regulation of Public Utilities.* The Macmillan Company, New York, 1928.
2. Conover, Milton, *Federal Power Commission; Its History, Activities, and Organization.* Johns Hopkins Press, Baltimore, 1923.

3. Cooke, Morris L., *Public Utility Regulation*. Ronald Press, New York, 1924.

ARTICLES IN PERIODICALS

1. *American City*, 39 : 112. October, 1928. "Two Towns and Their Hydro-electric Plants." E. E. Miller.
2. *Annalist*, 28 : 3. July 2, 1926. "The Investment Yield of Public Utility Securities." H. P. Gillerts and Alfred S. Malcomson.

The bibliography may or may not be divided into affirmative and negative divisions as it seems best. It is a good practice for students to star references that have been read in a bibliography that is to be handed in to an instructor. In every case the bibliography should be given a title as follows:

A Bibliography on the Proposition,
Resolved: THAT THE FEDERAL GOVERNMENT SHOULD
OWN AND OPERATE ALL HYDRO-ELECTRIC
PROJECTS.
by John H. Franklin

VI. READING

After the bibliography has been prepared, the student may then begin to look up the references and read the materials listed therein.

A. Reading from the General to the Specific. — It is a helpful rule in systematic reading to consult materials of a general nature first and turn to the more specific references later in the study. The investigator needs to see his problem as a whole and get at least a rough grasp of the entire situation before he is really competent to examine the more specialized points intelligently. For instance, in reading on the proposition that the Federal Government should own and operate all hydro-electric projects, it would be advisable to study materials relating to the nature and extent of hydro-electric development in the United States, the history of Federal regulations, and other broad subjects, before dipping into the successes and failures of specific projects, the economics of rate making, and other fine points of the proposition. To ignore this rule is to run the risk of misinterpreting the facts which are discovered, assigning disproportionate values to arguments, and the risk of losing sight of the real issues of the case.

B. Reading Discriminately. — It seems best also to warn the investigator against indiscriminate reading. To exercise discrimination in reading involves two points: (1) The ability to select references that are germane to the proposition; and (2) The ability to scan material for usable evidence. To read every word and line of every reference in a long bibliography is not worth the effort for purposes of argument. In reading a book, for instance, note the table of contents carefully, and then skim those sections that give meager returns and devote the major part of your time to those parts from which you can derive the most assistance. It is a real art to be able to sift the relevant from the irrelevant, and the important from the unimportant by scanning the material as we suggest, but only in this way can real proficiency in reading be acquired.

VII. Discussion and Correspondence

Aside from original investigations and reading it is helpful to confer with others about the proposition upon which research is being undertaken. Discussion groups and conversations, preferably with persons who are well informed on the question, are of distinct value in crystallizing the ideas of the arguer, in testing arguments, and in suggesting new arguments. It is good preparation to try arguments out with someone else before submitting them to the final test. Such practice is indispensable for successful debating; in fact, most debating teams engage in a whole series of practice debates before appearing in public.

Likewise, correspondence with authorities with whom conferences cannot be arranged frequently yields valuable information. In no case, however, should an investigator trouble another person for information which he can obtain through other channels, even though it does require a somewhat greater effort. Most men are glad to answer intelligent questions about matters upon which they are competent to speak as a result of their position, training, travel, or any other experience that they may have had ; but carelessly prepared interrogations and questionnaires are usually relegated to the waste paper basket.

VIII. RECORDING MATERIALS

A. What to Record. — It is always a problem to know just how much of one's reading and investigation he should record. Undoubtedly the nature of the argument for which a preparation is being made should be an important consideration in answering this question. However, there is a tendency among students to record too little. Many times only that evidence and argument is noted down which appears at the time to be something that can be used in the case. Of course in the early stages of investigation, it is difficult to know just what the best case may be, and for that reason it is decidedly unwise to limit one's note-taking to materials which tend to support any particular case. It is our suggestion, subject to exceptional cases, to record briefly at least all the significant evidence and argument uncovered by the investigation.

It is important also that enough be said regarding each item of evidence and argument to make its meaning perfectly clear when reference is made to it several days, or even months or years later.

B. Methods of Recording. — Perhaps the best method of recording materials is a card file properly indexed. For the debater as well as most ordinary usage, we suggest a 4″ × 6″ ruled card with a file box to accommodate cards of this size. If such a card system is not possible for some reason, a loose leaf notebook of any size may be used for the same purpose.

A number of headings or topics should always be chosen under which to organize references on the various materials collected. While these topics should be worked out independently for each proposition, it will be found that the various points included in Section IV will with some modification usually constitute an excellent basis for an index system, especially for propositions of policy. That is, practically all argument and evidence collected can be conveniently catalogued under the origin of the question, the history of the question, the immediate cause of the discussion, the definition of terms, or some one of the ten points included in the survey of the materials for proof. A separate file may or may not be kept for the affirmative and negative references depending upon the needs of the persuader. Ordinarily, however, it is best to make a complete division between affirmative and negative materials in the recording system.

The reference to all material that is filed should be complete, accurate, and standardized. The need for such documentation cannot be emphasized too much. Very often the results of hours of careful research are lost because of the failure to make a careful reference to the source of the material. We suggest the following form for file cards. It includes a suggestive title which will assist in filing; a statement of the source, including the man's name, his rank or position, and the place where it can be found; and finally a statement of the material to be filed (in this case, opinion evidence).

TOPIC	WRITER	WHERE FOUND
Private Ownership Successful	Charles A. Eaton	National Electric Light Association Bulletin
	United States Congress-man from New Jersey	Vol. 14, P. 444, July, 1927

"The electrical industry in America, as developed by private ownership and operation, constitutes the greatest, cheapest, most vital and universally used social service of a material kind ever rendered a civilized community.   And in this service the production and distribution of electric power stands in the first rank."

EXERCISES

1. Investigate some proposition of your own choosing upon which considerable library material is available. This proposition may be used in a later speech assignment.

    a. Record the material you find on 4 × 6 file cards. Have the cards ready to hand in for examination.

    b. Prepare a bibliography of at least twenty-five references. Star the references you have read.

2. Let the entire class investigate some simple proposition of policy agreed upon by the class. Be prepared to discuss as a group:

    a. The origin of the question.
    b. The history of the question.
    c. The immediate cause for discussion.
    d. The definition of terms.
    e. The present plan.
    f. The proposed plan.
    g. Other possible plans.

3. Prepare a five-minute argumentative talk based upon an original investigation.

4. Read Chapter V in *Argumentation* by James A. Winans and William E. Utterback; read Chapter II, Part III, in *The Art of Debate* by W. C. Shaw. In both cases compare the ten points

comprising the survey of proof presented in this chapter with those given in the collateral reading suggested.

5. Read a report of a university or college debate as recorded in one of the H. W. Wilson Company *University Debaters' Annuals*, and note what is done in respect to each of the seven points listed in Exercise 2 above. Write this up in the form of an analysis of the debate, organizing your comments around the seven points mentioned.

CHAPTER IV

ANALYZING THE PROPOSITION: THE ISSUES

I. The Purpose of Analysis

Analysis of a given proposition is the mental process of perceiving within the proposition the parts of which it is composed. It is the process of discovering the issues. Many writers include a survey of the background of the proposition, a definition of terms, and the survey of the materials for proof as steps in analysis.   These are not in our estimation strictly speaking a part of the analysis of the proposition.   They are rather steps in the investigation of the proposition which in many cases are necessary in order that the debater may have a clear understanding of what he is going to analyze.   To procure a clear conception of the proposition, it may be necessary to survey the background of the question, define the terms, and investigate the materials for proof; but doing this is not a matter of analysis; it is something done for the purpose of making clear what it is that must be analyzed.

In many cases the issues can be perceived without a great deal of investigation.   In most cases, perhaps, certain of the issues are manifest without investigating the proposition. Normally, however, one cannot be certain that he has discovered all the issues without undergoing a careful study of both sides of the question.

II. The Nature of Issues

A. Issues Defined. — " The issues are the inherently vital points, elements, or sub-propositions, affirmed by the affirmative and denied by the negative, upon the establishment of which depends the establishment of the main proposition." [1]

It seems well to direct attention to two words in this definition whose significance might perhaps be overlooked.   We have said that the issues are *inherent in* and *vital to* the proposition.   By inherent we mean that the issues exist in the very nature of the proposition; by vital we mean that the life of the proposition depends upon the issues.   It is thus the purpose of the persuader to *find* or *discover* the issues and not to *invent* or *select* them.   The action stated in the proposition

---

[1] O'Neill, James M., Laycock, Craven, and Scales, R. L., *Argumentation and Debate*, p. 43.   The Macmillan Company, 1917.

either should or should not be taken by the individual or by the group to whom it is addressed. The answer in each case turns on certain crucial elements in the situation. It is these elements which must be uncovered and determined upon by the analysis of the proposition before an accurate judgment on the proposition can be reached. To invent issues or trump up reasons to support a previously formulated opinion is to miss the whole point of an analysis.

B. Issues Illustrated. — Some illustrations will help to explain the inherency of issues and their vital relation to the proposition.

O'Neill, Laycock, and Scales cite a legal example which is very helpful.

"First let us say for example that A is accused of the crime of burglary at common law. Now this crime has five essential elements, (1) breaking, and (2) entering (3) a dwelling (4) at night, (5) with felonious intent. There are in the first place five issues here. The State (affirmative) must prove all five. They are all vital. If the defense (negative) prevents the affirmative from establishing any single point beyond any reasonable doubt, the case of the affirmative fails. Then the defendant is not guilty of burglary. He may be guilty of a number of other things, but that is another story. The defendant may admit that he broke and entered a dwelling at night, but deny that it was done with felonious intent — say he did it to put out a fire. The affirmative has established (or gained an admission of) four of the five necessary points, but the whole case falls. No affirmative case can stand after the loss of a single issue. Any point which the affirmative can fail on, and still establish the case cannot be an issue, though it may be very important. Importance is not enough — an issue is vital in the strictest sense of that word." [1]

The proposition, *Resolved:* That the several states should enact legislation providing for compulsory unemployment

[1] O'Neill, James M., Laycock, Craven, and Scales, R. L., *Argumentation and Debate*, p. 43.

insurance will give us another illustration. The issues in this proposition seem to be substantially these: (1) Are present unemployment conditions such as to warrant taking some form of action? (2) Is legislation providing for unemployment insurance the action which should be taken? (3) Should this unemployment insurance be compulsory? (4) Should this action be taken by the several States? If the affirmative on this proposition succeeds in establishing these four points, it will have a complete prima facie case for its proposition. On the other hand, if the negative can succeed in destroying any of these points, the affirmative position will necessarily fall. Each and every issue is inherent in and vital to the proposition.

C. Rules Governing the Issues. — A discussion of the rules governing issues will give us further assistance in understanding the nature of issues.

1. THE ISSUES MUST BE VITAL POINTS. — This rule is derived directly from our definition of issues and is undoubtedly clear from our previous discussion. Every issue is of such a vital nature that its destruction results in the destruction of the proposition regardless of the other issues involved. The mistake is sometimes made of assuming that if the affirmative establishes a majority of the issues, it will have proved its case. This, of course, is not the truth of the matter. Failure to establish any contested issue regardless of the number of the issues is fatal to the affirmative.

2. THE ISSUES MUST BEAR A DIRECT AND IMMEDIATE RELATION TO THE PROPOSITION. — In the process of discovering issues it is easy to confuse important arguments and significant points with real issues. Take as an example the proposition, *Resolved:* That all colleges and universities should abolish the distinction between amateurism and professionalism in sports to which admission fees are charged. There are three very evident issues in this question: (1) Do conditions in college

and university athletics demand some change in the present amateur status? (2) Is the abolition of the distinction between amateurism and professionalism the desirable change to make? (3) Should this abolition take place in those sports to which admission fees are charged? Let us say that in our investigation of the question we find considerable emphasis placed on the argument that the existing amateur rules are being violated on all hands. The question then presents itself as to whether or not this point is one of the issues. While it might at first appear to be such, closer observation will reveal that it is simply an aspect of the first issue. It relates to the proposition only as it tends to prove the first issue. The relation is not direct and immediate as in the case of the three issues named.

The argument is also current that the abolition of the distinction between amateurism and professionalism would result in the introduction of all the evils of professional athletics into college sports. But here again we can see that no matter how important the argument may be, it is an aspect of the second issue rather than an issue in and of itself. The relation to the proposition is through the mediation of another point rather than direct and immediate.

Because of the tendency to include important arguments as issues, when they really should not be so included, what appears to be a large number of issues can frequently be boiled down to an irreducible minimum of one, two, three, four, or five salient points. While efforts should never be made to select any particular number of issues, nor should a large number of issues necessarily be considered a sign of faulty analysis, nevertheless, in those cases where a multiplicity of issues appears to exist, a particularly close scrutiny of their relationships to the proposition is desirable.

3. THE ISSUES SHOULD BE MUTUALLY EXCLUSIVE POINTS. — Each issue on any proposition represents a separate and

distinct aspect of that proposition.   Any analysis which ends up with a group of points as issues, which overlap and encroach upon each other, constitutes a faulty analysis.   For example, in the proposition that the President should be elected for a single six-year term, there seem to be three issues : (1) Does the present four-year term with a possibility of reëlection need to be modified in some way?   (2) Is a single term the desirable modification?   (3) Should this single term be for six years?   It will be noted that these issues deal with wholly distinct and separate units or elements of the proposition.   The first issue has to do with the present situation, the second with a single term, and the third with a six-year feature.   Failure to observe these natural and logical lines of division between the various vital elements in the proposition will invariably confuse the real issues.

4. THE ISSUES SHOULD BE ALL INCLUSIVE POINTS. — In analyzing the proposition it is of course important that no essential element be overlooked.   The issues embody all the vital elements in the situation, no more and no less.   If there is but one such element, then there is but one issue, and if there are ten points of vital importance, there are ten issues. The weakness of the analysis which fails to reveal all the issues is evident.

5. THE ISSUES SHOULD BE STATED AS IMPARTIAL QUESTIONS. — Unlike the proposition, the issues should always be stated as questions.   They should be phrased in such a way that the affirmative will always answer " yes," and the negative " no."

D. Issues and Proving the Proposition. — Further insight into the nature of issues can be gained by observing their relation to the proof of the proposition.   The truth or falsity of the proposition is established through argument by defending or attacking the issues.   Proof of the truth of the proposition is attained when evidence and reasoning have been presented to demonstrate the truth of each and every issue. Proof of the falsity of the proposition is attained when evidence and reasoning have been set forth to establish the falsity of any one or more of the issues.

III. TYPES OF ISSUES

In our discussion thus far we have made no distinction between the different types of issues. We shall find it helpful to understand potential issues, admitted issues, ultimate issues, and stock issues.

A. Potential Issues. — Potential issues are the real issues in a proposition. They are the issues we defined earlier in the chapter and the issues we have been talking about up to this point. They are the inherently vital points upon which the truth or the falsity of the proposition hinges. In one sense of the term they are the only points which we can accurately call issues without some adjective to modify our label. We have used the word " potential " simply because it conveys the point that all the real issues may not materialize in any given argument. They are always potentialities, but they may or may not arise in any given argument.

B. Admitted Issues. — Admitted issues are those potential issues which are admitted by the negative and therefore are not significant in the argument where the admission is made. Since it is the affirmative that must account for every issue in order to prove its case, it is of course only the negative that can admit issues. Such admissions on the part of the negative immediately limit or at least should limit the argument to those potential issues which remain controversial.

C. Ultimate Issues. — By ultimate issues we have in mind those potential issues which do actually develop in the argument. They are the inherently vital points upon which the truth or falsity of the proposition hinges in any particular argument between a given affirmative and a given negative.

Thus, if three of five issues are openly or tacitly admitted, the other two become or should become the ultimate issues.

D. Stock Issues. — There have been many efforts to discover formulas for issues or type issues which will apply to all propositions. The very nature of issues, however, makes it impossible to set up any group of stock questions which will permit of such a wide application. The issues are specific to each proposition. The only helpful or legitimate use of stock issues occurs in the case of propositions of policy having to do with changes in necessarily continuing systems, as taxation, education, railways, water, light and power utilities, etc. In propositions involving changes of this nature, there are always two questions that are bound to arise: (1) Is the present system unsatisfactory? (2) Is the proposed action the proper remedy?

It will be noticed that there is a similarity between these two points and the ten guides for surveying the proof which are discussed in Chapter III. This similarity is apt to prove confusing unless it is understood that the ten guides, while ultimately reducible to these same two stock issues, do not in themselves constitute stock issues. Helpful as they may be, they do not meet the requirements of issues and it is inaccurate and confusing to speak of them as such.

In analyzing propositions which involve changes in a policy dealing with an activity which must be carried on, it is helpful *to begin* the analysis with the two stock issues we have named. As O'Neill, Laycock, and Scales state, " New systems will not be adopted while the present is satisfactory, nor unless the proposed scheme looks like a satisfactory remedy or improvement. So the man with a new scheme must always show somehow or other (or get it admitted) first, that there is something wrong and second, that his scheme will make it right."[1]

[1] O'Neill, James M., Laycock, Craven, and Scales, R. L., *Argumentation and Debate*, p. 57.

It should be emphasized, however, that these stock issues are not the exact issues on a proposition. The proposition that the Federal Government should own and operate the coal mines will illustrate this point. An analysis of this proposition reveals four potential issues: (1) Do conditions obtaining under private control make some action necessary? (2) Would governmental control of the coal mines be the desirable course to pursue? (3) Should this governmental control consist of ownership and operation of the mines? (4) Should the control be exercised by the Federal Government? In this case it can be seen that the first potential issue corresponds with the first stock issue, while all three of the remaining potential issues relate to the second stock issue. As this example tends to show, there is little or no relationship between the number of stock issues and the number of potential issues. It may also be noticed that the language of the potential issues is much more specific and concrete than that of the stock issues in that it is adapted to a specific proposition. We may say, then, that any set of stock or type issues is at best valuable only as a point of departure in the search for the real issues.

IV. METHOD OF ANALYSIS

We have defined analysis as the mental process of perceiving within the proposition the parts of which it is composed. As we stated earlier in the chapter, there are many propositions which can be analyzed quickly and accurately by persons with trained, analytical minds without any apparent method or system. On the other hand, there are a great number of propositions which will not submit even to the most competent analyst without considerable thought and application. Is there some method of analysis which will profitably direct this thought and application and help to cultivate competence in analysis? We are suggesting a method which involves the following four steps : (1) Arraying the arguments ; (2) Excluding matter that is not significant ; (3) Organizing the arrays ; and (4) Contrasting the affirmative and negative arrays.

A. Arraying the Arguments. — After having investigated the proposition thoroughly, the arguer may then list all the affirmative and negative arguments in separate columns. In preparing these arrays it is not advisable to be too discriminating at the outset. State all the arguments, regardless of their apparent importance, in coördinate lists of points without any effort at indicating their relationships. The array of arguments, then, consists simply of lists of affirmative and negative arguments in parallel columns. These lists may be made up as the investigation progresses, or drawn from one's records after the investigation has been completed.

B. Excluding Unimportant Matter. — After the arguments have been arrayed, it is then necessary to strike out all those points which are irrelevant, trivial, duplications of other points, or otherwise unimportant. This step will shorten the lists and leave only those points which bear significantly on the proposition.

C. Organizing the Arrays. — When the unimportant matter has been eliminated, each list of arguments should then be rearranged to show the relationships between the remaining points. The points of central importance should be listed coördinately and the less important topics should be placed under the main headings to which they apply. The array can be refined to as many series of sub-points as is necessary to display the relationships involved. Such an organization will almost always require several rewordings and regroupings before a satisfactory arrangement is reached. In performing this step in analysis, the rules governing the issues should constantly be kept in mind because it is the main points in the final array that will suggest the issues.

D. Contrasting the Arrays. — The object of contrasting the affirmative and negative arrays is to find the nature of the clash between the various topics or arguments in the two lists. If the previous steps in analysis have been carefully undertaken, this comparison should reveal a rather close, point-for-point clash throughout. That is, for every affirmative argument in the affirmative array, there should be a corresponding negative argument in the negative array. While this coincidence between points is seldom perfect, nevertheless the important points upon which the affirmative and negative arguments clash will be disclosed.

Since the issues are the inherently vital points affirmed by the affirmative, and denied by the negative, we would naturally expect to find the issues appearing in both the affirmative and negative arrays. And since the issues bear a direct and immediate relation to the proposition, we might expect the questions precipitated by a clash between the main points in the opposing arrays to be the issues. Ordinarily this is the case. A collaboration of the corresponding main arguments in each array, stated in the form of impartial questions, will usually constitute the issues, or at least *points which should seriously be considered as possible issues*. We do not mean to say that this contrast of arguments is an infallible method of determining the issues. Our only point is that it will call one's attention to significant points of clash between the affirmative and negative arguments which are apt to constitute the issues. It presents a method of bringing the results of one's investigation to bear in a helpful way on the problem of analyzing the proposition.

EXERCISES

1. Select five propositions for analysis; let each member of the class determine the issues on these propositions, and then compare results.

2. Analyze some proposition of your own choosing, employing the method of arrays suggested in this chapter. Write up the entire analysis, setting forth each step.

3. Give the potential issues on five propositions of your own choosing and indicate in each case which potential issues you would admit if you were in charge of the negative case.

4. Conduct class debates on a group of propositions and in each case compare the potential issues with the ultimate issues.

5. Study the debates in Appendix A. Compare the potential issues with the ultimate issues in each case.

6. Give the potential issues on each of the following propositions:

   a. *Resolved:* That you should cease trading in chain grocery stores.
   b. *Resolved:* That chain grocery stores should be abolished.
   c. *Resolved:* That chain grocery stores are detrimental to the people of Michigan (supply the name of your own State).
   d. *Resolved:* That chain stores practice unfair retailing methods.

CHAPTER V

ANALYZING THE AUDIENCE

CHAPTER OUTLINE

I. The Audience Defined.
    A. The Audience as a Unit.

II. The Audience and the Proposition.

III. The Audience and the Issues.

IV. The Relation of Audience Analysis to Proposition Analysis.

V. The Relation of the Audience to Building the Case.

VI. The Objectives of Audience Analysis.

VII. Communicating the Argument to the Audience.
    A. The Vehicle of Communication: Speech Symbols.
    B. Steps in Communicating Argument.
        1. Attention.
        2. Perception.
        3. Reasoning.
        4. Judgment.
        5. Overt Action.

VIII. Factors in Audience Analysis.
    A. The Existing Status or Needs of the Audience in Relation to the Proposition.
    B. The Environmental Background of the Audience.
    C. The Personality Type of the Audience.
    D. The Acceptance Attitude toward the Proposition.
    E. Familiarity with the Proposition.
    F. Emotional Attitude toward the Proposition.
    G. Attitude toward the Arguer.

I. The Audience Defined

The term " audience " in relation to our study is widely used with two quite different meanings. In the broader sense, it refers to any person or group of persons present at a given argument. That is, it comprises all those people in hearing (or seeing) distance of the argument whose attention is being given to it. The persuader's interest in them or his desire to modify their thinking or acting has nothing whatsoever to do with the situation, and in no way qualifies the membership of the audience when the term is used in this sense.

In its narrower meaning the audience consists of the person or persons called upon to think or act in some certain way by the proposition. If I am trying to persuade Mr. Jones to buy a new automobile, Mr. Jones is my audience even though there may be a dozen other persons listening to my argument. The audience in this sense consists specifically of that person or group of persons upon whom a demand for belief or action is made. A political speaker campaigning for votes, for example, might speak to a large group of people, but his real audience (in the narrower sense of the term) would consist only of those people in the group who had voting privileges. Likewise a lawyer in pleading a case before a jury, might be heard by a large group in the courtroom, but his real audience would be the jury, because it is this group whose thinking and acting he is trying to influence.

It seems to us that there is much to be gained from conceiving of the audience in this narrower sense — *as the person*

*or group of persons upon whom the demand for belief or action
is being made.* After all, this is the real audience. This is
the group from whom a response is being elicited. It is the
individual or individuals to whom the argument must be
adjusted. And in the final analysis, the success of the argument must be determined by its power to influence the thinking or acting of this real audience. We shall use the term
" audience " in this narrower sense.

A. The Audience as a Unit. — There are, of course, many
differences between an audience consisting of one person, and
an audience consisting of a group of persons. In the case
of the single individual, the persuader is concerned with the
needs and reaction tendencies of just one person and can
adjust his argument accordingly. In the case of the group,
he may be confronted with a great diversity of beliefs and
opinions. In both cases, however, it is usually best to treat
the audience as a single reaction unit. If this unity of
response does not exist in a group composing the audience,
then it must be achieved before anything like unanimity of
belief or action can be obtained on the proposition. Methods
of securing this unity of response from the audience are
discussed in Chapter XI. (Read section V in this connection.)
While it is ordinarily impossible to establish such common
bonds and ties as will mold every individual of a large group
of people into a single reaction unit, at the same time it must
be realized that most groups of people whose thinking and
acting the persuader has occasion to influence will almost
always have considerable group solidarity to begin with;
that is, they will usually have certain common needs and reaction tendencies which tend to unite the group and which
can be utilized by the arguer as a basis for furthering this
unity. We shall find it helpful, then, to look upon the audience, no matter how many people compose it, as a single
unit in the argument.

II. The Audience and the Proposition

Just how does the audience relate to the proposition? Should the unit constituting the audience be named in the proposition, or should the audience be considered as something entirely apart from the phraseology of the proposition?

In a situation in which I am trying to convince Mr. Jones that he should buy a new automobile, the formal statement of my proposition would undoubtedly be, *Resolved:* That Mr. Jones should buy a new automobile. Now dividing this proposition up into its two terms and copula, we can see that " Mr. Jones " is the first term; " should buy " is the copula; and " a new automobile " is the second term. Here is a case, then, in which the *audience is a term in the proposition,* because certainly Mr. Jones is the audience in this example. The significance of this term can readily be seen by changing the audience. Is it not clear that it is one proposition to propose that one person buy a new automobile, and ordinarily quite a different proposition to suggest that another person do the same thing?

It is not difficult to see that the audience constitutes a term in this proposition and for that matter in every other overt-action proposition. The proposition actually changes as you ask different audiences to perform the same overt act. And now the question arises, does this same relationship exist in other types of propositions? It does, but it is much less apparent. And it is probably not so apparent because it is much less significant for the persuader. Let us illustrate this point with a pure or unmixed question of fact, *Resolved:* That a straight line is the shortest distance between two points. Wording this question as it actually appears in an argument we might have the following, *Resolved:* That Mr. Smith should think that a straight line is the shortest dis-

tance between two points. In this case, " Mr. Smith " is the
first term; " should think " is the copula; and the noun
clause " that a straight line is the shortest distance between
two points " is the other term. Changing the audience here
would have little effect on the proposition, because Mr. Smith
or Mr. Brown or anyone else should and probably would
believe or disbelieve that a straight line is the shortest distance between two points for substantially the same reasons.
In fact, a careful scrutiny of the classes of propositions studied
in Chapter II will make it clear that changing the audience
affects overt-action propositions most; policy-endorsement
propositions somewhat less; propositions advocated as
theoretically sound, considerably less; and pure questions
of fact, least. That is to say, the audience as a term in the
proposition, ordinarily, becomes less significant as we leave
the realm of personal action and matters of policy endorsement, and approach unmixed questions of fact. The explanation of this observation lies in the fact that while propositions of fact are settled largely by impersonal convictions
and strictly logical considerations, questions of policy tend
more and more to be matters which are affected by individual prejudices, emotional differences, personal likes and dis-
likes, and other psychological considerations. We may say,
then, that the significance of the audience as a term in the
proposition is in direct proportion to the emotional and personal nature of the judgment; or conversely, it is in inverse
proportion to the logical and impersonal nature of the judgment.

III. The Audience and the Issues

We learned in Chapter IV that the issues are specific to
each proposition. It follows from this, of course, that any
change in the proposition will also affect the issues. Since
changing the audience alters the proposition in the way we

have just discussed, it may be inferred that the issues will also change with the audience and in that way be specific to each audience. We may say with certain qualifications that this is precisely the case. In overt-action propositions where we have seen the audience to be a most important term in the proposition, the issues are apt to differ greatly with different audiences. To return to the proposition of buying a new automobile for illustration, it can readily be seen that with one prospective buyer the matter of price might be the sole issue; with another individual, riding comfort might be an issue in addition to price, or it might be the sole issue. The issues on such propositions cannot possibly be determined apart from the individual or group of individuals called upon to act.

As might be expected, however, as we leave the realm of overt-action propositions, the audience plays a much less significant part in determining the issues for reason that the proposition is not significantly affected by changing the reaction unit. In fact, we are disposed to conclude that only in overt-action propositions and in certain policy-endorsement propositions need the audience even be considered in analyzing the proposition *for purposes of discovering the issues.*

IV. THE RELATION OF AUDIENCE ANALYSIS TO PROPOSITION ANALYSIS

While this relationship is fairly evident from what has already been said, perhaps it should be emphasized that in propositions of policy, particularly of the overt-action type, any complete analysis of the proposition must include an analysis of the audience. Only by understanding the position and needs of the reactor relative to the action he is being called upon to take, can the issues be determined. As stated above, however, this audience analysis is not signifi-

cant or at least much less significant in analyzing propositions of fact.

V. The Relation of the Audience to Building the Case

At this point it becomes necessary for us to make an important distinction between *analysis* and *synthesis* in argument. Whereas analysis is the process of breaking up a
proposition into its various elements, parts, or issues, synthesis is the process of putting materials together; it is the
process of building the case. A later chapter will define the
case as consisting of that evidence and argument upon which
the persuader rests his cause before any given audience. The
finished case, then, is the objective toward which we are proceeding. If the audience analysis plays an important rôle
in the analysis of the proposition, it certainly plays a much
more important part in case building. The case must be
planned to appeal to the audience. The success or failure of
argument, with certain exceptions, must be evaluated upon
its power to influence the thinking or acting of the audience.
It is hardly necessary for us to say that audiences react differently to the various forms of support, types of appeal, and
methods of approach in argument. Realizing this, it is
evident that a careful inquiry into the reaction tendencies of
the audience is necessary if the persuader is to draw up a
case which will be effective in a given situation.

VI. The Objectives in Audience Analysis

From what we have just said, it can be seen that the objectives of audience analysis are really two-fold: (1) To determine the action needs of the audience; and (2) To determine
the reaction tendencies of the audience. The first of these
objectives is occasioned primarily by the analysis of the proposition, and the second, primarily by the building of the case.
The analysis of the audience should be such as to reveal both

the needs of the audience in relation to the action it is being asked to take, and the method and approach which will be most persuasive in leading it so to act.

VII. Communicating the Argument to the Audience

Before going further into the matter of audience analysis, it seems best to explain briefly the nature of the process by which the argument is communicated to the audience. We feel that the rest of the chapter will be more meaningful in the light of this discussion. At this point we wish to give only such explanation of this process as will enable the reader to appreciate more fully the rôle of the audience in argument. A more complete description of the nature of communication is given in Chapter XIV, Section II.

A. The Vehicle of Communication: Speech Symbols. — The argument is communicated to the audience either orally or in writing. In either case it is conveyed through certain speech or language symbols. In oral communication these are of two kinds, audible symbols and visible symbols. Audible symbols consist of spoken language and other vocal utterances produced by vocalized and articulated breathing. Visible symbols consist of posture, movement, and gesture, and are produced largely by the different muscular dispositions of the speaker. A symbol may be defined as anything that suggests an idea or thing, either by resemblance to it or association with it. Thus, the persuader presents his ideas and feelings in sounds and movements which have symbolic significance for the audience, and in that way communicates his argument to the audience.

B. Steps in Communicating Argument. — There are five psychological states which must be experienced by the audience before effective communication takes place in argument. Our reference to them as *steps* refers to their sequence only, and is otherwise entirely figurative.

1. ATTENTION. — Attention is the first important step in communication. It can be defined as " a unified, coördinated muscular set, or attitude, which brings sense organs to bear with maximum effectiveness upon a source of stimulation and thus contributes to alertness and readiness of response." [1] The speaker's symbols are brought to bear on the audience as definite stimuli when a state of attention exists, assuming, of course, that the speaker is the source of stimulation. Attention is absolutely necessary to communication. When attention ceases, communication ceases.

2. PERCEPTION. — Perception can be explained simply as the process by which meaning is added to sensation. Certain speech symbols act as a stimulus to the sense organs. This stimulus is conveyed to the brain as a nervous impulse and the reactor experiences a sensation. If this sensation has been experienced before, it is interpreted in the light of its predecessors and meaning is thereby added to it. The more a given sensation has been experienced the more vivid is the percept upon its recurrence. If we never have experienced the sensation before, there is little perception, and the stimulus or symbol provoking the sensation is not understood. Woodworth explains perception as follows : [2]

"When the facts are presented to the senses, we speak of 'sense perception.' If they are presented to the eye, we speak of visual perception; if to the ear, of auditory perception, etc. But when we speak of a fact as being 'presented' to the eye or ear, we do not necessarily mean that it is directly and completely presented; it may only be indicated. We may have before the eyes simply the sign of some fact, but perceive the fact which is the *meaning* of the sign. We look out of the window and 'see it is wet today,' though wetness is something to be felt rather than seen; having previously observed how wet ground looks, we now

[1] O'Neill, J. M., and Weaver, A. T., *The Elements of Speech*, p. 301. Longmans, Green and Company, 1926.
[2] Woodworth, Robert S., *Psychology, A Study of Mental Life*, pp. 421-422. Henry Holt and Company, 1921.

respond promptly to the visual appearance by knowing the indicated state of affairs. In the same way, we say that we 'hear the street car,' though we must admit a street car is not essentially a noise. What we hear, in strictness, is a noise, but we respond to the noise by perceiving the presence of the car. — Sense perception, then, is responding to a stimulus by knowing some fact indicated by it either directly or indirectly.

"Perception that is not sense perception occurs when the fact perceived is not even indirectly presented to the senses at the moment. The fact is then presented by recall; yet the fact in question is not recalled. Recall not only gives you facts previously perceived, but may provide the data, the stimulus, for fresh perception. Putting together two recalled facts, you may perceive a further fact not previously known. Remembering that you took your umbrella to the office this morning in the rain, that it was fine when you left the office, and that you certainly did not have the umbrella when you reached home, you perceive that you must have left it at the office. Reading in the paper of preparations for another polar expedition, and remembering that both poles have already been discovered, you perceive that there is something more in polar exploration than the mere race for the pole. Perception of this sort amounts to 'reasoning' . . ."

3. REASONING. — Reread Woodworth's statement carefully, trying to discern the distinction between sense perception and reasoning. He says that reasoning is a particular kind of perception which culminates in inference, and as such is to be distinguished from sense perception. His words are as follows: [1] " Reasoning as a whole is a process of mental exploration culminating in an inference." Consider the following examples of the perceptive reaction in reasoning which we also take from Woodworth: [2]

"To bring out distinctly the perceptive reaction in reasoning, let us cite a few very simple cases. Two freshmen in college, getting acquainted, ask about each other's fathers and find that both are alumni of this same college. 'What class was your father in?' 'In the class of 1900. And yours?' 'Why, he

[1] *Ibid.*, p. 468.   [2] *Ibid.*, pp. 465–466.

was in 1900, too. Our fathers were in the same class; they must know each other.' Here two facts, one contributed by one person and the other by another person, enable both to perceive a third fact which neither of them knew before. Inference, typically, is a response to two facts, and the response consists in perceiving a third fact that is bound up in the other two.

"You do not infer what you can perceive directly by the senses. If Mary and Kate are standing side by side, you can see which is the taller. But if they are not side by side, but Mary's height is given as so much and Kate's as an inch more, then from these two facts you know, by inference, that Kate is taller than Mary."

4. JUDGMENT. — By judgment we mean the result of reasoning and inference, or a conclusion. It is the third fact which arises out of the comparison of two known facts. In our study of the proposition we defined the proposition as the expression of a judgment in language. The persuader arrives at this judgment as a result of his own reasoning processes, and argument is the process of getting the other fellow to accept this judgment. To do this the arguer must set forth argument which will enable the listener to arrive at this conclusion or judgment. Judgment is thus either directly or indirectly the objective of argument.[1] If the persuader is simply attempting to convince the reactor, his purpose is accomplished when the reactor accepts the judgment which constitutes the proposition for argument.

5. OVERT ACTION. — In discussing overt action, it must be kept in mind that there are many degrees of " overtness." Strictly speaking, verbal responses, raising the hand in assent, clapping the hands, winking the eye, and many other responses which have barely reached the overt level are overt

[1] It should be noted that there are cases in which a speaker attempts to secure action by the use of *suggestion* alone. It is probable that many acts so stimulated are not preceded by judgment, but are rather simply idea-motor reactions. We have discussed this whole matter of suggestion in relation to argument in Chapter XI, "Supporting the Proposition: Motivation."

action nevertheless.   In fact, it is believed that there is little if any qualitative difference between inner action such as judgment and overt action.   Both involve a stimulus and in all probability a muscular (or glandular) response.

But when we speak of overt action we have in mind more particularly such complex acts as mowing the lawn, going to the theater, getting to work on time, constructing a new plant, going to the polls, etc.   It is our belief that actions such as these, while ultimately reducible to stimulus-response mechanisms, when they are called forth by argument, must have had their conception in a previously formulated judgment.   (See footnote, page 72, for possible exception.)   We shall see in later chapters how this decision to act or judgment may be secured through argument by a logical case, confirming the proposition; by an explanation of the facts of the case; or by a motive appeal.   We may say now, however, that practical experience leads us to believe that somewhat different methods are ordinarily required to " stir up " overt action than are required to elicit action below the overt level, inner action, or thought.

VIII. FACTORS IN AUDIENCE ANALYSIS

With this explanation of the nature of communication, we are now in a position to examine those factors which an analysis of the audience should include.   We have seen that the objectives of such an analysis are, first, to determine the action needs of the audience, and, second, to determine the reaction tendencies.   The question now to be considered is what factors must be examined in order to reveal the *action needs* and *reaction tendencies* of the audience?   We suggest a consideration of the following factors.

1. The existing status or needs of the audience in relation to the proposition.
2. The environmental background of the audience.

3. The personality type of the audience.
4. The acceptance attitude toward the proposition.
5. Familiarity with the proposition.
6. Emotional attitude toward the proposition.
7. Attitude toward the arguer.

A. The Existing Status or Needs of the Audience in Relation to the Proposition. — An analysis of the audience from the standpoint of its needs in relation to the proposition is the factor whose examination will be most helpful in *analyzing the proposition*. This is especially true in the case of propositions of policy, and even more especially those of an overt-action type. The salesman's proposition illustrates this point; he certainly must know the needs of each prospective customer in relation to his sales' offering before he can hope to analyze his proposition and set up an effective selling argument. When the proposition calls upon the audience to perform some overt act or to endorse some policy change, the needs of the audience, socially, economically, politically, and otherwise, are important determiners of both the issues of the proposition and the reaction tendencies of the audience. People can be both logically and persuasively called upon to buy, to sell, to vote, or perform any overt act, when it can be shown that their needs demand such action. The analysis of the audience should always include a careful investigation of these needs in relation to the proposition.

B. The Environmental Background of the Audience. — One of the most illuminating inquiries that can be made in analyzing an audience is an investigation of its environmental background. We may say that this factor, as are all the others remaining to be discussed, is especially helpful in determining *the reaction tendencies of the audience*. If the audience consists of a single individual, questions such as the following should be considered: Is the reactor city or country bred? Has he attended an elementary school, high school, college, or university? Has he traveled widely? What is his occupation? With what success has he pursued this occupation? What is the nature of his family life? To what church, lodge, fraternity, or other organization does the reactor belong? Is he a leader in his community? How does he spend his leisure time? Knowledge concerning such points as these is helpful in analyzing many propositions and is often indispensable in case building.

The environmental background of larger audiences is also significant. Is the audience a city or country group? What professions are represented in the audience? These questions and many others relating to the political, economic, and social background of the audience will assist the persuader in sizing up the situation and shaping his argument accordingly.

C. The Personality Type of the Audience. — A third factor of importance in audience analysis is the personality type of the audience. This factor is probably more significant in the analysis of single individual reactors than it is in the analysis of groups, but it should be considered in either case. Most sales manuals and textbooks in salesmanship attest to the value of differentiating personality types. Many of these books present elaborate classifications of customs based largely upon personality differences. Such types as the garrulous customer, the vacillating customer, the argumentative customer, and many others are distinguished. Psychologists have long been talking about personality differences and making efforts to classify personality types. O'Neill and Weaver in their book, *Elements of Speech*, discuss the following types: (1) Intellectual and emotional; (2) Hyperkinetic and hypokinetic; (3) Extroverted and introverted; (4) Ascendent and submissive; (5) Social and reclusive; and (6) The suggestible and non-suggestible.[1]

[1] O'Neill, J. M., and Weaver, A. T., *The Elements of Speech*, pp. 340–344. Longmans, Green and Company, 1926.

Without attempting any classification of personality types here, we do wish to emphasize the importance of sizing up the type of person you have before you in an argument. Certainly the emotional personality, for instance, will require a quite different approach than the individual whose reactions are predominantly intellectual in nature.   Likewise the suggestible individual can be appealed to from points-of-view that will not influence the non-suggestible; and the tactics one would use in persuading an ascendant, dominant personality would in most instances differ widely from those employed to actuate or win the assent of the submissive type.

While most group audiences will be composed of personalities of many types, it is frequently if not usually possible to discover a *dominant or prevailing type in the group*.   For example, it is not at all unusual to find emotional group types, and there are many audiences which may quite accurately be described as intellectual types.   We wish simply to say that in many cases it is profitable to attempt to determine the personality type of the group audience as well as that of the single-individual audience.

D. **The Acceptance Attitude toward the Proposition.** — It is also important that the arguer ascertain the acceptance attitude of the audience toward the proposition.   Does the audience favor the proposition, oppose it, or is it merely indifferent?   Audiences have been classified on this basis as (1) Accepting; (2) Opposing; and (3) Considering.[1]   Very evidently a speaker must adjust his argument to meet these different attitudes.   In the case of the accepting audience, he needs only to strengthen his cause; with the opposing audience, he must attempt to break down the opposition; and with a considering audience, he must endeavor to replace indifference with positive conviction.   In every instance, the

[1] Collins, G. R., and Morris, J. S., *Persuasion and Debate*, pp. 61–62. Harper and Brothers, 1927.

cause of the audience's attitude is the important thing. Why does the audience accept the proposition? What is the basis of its opposition? What is the cause of its indifference? Only by knowing these causes can the persuader proceed intelligently with his argument. If an audience favors a proposition for certain positive reasons, and the arguer belittles, neglects, or states these arguments very poorly, he will injure his case greatly. Again, a failure to recognize the cause of the opposition to one's proposition may be equally fatal. Such opposition may be due largely to emotional prejudice; it may be based upon certain well defined, logical objections; or it may be due to inaccurate or insufficient information. In any case the persuader should analyze the situation and construct an argument designed to remove the cause. Likewise the cause of an indifferent attitude may be one of many possibilities, and here again the argument must be planned to strike at the specific causative factor. If it is a lack of information, supply the facts. If it is a failure to think the proposition through, construct a logical case for the proposition. *In every instance discover the cause of the attitude and then plan an argument which will remove this cause.*

E. Familiarity with the Proposition. — Audiences may also be classified in three ways on the basis of their familiarity with the proposition. An audience may be: (1) Uninformed regarding the proposition; (2) Well informed; or (3) Incorrectly informed. Regardless of the kind and degree of information, however, it is not unusual to find the audience definitely opinionated on the proposition. Many persons entertain opinions on questions about which they know little or nothing. On matters of national policy, election issues, religious questions, and in innumerable other affairs, a great number of individuals simply do what their parents have done before them, what most people seem to be doing, or

what strikes their fancy at the time. Of this group, there
are those who frankly admit their ignorance and yet just as
insistently maintain their position in the matter. Where the
audience analysis shows the reactor's opinion to be based on
inadequate information, the persuader's task is one of supplementing this fragmentary knowledge and correcting erroneous impressions. *Chapter X, "Supporting the Proposition:
Explanation," outlines a complete methodology to be used in
combating opinions based on inadequate information.*

   F. Emotional Attitude toward the Proposition. — A fifth
factor in the analysis of the audience is its emotional attitude
toward the proposition. The person who maintains a position because of emotional bias or prejudice is not to be confused with one who is inadequately informed. In fact, it is
doubtful whether there is any correlation between the two.
Irrespective of information, there are individuals who have
emotional sets on certain propositions which no informative
argument could move. Such indisposition may be the result
of long-standing opinions, aversions based on peculiar or
accidental experiences, stubbornness, anger, or some other
emotional cause. In this class, also, there are those who
admit themselves to be in error and yet are still disinclined
to alter their position.

   In cases of this kind the reactor must be " remotivated ";
that is, he must be supplied with motives which are sufficiently powerful to supplant those that are blindly holding
him to a given course. The following incident, related to the
writer by a friend who is engaged in selling life insurance,
illustrates this point exceptionally well.

   "I had an elderly man among my insurance prospects, an
intelligent, competent person, who was bitterly adverse to the
whole institution of life insurance. It seems that he had taken
out an insurance contract in his early years which had proved
costly and entirely unsatisfactory. In fact, he was eventually

forced out of the contract altogether by prohibitory rates. Despite irrefutable evidence that a repetition of the experience was utterly impossible under existing insurance laws and the contract I was offering, he could not be moved. He was perfectly willing to concede his insurance needs and liked my company. He didn't seem to have any logical objections to offer. Apparently, the only obstacle to the sale was this obstinate indisposition engendered by an unusual experience in another insurance company under conditions that could not occur again.

"The argument that finally sold this man was a contrast of motives. I knew his family well, his wife and three minor children; I knew of his concern about their future, and I thought he ought to have the insurance. So I didn't hesitate to compare the motive that prompted his consistent refusal with the motive for entering into the contract which I thought would 'hit nearest home.' When the love for his family and his regard for their welfare was brought to bear strongly on the issue, the egotistical satisfaction which he seemed to derive from his old grudge was driven to the background. A new and stronger motive had been supplied, and that motive prevailed."

This method of argument is treated in Chapter XI, " Supporting the Proposition: Motivation."

G. Attitude toward the Arguer. — The last factor to be considered in analyzing the audience is the attitude of the audience toward the speaker. Perhaps in most cases this is simply a matter of considering just what reaction you can reasonably expect the audience to make to you as an individual. Some questions for consideration are: Just how will this audience react to me? to my appearance? to my personality? what impression will I make? how will my statements be received? A careful analysis of the audience will invariably reveal information which will greatly assist the speaker in answering these questions and thereby in adjusting himself to the occasion. Any tactful individual can do much in the way of adapting himself, both in manner and in appearances, to fit into different audience situations, if he will only give the matter his attention.   Winans and Utterback say on this point : [1]

> "The speaker's reputation and his appearance and conduct on the platform almost inevitably lead the audience to adopt some particular attitude toward him personally. They may consider him well informed or ill informed on his subject, of sound judgment or of poor judgment. trustworthy or untrustworthy in his statements : they may respect and like him, or they may disrespect and dislike him.
>
> "This estimate of the speaker by the audience is an extremely important factor in argumentation. It is important, in the first place, because it determines to what extent the speaker may rely upon his own unsupported assertion for the acceptance of his premises. But it is important quite apart from the acceptance of premises. An audience is seldom impressed by argument coming from a speaker in whom they have no confidence, while the argument of a speaker who enjoys their confidence often exerts an influence, all out of proportion to its logical value. Le Bon, the psychologist, considers the speaker's authority the 'fundamental element in persuasion.'"

IX. USING THE AUDIENCE ANALYSIS

We have presented seven factors which may be investigated in analyzing the audience.   We do not wish to be interpreted as saying that every occasion for argument demands an investigation of all these factors.   Quite obviously there are many impromptu arguments in which the audience must necessarily be sized up on the spur of the moment and sounded out for its views and impressions as the argument progresses. There are occasions in which the nature of the audience cannot possibly be known in advance, and other situations in which an elaborate audience analysis is not at all necessary. It has been our purpose to submit a basis for analyzing the audience which may be used as completely and intensively

[1] Winans, James A., and Utterback. W. E., *Argumentation*, p. 172. The Century Company, 1930.

as the occasion seems to demand. We are particularly anxious that the reader at this point in our study fully appreciate the importance of the audience as a factor in the argument-situation. The two remaining sections briefly summarize the ways in which the audience analysis can be used in analyzing the proposition and in building the case.

A. In Analyzing the Proposition. — As we have pointed out repeatedly, the audience analysis, especially an investigation of the *needs* of the audience in relation to the proposition, will be of assistance in analyzing the proposition. Overt-action propositions, particularly, seldom can be adequately analyzed without considering the audience, or the person or persons called upon to act. The issues on such propositions are specific to each audience and necessarily must be determined in relation to the audience.

B. In Synthesis or Building the Case. — While the analysis of the audience is helpful in analyzing the proposition in the manner we have indicated, its greatest usefulness, without any question, lies in the assistance which it affords in building the case. The argument must be acceptable to the audience if it is going to carry conviction or stir up action. In our chapter on Evidence it is pointed out that audience acceptability is always a criterion of good evidence and in some cases it is the primary requisite. The beliefs of the audience in relation to the available evidence can be determined only by analyses of the type we have just discussed. Not only will an analysis of the audience assist in choosing acceptable evidence, but it should be a determining factor in selecting the type of argument or reasoning to be employed. Generally speaking, we may say that if the audience is open-minded and logical in its reaction, a *confirmation* of the proposition will be the best form of support; if the audience is inadequately informed, *explanation* will usually prove most effective; if the audience is predominantly emotional in its reaction, and in many other cases where immediate decision or prompt action is sought, *motivation* may be employed to an advantage. Chapters VIII–XI will develop these three basic forms of support, but it should be emphasized here that the audience analysis will largely determine which form of support or combination of forms will be most effective in a given situation.

EXERCISES

1. Prepare in writing two short arguments on the same proposition designed to meet two audience situations differing in respect to each factor discussed in Section VIII of this chapter.

2. Assume a situation in which you are to speak before a certain group on some proposition and then write up your audience analysis in 200–250 words, organizing it on the basis of the factors discussed in Section VIII.

3. Prepare a five minute oral argument designed to meet the situation you analyzed in the preceding exercise. Read your written audience analysis to the class before you give your argument, and after delivering the argument discuss its effectiveness in meeting the situation.

4. Word an overt-action proposition and illustrate how the issues may be altered by changing the audience (*i.e.*, assume different audience situations). Do you change the proposition when you change the audience? Explain.

CHAPTER VI

THE CASE

I. The Case Defined

Earlier chapters have developed the analysis of the proposition and the analysis of the audience. Subsequent chapters are devoted to building the case and the presentation of the case. At this point we wish to make clear just what the case is and what its requirements are. We shall use the term to designate the position or stand which either the affirmative or negative proposes to take on the proposition. It is the statement which the persuader presents to his audience. It is the evidence and argument upon which he chooses to rest his cause and upon which he must win or lose.

An understanding of the following relationships will further clarify the *case*.

A. The Case and Proving the Proposition. — Proof, as we are using the term, consists of that evidence and reasoning which establishes or tends to establish the truth or falsity of the proposition. A case with probative power, then, would be one which establishes or tends to establish the truth or falsity of the proposition which it has been constructed to support. It should not be thought, however, that all effective cases in argument either have, or necessarily should have, probative force. We have seen that the objective of argument is to influence the thinking or acting of the audience. Unquestionably the case which presents proof of the proposition is one method of achieving this objective. It may be argued from some points of view that this is the best way to convince or actuate an audience, and there are undoubtedly many occasions for argument where this is the only legitimate approach to the proposition. There are, nevertheless, methods of moving people through reasoned discourse which do not involve the proof of the proposition. It is possible to build highly persuasive cases which have little or no probative force. For this reason we do not propose to make the proof of the proposition the ultimate and final test of the case. It is possible to build a good case which does not prove the proposition.

B. The Case and the Issues. — We have defined the issues as those inherently vital points upon which hinges the truth or falsity of the proposition. Thus any affirmative case which attempts to *prove* the proposition must set forth evidence and reasoning which will logically support affirmative answers to each contested issue; and any negative case which attempts to *disprove* the proposition must set forth evidence and reasoning which will support a negative answer to one or more issues. Once again, however, it must be realized that it is possible in many instances to win the acceptance or rejection of certain issues with arguments which do not logically sustain one's position.

1. ISSUES AND POINTS IN PARTITION DISTINGUISHED. — Whether the case sets out to prove the proposition or not, it should not be thought that the issues necessarily constitute the main points in one's argument. This is a mistake that is often made by beginning students of the subject. The main points that are to be taken up in the case are known as the points in partition. Both the wording and grouping of these points may differ widely from the statement of the issues. In fact, we are probably justified in saying that the instance is rare in which it is best to make the language and sequence of the points in partition agree perfectly with that of the statement of the issues. In most cases an organization more adapted to the reaction tendencies of the audience will be found to be preferable.

C. **The Case and the Audience.** — Since the case consists of the evidence and reasoning through which you hope to convince or actuate the audience, it is obvious that it must be constructed and presented in the way that will make the strongest appeal to the audience. Both the selection of arguments and the arrangement of points in the case should be adjusted to take advantage of the reaction tendencies of the audience.

D. **The Case and the Forms of Support.** — The *Forms of Support* brings a new term into our study. By the forms of support we have reference to the types of reasoning or argument that can be set forth to support a proposition.

Later chapters will develop three such forms of support, Confirmation, Explanation, and Motivation. It is our position that a given case may attempt to convince or actuate an audience through confirming the proposition, explaining it, or by motivating its acceptance. Some cases are almost wholly confirmatory, explanatory, or motivational; others combine these three forms of support. The terms Confirmation, Explanation, and Motivation will of course be explained in later chapters and the relationship we are discussing in this section will undoubtedly be clearer at that point.

II. A Prima Facie Case

The prima facie case is a special concept with which students of argument should be familiar. It is defined as the case which is of sufficient strength to win if not refuted.[1] That is, it presents sufficient proof on one side of the proposition logically to maintain that side if the argument goes unanswered.

A. A Prima Facie Case and the Burden of Proof. — The theory of argument is that the affirmative, upon whom the burden of proof always rests in a correctly worded proposition, can discharge this burden only by building a prima facie case which establishes a presumption in favor of the proposition. At the outset of the argument, the obligation rests upon the affirmative to present proof of the proposition before it is entitled to an answer from the other side. The presumption is in favor of the negative when the argument begins, and a presumption is raised against the negative only by the presentation of a prima facie affirmative case. After the affirmative has presented such a case, it then becomes necessary for the negative to make a rejoinder which

[1] O'Neill, J. M., Laycock, Craven, and Scales, R. L., *Argumentation and Debate*, p. 35. The Macmillan Company, 1917.

will block this case, or, in other words, destroy the presumption which has been raised against it. To this attack the affirmative must make a rebuttal, and so the argument goes. From this it can be seen that in an argument in which both sides are represented, it is imperative that the affirmative present a prima facie constructive or opening case and that the negative present a prima facie rejoinder, if a good argument is to ensue. If one side fails, the argument is usually shortlived, or at least it should be, because the arguer who does not present a prima facie case has no grounds upon which to proceed.

B. A Prima Facie Case and the Burden of Rebuttal. — The *burden of rebuttal* is a concept which can be easily explained in the light of the above discussion. When the affirmative has built a prima facie case, there devolves upon the negative a duty or burden to respond. Some writers erroneously state that the burden of proof has shifted to the negative in this instance. The burden of proof has not shifted, however, and *never does shift*. True, the negative must make a rejoinder to the affirmative's prima facie case if the argument is to proceed, but that responsibility is known as the burden of rebuttal and should not be described as a shifting of the burden of proof. When the negative has made a prima facie rejoinder, then the burden of rebuttal is shifted to the affirmative, and if the affirmative can make a successful counter-rejoinder, the burden of rebuttal is pushed back to the negative. Thus, we may say that the burden of rebuttal can shift from one side to the other and usually does in a close argument, whereas the burden of proof never shifts.

It should perhaps be explained at this point that there are conditions under which the negative can assume a burden of proof. This is not an exception to the statement we have just made, however, because there is no shifting of the affirmative's burden of proof involved. When the negative uses a counter proposition or alternative plan as its rejoinder to the affirmative's prima facie case, then the negative assumes a burden of proof. For instance, on the proposition that (X) street be paved with brick, if the negative opposed the proposition with the alternative that the street be paved with concrete, the negative would have the burden of proof on this counter proposition. In this case, or in the case of any other alternative plan, the negative also is proposing a change from the status quo, and therefore has the burden of proof which a defense of this change entails. It should be emphasized, however, that the mere fact that the negative assumes a burden of proof does not relieve the affirmative of the burden of proof on the main proposition.[1]

C. Should Every Case Be a Prima Facie Case? — In one sense this question raises the same point that we made earlier in this chapter in discussing the relationship between the case and proving the proposition. We said in that connection that it is possible to build a good case which does not prove the proposition. Now, since a prima facie case is one which does prove the proposition, at least in a sufficient degree to shift the burden of rebuttal, we are brought face to face with the question as to what circumstances permit the persuader to present a case which does not constitute prima facie evidence and argument for the proposition under discussion. We shall consider this question both from the standpoint of the argument in which both sides are represented, and from the standpoint of the argument in which the affirmative or negative alone is represented.

1. ARGUMENTS WHERE BOTH SIDES ARE REPRESENTED. — In arguments where both the affirmative and negative are

---

[1] See O'Neill, Laycock, and Scales, *Argumentation and Debate*, pp. 37–38 for a discussion of the burden of rebuttal, and pp. 36–37, for a discussion of the effect of a counter proposition on the burden of proof.

represented by their advocates, especially formal arguments such as contest debates, for example, it is important that both sides present prima facie cases. Our discussion of the burden of proof and the burden of rebuttal has made it clear that logically the negative has no responsibility to respond until the affirmative has presented a prima facie case, and the affirmative in turn has no responsibility, having presented a prima facie case, until the negative makes a prima facie rejoinder. Of course, as we all know, what actually takes place in many arguments differs somewhat from this. Both the affirmative and negative will attempt to tear down the opposing case before it is ever completed and the argument becomes a give and take affair throughout. Notwithstanding, it should always be kept in mind that any arguer who confronts an opponent with a case which is not prima facie, no matter how persuasive it may be, is open to the danger of losing the argument by the very simple stratagem of having its shortcomings in this respect pointed out.

Perhaps it should be noted in this connection that admissions on the part of the negative very frequently eliminate the necessity of the affirmative proving points which it would otherwise need to prove in order to establish a prima facie case.

2. ARGUMENTS WHERE ONLY ONE SIDE IS REPRESENTED. — There are many arguments where but one side is represented in which the persuader is entirely justified in presenting a case which falls short of prima facie proof of the proposition. Time limitations play an important part here. It is certainly much more effective to take one aspect of the question in the time allotted and treat it thoroughly than it is to attempt a complete prima facie case and do nothing thoroughly. Furthermore, there are many situations in which only certain aspects of the proposition are significant

for the particular occasion at hand. For instance, in presenting an argument for a new municipal auditorium; before one group, the whole project might turn on the financing of the building; before another audience, the main consideration might be the need of such a building. In such instances, the arguer very evidently should build a case which will meet the controversial issues even though this case may not be logically complete.

In presenting a case which is not a prima facie support of the proposition, it is frequently a wise plan to partition the whole case in the introductory statement, and then state the particular points you plan to discuss in the speech at hand. In this way, the audience will get a perspective of the whole proof even though it is argued only in part. This is an excellent plan to follow in class talks where time does not permit the development of the entire case.

Another expedient which may be resorted to when time will not permit a discussion of all the issues is that of narrowing the proposition. The proof of any proposition resolves itself into the establishment of one or more sub-propositions. By narrowing the proposition we mean the substitution of one of these sub-propositions for the original proposition as the topic for discussion. Thus, if I am thinking of arguing the proposition, *Resolved:* That the Equity Courts should be deprived of the power of issuing injunctions in labor disputes, and I find that I shall not have time to handle the proposition as stated, I may narrow my topic by choosing one of the aspects of this proposition. Thus, I might argue the proposition, *Resolved:* That the labor injunction has been detrimental to American Labor; or, *Resolved:* That the labor injunction is unfair to American Labor. What this process amounts to, of course, is simply the substitution of a narrower proposition, which embodies one phase of the broader subject.

Entirely apart from the situations discussed, however, there are countless occasions on which highly persuasive arguments can be given without proving the proposition. We certainly see evidence of this in political speeches, sermons, sales talks, argumentative conversations, and in arguments of all kinds, especially where only one side is represented, or at least where only one side is represented by an advocate who has prepared to meet the situation.

III. DIVISIONS OF THE CASE

There are three divisions to every case: (1) The Introduction; (2) The Body; (3) The Conclusion. Since the outlining, composing, and presenting of these divisions of the case are given specific treatment in other chapters, we shall be brief in our discussion of them at this point.

A. The Introduction. — The introduction is that part of the case which appears at the beginning of the argument and prepares the audience for the argument which is to follow.

B. The Body. — The body is that part of the case which presents the argument proper and constitutes the main support of the proposition.

C. The Conclusion. — The conclusion is that part of the case which closes the argument and attempts to clinch a favorable decision.

IV. THE TYPES OF CASES

While cases may be classified on several bases, we shall consider simply the affirmative and negative cases.

A. The Affirmative Case. — We have already stated that the affirmative has the burden of proof and that it must present a prima facie case if it is logically to discharge this burden. The question next to be considered is: What must the affirmative do to establish such a case? This question cannot be answered specifically except in the light of specific propositions. In terms of the issues, however, we may say that the affirmative case, if it is to prove the proposition, must present an argument which, taken as a whole, will support an affirmative answer to the question raised by each issue. In terms of the stock issues cited in Chapter IV, a prima facie case on a proposition of policy may be set up by establishing the two stock issues: (1) Is the present system unsatisfactory? and (2) Is the proposed action the proper remedy?

The affirmative's case for the proposition is known as the affirmative constructive case, and, properly, should open the argument on any proposition.

B. The Negative Case. — We have already explained that the negative case must make a rejoinder to the affirmative constructive case. Here again we cannot be specific as to what should constitute such a rejoinder except in the light of specific propositions. However, in terms of the issues, any argument which can support an unconditional negative answer to one or more of the questions raised by the issues constitutes a prima facie rejoinder. In terms of the stock issues, an argument on a proposition of policy which successfully negates either one or both of the stock issues constitutes a valid negative case.

The negative's case against the proposition is known as the negative constructive case and should follow the affirmative constructive case in an argument.

V. Summary

It has been the purpose of this chapter to explain what is meant by the *case* in an argument, and to prepare the reader for subsequent chapters on supporting the proposition and on outlining, composing, and presenting the case.

EXERCISES

1. Prepare for presentation in class a short prima facie case on some simple proposition of your own choosing. Be prepared to state the issues on your proposition and explain the relation of your case thereto.

2. Conduct a series of debates under the following plan. Pay particular attention to the cases.

   a. One person on each side.
   b. Seven minute affirmative constructive case; ten minute negative rejoinder; and three minute affirmative rebuttal.
   c. Discuss each debate in respect to the burden of proof, the burden of rebuttal (how many times did it shift), and the prima facie adequacy of the affirmative and negative cases.

It might be well to read Chapter XVIII before conducting this series of debates.

3. Study the debates appearing in Appendix A (or others of your own choosing in the H. W. Wilson Company's *University Debater's Annual*) in respect to the following points:

   a. The issues and the points in partition. (How do they differ?)
   b. The prima facie adequacy of the affirmative and negative cases.
   c. The burden of rebuttal. (How many times does it shift?)

CHAPTER VII

EVICENCE

B. Audience Acceptability.
    1. Is the Evidence Already a Belief of the Audience?
        a. Mental Stereotypes.
        b. Some Factors Determining Belief.
    2. Has the Evidence Been Attributed to Authority Which the Audience Is Willing to Accept?

IV. Summary.

I. THE NATURE OF EVIDENCE

A. Evidence Defined. — Evidence consists of those matters of fact and opinion which are used as a basis of argument.

All argument consists of *inferences* from *premises* to a *conclusion.* That is, it is the process of setting forth premises or propositions in relationships which will permit the inference of a new proposition or a conclusion. It is the function of argument to maintain these premises and display the relationships between them in such a way as to lead other people to accept the conclusion and act upon it. Thus, a premise can be defined as any proposition, either stated or assumed, which is used as a basis for inference; and an inference, as the mental process by which the relationships between premises is discerned. The matters of fact and opinion, which we have designated evidence, are either stated in the premises of an argument or arrayed in support of these premises. *Every premise must be so evidenced or else stand as an unsupported assertion.*

The following argument presented in an advertisement of Buick automobiles illustrates the relation of evidence to the other elements in argument.[1]

Premise   1. You should purchase an automobile upon which other people bestow confidence and preference.

[1] An advertisement of the Buick Motor Company, Flint, Mich. *The Saturday Evening Post*, Vol. 203, No. 2, July 12, 1930, pp. 70 and 71.

Premise   2. People have bestowed rewards of confidence and preference upon the Buick not accorded any other car in its field.

Evidence   a. "Two people have purchased Buicks, year after year, for one buyer of any other automobile priced above $1200."

b. "There are 700,000 more people driving Buicks than any other of the fifteen makes of cars in Buick's class."

c. "Women, in every section of America, purchase more than twice as many Buicks as any other automobile priced above $1200."

d. "More than four out of every five — 88 per cent of the great army of Buick owners — buy Buicks again and again."

e. "Month after month, today's Buick has won from 30 to 50 per cent of the combined sales of the fifteen makes in its price class."

f. "Buick owners alone purchase more Buicks than the total annual production of any other automobile priced above $1200."

Conclusion   3. Hence, you should purchase a Buick automobile.

In this example, the first proposition is a premise of opinion or theory, whose general acceptability is deemed such as to make evidence of its truth unnecessary. The second proposition is a premise of fact supported by six statements of fact. These six sub-propositions constitute evidence, with the definite implication that authentic records are available to establish each fact, if they are called for. The third proposition is the conclusion *inferred* from the relationship existing between the two premises.

B. Evidence and Proof. — All proof is composed of two great elements : (1) Basic premises of fact and opinion ; and (2) Certain inferential relationships. These are usually referred to as Evidence and Argument, respectively. Logicians speak of evidence and argument as the two elements of proof, and by proof, they refer to the establishment of the truth or falsity of the proposition in whose support the evidence and argument is being offered. Now the *proof of the proposition* under discussion is the objective of some arguments, perhaps of most, arguments. Later chapters will develop three forms of support or three basic methods of argument, Confirmation, Explanation, and Motivation. Of these, Confirmation is clearly probative; Explanation may have probative force; while Motivation makes no attempt to prove the proposition which it is advanced to support. The point we wish to make here, however, is that evidence should be set forth in all good argument, no matter what form of support is used. For that reason we have defined evidence as "those matters of fact and opinion *which are used as a basis of argument*." Shaw, writing on debating, defines evidence as "any matter of fact *that serves as a basis of proof*." [1] The limitations of this definition for our purposes are evident from the above discussion. It is true that evidence plays a more important part in those forms of support which depend upon *proof* for their persuasive power, but it does enter into all argument as we shall see later.

C. Evidence and the Beliefs of the Audience. — Another very interesting relationship which needs to be worked out at this point is that between evidence and the beliefs of the audience. One of the most recent books on argumentation very significantly omits any treatment of evidence as such.[2] This book does give an excellent treatment of the beliefs of the audience as basic premises, however. Read the following statement carefully:

"The term *premise* is used to indicate any statement in argument employed to support another statement. Such a support-

[1] Shaw, W. S., *The Art of Debate*, p. 49. Allyn and Bacon, 1922.
[2] We have reference here to Winans and Utterback, *Argumentation*, The Century Company, 1930.

ing statement may be a conclusion as well as a premise, for it in turn may be supported by other statements. It is obvious, however, that the argument must ultimately rest upon statements which are themselves left unsupported. These unsupported statements of fact or principle, upon which the superstructure of argument is erected, we shall call the *basic premises* of the argument. To be convincing an argument must rest upon basic premises which are acceptable to the hearer. Such a premise will be acceptable (1) if it is already a belief of the hearer, (2) if it is presented by a speaker whom the hearer accepts as an authority, or (3) if it is presented as the opinion of some one other than the speaker whom the hearer accepts as an authority." [1]

The sentence in this quotation to which we would call particular attention is this — " To be convincing, an argument must rest upon basic premises which are acceptable to the hearer." While this statement is true beyond any question, we feel that as a bit of advice to students of argument it should be given some very careful interpretation. Are we to conclude that the evidence or basic premises in an argument should be made acceptable to the audience *at the time the argument is presented?* If so, might there not be many instances when more mature reflection and later investigation would cause many an auditor to become unconvinced, having discovered that the basic premises were not as " basic " as he originally thought them to be? Might there not be instances when evidence or basic premises constituting the " cold, unvarnished facts," supported by the best possible authority, and presented without regard to personalities or the whims and prejudices of the audience, would eventually be more acceptable and hence more convincing than premises selected to cater to the audience at the time of presentation?

We are not raising the question of the rightness and wrongness of employing false premises which are acceptable to the

---

[1] Winans and Utterback, *Argumentation*, pp. 140–141.

audience. That is purely an ethical question which in the words of Professors Winans and Utterback, " . . . must be decided according to the same principles of honor and decency that govern the speech of honest men in private conversation." The question we are raising is purely a rhetorical problem. Is it advisable to weaken one's evidence from the standpoint of logical adequacy in order to secure immediate acceptability, and run the risk of losing all conviction, to say nothing of the respect of the audience, by having this superficiality discovered at a later date? There seems to us to be little question but what there are many occasions both in oral and written argument in which the first and primary test of evidence should be its logical adequacy. Certainly this is true in those cases where the speaker is attempting to convince by confirming or proving the proposition. Of course, even in argument of this type, if evidence is acceptable to the audience, so much the better ; and in choosing between two equally sound items of evidence, by all means choose the one which you believe to be more acceptable to the audience.

We have no desire to underestimate the importance of audience acceptability as a criterion of good evidence. There are undoubtedly many occasions for argument where audience acceptability should take precedence over logical adequacy in the speaker's choice of evidence. This is especially true where an immediate decision or prompt action is sought. The point we are making is that both of these tests ought to be considered ; in some cases, it is advisable to be guided primarily by one test, and in other cases, primarily by the other test.

In the remaining sections in this chapter we shall classify the kinds of evidence and discuss these two basic tests of evidence.

II. Kinds of Evidence

A. Facts and Opinions Distinguished. — We have already stated that evidence consists of matters of fact and opinion which are used as a basis of argument. A matter of fact may be said to be a known truth which is concerned with the existence of things, the occurrence of acts, the classification of objects, or the connection of events.[1] An opinion on the other hand is some person's belief, idea, or conjecture, which may or may not represent the truth. It is sometimes difficult to distinguish between a fact and an opinion, because what is thought to be a fact may turn out to be only a mistaken opinion, and what is taken as an opinion may prove to be a fact. On the whole, however, the distinction is a very useful one. In most arguments there are usually certain data which in no way involve the opinions of persons and which constitute the facts of the case. In addition to evidence of this type there is commonly available a number of opinions interpreting these facts which are quite readily distinguishable from the facts of the case and which are known as opinion evidence. A discussion of fact witnesses and opinion (usually called " expert ") witnesses in Section III of this chapter will give further consideration to this distinction between facts and opinions.

B. Methods of Classifying Evidence. — While facts and opinions constitute the two kinds of evidence and should be remembered as such, there are several bases upon which evidence can be classified.[2]

1. Direct and Circumstantial. — Evidence can be classified as direct or circumstantial depending upon the relation it bears to the conclusion. If the conclusion follows from the premises *without inference*, the evidence is direct; and in

---

[1] Shaw, W. C., *Art of Debate*, p. 49.

[2] O'Neill, J. M., Laycock, Craven, and Scales, R. L., *Argumentation and Debate*, pp. 88–101. The Macmillan Company, 1917.

those cases in which the conclusion *must be inferred,* the evidence is circumstantial or indirect. For example, if a person were seen to enter an apple orchard empty-handed and come out with a sack of apples, it would probably be inferred that he picked the apples in this orchard. If further evidence were introduced to show that he entered stealthily and at night, the inference would likely be that he stole the apples. The evidence in either case, however, would be circumstantial because the facts, while creating a high degree of probability, are still indirect. If the man were seen picking the apples in this orchard, evidence to that effect would directly bear out the conclusion that he obtained the apples in that way. The evidence would be direct, because the conclusion follows without inference, — or is identical with the evidence.

It is impossible to classify evidence as direct or indirect without first knowing the conclusion that is being drawn, because these are only labels of the relation of the evidence to the conclusion. As we have just said, evidence showing that the man was seen to pick the apples would directly evidence the conclusion that he did so procure them ; on the other hand, this same evidence would be circumstantial, if the conclusion alleged that the man stole the apples. Never attempt to pass upon the directness of evidence until you know the conclusion that the evidence is being advanced to uphold.

Needless to say, direct evidence is much to be desired in argument wherever it can be found. It is much more conclusive and highly persuasive. It should not be thought, however, that it is impossible to argue from circumstantial evidence. On the contrary, most of the available evidence on questions which permit of argument is circumstantial. If there is much direct evidence bearing out the proposition, the argument is apt to be short-lived.

2. WRITTEN OR UNWRITTEN. — Evidence can be further classified as written or unwritten. Any facts or opinions

which have been reduced to writing or print constitute written evidence, while those rendered orally constitute unwritten evidence. Written evidence is ordinarily considered more valuable than unwritten, because it usually represents more careful and mature thought, is less apt to be influenced by passing whims and prejudices, and is not as subject to error when it is being reproduced in argument.

3. REAL OR PERSONAL. — Real evidence consists of any object or thing which is itself used as evidence. Personal evidence, as opposed to real evidence, consists of the statements of people. The best examples of the use of real evidence are the exhibits produced in court trials, such as the weapons or instruments used in committing the crime, or any other object that has an evidential bearing on the issues. In a recent intercollegiate debate on chain retailing, the team opposing the chain stores made use of real evidence. It was argued that the chains were deceiving the buying public by selling standard brands of goods in containers holding less merchandise than those dispensed by independent dealers. The point was evidenced by producing a number of chain store containers and comparing them with the larger cans and tins of the independent merchant. The important thing to remember in regard to real evidence is that the objects so used must be presented directly to the senses of those who are to judge — wounds to the eyes, odors to the nose, sounds to the ears *of the judges*.

4. ORIGINAL OR HEARSAY. — Evidence originating with the witness or one presenting it is known as original evidence as distinguished from hearsay evidence, which is derived from someone else. Where the persuader is as competent a witness as any one else that might be quoted, his own testimony is ordinarily considered more valuable because he has made the observation or investigation for himself. Certainly, if other things are equal, the person who speaks from first hand

information is more persuasive than one who must rely on the statements of others. The attitude of the courts is very much opposed to hearsay evidence, and its use is permitted only in certain exceptional cases. In general argumentation, however, much reliance must be placed on the experiences and observations of others as they are told to you, or as they are printed in books and magazines. For this reason we suggest two considerations upon which the value of hearsay evidence can be estimated : (1) Is the nature of the evidence such that it is likely to be passed from one person to another without being exaggerated or altered? (2) Has it passed through reliable hands? If these two questions can be answered affirmatively when applied to a given piece of hearsay evidence, the persuader can usually use the evidence confidently.

5. PRE-APPOINTED OR CASUAL. — Where material is deliberately and consciously prepared or preserved to be used as evidence at a future date, it is known as pre-appointed evidence. Where this intent and preparation is lacking, the evidence is known as casual. Casual or undesigned evidence has particular value because it is almost certain to be freer of prejudice and bias than material which has been prepared to win a particular cause. On the other hand, it can be argued that casual evidence is less apt to be the result of careful observation and study, and therefore less accurate than that which has been designed. As a general rule, however, we may say that those facts and opinions which are gathered and formulated without any intention of using them as evidence in any particular argument are more valuable as evidence than those designed as such, providing the casual statement is one that can meet the other tests for accuracy and honesty.

6. POSITIVE OR NEGATIVE. — It is possible, further, to classify all evidence as either positive or negative, depending

upon the existence or non-existence of pertinent facts and opinions. Positive evidence has little value as a separate category except as it opposes negative evidence, which can be defined as a significant lack of evidence to the contrary. In many cases the very lack of any materials that can be used as positive evidence, constitutes the most convincing evidential fact that can be produced. For example, the absence of campfires might be used to support the conclusion that there were no campers; or a photograph of a group of people on a picnic could be used as negative evidence to prove that one whose picture did not appear, was not present at the picnic. Another common example of negative evidence is the empty pail which has stood out all night, presented as evidence that no rain fell during the night.

7. ORDINARY OR EXPERT. — Ordinary evidence consists of those matters of fact which can be observed and reported upon by an average individual without the use of any professional knowledge or training. Expert evidence, or opinion evidence, as it is quite generally known, springs from an individual whose training and ability renders him competent to pass a judgment on the point under question which could not be authoritatively given by one who does not have such training and ability. This distinction will be elaborated further in our discussion of the sources of evidence in the next section.[1]

III. TESTS OF EVIDENCE

A. Logical Adequacy. — The first basic test of evidence which we shall discuss is that of logical adequacy. Is the evidence logically sufficient to justify the conclusion that is being drawn from it? Three factors must be considered in

[1] It should be explained, perhaps, that each of the seven pairs of evidence we have given are all inclusive classifications. That is, all evidence is either direct or circumstantial, written or unwritten, etc. Any given piece of evidence can be classified in these seven different ways.

answering this question: (1) Is the source of the evidence reliable? (2) Is the evidence consistent? and (3) Has enough evidence been presented?

1. IS THE SOURCE OF THE EVIDENCE RELIABLE? — All evidence is derived from *persons* except those facts which are made apparent by *objects* and *things*. For instance, the exhibit of an object, *i.e.*, real evidence, constitutes evidence whose source is the object exhibited. Thus, the gun that was used in the crime, the car with a broken windshield, or any other such object has its evidential origin in the object itself. Usually, however, evidence has its origin in the oral or written expressions of persons. People who report facts or give opinions which are used as evidence are known as *witnesses*. The courts recognize two kinds of witnesses which should also be distinguished by students of argument: (1) An ordinary witness; and (2) An expert witness. In the case of the collision of two automobiles, for instance, any person of ordinary ability who witnessed the accident could testify as to how many people were involved, from which direction the cars approached the intersection, approximately where the two machines met, and other such facts; but this individual is not permitted to supply any evidence beyond these facts. The courts will only in certain unusual cases accept this man's opinion as evidence. The ordinary witness has just two functions, the first of which is *to find out* the facts, and the second, *to report* these facts as he found them. If there are any questions in the case upon which an opinion is necessary, the court calls in an expert or specialist, whose training and experience render him competent to pass authoritative judgment on the point in question.

While it is the general rule in law that ordinary witnesses report facts, and expert witnesses give opinions, it is true that there are situations in which an ordinary witness is permitted to give an opinion and expert witnesses are asked to report facts. This whole matter is explained in the following quotation from O'Neill, Laycock, and Scales.

"Most evidence is *ordinary*. This term covers all that is not *expert*. Expert testimony strictly speaking is called in law 'opinion evidence' and in general argumentation 'argument from authority.' These two terms cover practically parallel things, and we will gain considerably in general argumentation if we understand the legal doctrine of 'opinion evidence' and follow it in dealing with 'argument from authority.' In law the testimony of an 'ordinary' witness is not always limited strictly to matters of fact. There are circumstances under which an ordinary witness is allowed to testify in regard to matters of opinion, such for instance as his opinion regarding the 'character' or the 'sanity' of some other person. Also, there arise at times in law trials circumstances under which an 'expert' witness testifies as to matters of fact rather than to matters of opinion. For instance, an expert chemist might well testify as to matters of fact in the realm of chemistry, under which circumstances he could not be called strictly an 'opinion' witness. However, the expert is usually asked to interpret facts which he or other witnesses establish, and this interpretation, which is the expert's principal function, usually is, of course, opinion evidence in law, or argument from authority in general argumentation." [1]

Both facts and opinions must be derived from reliable sources if they are to be given much credence in argument. O'Neill, Laycock, and Scales suggest that the following tests be applied to the sources of evidence: [2]

"*Ordinary ('fact') Witnesses:*
1. Is the witness physically qualified?
2. Is the witness mentally qualified?
    a. Does the witness have a reliable memory?
    b. Is the witness accurate?
        (1) Is the witness subject to thoughtless exaggeration?

[1] O'Neill, J. M., Laycock, Craven, and Scales, L. M., *Argumentation and Debate*, pp. 96–97. The Macmillan Company, 1917.
[2] *Ibid.*, pp. 107–112.

3. Is the witness morally qualified?
    a. Is he unduly interested in the case?
    b. Is his general moral character good?
4. Did the witness have the opportunity to get the truth?

"*Expert* ('*opinion*') *Witnesses:*
  1. Is opinion evidence necessary?
  2. Is the authority qualified?"

    a. The Reliability of Ordinary (Fact) Witnesses. — A brief
explanation of the points outlined above will make clear the
conditions under which reliance can be placed in an ordinary
(fact) witness. First of all, any individual reporting facts
must be *physically* able to find the facts he proposes to report.
A blind man is not competent to find facts which can be detected only by seeing, and a deaf person cannot discover facts
whose discernment is dependent upon hearing. The testimony of any individual, who can be shown to be physically
unable to discover the facts which he purports to have
found, is rendered valueless by such an exposure. Likewise,
a fact witness must be *mentally* qualified. Some witnesses,
even though they are well intentioned, have bad memories,
are incapable of accurate expression, or are subject to thought-
less exaggeration. If a person can be shown to possess any
of these weaknesses, it raises a strong presumption of error
against any evidence derived from this source. The *moral*
competence of the witness is conditioned by his personal interest in the case and his general moral character. If it can
be shown that a witness will gain from certain testimony, a
motive for dishonesty or deliberate exaggeration has been
established which will weaken this testimony. Or, if it can
be proved that the witness is inclined to prevaricate in other
matters and is chronically dishonest, there is established a
high degree of probability that he will pervert the truth in
the matter under question.
    The final test of a fact witness is his *opportunity to get the*

truth. Regardless of the physical, mental, and moral competence of the witness, if it can be shown that he did not have an opportunity to make an accurate observation, his testimony falls. For instance, a football fan, who is seated on the five yard line in the stadium, is hardly in a position to pass judgment on the ruling of the referee made at the other end of the playing field, no matter how qualified he may be otherwise.

b. The Reliability of Expert (Opinion) Witnesses. — In testing opinion evidence, the first consideration is whether there is any necessity for evidence of this kind. In those cases in which the opinion of the audience is just as good as anyone else's, there is no occasion for opinion evidence. Wherever it is possible to cite the facts of the case and draw acceptable conclusions without the use of the opinions of others, it is far better to do so. At least, if expert testimony is to be used in cases where the facts are comprehensible to the audience, this testimony should be brought in as a confirmation of the judgment you expect the audience to make, rather than quoting it as the only evidential support. This point should be emphasized for the benefit of debaters who seem to prefer to cite a long list of references rather than reason a point out with the audience. Under ordinary circumstances, it is much better debating to give the facts which have led authorities to certain opinions than it is simply to quote those opinions.

If the facts of the case are such that the audience is incapable of passing competent judgment on them, then the persuader is not only justified, but should support his argument with the opinions of others. And when he does so, he should select witnesses who are qualified to give an opinion. It seems necessary to observe, however, that competence to pass judgment in one field does not imply a similar competence in other fields. It is amusing to hear young debaters quote men of national reputation as authorities in matters about which their opinion is of no more value than that of any intelligent person in the audience. Opinion evidence is valuable only when it is the opinion of a recognized specialist, given in his field of specialization, and upon matters of fact which ordinary persons cannot interpret adequately.

c. Documenting Sources. — The persuader should be able to document all his evidence. In the case of facts, it is a matter of stating who discovered the facts and where they are reported. When opinion evidence is used, the persuader should know whose opinion it is and where it is recorded. If the evidence is gotten from books, magazines, pamphlets, newspapers, or printed material of any kind, an *exact* and *complete* reference to the source of the material should be kept, as suggested in an earlier chapter. If the persuader is documenting his evidence so that the audience may refer to it later, the entire reference should be given in the argument. Otherwise, only as much of the citation needs to be stated as seems necessary to establish the authenticity of the evidence that is being documented. In the case of unwritten materials it is best to explain the exact channels through which the facts or opinions have reached you. While there is probably less danger of excessive documentation than there is of inadequate reference, it should be remembered that the constant citation of pages, numbers, volumes, and other symbols of identification is wearisome to the average audience, and should be limited to that evidence which the audience is inclined to doubt or question.

Some students seem to confuse the documentation of evidence with the evidence itself. It should be understood that documentation is nothing more than stating the source of the evidence in order to lend it greater authenticity or to enable others to refer to it at a later date. A long list of sources has little or no value as evidence unless the facts and opinions to be obtained from these sources are also cited.

2. Is the Evidence Consistent? — By the consistence of evidence we refer to its agreement or harmony with human nature, known facts, other evidence, and the beliefs of the audience. If evidence is to be accepted by the audience, it must either meet these tests of consistency or the inconsistency must be capable of a satisfactory explanation.

a. Consistence with Human Nature. — There are certain things which we expect normal persons to do under normal circumstances, and we are inclined to doubt any allegations of fact or opinion which do not fit in with our expectations. For instance, evidence to the effect that a farmer shot himself because of a bumper crop, would hardly be acceptable without some explanation of this incongruous behavior. Wherever such an inconsistency exists, the accuracy of the evidence should be carefully ascertained and explained to the audience, or else the evidence should be abandoned.

b. Consistence with Known Facts. — Evidence that is inconsistent with known facts has no probative or logical value. Of course, as we pointed out earlier in the chapter, if the audience is unaware of the facts with which the evidence is inconsistent, it may be willing to accept it. Such acceptance, however, does not make the evidence any truer or any more logically adequate. This whole matter of using false premises in argument is nothing more nor less than deliberate prevarication. The ethical question of lying is not particularly different in debate than in ordinary conversation. Honest men are honest men, and liars are liars, in both situations. This rhetorical consideration remains, however — whenever an arguer, for the sake of winning immediate favor, employs any evidence which is logically weaker than other material at his disposal, whether the evidence chosen is false or not, he runs the risk not only of losing conviction on the point in question, but also of seriously impairing the confidence of people in his ability and integrity as a speaker.

c. Consistence with Other Evidence. — One of the worst inconsistencies into which an arguer can fall is to present two or more matters of fact or opinion which cannot consistently stand together. An inconsistency of this kind is especially damaging if the discrepancy exists between two items of evidence presented in the same proof or in the same argument. The confidence of the audience will be badly shaken, however, even if it can be shown that the speaker has presented evidence in another argument or on some previously recallable occasion which is inconsistent with that set forth on the occasion at hand. There is no better way to avoid such an embarrassing circumstance than to check all the evidence to be offered in an argument with this possibility in mind before the argument is ever presented.

d. Consistence with the Beliefs of the Audience. — Facts and opinions which are inconsistent with the beliefs of the audience are not convincing no matter how fundamental they may be. If their acceptability cannot be established at the time of presentation, the speaker can do one of three things: (1) He can disregard the beliefs of the audience, use what he considers to be the strongest evidence at hand, draw his conclusions, and urge the audience to investigate for themselves. (2) He can argue hypothetically, *i.e.*, accept the beliefs of the audience for the sake of argument, and establish the case on the basis of these beliefs without ever alleging their logical adequacy or giving his personal sanction to them. When arguing on a hypothetical basis of this kind, the speaker should make it clear to the audience that he is making an assumption, and in that way avoid any variance with his own convictions in the matter. (3) If immediate conviction or prompt action is sought, he can premise his argument on the existing beliefs of the audience or on evidence that can be made immediately acceptable. Of course, when the strongest evidence, logically considered, is at variance with the beliefs of the audience, and the arguer sees fit to premise his argument on these beliefs, he should know that the tests of logical adequacy can be applied with telling effect by an opponent or anyone else who is disposed to do so.

3. HAS ENOUGH EVIDENCE BEEN PRESENTED? — A final test of the logical adequacy of evidence is the amount of evidence presented. Has enough evidence been presented to prove the point which it is set forth to support? This is a purely quantitative consideration and should not be confused with the tests of source and consistence just discussed. While it is of course impossible for us to say just how much evidence should be presented on any occasion, we do wish to caution the student against jumping to conclusions from too little evidence. Be certain that you have enough evidence logically to sustain the conclusions you are drawing.

B. Audience Acceptability. — Audience acceptability is the second basic test which should be applied to evidence. If a situation exists where the evidence which is most *logically adequate*, is also most *acceptable to the audience*, the problem of choosing evidence or the basic premises of the argument is then a relatively simple one. But if the evidence which is most desirable from a purely logical standpoint is at variance with the beliefs of the audience and cannot be made immediately acceptable to them, the speaker is then confronted with a real problem. Which test shall be the primary guide in selecting evidence? This question the arguer must answer for himself. Generally speaking, if immediate conviction or prompt action is sought, audience acceptability should be the primary consideration; and if studied, deliberative judgment or action, based on investigation and mature consideration, is desired, then logical adequacy should take precedence. Even this is a rough generalization, however, and the best that we can do is to set forth the factors involved. We have gone into the matter of logical adequacy so that any careful reader should understand the logical tests of evidence. We shall now consider audience acceptability, so that the reader may have some insight into the many factors involved here.

1. IS THE EVIDENCE ALREADY A BELIEF OF THE AUDIENCE? — If the basic premises are already the beliefs of the audience, they will of course be altogether acceptable. But in order to premise an argument on the beliefs of the audience, we must first know what these beliefs are, or at least what they are likely to be and how to discover them. In Section VIII of Chapter V, we set forth seven factors which might be looked into in analyzing the audience. A consideration of the audience from these points of view will certainly be helpful in discovering its beliefs relative to the proposition. We would suggest a careful rereading of that Section at this time. A few additional facts about the nature of belief will also be helpful.

a. *Mental Stereotypes.* — Walter Lipmann in his interesting book, *Public Opinion,* has developed a concept with which students of argument should be familiar. That concept is the " mental stereotype." Lipmann defines stereotypes as follows:

"They are an ordered, more or less consistent picture of the world, to which our habits, our tastes, our capacities, our comforts and our hopes have adjusted themselves. They may not be a complete picture of the world, but they are a picture of a possible world to which we are adapted. In that world people and things have their well-known places, and do certain expected things. We feel at home there. We fit in. We are members. We know the way around. There we find the charm of the familiar, the normal, the dependable; its grooves and shapes are where we are accustomed to find them. And though we have abandoned much that might have tempted us before we creased ourselves into that mould, once we are firmly in, it fits as snugly as an old shoe."

"No wonder, then, that any disturbance of the stereotypes seems like an attack upon the foundations of the universe. It is an attack upon the foundations of *our* universe, and, where big things are at stake, we do not readily admit that there is any distinction between our universe and the universe." [1]

We may say, then, that every individual, as a result of his experiences and capacities, develops a more or less definite system of beliefs into which he tends to adjust all new ideas. Ideas that will not fit, he is inclined not to believe, because believing will disturb his ordered picture of things, his mental stereotype. Regarding the reception of new ideas, Lipmann says :

"In some measure, stimuli from the outside, especially when they are printed or spoken words, evoke some part of a system of stereotypes, so that the actual sensation and the preconception occupy consciousness at the same time. The two are blended, much as if we looked at red through blue glasses and saw green. If what we hear or read corresponds successfully with what we anticipated, the stereotype is reinforced for the future, as it is in the man who knows in advance that the Japanese are cunning and has the bad luck to run across two dishonest Japanese."

"If the experience contradicts the stereotype, one of two things happens. If the man is no longer plastic, or if some powerful interest makes it highly inconvenient to rearrange his stereotypes, he pooh-poohs the contradiction as an exception which proves the rule, discredits the witness, finds a flaw somewhere, and manages to forget it. But if he is still curious and open-minded, the novelty is taken into the picture, and allowed to modify it. Sometimes, if the incident is striking enough, and if he has felt a general discomfort with his established scheme, he may be shaken to such an extent as to distrust all accepted ways of looking at life, and to expect that normally a thing will not be what it is generally supposed to be." [2]

The arguer, to be effective, must realize that his hearers will interpret his arguments in the light of their individual

[1] Lipmann, Walter, *Public Opinion*, pp. 95–96.   Harcourt, Brace, and Company, 1922.   [2] *Ibid.*, pp. 99–100.

stereotypes, and he must fit his proposition into these stereotypes. The national prohibition question presents an excellent illustration of this point. People who have been brought up in dry families and communities, and who have been taught that liquor is evil and immoral, simply cannot be brought to believe many premises which are very sincerely believed by those who have had drinks served at the family table all their lives. The stereotypes of these people on this subject are very different, and the same type of argument will not be persuasive to both groups. If one is trying to convince a dry that the national prohibition act should be modified to permit the sale of light wines and beers, he might win conviction by citing as evidence the increasing number of bootleggers and other lawless elements, and the poisonous " moonshine " liquor which is being sold, providing he did this without ever questioning the basic evil of all drink and the ultimate desirability of wiping it out completely. Whereas with a wet, it could be convincingly argued that prohibition is basicly wrong, administratively ridiculous, and for that reason the quickest, surest way to its abolition would be through the entering wedge of light wines and beers.

   b. *Some Factors Determining Belief.* — The prohibition example is not an extreme case. There is hardly a subject upon which people are apt to differ and argue about but what presents the same situation. It will be seen that beliefs and belief systems or stereotypes are largely determined (1) By the experiences of the individual, (2) By his own personal desires, and (3) By the opinions of the social group with whom he is associated. Every individual believes fundamentally what his experiences and contacts have led him to believe. Where his desires counter these beliefs, he usually succeeds in rationalizing and modifying his mental picture to accommodate ideas consistent with the satisfaction of these desires.

And where his ideas are inconsistent with those of his social group, there is a strong tendency to swing in line with the group. Pillsbury refers to this last factor as the " illusion of universality," the idea that they " all are doing it " and they " all are believing it "; therefore, it is the thing to do and believe.

2. HAS THE EVIDENCE BEEN ATTRIBUTED TO AUTHORITY WHICH THE AUDIENCE IS WILLING TO ACCEPT. — Sometimes evidence which is not already believed by the audience can be made acceptable by attributing it to authorities whose words they are willing to accept. In some cases, the statement of the speaker will be accepted as authority and for that reason, if none other, it is advisable for the speaker to use language, and maintain an attitude and bearing, which will be conducive to such acceptance. In other instances, the testimony of others will carry conviction. In either case, of course, the authority must be one whose competence to speak on the subject, and whose veracity, is accepted by the audience. As pointed out in a previous section, the careful documentation of sources will frequently lend credence to evidence which would otherwise be questioned.

IV. SUMMARY

In summary we may say that every good argument should be premised on evidence. In selecting this evidence there are two basic tests which should always be considered, logical adequacy and audience acceptability. Sometimes these tests may be entirely consistent; in other cases, they may be quite inconsistent. In the latter case one or the other must be given precedence, depending upon the situation at hand. A competent and thorough student of argument should be able to construct a logical confirmation of a proposition where the evidence used represents the facts as he knows or at least believes them to exist; he should also be able to build a per-

suasive case on evidence which he believes to be most acceptable to the audience.   This is indeed a big order, and a careful
study of the various kinds of argument will be required,
before evidence can be so used.   We shall undertake a study
of the forms of support or the types of argument in the next
four chapters.

EXERCISES

1. Bring to class original examples of each of the kinds of evidence
discussed in Section II. B.

2. Give examples of items of evidence which meet the following
descriptions:

 a. Personal, circumstantial, and original.
 b. Negative, real, circumstantial, and ordinary.
 c. Direct, unwritten, hearsay, personal, and casual.
 d. Negative, real, casual, and circumstantial.

3. Clip ten advertisements from magazines or newspapers.
Phrase the proposition argued by each advertisement and discuss
the evidence as to kind, logical adequacy, and audience acceptability.

4. Clip a short argumentative article from some magazine or
newspaper and discuss the evidence used as to kind, logical adequacy, and audience acceptability.

5. Study the debates in Appendix A (or others of your own choosing from the H. W. Wilson Company's *University Debater's Annual*)
and discuss the evidence used as to kind, logical adequacy, and
audience acceptability.

CHAPTER VIII

SUPPORTING THE PROPOSITION: CONFIRMATION BY INDUCTION

Chapter Outline

I. Methods of Supporting the Proposition

The central problem for the persuader is that of supporting the proposition, advancing argument which will cause the audience to believe in and act upon the proposition. As stated before there are three important methods of support, Confirmation, Explanation, and Motivation. Confirmation is an attempt to win conviction and action by establishing the truth of the proposition through the medium of inductive and deductive reasoning. Chapters VIII and IX are devoted to a study of inductive and deductive types. Explanation is a method of support which, as its name suggests, attempts to win acceptance by explaining the facts relating to the proposition in such a way as to cause its truth to be implied. It involves the use of the implicative system, a concept explained in Chapter X. Motivation, the third method of support, relies for its persuasive power upon the desires and wishes of the audience in relation to the proposition. It is an attempt to associate the desire of the reactor with the proposition in such a way as to cause him to wish to think and act as the proposition suggests. Chapter XI presents this very interesting method of argument.

II. THE RELATION OF THE FORMS OF SUPPORT TO EVIDENCE

We have learned that evidence consists of those matters of fact and opinion which serve as a basis for reasoning or argument. As such it constitutes the basis for Confirmation, Explanation, and Motivation. These are the forms and methods of reasoning. In *confirming* a proposition evidence is placed before the audience and the truth of the proposition is inferred through certain inductions and deductions made by the persuader. In *explaining* a proposition evidence is set forth in such relationships as will cause the audience itself to imply the truth of the proposition. In *motivation* evidence plays a different and somewhat less significant rôle because proof of the proposition is not attempted. Nevertheless, even in awakening desire and associating it with the proposition as is done in motivation, the use of evidence enters in, as we shall point out later.

It is helpful to compare evidence and reasoning to a bridge with its concrete piers, steel supports, and superstructure.

Evidence may be likened to the piers; reasoning to the steel girders which rest on the piers, and support the traffic runway or the proposition for argument. Both evidence and reasoning are necessary to support the proposition just as the piers and girders are required to support the runway.

III. The Nature of Confirmation

Confirmation may be defined as that form of support in which conviction and action are sought by proving or pretending to prove the proposition through inductive and deductive reasoning. It is the process of setting up pertinent facts and opinions (evidence) and making such inductions and deductions as will prove or tend to prove the proposition.

From time to time in our study thus far we have met with the problem of making argument conform to the requirements of logical adequacy and at the same time, making it acceptable to the audience. We have learned, in connection with evidence at least, that these two criteria may at times be quite opposed. The following quotation from Tompkins is an excellent statement of this problem in relation to argument as a whole. It should be studied very carefully.

"The practical value of an argument is not measured by its absolute logic, but by the progress from one mental condition to another, made in the minds of those addressed. Such progress may require the closest logical articulation of the subject matter; as, when the purpose is to present the logic of the subject for its own sake. In this case those addressed are supposed to be seeking the reason involved in the question for the sake of that reason. The mind desires the whys and wherefores of things, and it appeals to argumentation to gratify this desire. In this case the argument has no end beyond the logic of the argument itself; hence, the logical continuity in the argument measures the progress desired in the mind addressed. The arguments in geometry are of this class. It is possible to argue questions of free trade and protective tariff in the same spirit; that is, not as an advocate who has an ulterior end, but as one investigating truth for truth's sake. In such cases the mind addressed is supposed to be in search of the truth, and needs no rhetorical device to stimulate it to active appropriation. Such arguments are supposed to fall outside the subject of rhetoric into that of logic; yet the strictest logical argument must form the basis of adaptation to minds in other conditions than that above described. . . . The rhetorical argument is called into exercise in the stress and art of producing volition and action; especially when the mind is indifferent or hostile to the truth advocated."

"The argument must have unity, not only in itself considered, but in relation to the mind addressed, — must have rhetorical as well as logical unity. Everything must progressively tend to establish belief in the truth asserted, and this is subject to other conditions than those imposed by the laws of thought alone; namely, by the capacity, beliefs, and prejudices of those in whom the new belief is to be established. The argument, to have unity, must be presented from the standpoint of the audience's present knowledge, interests, and desires. The most closely unified and logical argument in itself considered may have no unity with the mind addressed. A progressive argument toward belief is the law of rhetorical unity in argumentative discourse." [1]

Generally speaking, of the three principal types of argument, Confirmation may be considered to be the most strictly logical, Explanation somewhat less logical, and Motivation the least logical. Entering into each of these forms of argument, however, there are two elements which may affect their logical adequacy; one is evidence, and the other is reasoning or inference. Thus the confirmation of a proposition premised on evidence selected for its audience acceptability rather than its logical adequacy might not be any more logically perfect than an implication based upon a careful, unbiased explanation. Of course, the strongest possible argument, from the standpoint of logical adequacy, would

[1] Tompkins, Arnold, *The Science of Discourse*, pp. 160–164. Ginn and Company, 1897.

be a confirmation based on sound evidence, from which inferences are drawn with regard only to their logical unity and continuity. From this same point of view, the weakest arguments would probably be those forms of Motivation which attempt to stir up desire by the presentation of evidence designed especially for that purpose, and which then reach a conclusion solely by suggestion or by rationalization of this desire.

We may summarize some of the more important characteristics of Confirmation, then, as follows: (1) It always proves or at least pretends to prove the proposition which it is designed to support; (2) It is generally speaking the most probative and most logically perfect method of argument, and for that reason, lends itself to the proof of unmixed questions of fact or to any other proposition where logical unity is especially desired; and (3) It can be made to subserve the demands of audience acceptability, although less completely and less satisfactorily than other methods of argument, by selecting evidence which conforms or can be made to conform to the beliefs of the audience, and by choosing those inductive and deductive inferences which will most nearly represent unity to the mind addressed.

IV. INDUCTION AND DEDUCTION DISTINGUISHED

Having defined Confirmation as a form of support employing inductive and deductive reasoning, let us now make a distinction between induction and deduction. Induction may be said to be that process of thought by which the mind is led to draw principles, rules, or conclusions from the observation of particular facts, instances, and cases. It is frequently described as reasoning from the particular to the general. Deduction, on the other hand, is that process of thought by which the mind is led to draw conclusions regarding specific instances of any phenomenon from related principles, rules, or laws already known or presumed to be true. It may be described as reasoning from the general to the particular.

It will be helpful to remember that induction is derived from the Latin " induco " meaning to " lead into "; from a particular instance or group of instances the mind is led into a general conclusion. For example, if capital punishment has reduced crime in Illinois, Ohio, and New York, it may be induced that capital punishment is a general means of reducing crime. It will also be helpful to remember that deduction is derived from the Latin " deduco " meaning to " lead out " or " to lead away from "; the mind is led out from a general truth or principle to a conclusion regarding some particular case which is covered by this principle. For example, we may deduce from the generalization that capital punishment is an effective deterrent to crime, the conclusion that capital punishment will deter crime in Michigan.

V. The Thought Relationships Involved in Induction and Deduction

There are two important thought relationships involved in induction and deduction. They are cause-effect relationships, and substance-attribute relationships.

A. Cause-Effect Relationships. — Every activity has its cause and its effect. The laws of causation, or as they are sometimes called, the natural laws, are universal in their application. The establishment of such relationships constitutes an important part of argument and enters into the support of almost every proposition where Confirmation is employed. In induction, for example, when a causal relationship is observed to exist in a number of particular instances of the phenomenon, a general rule of causation may then be induced therefrom. The capital punishment illustration cited in the previous section involves a cause and effect relationship. If the death penalty causes crime to decrease in Illinois, Ohio, and New York, it may be induced that the death penalty will cause crime to be reduced in all States. There are, of course, countless illustrations of both inductions and deductions involving causal relationships. I observe that temperatures of 32 degrees Fahrenheit or below cause water to freeze and generalize to that effect. I infer that the river will rise, knowing that it rained the night before and knowing that rain causes it to rise. Innumerable experiences with fire permit the induction that fire causes heat. I deduce from the statement that the recent fires in our neighborhood have been caused by willful and malicious incendiarism, that the burning of my house was so caused.

B. Substance-Attribute Relationships. — Just as every cause has its effect, so every substance has its attribute. The following statements express substance-attribute relationships: Men are mortal; Whales are mammals; Ripe strawberries are red; Chain stores are detrimental to the people of Michigan. Each of these statements alleges a certain substance to have a certain attribute. It will be observed that there is no causal relationship involved in these cases. The cause-effect and substance-attribute connections are quite different and distinct relationships.

Many inductions and deductions are made regarding substance-attribute relationships in the confirmation of a proposition. From the observation of such a relationship among the particular instances of a phenomenon, we induce a generalization of classification; and from general rules of classification we deduce conclusions regarding the attributes of particular substances.

We have referred to this substance-attribute relationship as being one of *classification*. It really is such, because all substances are classified on the basis of their attributes.

When we say that whales are mammals, we are classifying whales in a definite category ; when we say ripe strawberries are red, we have classified ripe strawberries in the category of red substances, a rather rough classification to be sure, but nevertheless a classification. We shall refer to the substance-attribute relationship as being one of classification just as we speak of the cause-effect relationship as being one of causation.

VI. Inductive Types

Inductive reasoning is frequently referred to as Example. We shall discuss two types of induction or reasoning from example, generalization and analogy. Both of these types are common in argument.

A. Generalization. — Generalization is the typical inductive form. A series of particular instances are cited, all of which display a certain relationship either of causation or classification, and a general conclusion is then drawn to the effect that this relationship obtains in all instances of the phenomenon.

The following examples will illustrate generalizations establishing cause-effect relationships and those establishing substance-attribute relationships.[1]

> Case 1. The Michigan State Police Patrol stationed at X is efficient.
>
> Case 2. The Michigan State Police Patrol stationed at Y is efficient.
>
> Case 3. The Michigan State Police Patrol stationed at Z is efficient.
>
> Therefore : The Michigan State Police Patrols are efficient.
>
> Case 1. The change from a Republican to a Democratic administration in 1885 (Arthur to Cleveland) caused a period of business unrest.

[1] The examples cited in this chapter are for illustrative purposes only.

Case 2. There was a period of business unrest in 1889 (Cleveland to Harrison).

Case 3. In 1893 (Harrison to Cleveland).

Case 4. In 1897 (Cleveland to McKinley).

Case 5. In 1909 (Taft to Wilson).

Case 6. In 1913 (Wilson to Harding).

Therefore: Changes from one party administration to another cause periods of business unrest.

Stated in brief form generalization appears as follows:[1]

I. An increase in the rediscount rates to member banks by the Federal Reserve Board causes a slump in the general price level, because

    A. A slump in prices was caused by the increase in the rediscount rate in 1919.

    B. A slump followed an increase in the rediscount rate in 1920.

    C. A slump followed an increase in the rediscount rate in 1921, etc.

1. RULES GOVERNING THE USE OF GENERALIZATION. — There are certain rules governing the use of generalization in argument which need to be observed if it is to be effectively employed.

a. A Reasonable Number of Instances Must Be Cited. — There is the ever present danger in argument of this kind of generalizing from two few instances of the phenomenon. Since the number of instances that need to be cited varies with the different phenomena under observation, however, it is impossible for us to stipulate any set number of cases which must be presented in order to lend probative force to the argument. We can simply say that, generally speaking, the greater the number of the cases, the stronger the generalization; and unless a reasonable number of cases

---

[1] The brief is a type of outline particularly adapted to the statement of the inferences in Confirmation. See Chapter XII, "Outlining the Case," for a discussion of the brief.

are given, the conclusion is of little significance as a confirmation of the proposition.

In some cases of induction it is possible to examine *all* the instances in which the phenomenon has occurred. For example, many generalizations regarding the States of the United States enable the persuader to consider all forty-eight States and draw an infallible conclusion. Such induction is really not induction at all. It is merely a process of adding up or putting together the various cases. No inferential progress takes place and hence no reasoning is involved.

b. Typical Instances Must Be Cited. — Not only must a reasonable number of instances be cited, but these cases must be typical. It is possible in most inductions to select a few unusual or exceptional cases from which some highly misleading conclusions can be induced. The persuader should make certain that the cases upon which he rests his generalization are representative instances of the phenomenon.

> For instance in a recent debate on old age pensions the advocates of the pension system attacked the county poorhouses of the state in which the system was to be introduced as a means of poor relief. The negative rejoindered by charging that the affirmative had used only the poorest counties in the state as a basis for their generalization. The position of the affirmative was greatly weakened when it was shown that the poorhouses they had described were not representative of the poorhouses of the state about which they were generalizing.

c. Negative Instances Must Be Accounted For. — Whenever a generalization is drawn in which there are negative instances, that is, instances in which the relationship that is sought to be established is not borne out, steps must be taken to account for these cases. Failure to do this paves the way for an opponent to produce these cases and thereby greatly weaken the generalization. The persuader must either be in a position to show that there are no instances of the phenomenon in which the relationship does not occur, that the negative instances are exceptional cases, or that they are not significant for some other reason.

d. The Relationship Must Be Proved to Exist in Each Particular Instance. — This final rule governing generalization may be stated more fully as follows: The relationship of causation or classification about which a generalization is being made must be proved to exist in each particular instance of the phenomenon *which is used as a basis for the generalization.* It is not sufficient simply to assert that a certain cause-effect or substance-attribute relationship exists in the various cases under observation. The relationship must be proved to exist in each case if a valid generalization is to be drawn.

For example, let us assume that we are trying to prove that the intervention of the United States by force of arms to protect American capital invested in foreign countries causes trade to decrease between the United States and the countries in which this intervention takes place. To prove the point we cite the cases of Nicaragua, Haiti, and China. Three things would need to be proved regarding each of these cases. It would be necessary to show that the United States has intervened, that trade has fallen off, *and that the intervention was the cause of this reduction in trade.*

Another illustration will show the necessity of proving the substance-attribute relationship in each particular instance from which a general rule of classification is to be induced. If one were to prove that all whales are mammals, it would be necessary to prove in connection with each specimen examined, first, that it was a whale, and second, *that it possessed the attributes or characteristics of the mammalia.*

B. Analogy. — Analogy is the second inductive form we shall discuss. It is frequently more valuable for its illustrative power than it is for its probative force. In fact, it is little more than a generalization from a single case which is selected because of its close parallel to the instance in which the persuader is endeavoring to establish a certain relationship of causation or resemblance. Theoretically, an analogy *generalizes* from *one* instance in which the phenomenon occurs, and then *deduces* immediately to the instance about which a conclusion is being drawn, thus combining induction and deduction. Practically, however, it amounts to a comparison of two instances, one in which a certain relationship is known to exist and the other in which it is alleged to exist or will exist. An analogy proceeds upon the theory that if two things are alike in most basic points, they will be alike in the point under question. Thus, it might be argued analogically that a governmental project which is successful in Canada would succeed in the United States by showing the conditions essential to this project to be alike in both countries.

In a debate on the proposition that the several States of the United States be permitted to adopt the Ontario system of liquor control, the affirmative team showed Ontario and several States of the United States to be similar in all essential respects relating to liquor control. Then, after proving the Ontario plan to be successful in Ontario, they reasoned analogically that it would be successful in each of the States where they had shown the conditions to be comparable with those obtaining in Ontario. Each State that was compared with Ontario constituted an analogy.

The complete form for an analogy is as follows :

1. Ontario and the State of Michigan are alike in all essential conditions relative to liquor control.
2. The Ontario system of liquor control is successful in Ontario.
Therefore : The Ontario system of liquor control would be successful in Michigan.

This same analogy may be stated in brief form as follows:

I. The Ontario system of liquor control would be successful in the State of Michigan, because
    A. It has been successful in Ontario, and
    B. Ontario is comparable with Michigan.

1. RULES GOVERNING AN ANALOGY. — The following rules should be observed in arguing analogically.

a. *The Instances Being Compared Should Be Alike in All Essential Respects.* — The significant word in this rule is *essential.* Two cases can be unalike in many ways and yet form an excellent comparison for the establishment of certain relationships. The important thing for purposes of analogy is that the instances be alike in all the essential conditions relative to the phenomenon under consideration. In a debate on the advisability of establishing a Federal Court of Industrial Relations the writer heard some excellent analogies established between New Zealand and the United States and between the State of Kansas, where such a court was in operation, and the United States. In both of these cases many differences are readily apparent. The mere fact that differences exist between the cases being compared does not invalidate the analogy, unless these differences are shown to be essential matters.

b. *Differences in the Cases Being Compared Must Be Accounted for.* — Any differences or apparent differences between the cases being compared must be shown to be non-existent, non-essential, or disposed of in some other manner.

c. *Analogical Reasoning Should Be Cumulative where Possible.* — Analogical reasoning becomes cumulative when more than one comparison is adduced to support the conclusion. For instance, if we were arguing that a certain project would be successful in Michigan, it might be possible to draw analogies with several other states where this project was in operation. Cumulative analogy is not identical with generalization as it is sometimes claimed, because a particular conclusion regarding some specific case is always drawn in analogical reasoning, while a general conclusion pertaining to all cases is the result of generalization. From a series of analogies showing the success of a certain project, we argue that it will be successful in a particular case. From a series of cases in generalization we conclude that the project will be successful in all cases. Reasoning from analogy becomes increasingly strong as the number of comparisons are increased, or in other words, as the analogies are cumulated.[1]

VII. INDUCTIVE METHODS

Before leaving induction, it will be well to examine certain methods which are helpful in detecting relationships among the various particular instances of a phenomenon. We shall explain five such methods: (1) Method of agreement; (2) Method of difference; (3) Joint method; (4) Method of residues; and (5) Method of concomitant variations. These methods will be found to be especially helpful in detecting a general law of causation among its particular occurrences and should be employed in discovering and exhibiting generalizations of this type.

A. Method of Agreement. — The first inductive method, that of agreement, proceeds upon the following principles: " If two or more instances of the phenomenon under investigation have only one circumstance in common, the circum-

[1] The distinction is frequently made between literal analogies and figurative analogies. Literal analogies compare two instances which fall in the same general category, two houses, two states, two cities, etc. Figurative analogies compare two instances which fall in essentially different categories. For example, the analogy is figurative in the argument that "you wouldn't change horses in the middle of a stream, and you should not, therefore, change generals in the middle of a campaign." Whereas literal analogy has great probative force, particularly where it is cumulative, figurative analogy is purely illustrative and therefore not included in this chapter.

stance in which alone all the instances agree, is the cause, or effect of the given phenomenon." [1] This method is illustrated by the following example. Let us assume that we are trying to determine what causal relationship, if any, exists between a college education and the earning power of individuals who have completed a college course. We could select a thousand college men at random, graduates of different schools, residents of different sections of the country, and engaged in many different occupations. If we found this group of men to be uniformly above average in earning power, we might conclude that a college education was the cause of this ability. Before drawing this conclusion, however, we would need to make certain that the college education was the *only* condition which these men had in common. If it could be shown that another such common factor existed, it could be contended with equal force that this second condition constituted the causative agency. For instance, in the above illustration it might be shown that these college men were above average in intelligence and initiative, with the conclusion that their superior intelligence and initiative rather than the college education was the chief cause of the added earning power.

Another illustration of the method of agreement is presented in the following case : Assume that an effort is being made to establish a causal relation between chain stores and certain undesirable merchandising practices. If a hundred chain stores in different chain systems, dispensing different types of merchandise, and located in both large and small communities in different sections of the United States, were investigated and found to be uniformly resorting to these practices, it could be concluded with considerable

---

[1] We quote Mill's five principles from J. M. O'Neill, Craven Laycock, and R. L. Scales, *Argumentation and Debate*, pp. 124, 125, 126, 128, and 129 respectively.

certainty that the chain store principle or at least something peculiar to chain stores was the causative factor.

B. Method of Difference. — The second inductive method is that of difference. It embodies the following principle: " If an instance in which the phenomenon under investigation occurs, and an instance in which it does not occur, have every circumstance in common save one, that one occuring only in the former ; the circumstance in which alone the two instances differ, is the effect, or the cause, or an indispensable part of the cause, of the phenomenon." This method can also be illustrated by the chain store example. If a chain store is compared with an independent store and found to be alike in every essential respect except that one is organized on a chain basis and the other on an independent unit basis, and it can be shown further that the chain store displays certain undesirable merchandising practices which do not exist in the independent store, it can be inferred that the chain store principle is the causative factor.

This method could also be employed in exhibiting the causal relationship between a college education and increased earning power. Let it be shown that two men are alike in all respects, except that one has a college education and the other is not so educated, and that the one possessing this education earns more money than the one who is not college trained, and it can be inferred that the college education is the probable cause of this greater earning power.

C. Joint Method. — The principle of the joint method may be stated as follows : " If two or more instances in which the phenomenon occurs have only one circumstance in common, while two or more instances in which it does not occur have nothing in common save the absence of that circumstance ; the circumstance in which alone the two sets of instances always differ, is the effect, or the cause, or an indispensable part of the cause, of the phenomenon." As an illustration, assume that we again chose a hundred widely different stores all of which employed certain undesirable merchandising practices, and upon investigation found them all to be chain stores. By the method of agreement this would lead us to believe that the chain store principle was the factor causing these practices. Then, if we were to select a hundred different stores none of which employed these undesirable tactics and discovered them all to be independent stores, our original conclusion would be greatly strengthened.

From this illustration it can be seen that the joint method is simply a combination of the methods of agreement and difference. Two sets of phenomena are investigated independently by the method of agreement, and then the two sets are contrasted by the method of difference. If the results of one investigation are confirmed by the other, the rule of causation thereby established is in all probability correct.

As a second illustration of the joint method assume that a farmer selects at random fifty trees of various kinds from his several orchards none of which show any signs of worms, and upon examination finds that every one of these trees have been sprayed. Then he goes through his orchards and selects at random fifty more trees which do have worms and finds that none of these trees have been sprayed. The conclusion from these two sets of phenomena, which always differ in this one circumstance and display no other uniform difference, would be, of course, that spraying the trees caused the disappearance of worms.

D. Method of Residues. — In some phenomena there are many causes operating at the same time with their effects so blended as to make the isolation of any given cause and its effect a difficult task. For instance, the economist is confronted with this problem in determining what part of

any selling price represents profit. There are any number
of causes determining selling price, labor costs, transportation charges, interest charges, taxes, etc. There is no
better way to determine the amount of profit than to esti-
mate each cost element independently and deduct their total
from the selling price. The *residues* will then represent
the amount of the selling price (the effect) that can be attributed to profit. The method of residues which is illustrated
by the above example can be stated in the following principle :
" Subtract from any phenomenon such part as is known by
previous inductions to be the effect of certain causes, and
the residue of the phenomenon is the effect of the remaining
causes."

" ' If we know that the joint effect a, b, c, is due to the
causes A, B, and C, and can prove that a is due to A and b
to B, it follows that c must be due to C. There cannot be
a simpler case of this than ascertaining the exact weight of
any commodity in a cart by weighing the cart and load,
and then subtracting the tare or weight of the cart alone,
which has been previously ascertained.' " [1]

E. Method of Concomitant Variations. — " Whatever phenomenon varies in any manner whenever another phenomenon varies in some particular manner, is either a cause or an
effect of that phenomenon, or is connected with it through
some fact of causation." For instance, it has been observed
that when the Federal Reserve Board raises the rediscount
rates to member banks there is a tendency for loans to be
curtailed and prices to go down, and when the rediscount
rate is lowered there is a boom tendency in the opposite
direction, loans are increased and prices go up. The observation of these concomitant variations over a period of time
has led economists and bankers to believe that the rediscount

[1] O'Neill, J. M., Laycock, Craven, and Scales, R. L., *Argumentation and
Debate*, pp. 128–129.

rate is an important causative factor in the determination of the general price level. A simpler illustration of this method is the observation that the flow of water from the spout varies directly with the speed of the windmill, thus establishing a causal relationship between the windmill and the flow of the water.

In complicated phenomena concomitant variations can be detected best when they are graphed. Statisticians have long resorted to graphs to display causal relationships. Economists, for instance, reduce wage variations, prices of various commodities, transportation costs, and other such phenomena to standard units of measurement (Index figures), and place them on the same graph, so that any concomitant variation can be readily discerned. A high degree of either direct or inverse correlation between two phenomena is considered significant. Correlation is estimated by a measurement known as the coefficient of correlation. A perfect positive correlation is indicated by a positive one ($+$ 1) while a perfect inverse correlation is noted by a minus one ($-$ 1).

EXERCISES

1. Prepare to hand in two original examples of each of the five inductive methods.

2. Prepare to hand in five examples of sound generalization based upon cause-effect relationships, and five based upon substance-attribute relationships. (Set these examples up in the same form as is used in presenting examples in this chapter.)

3. Prepare to hand in five examples of literal analogy.

4. Prepare a five-minute argumentative speech embodying examples of generalization and analogy.

5. Select all the instances of generalization and analogy in one of the debates in Appendix A (or one of the debates in the H. W. Wilson Company, *University Debater's Annual*) and apply the appropriate rules to each example of argument.

6. Illustrate each of the rules governing generalization by preparing examples of generalization which are sound in every respect except that covered by the rule being illustrated. Submit these illustrations to the class and have them invoke the rule that is violated.

7. Illustrate each of the rules governing analogy as you did in the case of generalization in Exercise 6.

CHAPTER IX

SUPPORTING THE PROPOSITION: CONFIRMATION BY DEDUCTION

CHAPTER OUTLINE

I. THE SYLLOGISM

Before attempting to classify and study deductive types, it is important that the student of argument understand the syllogism.

A. The Place of the Syllogism in Logic and Argument. — The syllogism is the form in which deductive reasoning is stated in Logic. Fully expressed it consists of two propositions called the major and minor premises, respectively, and a third proposition which is called the conclusion. The major premise consists of a general rule, law, or statement expressing either a relationship of causation or one of classification. The minor premise relates some particular instance of the phenomenon under question to the generalization stated in the major premise, and the conclusion is then drawn regarding this particular instance. The following form illustrates the syllogism:

Major Premise: All men are mortal.
Minor Premise: Socrates is a man.
Conclusion: Therefore, Socrates is mortal.

Not only should attention be called to the fact that the major premise may state either a relationship of causation or classification, but also to the fact that either of these relationships may be expressed categorically, hypothetically, or disjunctively. It is on this basis that we classify syllogisms. If the major premise is a categorical statement of causation or classification, any deduction from it is stated in a categorical syllogism; if the major premise is a disjunctive statement, a disjunctive syllogism results; and if it is a hypothetical statement, the hypothetical syllogism results. These different kinds of syllogisms are explained and differentiated in the next section.

It should be understood that the syllogism is the full and complete form for all deductive reasoning. We do not meet the formal syllogism very frequently in argument, however, for reason of the fact that one of the premises or the conclusion is usually assumed without stating it in so many words. Thus the arguer will reason that Socrates is mortal because he is a man, or that he is mortal because all men are mortal.   In both of these cases one premise of a full syllogism is taken for granted without stating it.   Even though the arguer does not often meet the complete syllogism, it is quite necessary, nevertheless, that he understand syllogistic reasoning in order accurately to evaluate the deductions which are made in argument.   For that reason we recommend a careful study of the following section to every student of the subject.

B. Kinds of Syllogism. — We shall discuss three kinds of syllogisms, the Categorical, the Disjunctive, and the Hypothetical.

1. THE CATEGORICAL SYLLOGISM. — The categorical syllogism is the form in which categorical deductions are stated. It is characterized by the fact that its major premise is always a categorical or unqualified statement of either a relationship of causation or resemblance which admits of no conditions or exceptions.   The following syllogism is categorical.

I. Every school in the conference won a majority of its football games.
II. Michigan is a school in the conference.
III. Therefore: Michigan won a majority of its football games.

a. Rules Governing the Categorical Syllogism. —

(1) It Must Contain Three and Only Three Terms. — The three terms to which this rule refers are the major term, the middle term, and the minor term.   In the above illustration the major term is *the winning of a majority of its football games; the schools in the conference* is the middle term; and *Michigan,* the minor term.   Every term is used twice in the syllogism.   In composing a categorical syllogism the terms should be arranged as follows:

I. Major premise: Middle term — Major term.
II. Minor premise: Minor term — Middle term.
III. Conclusion: Minor term — Major term.

In ordinary speaking or writing, however, the terms do not appear in any definite order, and only a thorough understanding of the syllogism will enable the persuader to reduce an argument to the proper syllogistic form.

(2) The Middle Term Must Be Distributed in at Least One of the Premises. — By a distributed term is meant one that refers to a class of things in its entirety as *all men*, or *every law*. A term is distributed when it includes all the members of any category, or all the parts of a whole ; and it is undistributed when it is not universal or all-inclusive as *some men, a part of the group*, or *many animals*. In many cases terms are distributed or undistributed without such words as *all, every, some*, or *many* appearing in the term. Generally speaking, the following rules obtain in such cases : (1) The subjects of statements are usually distributed ; (2) The predicates of affirmative statements are usually undistributed ; and (3) The predicates of negative statements are always distributed.[1]

The fallacy in reasoning occasioned by the failure to distribute the middle term in at least one of the premises is illustrated in the following syllogism :

    I. Some college men belong to fraternities.
    II. John Smith is a college man.
    III. Therefore : John Smith belongs to a fraternity.

(3) A Term Must Not Be Distributed in the Conclusion unless It Is Distributed in One of the Premises. — Since the middle term does not appear in the conclusion, this rule applies only to the major and minor terms. The fallacies arising from violations of this rule are illustrated by the following syllogisms :[2]

[1] See Winans, James A., and Utterback, William E., *Argumentation*, pp. 69–70. The Century Company, 1930.

[2] The illustrations used here are adopted from O'Neill, Laycock, and Scales, *Argumentation and Debate*, p. 178.

I. Horses are animals.
II. Cows are not horses.
III. Therefore: Cows are not animals.

In the above syllogism the major term, *animals*, is undistributed in the major premise, and distributed in the conclusion. The fallacy becomes more apparent when the major premise is stated, " Horses are (some) animals."

I. All Senators are at least thirty years old.
II. All Senators are voters.
III. Therefore: All voters are at least thirty years old.

In this case, the minor term, *voters*, is undistributed in the minor premise and distributed in the conclusion. Here also the fallacy becomes more apparent when the word, *some*, is stated in the minor premise, " All Senators are (some) voters."

(4) A Valid Conclusion Cannot Be Inferred from Two Negative Premises. — The student can illustrate this rule for himself by taking any two negative premises. The precaution should be observed, however, that the mere occurrence of a negative particle in a statement does not necessarily make that statement negative. " Thus the argument:

'What is not a compound is an element;
'Gold is not a compound;
'Therefore gold is an element.'

contains negatives in both premises, but is nevertheless valid, because the negative in both cases affects the middle term which is really the negative term *not-compound*." [1]

(5) If One Premise Is Negative the Conclusion Must Be Negative. — The student can also readily illustrate this rule to his own satisfaction. Here again, however, care must be taken to ascertain that the premise thought to be negative is

[1] Jevons, W. S., *Lessons in Logic*, p. 134. Charles Scribner's Sons, 1901.

actually a negative statement, and not simply an affirmative statement containing the particles *no* or *not*, or the prefix *non*, as a part of one of the terms.

2. THE DISJUNCTIVE SYLLOGISM. — The disjunctive syllogism is the form in which disjunctive deductions are stated. It is characterized by the fact that its major premise is always a disjunctive statement setting forth certain alternative possibilities. Whereas a categorical statement expresses an unconditional relationship of causation or resemblance, a disjunctive proposition states alternative relationships of causation or resemblance as follows : " Either a cyclone or earthquake caused the destruction of the city " ; or " The books on this shelf are either biography or fiction." The following syllogism is disjunctive :

I. A Federal Department of Education must be justified either on the basis of its ability to subsidize education, or its ability to conduct educational research more efficiently than the existing Bureau of Education.

II. A Federal Department of Education cannot be justified on the basis of superior ability to conduct research.

III. Therefore : It must be justified on the basis of its ability to subsidize education.

a. Rules Governing the Disjunctive Syllogism. —

(1) The Alternative Possibilities Enumerated in the Major Premise Must Be All-inclusive. — Failure to include all the possibilities in a disjunction destroys its validity. Any conclusion deduced from an incomplete disjunction can be seriously weakened by presenting possible causes or classifications not contemplated by the disjunction. The following syllogism illustrates this point :

I. Crop failures are caused either by drouth or excessive moisture.

II. This crop failure was not caused by excessive moisture.

III. Therefore : It was caused by drouth.

In this case, the inference could be destroyed and the conclusion opened to serious question by showing that insects, frost, hail, as well as other causes might have operated to produce the crop failure.

(2) All the Possibilities Enumerated in the Major Premise Must Be Mutually Exclusive. — If the possibilities set forth in the disjunction overlap, the elimination of one alternative will seriously impair any others with which it may overlap. Consider the following case:

I. The American farmer must seek relief either through the provisions of the McNary-Haugen Farm Relief Bill, or through the control of surplus production.
II. It is impossible to control surplus production.
III. Therefore: The farmer must seek relief through the McNary-Haugen Bill.

Readers who remember the McNary-Haugen Bill will recall that it was a farm relief measure which proposed to assist the farmer by an elaborate plan to control surplus production. In the above syllogism, then, when the minor premise eliminates surplus control, it also eliminates the McNary-Haugen Bill in-so-far as it depends upon surplus control.

(3) If the Minor Premise Affirms One of the Possibilities, the Conclusion Must Deny the Other.

(4) If the Minor Premise Denies One of the Possibilities, the Conclusion Must Affirm the Other.

3. THE HYPOTHETICAL SYLLOGISM. — The hypothetical syllogism is the form in which hypothetical deductions are stated. It is characterized by the fact that its major premise always expresses a hypothetical or conditional relationship of causation or resemblance. We shall refer to the conditional or " if " clause in the major premise as the antecedent, and the clause to which the condition is applied as the consequent. Thus in the following syllogism, *if the drouth continues*, is the antecedent and, *the crop will be lost*, is the consequent:

  I. If the drouth continues, the crop will be lost.
 II. The drouth continued.
III. Therefore : The crop was lost.

a. Rules Governing the Hypothetical Syllogism. —

(1) If the Minor Premise Affirms the Antecedent, the Conclusion Must Affirm the Consequent. — This rule expresses the relationship between premises which obtains in most hypothetical reasoning, and is evident from the above illustration.

(2) If the Minor Premise Denies the Consequent, the Conclusion Must Deny the Antecedent. — In the following syllogism a valid conclusion is drawn by denying the consequent :

  I. If the United States will disarm, other nations will disarm.
 II. Other nations will not disarm.
III. Therefore : The United States will not disarm.

The reasoning in this syllogism is sound because the disarmament of other nations is alleged to be an absolute consequent of disarmament by the United States. If other nations will not disarm, it can be deduced infallibly that the United States will not disarm, assuming, of course, that the major premise is true. The student should understand that we are making an assumption of this kind in all the illustrations used in this chapter. In actual argument any premise is open to attack if it is not properly evidenced. In this chapter, however, we are concerned with inferences and the forms in which they appear rather than evidence. So, assuming the premises to be sound, we narrow our discussion to the validity of inferences.

(3) A Conclusion Drawn from a Minor Premise Which Denies the Antecedent Is Not Necessarily True. — Consider the following illustration :

  I. If a Federal Department of Education is established, the Federal appropriation for education will be increased.

II. A Department of Education will not be established.

III. Therefore: The Federal appropriation for education will not be increased.

The conclusion in this syllogism is not necessarily sound because the minor premise denies the antecedent. While the major premise states that the appropriation will be increased, if a Department of Education is established, so far as this hypothesis goes, there could be many causes other than the one stipulated which could operate to produce the same effect.

(4) **A Conclusion Drawn from a Minor Premise Which Affirms the Consequent Is Not Necessarily True.** — The following syllogism in which the minor premise affirms the consequent illustrates the weakness of a conclusion drawn from such hypothetical reasoning:

I. If a large crop is produced, prices will be low.

II. Prices are low.

III. Therefore: A large crop was produced.

Here again the conclusion does not follow from the condition stated in the major premise. Whereas high prices would prove beyond question that a small crop was produced, low prices would not necessarily prove that a large crop was produced. So far as the major premise in the syllogism goes, many other causes might have operated to produce low prices, but a large crop is alleged to be a certain cause. Thus, the existence of high prices must necessarily mean that a small crop was harvested, while the existence of low prices may or may not mean that a large crop was produced.

II. The Enthymeme

A. The Place of the Enthymeme in Logic and Argument. — We have already stated that the formal syllogism is rarely met in argument. One premise or the conclusion is almost invariably omitted and simply assumed by the speaker or writer. This contracted syllogistic form is known to students of logic as the enthymeme. It may be defined as a deductive form which is identical to the syllogism except for the fact that one of the premises or the conclusion is missing. Thus, enthymemes may be classified as categorical, disjunctive, or hypothetical just as syllogisms. It is more helpful, however, to classify them on the basis of the proposition which is omitted.

B. Kinds of Enthymemes. — There are three forms of the enthymeme, the first order, second order, and third order.

1. ENTHYMEMES OF THE FIRST, SECOND, AND THIRD ORDERS. — When the major premise is omitted, the argument is an enthymeme of the first order; when the minor premise is omitted, the enthymeme is of the second order; and an omission of the conclusion gives an enthymeme of the third order. These orders are illustrated as follows :

First Order

I. (?)
II. The tariff is being reduced.
III. Therefore : Prices will have to go down.

Second Order

I. Accidents curtailing one's earning power are likely to occur to any man.
II. (?)
III. Therefore : You should protect yourself with accident insurance.

Third Order

I. Either Smith or Ferry is bound to win the tournament.
II. Smith's chances of winning were lost when he sprained his ankle.
III. Therefore : (?)

C. Rules Governing the Enthymeme. — The rules governing the enthymeme are identical to those governing the various forms of the syllogism. Since any type of the syllogism may be reduced to an enthymeme of any order, to test the validity of the enthymeme, the persuader needs only to supply the missing proposition and apply the syllogistic rules which pertain.

D. The Use of the Enthymeme in Argument. — Most deductive argument appears in the form of an enthymeme. In fact argument is rarely stated in the form of a complete syllogism. Either one of the premises or the conclusion is usually knowingly or unwittingly assumed. It is important both in the construction of an argument and in the refutation of argument that the persuader be able to supply the missing proposition and test the logic of the reasoning by an application of the rules governing the syllogism.

Chains of reasoning or logical outlining is the form in which most argument is stated. It usually consists of a series of enthymemes of the first order. Consider the following excerpt from a brief on the proposition that the jury system be abolished :

I. The jury system is impractical as a means of securing justice, because
    A. The jury makes justice uncertain, because
        1. It is incapable of determining facts in litigation.
        2. It is governed by bias, prejudice, and emotion.
    B. The jury delays justice, because
        1. Time is consumed in impaneling a jury.
        2. Appeals and retrials are more numerous.

Reducing a portion of this outline to a series of enthymemes, we have the following :

    I. (?)
   II. The jury system is impractical.
  III. Therefore : It should be abolished.

    I. (?)
   II. The jury makes justice uncertain.
  III. Therefore : It is impractical.

I. (?)
II. The jury is incapable of determining facts in litigation.
III. Therefore: The jury makes justice uncertain.

In each case we have an enthymeme of the first order because the major premise is assumed. It should be observed that in each case either a hypothetical or categorical statement could be supplied as the major premise, thus making the enthymeme either a hypothetical or categorical syllogism.

In a recent debate on the jury system the reasoning outlined above appeared substantially as we have briefed it. In responding to the enthymeme that the jury is impractical because it delays justice, the negative team attacked the assumed major premise upon which this argument rests. They pointed out that the affirmative was simply assuming that justice was impaired by delay, and proceeded to argue that a reasonable amount of delay (which they contended was all that could be fairly charged to the jury) was indicative of a caution and conservatism which made for more certain justice, and therefore was an advantage of the jury which would be lost by its abolition, rather than a disadvantage.

III. DEDUCTIVE TYPES

Now that we understand the syllogism and the enthymeme, we are ready to consider deductive types. There are two important kinds of deductive reasoning in argument: (1) Antecedent probability; and (2) Sign. Our presentation will be clear if it is kept in mind that both antecedent probability and sign, when expressed in complete form appear as syllogisms, and when expressed in argument, usually take the form of enthymemes.

A. Antecedent Probability. — Antecedent Probability, or *a Priori* reasoning as it is frequently called, is that type of deduction in which an effect is inferred from a given cause, or an attribute is inferred from a given substance. It is the process of reasoning from a known cause to an unknown or alleged effect; or from a known substance to an unknown or alleged attribute. Antecedent probability appears in complete syllogistic form as follows:

> All fire causes heat.
> This is a fire.
> Therefore: It will cause heat.

> All whales are mammals.
> This animal is a whale.
> Therefore: It is a mammal.

It will be noted that the first syllogism illustrates reasoning from cause to effect, and the second, reasoning from substance to attribute. This type of reasoning usually appears in argument with the major premise omitted, or in other words as an enthymeme of the first order.

1. ARGUMENT FROM CAUSE TO EFFECT. — In treating antecedent probability, it has seemed best to divide our discussion on the basis of reasoning from cause to effect and substance to attribute. Proceeding to argument from a known cause to an alleged effect, it should first be pointed out that from a given cause we may infer either the entire effect or any part of it. Day illustrates this point as follows: " From the rise of the sap in the tree we infer that there will be foliage, bloom, fruit, and other particulars of vegetable growth — all or any one. The circulation of the sap is in this instance that which we represent to ourselves as the cause which, unless something interfere to hinder its operation, necessarily involves these effects." [1]

Reasoning from cause to effect is one of the most important kinds of reasoning in argument. In discussing matters of policy, for instance, much of the argument is of this type. The advocate of any policy or institution attempts to set this

[1] Day, Henry N., *The Art of Discourse*, p. 133. Charles Scribner and Company, 1867.

institution up as the probable cause of certain beneficial effects while his opponents will endeavor to establish the probability that certain detrimental effects will be caused by the suggested policy. This is just one illustration of the many ways in which the arguer is concerned with reasoning from cause to effect. Very evidently it is important that he know the rules governing argument of this type.

a. Rules Governing Argument from Cause to Effect. — The following rules should be observed in reasoning from cause to effect.

(1) The Connection between the Cause and Alleged Effect Must Be Complete. — The two facts, one of which is called the cause and the other the effect, are rarely in immediate connection with each other. There are almost always several intermediate steps between the two. Sidgwick says on this point, " Intermediate links in a chain of causation are so many opportunities for counteraction, in the same way as the length of a piece of railway provides opportunities for any accident. They are intermediate conditions. The pull on the trigger will fire the shot if, and only if, the catch, the spring, the hammer, the cap, and so on, all act in the expected manner." [1] The salesman attempting to sell a farmer quantities of fertilizer argues that a greater yield will result from its use. The causal connection here is also subject to several intermediate conditions. The yield will be increased provided the soil is capable of responding to the fertilizer and provided the crop is one which will flourish in a rich soil.

As we have already said, most arguments from cause to effect involve such intermediate provisos. It is necessary, of course, to make certain that all the intermediate conditions are fulfilled, that none of the links between the known cause and the alleged effect are missing. We may say that the

[1] Sidgwick, A., *The Process of Argument*, p. 153. London, 1893.

closer the causal connection, the surer is the argument, and that any argument may be destroyed by showing that some of the necessary intermediate links are lacking.

(2) No Other Cause Must Operate to Prevent the Action of the Cause under Discussion. — This rule should not be confused with the rule we have just stated. No matter how close the causal connection may be, if another cause operates to prevent the action of the cause under question, the alleged effect will, of course, not follow. This much is true, however; it is generally a fact that there are fewer causes which may operate to prevent the action of the cause under question in those cases in which there are few links between the known cause and the alleged effect than in those instances in which the causal connection is more remote.

" Many times the normal progress between the cause and the effect is stopped or turned from its course by the intervention of some other cause which destroys or turns aside the natural result of the first cause." O'Neill, Laycock, and Scales go on to illustrate this point, " If a man takes a dose of deadly poison, the chances are that it will cause his death; but it may be shown that this effect will not naturally follow in this case, by showing that the man took an antidote. The antidote prevents the occurrence of the natural effect. One may argue that the Chinese race are very numerous, that as a people they are physically formidable, that they are peculiarly fortunate in climate and in economic resources, and, consequently, that there is a great danger of a commercial ' Yellow Peril.' This is a clear inference from cause to effect. But this reasoning may be attacked, by arguing that certain racial peculiarities of the Chinese prevent them from being aggressive competitors, and make them thus incapable of the powers of initiative and self-advancement necessary for independent commercial progress as a race. The operation of this second cause will destroy the connection of cause and effect upon which the argument depends." [1]

In a recent debate on the proposition that all colleges and universities abolish the distinction between amateurism and professionalism in college sports, the negative argued that such a step would result in the introduction of all the evils of professional athletics into college sports. The affirmative attempted to break down this reasoning by responding that the operation of other eligibility rules, scholastic requirements, residence requirements, etc., would prevent these evil results even though the distinction were abolished. This is a case of pointing out other causes which would prevent or tend to prevent the anticipated effects by preventing the operation of the cause under discussion.

(3) The Extent to Which the Alleged Effect Is the Result of the Known Cause Should Be Known. — The failure to realize that an alleged effect may be only partially due to a known cause is one of the most subtle fallacies arising out of reasoning from cause to effect. This may be illustrated by an article written by an athletic director in which he sets forth data to show that college athletes live longer and are generally healthier than college non-athletes. Beginning with college athletics as the cause, he attempts to reason that health and longevity are the probable effects. The reasoning in the article may be open to serious question, however, when it is realized that the group of students which goes into athletics is on the average more healthy and robust than the non-participating group. Without ever stepping into a gymnasium or on to an athletic field the group entering athletics would, it is highly probable, live longer and more healthy lives because of their natural healthy condition than would the other group. While the longevity and better

[1] O'Neill, J. M., Laycock, Craven, and Scales, R. L., *Argumentation and Debate*, p. 144. The Macmillan Company, 1917.

health of the athletic group may be partially attributed to their participation in athletics, it is hardly reasonable to infer that this is the whole cause.

The fallacy of part cause is particularly hard to expose because of the very fact that the causal reasoning usually is part right. Thus, the added earning power of college graduates is attributed to their college education; it is forgotten that the very qualities which enabled them to graduate from college would, in all probability, contribute to their earning power with or without a college education. Here even more surely than in the previous illustration, at least part of the alleged effect may be attributed to the known cause, and that very fact makes it very difficult to discredit the reasoning which attempts to attribute the whole effect to the cause under discussion.

(4) The Cause Must Be Adequate to Produce the Effect in Question. — The probability of predicted results can profitably be investigated by inquiring into the adequacy of the known cause. Is the cause of sufficient size to produce the alleged effect? O'Neill, Laycock, and Scales present an interesting illustration of this point: " In 1893 the so-called ' hard times ' from 1892 to 1896 were said by some people to have been caused solely by the unexpected failure of a prominent English banking house. The failure in question might have been a startling incident of the day, it might perhaps have precipitated failures and misfortunes elsewhere; but it was clearly no adequate cause for such a wide-spread and prolonged misfortune." [1]

In a recent debate on compulsory unemployment insurance, the negative charged that such insurance would remove the incentive to work, and result in a class of laborers who would prefer to collect the insurance rather than retain their

[1] O'Neill, J. M., Laycock, Craven, and Scales, R. L., *Argumentation and Debate*, p. 143.

positions. The affirmative responded to this argument by pointing out that the amounts paid under such insurance plans were in no instance large enough to cause any great group of men deliberately to seek unemployment in order to collect the insurance. In other words, the affirmative argued that the cause was not adequate to produce the evil effects predicted by the negative.

2. ARGUMENT FROM SUBSTANCE TO ATTRIBUTE. — The second kind of antecedent probability is argument from substance to attribute. Day says of this kind of reasoning, ". . . from a proper substance-whole we may infer the aggregate of attributes, or any particular attribute, whether it be attribute of quality, of action, of condition, or of relation proper." [1] He illustrates his point that from a given substance there may be inferred both the aggregate of its attributes and also any one attribute, with the following example: " From the existence of man, we may infer all that can be attributed to man as essential to his being a man, — that there is reason, that there is animal body. Not only this, but any constituent attribute of either of these composite attributes down to the last degree; as, for instance, that there is intelligence, feeling, will; that there is perception, intuition, thought; that there are, moreover, all material attributes, and also organization; and that there is, further, life, growth, etc.; in short, any one of all the manifold capacities and qualities inherent in man, as man." [2]

a. *Rules Governing Argument from Substance to Attribute.* — We shall mention two simple rules applicable to reasoning from substance to attribute.

(1) The Substance Must Be Identified Accurately. — Very evidently the substance from which certain attributes are to be inferred must be identified very carefully before any sound inference as to its attributes can be drawn. For ex-

[1] Day, Henry N., *op. cit.*, p. 133.   [2] *Ibid.*, p. 131.

ample, many arguers will rather hastily pronounce some plan or proposal under discussion to be this or that type of institution, and then infer that it will display certain attributes because of that fact without stopping to prove its identity. Thus, in a recent debate on chain stores one speaker characterized chain stores as monopolies in the opening sentence of his argument and then spent the rest of his time pointing out the undesirable attributes of monopoly. He was attacked not on the point that monopolies had undesirable characteristics, but on his assertion that the chain stores constituted a monopoly. His argument from substance to attribute fell because he failed to prove the identity of the substance about which he was arguing.

(2) The Attributes Must Be Inherent in the Substance. — The second precaution to observe in reasoning from substance to attribute is that the alleged attributes be inherent in and essential to the known substance. Returning to the illustration used in the preceding section, even though the chain stores were proved to be retail monopolies, it would not necessarily follow that they possessed undesirable attributes. High prices, for example, is not an essential attribute of monopoly. In such public utilities as light, water, and transportation, commonly known as natural monopolies, lower prices and increased efficiency are very often attributes of monopolistic control. In other words, unless the alleged attributes are clearly inherent in the subject, their attribution to the known substance must be proved before the reasoning is valid.

B. Argument from Sign. — Argument from sign is the second important deductive type we shall study. Like antecedent probability it can most profitably be discussed from the standpoint of the cause-effect and substance-attribute relationships involved. Argument from sign reverses antecedent probability, however, in that the reasoning is from effect to cause and from attribute to substance rather than from cause to effect and substance to attribute. This type of argument is frequently called *a Posteriori* reasoning. It may be expressed in complete syllogistic form as follows:

> If there is smoke, there is fire;
> There is smoke;
> Therefore: There is fire.

> If the blue of the ocean increases, the depth of the water is
>   decreasing;
> The blue of the ocean is increasing;
> Therefore: The depth of the water is decreasing.

In the first of the above syllogisms, the reasoning is from the known effect (smoke) to the alleged cause (fire); in the second example, the inference is from the known attribute (increasing blueness of the ocean) to the alleged substance (decreasing depth of the water).

1. ARGUMENT FROM EFFECT TO CAUSE. — Argument is replete with examples of reasoning from a known effect to an alleged cause. The advocate of every policy change, for example, must point out certain existing evils and argue that they are caused by the institution he purposes to change or modify in some way. His opponent may question this causation and contend that some other agency is the causative factor. Since every effect must have a cause, when that effect is under discussion and its cause is unknown, the arguer must be able to reason cogently and persuasively from effect to cause.

a. Rules Governing Argument from Effect to Cause. — The following rules are applicable to argument from a known effect to an alleged cause.

(1) The Alleged Cause Must Be Capable of Being the Real Cause of the Effect in Question. — This first rule is a counterpart of the rule governing argument from cause to effect which

requires that the known cause must be adequate to produce the alleged effect. In reasoning from a known effect to an alleged cause, it is of course equally important that the adequacy of the cause be established. The validity of the reasoning can be open to serious question if it can be shown that the alleged cause could not have been powerful enough to have produced the known effect. In a recent debate on the advisability of a whipping post as a non-mandatory punishment for major crimes, the advocate of this measure pointed to the low crime rate in Canada, where the whipping post is used, as evidence of its deterrent power. The negative attacked this causal reasoning by questioning the adequacy of the alleged cause, and going on to contend that other factors were responsible for this low crime rate.

It should be pointed out that proof of the inadequacy of the cause does not in and of itself prove that the known effect is not a sign of the alleged cause. For example, in the illustration we have just cited, the affirmative immediately responded by saying that it was not its intention to argue that the whipping post was solely responsible for the low crime rate in Canada, but rather that it was a contributing cause. To make the refutation complete in such a case, it must be shown (by the negative in this case) either that these other causes, whose coöperation was necessary, did not exist; or that the other causes did operate, and were adequate in and of themselves without the coöperation of the alleged cause.

(2) The Known Effect Must Be a Certain Sign of the Alleged Cause. — Most argument from effect to cause is open to attack on the charge that it is not a certain sign of the alleged cause, or in other words, that the effect may be due to some other cause. Unless the known effect is a certain sign of the known cause, every reason should be advanced to establish the probability of the causal relationship which is contended to exist.

(3) The Cause and Effect Connection Must Be Complete.
— We have already discussed this rule in argument from
cause to effect. It is of course just as important that
no links in the chain of causation be missing in reasoning
from effect to cause as it is in reasoning from cause to effect.

2. REASONING FROM ATTRIBUTE TO SUBSTANCE. — Our
discussion up to this point will undoubtedly enable the reader
to understand this type of reasoning with little additional
comment or illustration. It should be pointed out, however,
that there is a great group of inferences arising out of the
arbitrary symbols of man which must be classified here as
well as natural attributes. For example, we infer from a
black flag that the weather will be stormy, and from a white
flag that the weather will be fair. In another connection the
white flag is a sign of surrender, and the red flag is a sign of
danger. These and the many other conventional signs which
we have, very evidently differ from such natural attributes
as smoke serving as the sign of fire, green grass the sign of
spring, etc. We may say that we infer the existence of substance wholes not only from their natural attributes, but also
from the many symbols which man has set up as arbitrary
attributes or signs of given substances.

a. Rules Governing Argument from Attribute to Substance. —
The following rules will be clear without discussion.

(1) The Attribute Should Be Identified Accurately. — Failure to identify an attribute or aggregate of attributes accurately will very obviously cause one to mistake the substance
in reasoning from attribute to substance.

(2) The Attribute Must Be a Certain Sign of the Substance. — This rule should perhaps be modified by saying
that unless the attribute is a certain sign of the substance,
every possible reason should be advanced to prove that it is in
all probability such a sign.

IV. A DIAGRAMMATIC REPRESENTATION OF THE INDUCTIVE AND DEDUCTIVE INFERENCES IN CONFIRMATION

The following diagrammatic representation of the inductive and deductive inferences in confirmation will help to summarize and fix the argumentative types studied in Chapters VIII and IX.[1]

A DIAGRAMMATIC REPRESENTATION OF THE INDUCTIVE AND DEDUCTIVE INFERENCES IN CONFIRMATION

A Relationship of Causation in several particular instances of the phenomenon   or   A Relationship of Classification in several particular instances of the phenomenon

will permit the

INDUCTION

of a

GENERALIZATION OF CAUSATION OR CLASSIFICATION

which may be

CATEGORICAL or DISJUNCTIVE or HYPOTHETICAL

and

which may be the basis of the

DEDUCTION

of an

alleged effect or *alleged attribute* or *alleged cause* or *alleged substance*

in the case of some

PARTICULAR INSTANCE OF THE PHENOMENON UNDER OBSERVATION

[1] Analogy is the only argumentative type studied in Chapters VIII and IX which is not shown in this diagram.

EXERCISES

1. Bring to class three valid examples of each of the following types of reasoning stated in syllogistic form:

    a. Cause to effect.
    b. Substance to attribute.
    c. Effect to cause.
    d. Attribute to substance.

2. Write out in composition form a short argumentative paragraph embodying a single illustration of one of the argumentative types named in Exercise I. Illustrate each of the four types with such a paragraph and then restate the argument in syllogistic form in each case. Read your paragraphs to the class and have them set the arguments up in syllogistic form. Compare your syllogisms with those of the class.

3. Explain the diagrammatic representation of the inductive and deductive inferences in Confirmation as it appears in this chapter, in your own words.

4. Illustrate each of the rules governing argument from cause to effect by preparing examples of argument from cause to effect which are sound in every respect except that covered by the rule being illustrated. Submit these illustrations to the class and have them invoke the rule that is violated. Do the same thing for the other types of argument named in Exercise I.

5. Select all the instances of antecedent probability and sign in one of the debates in Appendix A (or one of the debates in the H. W. Wilson Company, *University Debater's Annual*) and test the validity of each argument by applying the appropriate rules.

6. State the arguments found in Exercise 5 in syllogistic form.

7. Prepare an argumentative speech embodying examples of antecedent probability and sign.

CHAPTER X

SUPPORTING THE PROPOSITION: EXPLANATION

CHAPTER OUTLINE

I. The Nature of Explanation.
   - A. Explanation Defined.
   - B. Explanation and Confirmation Distinguished.
   - C. The Persuasive Values of Explanation.
     1. It Dispels Unfamiliarity.
     2. The Audience Is Prepared for the Conclusion by Its Own Thinking.
     3. It Avoids the "Contrarient Idea."

II. The Theory of the Implicative System.
   - A. What the Implicative System Is.
   - B. The "This or Nothing" Disjunction.
     1. Must Be All-inclusive.
     2. Must Be Mutually Exclusive.
     3. Must Avoid the Possibility of a Wrong Choice.

III. Types of Explanation.
   - A. Analytic.
     1. Definition.
        - a. Definition by Classification.
        - b. Definition by Negation.
        - c. Definition by Example.
        - d. Definition by Context.
     2. Division.
        - a. Partition.
        - b. Summary.
        - c. Outline.
   - B. Synthetic.
     1. Description.
     2. Narration.
     3. Exposition.

IV. Concrete Helps in Explanation.
   A. Charts.
   B. Models and Samples.
   C. Demonstrations.

V. Using Explanation in Conjunction with Other Forms of Support.

VI. Summary.

I. The Nature of Explanation

In Chapters VIII and IX Confirmation was presented as one method of supporting the proposition. In this chapter we shall set forth a second form of support which we shall call *Explanation.*

A. Explanation Defined. — Explanation is that form of support in which belief and action are sought by explaining the data connected with any proposition in such a way as to cause the audience to accept the proposition by implication. It is a process of argument in which the speaker analyzes and synthesizes the materials bearing on the proposition, thereby leading the audience to imply its truth. The method has been described as follows:

"Its plan (that of support by explanation) is simply to portray a situation which gradually, of itself, without compulsion or contention on the part of the speaker, through the compelling power of a developing situation, makes evident to the mind of the hearer the necessity of one certain solution. The method is not in the orthodox and generally accepted sense argumentative; rather it is that of exposition with a goodly dash of narration and description. It does not appear to argue; it merely sets forth — yet slowly, definitely as it proceeds, the lines of descriptive development begin to converge and it becomes compellingly evident to each thinking mind that such a set of conditions implies, necessitates, one thing, the conclusion toward which an approach has been made from the beginning. It is argument in a very true sense, its aim is to convince and persuade, yet it is argument of which exposition, narration, and description, are handmaidens." [1]

B. Explanation and Confirmation Distinguished. — The distinction between Confirmation and Explanation as forms of argument must be sought (1) In the methods of procedure employed, and (2) In the nature of the inferences involved. We have seen in the two preceding chapters that the method of Confirmation is essentially that of arranging a chain of syllogisms or enthymemes in a logical progression and supporting their premises where necessary by a group of cases (generalization) or by a comparison of cases (analogy) which prove or tend to prove these premises. This method is argumentation in the old and generally accepted sense. Now the methods of Explanation are essentially those of description, narration, and exposition, intended to convince and actuate, and thereby made to subserve the ends of argument. Thus the explanatory development abandons the syllogistic approach characteristic of Confirmation and relies upon a systematic exhibition of the data connected with the subject to imply the proposition, the acceptance of which is being sought.

That the methods of Confirmation and those of Explanation are quite different is readily apparent. The question now to be considered is whether the difference between these two forms of argument is one of method only. Are there any differences in the nature of the inferences involved? The inferences employed in Confirmation are frequently referred to as *linear inference*.[2] This linear conception of inference, which is that of the syllogism and generalization from recurrent particulars, we wish now to distinguish from a theory

[1] Graham, Gladys Murphy, "The Natural Procedure in Argument." *Quarterly Journal of Speech*, Vol. XI, No. 4, p. 321.

[2] See Bernard Bosanquet, *Implication and Linear Inference*, Chapter II, "The Linear Conception of Inference," pp. 21–30. Macmillan and Co., London, 1920.

of inference known as *implication*.[1] Implication has been defined as " the connection between terms or sets of terms in virtue of a common nature which binds them into parts within a continuous system such that you can tell from one or more parts of it what the other parts of it, or some of them, are and how they are behaving."[2] This, we feel, is the essence of the inferences in Explanation. It consists of a juxtaposition of the original data connected with the proposition, and out of the necessities which impose themselves when these data are thus arranged and exhibited to the audience arises a datum — a premise which partakes of the nature of a conclusion and is so accepted by the hearers.[3] Bosanquet, who speaks of this as " the natural procedure in argument " states, " I believe that the natural method of opening the case descriptively, and placing the reader or hearer within the system which is the development of our subject, not merely follows an instinct of common sense, but is a well grounded logical procedure and ultimately fundamental."[4]

The theory of implication in relation to argument will be discussed in this chapter. The thought has been expressed previously that " a clear explanation of a subject will often constitute a wholly persuasive treatment of it."[5] This is exactly the thesis we wish to develop.

C. The Persuasive Values of Explanation. — The following are certain advantages of Explanation as a method of argument.

1. It Dispels Unfamiliarity. — In Chapter V, Analyzing the Audience, we pointed out the value of Support by Explanation as a means of persuading an audience which is

---

[1] *Ibid.*, Chapter I, "The General Nature of Implication," pp. 1–21.
[2] *Ibid.*, p. 14.   [3] *Ibid.*, p. 116.
[4] *Ibid.*, p. 113.
[5] O'Neill, J. M., and Weaver, A. T., *The Elements of Speech*, p. 434. Longmans, Green and Company, 1926.

inadequately informed on the proposition. What argument could be more persuasive to a person who is indifferent or opposed to a proposition because he is not informed regarding it, than one which supplies him with this information? Almost invariably when the opposition has its basis in unfamiliarity, the persuader has but to explain the proposition in order to dispel this opposition and secure the desired action.

2. THE AUDIENCE IS PREPARED FOR THE CONCLUSION BY ITS OWN THINKING. — That you cannot pour conclusions into the heads of people as you would pour water into a receptacle is a matter of common knowledge. Only as the reactor is stirred up to " purposeful activity " can you expect to influence his thinking or overt conduct. Conclusions arrived at by one's own thinking are thus infinitely stronger than those imposed by others, so far as the individual is concerned. In the explanatory method the persuader does not simply recite his own conclusions before the audience. Rather than that he sets forth those facts and opinions which led him to conclude as he did, in such a way that the hearers will be led to go through the same reasoning process.

3. IT AVOIDS THE "CONTRARIENT IDEA." — This method also avoids what some writers have called the " contrarient idea." [1] When a persuader starts his presentation with certain conclusions, the very announcement of these conclusions invariably sets off inhibitions which might never otherwise occur. People seem to have an inborn antipathy against assuming other people's conclusions. They question at the slightest opportunity. They immediately begin a mental argument with the speaker and fight him from the first word to the last. It is believed that in many situations these obstacles can be avoided or at least greatly minimized by the method of explanation.

[1] MacPherson, William, *The Psychology of Persuasion*, p. 161. E. P. Dutton and Company, 1920.

II. The Theory of the Implicative System

Really to understand Explanation as a method of argument, it is necessary that we bring another logical concept into our study. That concept is the Implicative System.

A. What the Implicative System Is. — The Implicative System may be defined as a logical thought-whole consisting of a set of propositions so related (by implication) that the truth of one is implied by the truth of the others. A proposition may be looked upon as a part of this whole or system. In argument by Explanation, the proposition for discussion always comprises one of the propositions of an implicative system. It is the task of the persuader to present the other related propositions in such a way that the truth of the proposition under discussion will be implied. The accompanying figure illustrates the point we are making. Let us say that the

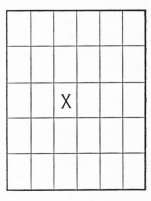

larger square represents an implicative system and each of the smaller squares a proposition. If we let the square marked by the x indicate the proposition for argument, we may say that its truth may be implied as we explain the propositions or data represented by the other squares. The more of these related propositions we explain, the more evident will become the proposition under discussion. The whole process is comparable to a picture puzzle which is unintelligible until its various parts are assembled. As the fragments are pieced together, the place of each remaining part becomes increasingly evident from the nature of the picture which is beginning to take form. Propositions, like the pieces of the puzzle, are not intelligible as isolated entities. Their identity as true or false statements, so far as any individual is concerned, is determined by many relationships. It is the task of the persuader to bring these relationships to light. If the proposition under discussion can be identified with a group of other propositions which cannot be logically denied or which are accepted by the audience, the truth of the proposition is thereby implied. A proposition is thus related to a system as a part is related to the whole. It is the persuader's task to make it clear that the proposition he is defending is a part of a system which the listener cannot safely or logically deny. When that system has been explained the truth or falsity of the proposition can be implied from it. In most cases the implication is perfectly obvious if the persuader's work has been well done. The conclusion simply rushes ahead of the argument.

The following examples of explanatory support will illustrate the implicative system:

In a recent argument defending the proposition that the United States should recognize the Russian Soviet Government, the speaker placed his proposition in an implicative system which included a sketch of Russia's history previous to the Soviet Government and a description of present conditions in Russia. It included bits of narrative from our own early history which paralleled that of Russia's. It explained the positions of the different classes in Russia and in this country. In short, it placed the proposition in a setting which compelled its acceptance. When the speaker had completed his picture the implication was obvious; and that implication was that the United States should recognize Soviet Russia. It was a highly persuasive argument and yet there was none of the forcing or contending or driving which so frequently characterizes speeches of this kind.

Another illustration of the implicative system is a speech of John Langdon Davies delivered in the 1930 lecture series of the University of Michigan Oratorical Association. The subject of this lecture was "The Political Scene in England." In this case, the speaker was an educated Englishman thoroughly conversant with political conditions in his country. He contrasted conditions in the United States and England where those conditions had a bearing on the English political situation. He related sketches of English party history in almost narrative form. He described the types of people composing the different parties in England. He explained England's greatest needs as a nation. Like the speaker in the previous illustration, he built up an implicative system which permitted but one conclusion, and that conclusion was that the Labor Party then in power in England should be continued in power.

It is interesting to note that this proposition was never once enunciated in so many words, and yet such was clearly the implication of the system the speaker constructed. It was an excellent illustration of a case in which a controversial objective was gained without a struggle.

B. The " This or Nothing " Disjunction. — It is helpful to observe that when an arguer builds an implicative system such as we have just discussed, he leads his audience to infer the truth of the proposition under discussion by confronting them with a rough disjunction, "This or Nothing."[1] That is, the audience must either accept the proposition under discussion or reject the propositions which imply its truth. The " This " in the disjunction refers to the persuader's proposition, and the " Nothing " refers to those related propositions whose truth is so evident that their rejection is well nigh impossible. The " Nothing " in the disjunction implies the absence of all logical grounds, the denial of truth as we know it and commonly accept it. For instance, in the illustrations cited in the preceding section, the argument in each case can be reduced to a " This or Nothing " disjunction. In the plea for the recognition of Soviet Russia, the persuader ex-

---

[1] "The Essence of the Inference in Implication, then, would be in showing of any suggested proposition, that unless we accepted it, our province of truth would as a whole be taken from us."   Bernard Bosanquet, *Implication and Linear Inference*, p. 3.

plained the Russian situation in such a way that to refuse to accept the proposition meant (or appeared to mean) a denial of truths and principles which were beyond reasonable question. Likewise, the speech of John Langdon Davies explained the English political situation in such a way that the audience was impelled to accept the conclusion that the Labor Party should be continued in power, because a refusal to accept this proposition, it seemed, would compel an abrogation of many principles which are unquestionably sound and a denial of many conditions which unquestionably existed.

In supporting a proposition by Explanation, it is the objective of the persuader, then, to set up an implicative system, or in other words, to confront the audience with such data as will cause the implication of the proposition in question. To make certain that the proper implication will be made, the arguer needs to present a case which will compel the audience either to accept his proposition or adopt the questionable alternative of rejecting the data he has presented. This disjunction with which the audience is confronted may be tersely phrased as we have explained as " This or Nothing."

We now wish to set forth three rules which need to be observed in arguing by Explanation in order to make certain that the implicative system constructed by the persuader will confront the audience with the " This or Nothing " disjunction.

1. MUST BE ALL-INCLUSIVE. — In the first place the disjunction must be all-inclusive. That is, the persuader must be certain that the reactor will not reason to himself, " I will accept neither This or Nothing. I will not accept your proposition nor will I deny the facts you have submitted. I can consistently imply another proposition from these same facts. I will take another course of action which you have not contemplated." Here would be a case in which the

audience implied a conclusion from the system presented which had not been considered by the speaker.

> This mistake was recently made by a speaker who addressed a state teachers' association on the proposition that a Federal Department of Education should be established. His explanatory development built up a system which compelled an implication all right; but the difficulty was that the wrong proposition could easily be implied. And that was exactly what happened. Most people were persuaded that the federal government should do more for education than it was then doing, but a need for a department was not at all apparent. He lost his cause to many listeners because his disjunction was not complete. Instead of concluding that a department of education should be established, the listeners concluded variously that the existing Bureau of Education should be given an improved status, that more money should be appropriated, etc.

To be conclusive argument the system developed must imply the proposition defended by the speaker to the exclusion of all other propositions. The listeners, truly, must be confronted with the necessity of either accepting the proposition at hand (This), or rejecting their province of truth as a whole (Nothing).

2. MUST BE MUTUALLY EXCLUSIVE. — Secondly, the two members of the disjunction must be mutually exclusive. Unless this precaution is taken the audience is likely to reason, " Accepting This means accepting Nothing. To accept your proposition is to deny many truths and facts which are beyond question. Therefore, I am opposed to your proposition."

The most complete violation of this rule would be the instance in which the system built up by the persuader implied the exact opposite of what he was trying to prove; that is, where the system implied the negative of the proposition rather than the affirmative or the affirmative rather than the negative. Here the speaker's proposition, or the This in the disjunction, would be exactly equivalent to the Nothing, and would, of course, be entirely rejected. Had the advocate of a department of education mentioned in the preceding section so completely bungled the situation as to have led his audience to conclude that it was the acceptance of his proposition rather than the rejection which would necessitate a denial of their province of truth, we would have an illustration of this point.

While it is true that such complete failures rarely take place, it is also true that this error occurs very frequently in lesser degrees with results almost as damaging. For instance, failure to dismiss any salient objections to the propositions, to that extent identifies the proposition with the Nothing in the disjunction. If your chief objection to a department of education lies in your belief that it will lead to federal domination of education, quite obviously no system will imply that proposition to your satisfaction until it removes your fears in that direction.

Is it not clear, then, that in direct proportion as the persuader fails to make the proposition and the Nothing in the disjunction mutually exclusive, his proposition becomes less and less evident from the system presented.

3. MUST AVOID POSSIBILITY OF WRONG CHOICE. — Finally, the persuader must beware lest the audence accept the Nothing in the disjunction in preference to the This. In such case the listener would reason, " You have presented me with two alternatives, This or Nothing. I think you are right in saying that I must either accept your proposition or deny certain facts and truths. However, I prefer to make this denial rather than accept your proposition." To avoid a choice of this kind the persuader must make the alternative to acceptance of his proposition so completely undesirable that the possibility of such a choice will be entirely removed, or at least made exceedingly remote. The following case

illustrates an argument in which the speaker did not take sufficient care to avoid a wrong choice.

> In a recent mayoralty campaign a speaker arguing in behalf of one of the candidates before a certain fraternal organization to which the candidate belonged, built up an implicative system which made it evident that the audience must either vote for this candidate or sacrifice both party and fraternal loyalty. His argument very apparently failed with most of the audience, because, granting the truth of his disjunction, they preferred the alternative to casting their vote for the candidate in question.

A choice of the " Nothing " in the disjunction in preference to the " This " most frequently occurs in highly controversial matters in which the reactor is very much opposed to the persuader's proposition. In the case of the proposal that a department of education be created, for instance, the question is sufficiently controversial to make it necessary that the persuader show the denial of a great province of truth to be coincident with its rejection. To impel an opponent of this proposition to imply its adoption, the persuader would need to build a system which tied his cause by descriptive, narrative, and expository relationships to beliefs, principles, and facts which could hardly be denied. Anything less than this would lead the reactor to reject the beliefs, principles, and facts rather than accept the proposition.

III. TYPES OF EXPLANATION

The Implicative System has been set forth as the logical basis of Explanation. We are now about to examine the different types of Explanation, Analytic and Synthetic. These in turn are divided into Definition and Division, and Description, Narration, and Exposition, respectively. While these terms are undoubtedly familiar to most students, the significant thing is that we are advancing them here as tools of argument. It is their use in an implicative system which gives them persuasive values. In fact, it is through Definition, Division, Description, Narration, and Exposition that any implicative system is constructed. We shall see how the use of these types enables the persuader to build a system which will confront the audience with the disjunction we have just discussed, " This or Nothing."

A. Analytic Explanation. — Analytic Explanation is of two kinds, Definition and Division. Not infrequently propositions can be persuasively supported by a clear definition of terms and a careful division of the subject matter.

1. DEFINITION. — Definition is the process of clarifying the terms which are to be used in the argument. These terms may appear in the proposition or may occur during the course of the argument. While Definition is not usually sufficient explanation to lead the reactor to imply the proposition, it is usually an important part of an explanation.

In general there are two types of terms which must be carefully defined before intelligent argument on any proposition can take place. They are unfamiliar terms and ambiguous terms. An unfamiliar term is simply a language symbol which does not stir up the proper meaning in the minds of the listeners, and must therefore be carefully conditioned or defined in terms that do carry adequate meaning. An ambiguous term is one which, in its correct usage, can convey two or more meanings. As suggested in the rules governing the proposition such terms should be avoided in phrasing the proposition, and this same precaution can well be applied to all persuasive discourse. However, where it becomes necessary to clear up any ambiguity, the exact meaning in which you are using the term under question should be carefully stated.

Quibbling is a term which frequently arises in this connection. It characterizes the improper act of employing an attack on terms as a guise to conceal one's inability to meet the argument. It is the practice of promiscuously questioning the definition of terms without regard to the real import of the argument. It should not be implied from this that all discussion of definition is quibbling. It seems to be a rather common practice among debaters to try to dismiss any discussion of terms on the part of their opponents with the charge that they are quibbling. Such indiscriminate charges are entirely unjustified. No argument can proceed intelligently until the terms are clear. If an opponent insists on using a term wrongly or equivocates on its meaning, this error should be insistently pointed out by all means; such insistence is not quibbling.

There are various methods of definition, but the following four seem to be most useful in argument: (1) By Classification; (2) By Negation; (3) By Example; and (4) By Context.

a. Definition by Classification. — A definition by classification identifies the term being defined with a certain class or category and then properly allocates the term in that category.

For example, if you were to define the term *horse*, you would first identify it as being a mammal and then cite those specific attributes which distinguish it from other mammals. The following definitions selected at random from Webster's *Collegiate Dictionary* illustrate this method:

> "**Aster** — Any of various herbaceous plants having heads with both discoid and radiate flowers."
>
> "**Athena** — One of the greater Olympian deities, preëminent as a civic goddess, wise in industries of peace and the arts of war."

b. Definition by Negation. — Definition by negation is the opposite of classification. It attempts to define by telling what a term is not. It excludes the term under question from various categories and makes clear that it does not possess certain attributes. The instance would be rare in which this method would be adequate in and of itself. It may become highly definitive, however, when used in connection with classification. It is also valuable as a device to exclude any connotations or denotations which you do not wish a term to convey.

Take the term *socialism* for example. Now most of us are more or less familiar with this term and we all have ideas as to what it means. To define it by classification as " a political and economic theory of social reorganization " and point out certain specific attributes is not enough. The term would still mean one thing to one individual and quite another thing to another. One would be thinking in terms of Marxian socialism, the other in terms of our modern Russian socialism, etc. Let the persuader say, " By socialism I do not mean communism; I do not mean Bolshevism, etc." By this process of exclusion or negation the exact meaning of the term can be worked out.

c. Definition by Example. — Definition by example is also commonly used in connection with classification. It defines by citing certain illustrations or instances which are familiar to the audience. For instance, in defining the term machine, after classifying the term, it would be helpful to cite typewriters, engines, etc., as examples of machines.

d. Definition by Context. — In some instances definition by context is the best way to clarify a term. Use the term in a sentence which brings out the exact shading of meaning which you wish to convey. If an ambiguous term is used in the proposition or in quoted language, the connection in which it is used may be the best defining agent. As in the case of negation and example, it should be observed that this method is valuable as a means of corroborating definition by classification.

There is frequently question as to where in the argument a definition should be given. There is no invariable rule on this. Probably the most common practice is to set forth the necessary definitions in the introduction to the argument. This method is preferable when the term occurs in the proposition or when it is to be used repeatedly during the course of the argument. Sometimes, however, it is more opportune to define the term when it arises. If a term does not occur in the proposition and arises more or less incidentally during the course of the argument, quite obviously its definition should be given when the need arises.

2. DIVISION. — Division is the second type of Analytic Explanation. It consists of the process of explaining a subject by exhibiting its parts. Division may be made on many different bases depending upon the purpose of the speaker. For example, if you were to divide the subject *kinds of apples*, it would be possible to make the division on the basis of color, taste, size, variety, or any one of a large number of other points which readily suggest themselves. Similarly, propositions for argument can be divided up into topics and subtopics on various bases. Take the salesman's proposition for illustration. An automobile salesman might divide his proposition in many different ways. He could make his selling points beauty, economy, and comfort, or he could talk engine, body, chassis, and running gears. Again he might follow the common sales method of first showing his customer that he needed an automobile, and secondly, pointing out the practicality of the particular car he is offering for sale. Here again many other possible divisions of subject matter will suggest themselves, but the point that we wish to emphasize is that some such division is imperative in persuasive speaking. Like Definition, Division is not usually sufficient explanation in itself to lead the reactor to imply the proposition, but it plays an important part in every argument.

Division evidences itself in argument in three ways: (1) Partition; (2) Summary; and (3) Outline.

a. Partition. — A partition is a statement of points or topics which will be taken up later in the argument. It may vary from a careful introductory statement laying out the plan of the entire case before the audience, to the announcement of new topics as the persuader makes transition from one point to another.

b. Summary. — Whereas the partition states what is about to be taken up, the summary recalls what has been already treated. As in the case of the partition, the summary may vary from a complete review of the argument in the conclusion, to a summary of individual points in the course of the argument.

c. Outline. — The outline of the argument is the skeleton or plan which underlies the finished case. It consists of the divisions and subdivisions of the proposition stated in the form of an organized group of points. The principles and methods of outlining are discussed in Chapter XII.

It should be understood, then, that Analytic Explanation consists of Definition and Division, two of the methods of building a clear implicative system. It is hardly necessary to observe that these devices are constantly used in connection with Confirmation and Motivation, the other forms of support. In fact, good argument of any kind is inconceivable without an understanding of terms and a careful division of subject matter. This observation, however, in no way invalidates the fact that in argument we are dealing with three essentially different forms of support, *i.e.*, Confirmation, Explanation, and Motivation. We will see other instances in which they are used together as our study progresses.

In some cases propositions can be adequately supported by Definition and Division alone. Let the full import of the terms be known and the salient issues stated, and many arguments can be won without more being said. This is particularly true where indifference or opposition to the proposition is based on ignorance or lack of knowledge concerning it.

B. Synthetic Explanation. — Synthetic Explanation is of three kinds, Description, Narration, and Exposition. Once more we are placing some old symbols in a new setting which we hope will add to their significance. Like Definition and Division, they are methods by which an implicative system can be built. They place the history, the attendant circumstances, and the various relationships before the audience in such a way as to imply the truth of the proposition.

1. DESCRIPTION. — "Description is that process or form of Explanation which exhibits the properties, attributes, and relations of *spacial* objects in their proper order." [1]

To illustrate Description as a factor in argument let us again consider the salesman's proposition. The orderly description of the commodity for sale is a vital part of most sales talks. Such a description should do exactly the things suggested by the above definition. It should point out the properties and attributes of the article for sale and relate it to the customer's needs and demands in such a way as to lead the customer to infer the advisability of its purchase. In this manner the clever salesman can build up an implicative system which will avoid many of the objections and inhibitions which might occur through the use of other forms of support.

A very persuasive talk recently given was an argument for the leasing of a tract of land to be used as a boy scout camp. The speaker proceeded descriptively almost altogether, telling of the woods, the lake, and other available factors which argued for a good camp-site. This speech, while almost wholly descriptive, proved to be a winning argument. The description implied the advisability of favorable action on the lease,

[1] Hyslop, James H., *Logic and Argument*, p. 66. Charles Scribner's Sons, 1899.

and in that way supported the proposition, probably better than could any other form of support.

2. NARRATION. — "Narration is that process or form of Explanation which presents a proposition in its *time* relations, or which exhibits events in their proper order." [1]

It will be seen from the definition that the process is essentially history no matter what the proposition may be. The value of Narration as a factor in argument is particularly well illustrated with any proposition of policy. In arguing for or against a policy of any kind it is highly persuasive to place it in a historical setting which implies its adoption. It should be made apparent that the policy advocated is the logical next step, that all that has gone before points to the adoption of this policy. Listeners will draw such conclusions from the argument without compulsion if these narrative lines are effectively drawn.

In a recent debate on the proposition that a lake to ocean canal be constructed via the St. Lawrence which would accommodate ocean-going vessels, the affirmative team abandoned the usual confirmatory method of support, and proceeded to build its case through an explanation consisting mainly of Narration and Description. The history of the canal was told with the aid of a chart, pointing out that huge sums of money had already been expended on portions of the canal to make it navigable for ocean-going vessels, that appropriations had already been made for other sections of the canal, and that there was an increasing demand for the use of the canal. These facts, along with others, were presented in a simple and straightforward explanation of the situation which permitted but one implication, and that was that funds should be provided so that the remaining sections of the canal could be made navigable for ocean vessels.

3. EXPOSITION. — "Exposition is that process or form of Explanation which exhibits a proposition as a logical thought whole independent of time or space relations." [2]

[1] Hyslop, James H., *Logic and Argument*, p. 68.   [2] *Ibid.*, p. 69.

From this definition it can be seen that Exposition deals largely with abstract and general conceptions, while pure description and narration are generally occupied with concrete things. Whereas description and narration deal with things seen, heard, depicted, as matters of observation, exposition is concerned with things conceived, identified, classified, as matters of penetrative and systematic thinking. Description and narration consider traits and acts that distinguish objects as individuals; exposition looks for the traits and acts that unite individuals into classes.[1] Assume, for instance, that you have occasion to explain some controversial religious doctrine or scientific principle. Neither Narration nor Description would suffice, because such a subject cannot usually be exhibited in relations of time or space. It is an abstract concept which can be adequately explained only by an exposition of its logical relations to other known concepts. These logical relationships are usually those of causation and classification or resemblance, and are expounded by *analyses, comparisons, and examples.* Thus to persuade an audience that socialism is a meritorious theory of government by Exposition, would require a statement of all causal and resembling relationships which would tend to establish the point. Socialism could be analyzed, compared with other forms of government, and examples cited. In this way an implicative system could be built which would imply the proposition.

Of the various types of Explanation it can be seen that Exposition most nearly approximates Confirmation. It displays essentially the same relationships as are used in Confirmation, but they are approached from the explanatory point of view, that of the implicative system, rather than being stated in the usual inductive or deductive forms. The

[1] See Genung, J. F., *The Working Principles of Rhetoric*, p. 554. Ginn and Company, 1900.

following hypothetical case illustrates the persuasive possibilities of Exposition:

> Assume that you are a firm believer in the World Court of International Justice, and you wish to win another to your point of view, who is opposed to the Court because of its connection with the League of Nations. The best argument you could advance would be to explain that while the court is a creation of the League and handles the cases of the League, it is otherwise independent of it. It could also be explained that adherence to the Protocol providing for the World Court would in no way necessitate adherence to or subjection to the Covenant of the League of Nations. Through an exposition of this kind the objection to the Court could be removed and the argument won, probably more readily than by any other method.

IV. Concrete Helps in Explanation

A. Charts. — Charts, curves, and maps are frequently helpful in explaining a subject. Wherever it seems that these devices can be used more effectively than a purely verbal explanation, and the occasion is propitious for their use, the persuader should by all means use such devices. If they are to be used in public address, however, ready visibility is a problem which needs to be carefully considered.

B. Models and Samples. — Models and samples are also aids to Explanation on certain occasions. Probably no single class of persuasive speakers use these devices more than salesmen. They can be displayed before the audience or passed around for individual inspection. The precaution should be observed, however, that these devices are introduced only at the time when the speaker wishes the attention of the audience directed to them. A persuader who fails to do this is apt to find himself talking to a group which is busily engaged in attending to his models or samples, with the result that the argument falls on deaf ears.

C. Demonstrations. — Perhaps the most persuasive concrete help to an explanation is a demonstration of the object under explanation. For example, if a salesman is selling an automobile, he invariably demonstrates the machine to the prospective buyer. A demonstration should be carefully planned before it is undertaken to make certain that it coördinates well with the arguments and proceeds smoothly.

V. USING EXPLANATION IN CONJUNCTION WITH OTHER
FORMS OF SUPPORT

At several points in this chapter we have indicated that Explanation is frequently used in conjunction with other forms of support. We wish to explain that point further here.

The use of Explanation is particularly common in the introduction. In many argumentative speeches it has become almost the rule to introduce the case with an explanation, usually of the Analytic type. Terms are defined and partitions set forth. These very same arguments, then, may proceed to develop the proposition by Confirmation or Motivation. It is probably safe to say that this is exactly what happens in the average argumentative speech. After an explanatory introduction, the proposition is supported by Confirmation, with an effort at Motivation in the form of a peroration.

It should also be pointed out that Explanation may be used in immediate connection with Confirmation and Motivation. That is to say, these forms of support may be used side by side to support a given point. Any single point in an argument may be supported by an Explanatory argument, a Confirmatory argument, and by Motivation.

While emphasizing the value of Explanation as means of supplementing other forms of support, the student should not overlook the fact, that through the implicative system, it presents a definite methodology which can be used independently of other forms of support as a means of argument.

VI. SUMMARY

In studying and applying the theories set forth in this chapter, the implicative system, the This or Nothing disjunction, and others, it will be decidedly helpful if the student will constantly keep in mind the relatively simple thesis which this chapter seeks to develop; and that is, that in many cases people can be led to believe in a proposition and to act as it suggests, by an orderly explanation of the proposition. This chapter has endeavored to make it relatively easy for the reader to present an explanation which will have such persuasive values.

EXERCISES

Note: Students will be able to prepare the exercises suggested here and use the Explanatory method much more readily after having read Chapter XII, "Outlining Argument."

1. Write a 500-word Explanation on one of the following subjects. In each case have in mind a definite proposition and make your treatment as persuasive as possible, but confine yourself to the types of Explanation discussed in this chapter.

   a. A book to read.
   b. A place to go for a vacation.
   c. An athletic event to attend.
   d. A moving picture to see.

2. Prepare a five-minute argumentative speech on some proposition of local, state, or national policy in which you use the Explanatory method. Hand in an outline of this speech and an explanation of the implicative system you have tried to construct.

3. Read the Explanatory argument in Appendix B and do the following things regarding it.

   a. State the proposition.
   b. Enumerate the types of Explanation used and in what connection they are used.

    c. In what way does this speech confront the reader with a "This or Nothing" disjunction? Explain fully.

    d. What related propositions would the audience have to accept or reject before it could reject the proposition of the persuader? In other words, what is the "Nothing" in the disjunction?

4. Prepare a five-minute Explanatory argument, using some of the concrete helps discussed in this chapter.

5. Divide the class into groups of two and assign a proposition to each group. Let one member of each group support the assigned proposition with a Confirmatory argument and the other member support the same proposition with an Explanatory argument. Compare methods and results.

6. Define five terms of your own choosing using the four methods of definition explained in this chapter in each case.

CHAPTER XI

SUPPORTING THE PROPOSITION: MOTIVATION

CHAPTER OUTLINE

186

I. The Problem of Motivation

What are the motives which lead people to act as they do? How can the action tendencies of people be modified in desirable directions? These are the problems of human motivation. The business man is interested in these questions because he must play on the motives of other men so that they will buy his goods or services. The clergyman, the lawyer, in fact every person who wishes to exert an influence on the conduct of others, whether for personal gain, for the advancement of society, or for both, must of necessity be interested in human motives.

From time immemorial philosophers, economists, rhetoricians, and psychologists have been endeavoring to reduce human motives to workable theories and categories. Generally speaking, these motives have evaded satisfactory classification and have not submitted readily to acceptable hypotheses. The problem of motivation is primarily a psychological one and many worthwhile contributions to a better understanding of human motives are coming from this field today. Within the last ten or fifteen years, there has been a tendency toward the experimental study of motivation. Most of this has been animal experimentation with such activities as feeding, mating, nestbuilding, fighting, migrating, etc. While as yet only in their infancy these studies have made notable headway and will perhaps yield results far more reliable than the older introspective studies.

II. Motivation in Argument

The problem of motivation is of particular interest to the student of argument. As we have seen, it is the arguer's objective to influence the thinking and acting of other people. To do this successfully, it is imperative that he understand human motives and how to utilize these motives in the support of propositions. Chapters VIII, IX, and X have set forth Confirmation and Explanation as two methods of support, and it is our purpose in this chapter to discuss a third method which we shall call Motivation.

A. Motivation Defined. — As a methodology in argument, Motivation proceeds upon the theory that people think and act in response to their own desires. Hence it may be defined as a form of support by which the reactor is led to desire to act as the proposition suggests. The crux of the whole problem of motivation is to associate the effective desire of the reactor with the activity expressed in the proposition. To approach this problem we must understand the nature and source of desire, how it is stimulated, and how it can be focused on a given proposition.

B. The Relation of Motivation to the Other Forms of Support. — One of our colleagues in reading the manuscript of this chapter raised the question as to whether every good argument ought not to enlist the desire of the audience in the cause for which the argument is being advanced. This very interesting question again brings up the old problem of the logical adequacy of argument and its audience acceptability. In the first place, as explained before, we feel that there are occasions for argument when the speaker should make *logical unity*, *continuity* and *completeness* the first consideration, irrespective of the desires of the audience or any other psychological considerations which may interfere; and in the second place, we feel that it is possible under certain circumstances, even when *audience acceptability* is taken as the primary test of argument, to premise the argument on existing beliefs of the audience and reason both persuasively and convincingly by either Confirmation or Explanation without giving any special attention to the desires of the listener. While we feel that desire is the important factor in motivation, it is true nevertheless that people can sometimes be convinced of things which they would prefer not to believe, and " argued into doing things " which they do not desire to do.

We are not attempting, however, to belittle the persuasive force of desire. Argument must take account of this factor; and in our analysis, that argument which especially is designed to arouse desire and associate it with the proposition, we term *Motivation*. It is quite true that either confirmatory or explanatory argument may be employed to focus desire on a proposition; but since this function is not a vital or integral part of either of these separate and logically distinct methodologies, and since there are many special problems and methods in utilizing desire which have nothing whatever to do with Confirmation or Explanation, we have seen fit to treat this whole matter as a separate method of argument under the head of *Motivation*.

C. The Persuasive Values of Motivation. — It may be helpful at this point to single out some of the more important advantages of support by Motivation.

1. IT TAKES ADVANTAGE OF THE DESIRES OF THE REACTOR. — The outstanding advantage of motivation lies in the fact that it takes advantage of the wishes and desires of the reactor. It attempts to capitalize upon the oft observed fact that " the wish is father to the thought." That this is a positive advantage is revealed by an interesting

experiment recently conducted by Dr. F. H. Lund.   Employing as objective data as the experiment would permit, Dr. Lund found a coefficient of correlation of .88 between belief and desire, and a coefficient of but .42 between belief and evidence.   In other words, he found the use of evidence less than half as effective as a means of obtaining belief as a method which associated the proposition with the desire of the reactor.   Since this was true in the case of belief, it would seem that it would be equally true, if not more pronounced, in those cases where overt activity is the objective of the persuader.[1]   In citing Dr. Lund's conclusions we do not wish to appear to be belittling the value of carefully evidenced argument; on the contrary, we simply wish to point out the persuasive power of the motive appeal.

2.   IT IS HIGH IN ATTENTION VALUES. — Another advantage of Motivation lies in the fact that it commands the attention of the reactor.   While this factor is likely a corollary of the point that Motivation enlists the desires of the audience, it is worthy of special mention, nevertheless. Many eminent psychologists, and more lately several writers in the field of speech, have said that persuasion is the process of inducing others to give favorable or undivided *attention* to propositions.   Professor Winans states, " To persuade a man, then, seems to be nothing more or less than to win his undivided attention to the desired conduct, to make him think of that and stop thinking of other courses, or of any inhibiting ideas." [2]   We wish to subscribe heartily to this doctrine.   In fact we would add that perception of speech stimuli of any kind is contingent on attention.   From the standpoint of argument there is probably no more effective

[1] Lund, F. H., "The Psychology of Belief: A Study of Its Emotional and Volitional Determinants," *The Journal of Abnormal and Social Psychology*, 1925, Vol. XX, Nos. 1 and 2.

[2] Winans, James A., *Public Speaking*, p. 194.   The Century Company, 1924.

way to maintain attention than through enlisting the desire of the reactor in the cause being argued. This method of support avoids the questioning, inhibiting, and objecting attitude which so frequently accompanies disagreement. It subtly stimulates the audience to follow the persuader and to acquiesce in his conclusions.

III. THE NATURE AND BASIS OF DESIRE

We are now about to consider the important question, what is the basis of desire. To answer this question we must examine the reflexive, instinctive, and habitual behavior of the individual, from which his fundamental needs and wants arise. This study carries us into some rather technical psychological considerations which may appear to some students as being rather far removed from argument. We can see no way to a thorough understanding of Motivation, however, which neglects to explain the fundamental basis of desire.

A. Reaction Tendencies as a Basis of Desire. — Reaction tendencies as the name suggests are tendencies or dispositions to react in a certain way because of the internal state of the individual. They can best be explained in relation to the reflexes, instincts, and habits which are causative of them.

The infant is brought into the world with certain inherited neural connections. That is, his nervous system is so constructed as to cause certain responses to follow given stimuli more or less automatically. Certain of these native reactions are called reflexes and others instincts.[1] Without pausing to discuss the distinction between reflexes and instincts, which incidentally is highly controversial, we may say that

---

[1] Some authors have abandoned the term "instinct" altogether and characterize all native reactions as reflexes. Others make a distinction between the two, but there is no unanimity of opinion as to the basis of this distinction. See Woodworth, *Psychology: A Study of Mental Life*, pp. 107–109.

all native reaction tendencies constitute inner forces which drive the individual in a given direction. It should be borne in mind that these inner urges are not always clearly conscious or definite and in many cases constitute little more than a general uneasiness or feeling of dissatisfaction.

It is from these reflexes and instincts that our habitual behavior is developed. By a two-fold process of conditioning and trial and error, the individual builds up a comprehensive group of habitual or acquired responses. As we have intimated, these habitual responses may be thought of as acquired reaction tendencies, — reaction tendencies not present at birth which develop from the native responses by the regular learning process.

Now it is important for our purpose to see that both these native and acquired reaction tendencies are basic to desire. They represent inner drives or urges which impel the individual instinctively or otherwise to certain courses of action. The demands set up by these drives constitute desire. In other words, desire is really the uneasiness or dissatisfaction attendant upon environmental or physical conditions which thwart the full and complete consummation of established reaction tendencies. It may be said to be the drive, wish, need, or want, originating in a certain organic or environmental maladjustment which prevents the normal reflexive, instinctive, or habitual reactions of the individual from expressing themselves to the satisfaction of the individual. The organism exists in an environment which is constantly bombarding it with stimuli of all kinds. So long as it can make normal adjustments to these stimuli, satisfaction and contentment reigns. As soon as these adjustments are made impossible or difficult, dissatisfaction and discontent result.

Allport says on this point, "The original motive power arises from one or more of the prepotent reflex groups. Early in life a habit is built upon these reflexes by the usual learning processes, which, because of its high adaptive value and affinity with the special talents of the individual, acquires a widespread and basic position in the action system. It takes on a seeming prepotency of response upon presentation of the stimulus. Since it began to form in the individual at an early age and gradually and unconsciously penetrated his whole life, it is considered by him to be an end in itself. . . . It behaves like a prepotent reflex in that anger is aroused if its operation is thwarted. A drive (or desire) may therefore be defined as a prepotent habit or group of habits which acquires a compelling power similar to that of a prepotent reflex, and which controls the integration of other habit systems in the individual's development." [1]

Dewey says of habits, "All habits are demands for certain kinds of activity. . . . They form our effective desires and they furnish us with our working capacities." [2]

Woodworth says, "A habit is a drive, as we may see from the tension and uneasiness that occur when a habitual reaction is called for but prevented from realizing itself. To perform a habitual reaction gives satisfaction: or, at least, to forego the performance brings dissatisfaction and uneasiness." [3]

B. The Emotional Reënforcement of Reaction Tendencies.
— It is probable that any reaction tendency can be emotionally reënforced. Introspectively, we are all familiar with the impetus which such emotions as joy, sorrow, fear, anger, disgust, amusement, and others may give to our desires. Physiologically, the chief difference between a reaction tendency which is emotionally reënforced and one which is not lies in the fact that in the first case there is an accompanying innervation through the autonomic nervous system causing widespread muscular and glandular reactions which would otherwise not be present. It is thought that the secretions of the endocrine glands, particularly

---

[1] Allport, Floyd H., *Social Psychology*, pp. 109–110. Houghton Mifflin Company, 1924.
[2] Dewey, John, *Human Nature and Conduct*, p. 76.
[3] Woodworth, R. S., *Dynamic Psychology*, p. 162.

the thyroid and adrenals, are responsible for most of the characteristic, emotional responses.

Unquestionably the emotions play an important part in determining and conditioning our desires. While we have no very complete data upon which to generalize, it is thought that *the usual effect of the emotional reënforcement of a reaction tendency is to heighten and increase the desire to consummate this reaction.*

C. The Place of Purpose in Desire. — Thus far our explanation of desire has conceived of it as merely an unrest or discomfort resulting from a blocking of our normal organic urges, which may or may not be emotionally reënforced. It is probable, however, that in addition to these factors there is a positive seeking process involved in which some representation of the desired end plays an important rôle. Physiologically, it is difficult to explain *purpose* satisfactorily, and for that reason many students of motivation part company at this point. However, a complete explanation of desire seems to necessitate an inclusion of purpose.

Troland says of purpose, "It is a representation in consciousness, in imaginal form, of something which is desired. . . . The most primitive kind of desire presents no definite images of the 'end'; such desire — prior to any experience which can establish associations informative as to the means by which the desire can be satisfied — will involve a process of volitional unrest. However, nearly all of the desires of human beings who have passed beyond the stage of early infancy are based upon previous, more or less accidental, affective experiences, or upon verbal information in association with such desires." [1]

Troland sums up this position in a later statement, "Purpose, then, differs from primitive desire namely by being more explicit in advance. It is an educated form of desire; or desire is purposive in so far as it represents in advance the form of consciousness or experience which will bring satisfaction." [2]

[1] Troland, Leonard T., *The Fundamentals of Human Motivation*, p. 348. D. Van Nostrand Company, 1928.   [2] *Ibid.*, p. 351.

Whether or not Troland's explanation of purpose in terms of conscious images is ultimately fundamental, we find it a very useful concept nevertheless in setting forth our views on the motivation of argument. We shall view desire, then, not alone as a restlessness or uneasiness arising out of the blocking of normal organic urges, but as a purposive urge prompted by an image in consciousness of a desired end, or as Troland calls it, " an image of the desideratum."

D. The Biological Utility of Desire. — Having explained desire as a physiological unrest caused by the blocking of response tendencies and accompanied in most cases by a conscious purposiveness, it is now important to observe that most desires have definite biological utility. In other words, most human desires are favorable to the survival of the organism and the race in the struggle for existence. This is particularly evident in the case of innate drives such as food, reproduction, protection, and aggression, which are unquestionably the most basic and most powerful motivating factors.

Nor should the fact that certain desires are very evidently lacking in biological utility be permitted to hide this powerful average tendency in the biological direction. It is perfectly logical to expect such exceptions. In our discussion of reflexive, instinctive, and habitual behavior, we saw that new response tendencies were developed by trial and error, or in other words by the selection and fixation of certain random responses. It is known that responses which are successful or beneceptive [1] in a particular situation tend to become fixed while the neural connections producing unsuccessful or nociceptive [1] responses are rendered less conductive.

[1] The terms "beneceptive" and "nociceptive" originate with Troland. He defines them as follows: "Beneception — a process in a sense organ or afferent nerve channel which is indicative of conditions or events that are typically beneficial to the individual or species. . . . Nociception — a process in a sense organ or afferent nerve channel which is indicative of conditions or events that are typically injurious to the individual or species." See *ibid.*, pp. 511 and 513.

Thus it is possible to fix responses which are biologically serviceable in certain more or less accidental situations, which will be generally lacking in biological utility. It should be understood, however, that these instances are exceptions rather than the rule.

Troland says of these exceptions to the rule that human motives have biological utility:

> "Random action is a necessary foundation for learning, but will constantly introduce particular neurological and mental factors which have no survival value, or which may be opposed to a successful struggle for existence. These random phenomena are exactly analogous to the 'accidental variations' which lie at the foundation of the Darwinian Theory. We cannot expect purposes to be any more rigidly determined by biological exigencies than are other factors in the evolutionary situation." [1]

E. The Hedonistic Implications of Desire. — It has long been the supposition of certain philosophers and psychologists including Epicurus, Hobbes, Bentham, J. S. Mill and Spencer that pleasure and pain play an important part in the determination of human and animal conduct. The common sense individual seems to accept as axiomatic the principle that a conscious being will naturally seek the pleasant and avoid the unpleasant. There are other thinkers, however, who question the causal efficacy of pleasantness and unpleasantness in determining action. Notable among these is John B. Watson, representing an extreme behavioristic position. Watson is quoted as saying:

> "It is our aim to combat the idea that pleasure or pain has anything to do with habit formation. . . . To call those stimuli pleasant to which the animal positively reacts, and unpleasant those to which he negatively reacts, is making a wholesale gratuitous assumption on a par exactly with the assumption made

[1] Troland, Leonard T., *The Fundamentals of Human Motivation*, pp. 356–357.

by unreflective individuals who maintain that the moth flies into the candle because he likes the light, or because the light is pleasant to him."

It seems to us that these two positions are not as wholly inconsistent as they may at first appear to be. We have found the basis of desire in those basic reflexive, instinctive, and habitual action tendencies with varying degrees of emotional accompaniment and enforcement. We have suggested that in all probability in the less primitive desires there is an element of conscious purposiveness, the physiological explanation of which we are at present unable to state. We have also seen that these desires are usually developed from beneceptive responses or responses of high biological utility. We now wish to add that there appears to be a close correlation between what the man on the street calls pleasantness and these so-called beneceptive responses. In other words, generally speaking, those responses which have biological utility are pleasant, and those which do not have such survival values are unpleasant. Troland says on this point:

"We may generalize our findings in our terminology by saying that affective intensity (pleasantness or unpleasantness) shows a high degree of positive correlation with beneception and nociception." [1]

The practical problem for the student of argument is, of course, just how and to what extent the desires of individuals are affected by pleasure and pain. We are disposed to agree with Troland when he says that most biologically serviceable reactions are pleasant. In other words, we feel that the strongest and most impelling motives in life are usually those which are pleasant to the individual; and further, that they are pleasant because they are high in biological utility.

[1] *Ibid.*, p. 286.

In summary of Section III, it may be helpful to reiterate at this point that a desire is: (1) A physiological uneasiness or dissatisfaction resulting from native or acquired reaction tendencies; (2) which may be intensified by emotional reënforcement; (3) which may be represented in consciousness by a definite purpose or goal; (4) which is usually consummated by a biologically serviceable response or what is thought to be such, and (5) which usually leads to a pleasant reaction.

IV. THE TWO GREAT PROBLEMS IN SUPPORTING A PROPOSITION BY MOTIVATION

Having discussed the basis of desire, we wish now to explain how the desires of the audience may be most effectively utilized in argument. We have defined Motivation as that method of support by which the audience is led to desire to think or to act as the proposition suggests. We may point out now that motivation involves two great problems for the persuader: (1) He must awaken and intensify desire; and (2) He must associate this desire with the proposition he is arguing. The remainder of this chapter will be devoted to a study of these two problems.

V. AWAKENING AND INTENSIFYING DESIRE

We have seen in connection with our discussion of the nature and basis of desire that many of our desires are quite indefinite. In fact some of them may be nothing more than an organic uneasiness or dissatisfaction of which we are only vaguely conscious, if at all. Professor A. J. Snow states on this point:

"There are many levels of desire ranging from only a general organic need amounting to an unrest or an uneasiness to well defined desires of which the reactor is entirely conscious. Sometimes they are on the surface, sometimes below at various depths of attention. Frequently every resource and method of stimulation and appeal must be called in to bring about their emergence in the reactor's consciousness." [1]

We may say then that the first important question for the arguer is how to awaken and intensify those desires which are not keenly and clearly experienced by the audience.

A. Through the Motives of Action. — Self-satisfied complacency is the greatest barrier to the effective use of motivation. The reactor must be aroused; reaction tendencies must be stimulated; he must be made vividly to experience the uneasiness and unrest attendant upon his reflexive, instinctive, and habitual tendencies to react; and where possible and feasible, these inner drives so aroused should be emotionally reënforced and facilitated.

To this end we shall classify and discuss the principal motives of action.

1. A CLASSIFICATION OF THE MOTIVES OF ACTION. — From time to time writers have attempted to set forth the motives which determine people's thinking and acting. Very evidently any such classification is bound to be more or less arbitrary and incomplete. From our earlier explanation it can be seen that the motives of action are just as varied as the reflexive, instinctive, and habitual behavior from which they spring. Nevertheless, it is possible and unquestionably helpful to the arguer to set forth the basic drives which all people experience and from which the countless needs and wants of our present day civilization arise.

Some writers have attempted to reduce all human desires to a single basic motive. Notable among these are Freud with his libido or sex drive, and Adler with his drive for superiority or " Will to Power." It is felt, however, that there is no single motive to which all the behavior of man can accurately be attributed. Almost innumerable classifica-

---

[1] Snow, A. J., *Psychology in Personal Selling*, p. 369.

tions of the basic motives of action have been presented
from Aristotle down to the present day. For our purposes
here we feel that the following classification will be most helpful: (1) Food; (2) Sex; (3) Protection; and (4) Power.

   a. Food. — The need for food is, of course, universal,
and from this universal need spring many of the motives
which actuate the conduct of people. This powerful motive,
strongly reënforced by the emotion of fear, has been the
causative factor back of many of the great struggles of mankind. It has been the motive force in most wars and industrial strife; it is the drive which keeps millions of people
working and toiling from day to day.

   b. Sex. — The desires associated with sex are equally
fundamental. This drive is basic to the desire to mate and
the desire to please the opposite sex. Many of the institutions of today such as the home and the family, together
with many of the needs and wants which they occasion,
must largely be attributed to this motive.

   c. Protection. — Protection of self and others is another
basic drive to which many of our present day wants and
needs must be attributed. All devices and activities to
protect the health and happiness of ourselves and others who
are near and dear to us are to be considered here. Thus
we are motivated to clean our teeth twice daily, to equip
our automobiles with safety glass, to get our vitamins and
our iron, to take out insurance policies, and to do countless
other things which serve to protect.

   d. Power. — The fourth basic motivating factor in our
lives is the " will to power." It is the desire to dominate
over others, the desire to excel, and the desire for good reputation. Thus, men will strive for economic and social position
far beyond that which is necessary to their physical well-being,
simply to satisfy this urge for position and influence. Others
will risk their lives to conquer nature, to climb high moun-

tains, to pioneer in new countries, because of this drive to dominate. We see this same factor motivating the lives of great scholars and scientists who are attempting to solve challenging problems.

In connection with this classification of the motives of action it should be pointed out that there are many *derived motives* which we have not discussed. It is believed, however, that at least the great majority of motives which determine human behavior are either directly or indirectly attributable to the four basic drives which we have explained. While the task of classifying these derived motives is both too exhaustive and too precarious for this chapter, may we suggest that each student will find it profitable to list as many motives as he can discover and then trace them back to the basic drive or drives which appear to be causative of them.

2. Using the Motives of Action in Argument. — There is perhaps no better way to appreciate the use to which the motives of action can be put in argument than to study the advertisements in almost any current magazine or newspaper. Most advertisements will picture some scene or object which stimulates desire and then rather tersely and suggestively associate this desire with some particular commodity or service that it is attempting to sell. Not infrequently there is little logical connection between the motive stimulated and the action suggested, but even in many of these cases the argument is impelling nevertheless, because some basic reaction tendency has been stirred, and strongly associated with a given course of action. We would like to suggest that each reader select a dozen different advertisements at this point in our study; note in each case the motive or motives which the advertisement aims to employ and observe how it attempts to associate this motive with the goods or services it is designed to sell.

In motivating any proposition it is the arguer's task to select the motive or motives which can be most effectively associated with the proposition and through them, make the audience keenly aware of the desire or desires he is endeavoring to bring to consciousness. Like the advertiser he must paint a picture or create a situation which will excite desire; the listener must be made to wish, to want. Such wishes, wants, and desires will be the result of a conscious appreciation on the part of the listener of some uneasiness or dissatisfaction or sense of incompleteness created by the motives stimulated. Elements may be brought into the picture which will emotionally reënforce the desire the argument is designed to stimulate. In short, it is the persuader's task to create vivid word pictures, to cite striking examples and illustrations; it is his task to employ every rhetorical device and every personal appeal which will bring the reactor's attention to bear on a specific maladjustment already existent or likely to occur, in the most striking and impelling manner possible. The objective as we have said is to produce a sense of dissatisfaction and incompleteness, to incite a desire for some course of action or method of procedure which will relieve the situation.

The following advertisement of Grinnell Automatic Sprinkler Systems presents an excellent illustration. Note how the basic motive of protection is used and emotionally reënforced as a means to arouse and intensify desire. The picture which heads this advertisement is that of a group of people, their horrified faces lighted up by the flames of a burning building. In the foreground is a mother with her arms outstretched. Under the picture is the caption, " How often is this tragedy enacted — little children in smoke-filled windows crying for a rescue? When is it due to happen in your city? " This story follows:

"After the fire in the Ninth Ward school was anybody tarred and feathered? After the heroism of teachers and firemen — after the impressive funeral of the little victims who perished — after the débris ceased to smoke and other visible reminders of the tragedy were gone — after the official investigation and the report — what reforms were recommended?"

"Did the report exonerate officials and attempt to clear the city of the disgrace?"

"Did it say that fire escapes and everything that was humanly possible had been done to safeguard the school against fire?"

" If so, the fathers and mothers of the victims would like to cry out in protest and reproach. 'Everything was NOT done that was humanly possible.' The simplest, sanest, surest thing of all was not done."

"If the fire had started in a business building owned by a private individual instead of a public building owned by a lot of tax payers, it would have been put out quickly by automatic sprinklers. Mere merchandise gets the protection of the finest fire-fighting device ever devised because the insurance expense is thereby cut from one-half to nine-tenths. But human beings in schools and hospitals must trust to their own cool-headedness under panic conditions or to the lucky chance of some heroic rescue."

"When human life and not mere merchandise is at stake, nothing else should be considered but this system — the highest type of fire-fighting device ever devised — the Grinnell Automatic Sprinkler. It is automatic. The heat of the fire works it. It is always on guard. Always ready. No human aid is required. When the fire starts the water starts."

"Write today for the free booklet, *Fire Tragedies and Their Remedy*."

The above illustration not only arouses and intensifies desire, which is the point we are illustrating here, but goes on to associate a definite proposition with this awakened desire. Just as the motive of protection is employed here to stir up desire, so can the other motives we have studied be utilized to this same end.

B. By Emphasizing the Obstacle. — Another method of awakening desire is by emphasizing the obstacle.[1] While this is in one sense merely a corollary of the method already discussed, it seems worth mentioning. Writing for salesmen, Professor Strong has defined the obstacle as follows:

"The obstacle is that which prevents the prospect from getting what he wants; either the presence or absence of an object may constitute an obstacle." [2]

Thus a shabby suit may be the obstacle to a desire to look well; a bad complexion, the obstacle to a good appearance; a dilapidated residence, the obstacle to desired social prestige, etc. The obstacle is the real reason why the reactor is dissatisfied; it is the maladjustment we have spoken of; it is the source of the uneasiness and unhappiness. Emphasizing the obstacle stirs up desire, because it serves to break down self-satisfied complacency and security.

Awakening and intensifying the desire of the audience is the first step in Motivation, then; it paves the way for the presentation of a solution, which is the next problem to be discussed.

VI. Associating Desire with the Proposition

A. Effective Desire. — Desire does not become effective for purposes of argument until it is associated with the proposition, in the mind of the reactor. There is little point in stirring up a feeling of dissatisfaction or a sense of need unless the listener can be led to see that the activity suggested in the proposition presents the necessary adjustment. Establishing this association is the second task of the motivator.

B. Methods of Associating Desire with the Proposition. — There are four rather distinct methods by which the per-

---

[1] Strong, E. K., *Psychology of Selling and Advertising*, p. 254.
[2] *Ibid.*, p. 288.

suader can associate desire with the proposition. They are:
(1) By Suggestion; (2) By Rationalization; (3) By Open
Explication; and (4) By Demonstration.

1. SUGGESTION. — The following quotation from Dr.
Walter Dill Scott, taken from his interesting little book
Influencing Men in Business, expresses an attitude toward
the use of suggestion with which every student of argument
should be familiar.

> "In moving and inspiring men, suggestion is to be considered
> as in every way the equal of logical reasoning, and as such is to
> be made a subject of consideration for every man who is inter-
> ested in influencing his fellows. While tradition regards man as
> wholly logical, the modern conception, as already intimated,
> makes him largely a creature of suggestion." [1]

a. Suggestion Defined. — " Suggestion can be defined as
the introduction of an idea into the mind, unopposed by
conflicting ideas, and leading to whatever action the idea
is associated with." [2]

It should be understood that thoughts and ideas are
dynamic; they lead to action unless they are in some way
inhibited. Sensory impulses tend to discharge themselves
through motor channels. Since these motor pathways in
the body lead to either muscles or glands, we can expect
ideas to set up various muscular and glandular activities.[3]
The explanation of suggestion, then, is to be found in the
ideo-motor theory. Stating this as nontechnically as possible, we may say that stimuli emanate from the speaker in
the form of word symbols or visible action which stir up an
idea in the reactor. This idea, unless inhibited by other
ideas, will normally express itself in action.

A significant characteristic of suggestion is that it does

---

[1] Scott, W. D., *Influencing Men in Business*, p. 36.
[2] Snow, A. J., *Psychology in Personal Selling*, p. 455.
[3] Thomson, M. K., *The Springs of Human Action*, Chapter VIII.

not attempt to prove the logic of the act it suggests. In fact, there is nothing of the probative element in it. The persuasive power of suggestion is to be found entirely in the ideo-motor reaction. Logically considered, the reaction from effective suggestion is much greater than the evidence submitted can justify.

b. Factors of Suggestion. — The effectiveness of suggestion varies greatly with different individuals and with different occasions. For that reason a brief consideration of the factors necessary to its most successful application in argument will be helpful.

(1) Authoritative Giver. — One of the chief factors in effective suggestion is the authority of the giver. All we say in Chapter XV about the speaker's personality should be emphasized here. A weak, hesitant, reticent persuader simply cannot get results with this method. The situation demands a confident, perhaps even dominant personality.

(2) Submissive Subject. — A submissive subject is another helpful factor in suggestion. Suggestion is not persuasive when it is examined critically and analytically by the reactor. Some people are normally more critical than others, and any person is more critical at certain times than he is at others. The time is ripe for suggestion when the reactor is in a receptive, non-critical frame of mind.

Undoubtedly there is a close reciprocal relation between the two factors just discussed. That is, any listener is much more apt to be submissive in the presence of a strong, dynamic speaker than he would be in the presence of a weak personality. It is also undoubtedly true that the speaker is much more apt to be confident and authoritative in the presence of a submissive reactor.

(3) The Psychological Crowd. — A third factor of importance in suggestion is the psychological crowd. " The psychological crowd is a group of individuals who by virtue

of the fact that they are stimulating each other, show a tendency to respond in a more or less uniform manner." [1] Such a group is to be distinguished from the heterogeneous group which lacks group solidarity, leadership, and unity. The submersion of individuality in the group, the tendency to inhibit anything which would differentiate the individual from the group, and high suggestibility are characteristics of the psychological crowd.   Since this unity ascribed to the psychological crowd is an important factor in suggesting ideas to a group of people, the persuader is frequently confronted with the task of molding his audience into a psychological crowd before he can attempt to motivate them through suggestion.   O'Neill and Weaver state :

> "The skillful speaker, when dealing with more than one person at a time, tries in every way possible to unify the mass of individuals so that he can deal with them all in the same way.   No speaker has very much chance to control the behavior of five hundred individuals in each of whom unique reaction tendencies are dominant." [2]

This process of fusing the audience into a psychological crowd is called *social facilitation* or *polarization*.   Doubtless every reader has attended some political rally, evangelistic service, labor meeting, or pep rally, where social facilitation has been practiced.   If you have observed the leader at such a gathering, you will probably recall that he elicited a large number of overt responses from the audience.   These responses may have been in the form of cheers, enthusiastic affirmations or denials of questions, stirring songs, or rituals of various kinds.   In any case group activity was stimulated. Allport says of this :

> "In our study of group influence we found that the social increment was in direct proportion to the coworking of others.

[1] O'Neill, J. M., and Weaver, A. T., *The Elements of Speech*, p. 332. Longmans, Green and Company, 1926.   [2] *Ibid.*, p. 332.

The same rule applies to crowd excitement, and is practiced by all those skilled in the art of public control. Speakers who wish to stir up their audiences use special methods for eliciting responses of a demonstrative sort, so that an abundance of contributory stimuli may be in evidence." [1]

Any persuader who hopes to use suggestion with a group of people should make an effort to polarize his audience. He may not care to resort to all of the methods described above, but at least he can stimulate a number of favorable group responses (preferably overt) from the audience by telling humorous stories, by citing experiences which he knows a majority of the audience has had; in short, by doing anything which will elicit a large number of agreeable responses. When unity of action is established, when the members of the group begin to respond together, he can then reasonably expect the action he is seeking to be undertaken with some degree of unanimity when the proper suggestion is given.

c. *Examples of Suggestion.* — A few illustrations will serve to point out the force of suggestion as a factor in motivation.

The American Tobacco Company, advertising Lucky Strike Cigarettes over the radio and in leading periodicals, has attempted to build up an association between *moderation* and the use of their cigarettes. The argument goes to some length to emphasize the value of moderation in all things, and then closes with the suggestion, "When tempted to excess, be moderate; reach for a Lucky." Here we have a subtle attempt to divert the customer's desire for moderation into the purchase of a commodity which by the wildest stretch of the imagination has but little causal relation if any with this quality. The advertisement depends entirely upon suggestion to initiate the desired action.

We take another illustration from a florist's display card which pictures a spray of roses over the question, "How long since you sent her some?" The question suggests to the reader

[1] Allport, F. H., *Social Psychology*, p. 300.   Houghton Mifflin Company, 1924.

his wish to please "her" and a possible way of doing so. A latent want is stimulated and directed into specific activity.

J. A. Stevenson in his book *Constructive Salesmanship* reports an interesting instance in which suggestion saved a five million dollar sale. We report the case in his words:

"One of the greatest real estate men of the country, J. P. Day, tells of negotiating with Judge Gary for the sale to the United States Steel Corporation of the building at 71 Broadway, which has always contained its offices.

"I thought I had closed the sale," says Day, "when, calling upon Judge Gary, he said, very gently, but very decisively:

" 'Mr. Day, we have had the offer of a much more modern building near here and it would seem to answer our purpose better. It is a better furnished building. This building is too old fashioned; you know it is a very old structure. Some of my associates think that, all in all, the other building will answer our purposes more adequately than this one.' There was a five million dollar sale drifting out of the window. I did not answer for a moment and Judge Gary did not go on. I did not attempt to answer. I, instead, asked:

"Judge Gary, where was your first office when you came to New York?"

" 'Right here,' he said, 'or rather, in the room on the other side.'

"Where was the Steel Corporation organized?"

" 'Right here in these offices,' he mused rather than answered. And then of his own accord: 'Some of the younger executives have from time to time had more elaborate offices than this. They have not been quite satisfied with the older furniture. 'But,' he added, 'none of these men are with us now.'

"The sale was over. The next week we closed the deal."

The particular sentiment which was appealed to in this last illustration and which made this big deal after it seemed lost is a sentiment not peculiar to Judge Gary, but it is possessed by the whole human race. It was the power of suggestion which brought back the many traditions surrounding the old building, and focused them on a specific activity in a highly persuasive way. Once desire has been brought to the conscious level and intensified, a strong idea suggestively planted in the mind of the reactor will usually lead to the response suggested.

2. RATIONALIZATION. — A second way of associating desire with the proposition is by rationalization. The average individual decides what he wants to do and then tries to find reasons to justify the act both for his own peace of mind and for explanations to others. This process is known as rationalization. It is the process by which an individual attempts to justify a given course of conduct by disguising his real motives and supplying other semi-plausible reasons as justification for the act. We are interested in rationalization because almost invariably when desire has been established, the reactor begins rationalizing that desire. It is the responsibility of the persuader to assist and direct this rationalizing process.

A simple hypothetical case will explain the persuader's part in this process quite clearly : Assume that you are attempting to persuade a friend of yours to attend an evening show with you during an examination week. Your friend desires to go, but knows that he ought to study. To break down this inhibition you will try to supply him with some reasons for acting as you wish him to act. You will likely intimate that it doesn't pay to cram for exams, that the rest will do him good, that he can study better after the show, etc. You do not pretend to prove your point ; you are simply trying to utilize his desire as a means of effecting your proposition by helping him to rationalize the situation.

3. OPEN EXPLICATION. — This method of associating desire with the proposition proposes to make the association by a frank and open explanation. Rather than suggesting that the action embodied in the proposition might gratify the desire, or rationalizing this desire for the audience, the persuader proceeds directly to prove this association by

either confirmatory or explanatory reasoning. The method, while resembling Confirmation or Explanation as the case may be, nevertheless has the desire of the reactor as its basis and is therefore studied as Motivation. It is a case in which desire is awakened and intensified and then associated with the proposition by Confirmation or Explanation. The method, thus, has the advantage of combining the persuasive values of Motivation with the probative force of these other forms of support.

4. DEMONSTRATION. — One of the most effective ways to show that a given course of action will gratify certain desires is to demonstrate that fact objectively. Quite obviously this is not always, perhaps not usually, possible, but it is highly persuasive when the nature of the proposition and the circumstances are such that a demonstration can be undertaken. There is perhaps no better way to associate a certain brand of confection with a desire for confection, for instance, than to give the prospect a sample, and thereby demonstrate its ability to gratify the desire. Likewise, with any other commodity or thing that can be demonstrated, a proposition suggesting its purchase or some other activity regarding it can be strongly motivated by directing the reactor's desire to the specific activity embodied in the proposition through such a demonstration.

VII. USING MOTIVATION IN CONJUNCTION WITH OTHER FORMS OF SUPPORT

In our discussion of *open explication* as a method of associating desire with the proposition, we pointed out that either Confirmation or Explanation might be used in conjunction with Motivation. In this case, you will recall, desire is established and then associated with the proposition by either Confirmation or Explanation. Another combination which is probably more often employed than any other, however, is that of an explanatory introduction, a confirmatory development, and a conclusion in the form of a motive appeal. This closing effort at Motivation is frequently known as a *peroration*, a term originating with the ancient rhetoricians. Motivation can also be used in immediate conjunction with either or both of the other forms of support to develop any given point in an argument.

VIII. Summary

It has been our purpose in this chapter to set forth a technique which will enable the persuader to take advantage of the desires of the reactor. The methodology is almost wholly psychological rather than logical and has little, if any, probative power. Nevertheless, its peculiar persuasive values and its wide usage make it a form of argument with which students of the subject should be thoroughly familiar.

EXERCISES

1. Discuss the following statement from Troland. Is it consistent with the position taken in this text? Explain.

"If an argument is between two scientific men or engineers, whose actual welfare lies in the discovery or utilization of objective truth, persuasion will depend largely upon adducing real evidence, and an application of approved principles of logical reasoning. Facts and logic in this case are conditioners of the ego, or other operative complexes. At a slightly lower level of intellectuality, the recognition of facts and logic coerces the individual by making him perceive himself to be a fool, when arguing or acting in opposition to the consequences of these processes. However, a commoner method of persuasion is to call up, or to create, associations which explicitly link the desired form of response with beneceptive mechanisms which tend to facilitate action, or the one which it is desired to prevent, with nociceptive mechanisms which tend to inhibit response." — Troland, Leonard T., *The Fundamentals of Human Motivation*, p. 444.

2. Select five advertisements and write out an analysis of their argumentative appeals. Are they designed to confirm, explain, or motivate? How do they do it?

3. Select advertisements illustrating each of the four basic motives of action.

4. Prepare a five-minute argumentative speech illustrating at least two of the four methods of associating desire with the proposition as discussed in Section VI of this chapter.

5. Prepare in writing an argumentative speech in which all three of the forms of support are used. Annotate the speech structurally; that is, note in the margin the exact argumentative types you are using.

CHAPTER XII

OUTLINING ARGUMENT

I. The Purposes of Outlining Argument

There are two purposes in outlining argument: (1) To aid in preparing the case; and (2) To aid in presenting the case. We shall see that the outlines which serve these two purposes are usually quite different forms.

A. To Aid in Preparing the Case. — In the first place, the drawing of an outline is an indispensable step in the preparation of the case. We pointed out in Chapter IV, Section IV that arraying the arguments pro and con on the proposition was a helpful step in the process of analyzing the proposition. This array makes an excellent starting point for a complete preparation outline, setting forth all the significant arguments on the side of the proposition that is to be argued. Such an outline differs from the array in the following respects: (1) It has to do with only one side of the proposition; (2) It is divided into an introduction, body, and conclusion; (3) It is supported by evidence; and (4) The points in the outline are organized on a different basis and arranged differently.

The particular advantage of a preparation outline is that it organizes all the significant evidence and argument on one side of the proposition in an orderly instrument which can be filed and used as the basis for drawing as many different case outlines as may be needed to meet different speech situations. It is a reservoir of information or an orderly storehouse of all the important evidence and argument on a given side of a given proposition.

B. To Aid in Presenting the Case. — An outline is equally necessary as an aid in presenting the case to the audience. It organizes and directs the speaker's material, and thus assists the persuader in maintaining his line of thought. It also enables the audience to follow the argument as it would be unable to do were such an organization of material lacking.

II. Kinds of Outlining

We shall consider two kinds of outlining: (1) Logical; and (2) Topical.

A. Logical Outlining. — Logical outlining is characterized by the fact that all of the subpoints stand as reasons for the truth of the points to which they are immediately subordinated. The following points illustrate logical outlining:

I. The regulation and control of child labor by the Federal Government is impractical, because
  A. The states are the proper agencies to cope with the problem, because
    1. The child labor problems of the several states differ widely.
    2. Existing state laws evidence the competence of the states to deal with the problem.
  B. The Federal Government can better approach the problem through other types of legislation, because
    1. Compulsory school attendance laws will keep the children in school.
    2. Minimum wage laws can set wage scales which will make child labor prohibitive to the employer.
    3. Legislation governing the hours and conditions under which children work can make industry safe for children during the time they are not in school.

1. A Chain of Causal Relationships. — The causal relationships which obtain in this type of outlining should always be indicated by the prepositions *because* or *for*. In fact, the logic of the outlining can be tested with considerable accuracy by reading the outline from the top to the bottom and connecting the subpoints with the point under which they are listed by *because* or *for*. A further check can then be imposed by supplying the word *therefore* in reading from the bottom of the outline to the top. If the reading makes " good sense " when these connecting words are used, the inference is that the outline is sound.

2. Adapted to Confirmation. — Logical outlining or a chain of reasoning as it is sometimes called is particularly well adapted to the inferences used in confirmation. Such an outline usually consists of a series of enthymemes whose premises are supported either by reasoning from generalization or analogy. A review of our discussion of the enthymeme in Chapter IX will help to make this point clear. Consider the following piece of outlining in the way of further illustration:

Resolved: That a Federal court of industrial relations should be established, because

I. Existing relations between capital and labor demand judicial determination.

II. Present governmental machinery for coping with industrial disputes is ineffective.

III. Industrial courts have proved their practicality, because

    A. Such a court is operating successfully in England.

    B. Such a court is operating successfully in New Zealand.

    C. Such a court is operating successfully in Australia.

It will be observed that this outline consists of a series of enthymemes of the first order which may be stated either categorically or hypothetically. For instance, the relationship between the proposition and the first main point may be stated as follows:

I. All countries whose existing relations between capital and labor demand judicial determination should establish a court of industrial relations.

II. The United States is such a country.

    Therefore: The United States should establish a federal court of industrial relations.

or

I. If existing relations between capital and labor demand judicial determination, then a federal court of industrial relations should be established.

II. Existing relations between capital and labor do demand judicial determination.
Therefore : A federal court of industrial relations should be established.

A similar relation exists between the proposition and point II and the proposition and point III. Point III is a generalization supported by three instances of the phenomenon. It is understood, of course, that both points I and II are unsupported assertions as the outline stands. Both need to be supported by further deductions and finally by specific instances of the phenomenon either in the form of generalization or analogical reasoning.

What we have shown to be true in this sample of outlining is substantially what obtains in all logical outlining. The student should experiment with it until he is able readily to reduce all confirmatory inferences to such outlining, and until he is able to pick up a logical outline and readily discern the confirmatory inferences contained therein.

B. Topical Outlining. — Topical outlining is characterized by the fact that all of the subpoints stand as explanations of the topics to which they are immediately subordinated. It differs from logical outlining in that the subpoints do not bear the causal relation to the main points which obtains in logical outlining. The following points illustrate topical outlining :

The Child Labor Problem

I. The state laws now existing.
   A. Laws governing hours of employment.
   B. Laws governing conditions under which people work.
   C. Laws governing wages.
   D. Existing child labor laws.
II. Some outstanding differences between states in conditions relating to child labor.
   A. Differences in the number of children employed.

    B. Differences in the kind of work.

    C. Differences in the time that children are employed.

III. Other possible federal legislative approaches to the problem.

    A. Compulsory school attendance laws.

    B. Minimum wage laws.

    C. Legislation governing the hours and conditions under which children will be allowed to work.

1. PART TO WHOLE RELATIONSHIPS. — It should be pointed out that the relationship existing between the subpoints and main points in the above outline in each case is really one of part to whole. That is, the various subpoints under any given topic stand as parts of the whole, which is expressed in the main topic. These subtopics may be descriptive parts, narrative parts, or expository parts of the main topic as illustrated below : [1]

"For an example of a case in which the subheads are descriptive parts of the main heads, let us suppose that a real estate agent wishes a distant owner to repair a building. The agent's plea is based on the present condition of the building. This he might describe in outline as follows:

I. The condition of the building.

    A. Exterior.

        1. The roof leaks in several places.

        2. The walls are cracked, and need paint.

    B. Interior.

        1. First floor.

            a. In the front room the paper is soiled.

            b. In the back room the plumbing is out of order.

        2. Second floor.

"Here, it is to be observed, the main head is a term which the subheads explain or amplify. The process is that of division, and the relation of the subheads is that of parts to a whole."

[1] These illustrations are taken from R. C. Ringwalt, *Brief Drawing*, Longmans, Green and Company, 1923. See Chapter XI.

The following is an example in which the subheads are narrative parts of the whole:

I. The facts leading to this action were:
   A. The defendant ordered of the plaintiff 500 barrels of flour, to be delivered 100 barrels in August, and the same amount each month thereafter until the order was filled.
   B. The plaintiff shipped, and the defendant accepted and paid for, four such monthly shipments.
   C. In December the plaintiff shipped the balance of the order.
   D. The defendant refused to accept the shipment on the ground that the last flour received was inferior in quality and that he so informed the plaintiff.

"Here the process is the same as the descriptive form. The main head is an inclusive term, a composite event, and the subheads consist of an analysis of this term. The relation of the subheads to the main head is again that of parts to the whole."

"A third form of topical outlining is that in which the subheads are expository parts of the main head; the explanation of an abstract idea. An example is:"

I. The defeat of the Germans was due to:
   A. Lack of reserves.
   B. Failure of morale.
   C. Breakdown in transportation.

2. ADAPTED TO EXPLANATION. — The reader has probably already noted that topical outlining is peculiarly adapted to set forth support by Explanation. The short outline on The Child Labor Problem, for instance, if properly developed, would imply the proposition that the federal government should not attempt to prohibit child labor. An implicative system on any proposition demands outlining of this kind, if the descriptive, narrative, and expository relationships are carefully and accurately to be set forth.

The reader should make certain that he understands how to outline Explanation, and how to set up an implicative system in outline form. Refer back to Chapter X, "Supporting the Proposition: Explanation" if this matter is not entirely clear at this point.

III. Types of Outlines

We shall consider three types of outlines: (1) The Brief; (2) The Case Outline; and (3) The Speaker's Outline.

A. The Brief. — The brief may be defined as a complete, logical statement which organizes and records all the usable evidence and argument on one side of a proposition. The brief does not outline the case, nor is it valuable as a speaker's outline. It is definitely a preparation outline.

1. A Step in the Preparation of Every Comprehensive Argument. — There has been considerable controversy as to the value of drawing up a brief in the preparation of every argument. It seems sound generally to take the position that a brief should constitute a step in the preparation of every *comprehensive argument*. While it is true that a brief is not well adapted to the expression of all kinds of argument (*i.e.*, Explanation and to some extent, Motivation), there is much to be gained, nevertheless, from reducing all argument to a linear statement such as you get in the brief, even though the subsequent presentation outline takes on a quite different form. As a step in preparation the brief compels the persuader to think the proposition through logically and completely. It compels a careful scrutiny of the evidence and argument necessary to a confirmation of the proposition. And unless the arguer does so exercise himself, it is usually true that his argument displays a rather decided lack of insight into the proposition and its various ramifications. The drawing of the brief will also assist the persuader in determining just what method of support is best suited to the case he plans to present.

2. A SPECIMEN BRIEF. — The following brief is a specimen prepared by a student in the University of Michigan.[1]

AN AFFIRMATIVE BRIEF

on the proposition

Resolved: That all colleges and universities should abolish the distinction between amateurism and professionalism in sports to which admission fees are charged.

Introduction

I. Statement of the proposition :
    A. *Resolved:* That all colleges and universities should abolish the distinction between amateurism and professionalism in sports to which admission fees are charged.

II. History of the Question :
    A. The amateur distinction evolved along with other rules formulated to control intercollegiate athletics.
        1. College sports began in earnest in the decade beginning in 1870.
        2. By 1890 serious evils were evident.
            a. Athletic conferences were formed to control these evils.
            b. Athletic rules of various kinds were set up.
                (I) At first these rules merely said what did not constitute an amateur ; *i.e.*, they listed a whole group of things which the amateur should not do if he desired to maintain his amateur status. This was known as a *negative definition.*
                (II) In 1916 a *positive definition* of an amateur was formulated by the Intercollegiate Association of Amateur Athletes of America.
                    (A) This definition still stands, and is as follows : " An amateur is one who engages in sport solely for the physical, mental, and social benefits to be

[1] Prepared by Wilbert L. Hindman, 1931, Junior in the College of Literature, Science, and the Arts, University of Michigan.

derived, and to whom sport is nothing more than an avocation."

B. In applying this new positive definition of an amateur, it became necessary to establish a number of rules. These rules, together with the definition itself, constitute the amateur distinction referred to in the proposition. They fall into two categories:

 1. Rules prohibiting the subsidization of athletes because of their athletic ability, through such means as,

  a. Scholarships where athletic ability is a qualification.

  b. Preferential or sinecure jobs.

  c. Gifts and loans from the alumni, the school, or any other source, when the award is given for excellence in athletics.

 2. Rules prohibiting an athlete from capitalizing on his athletic ability or reputation, by

  a. Playing summer baseball.

  b. Writing magazine articles on athletics for money.

  c. Giving athletic instruction for money, etc.

III. Immediate cause for discussion.

A. A recent bulletin by the Carnegie Foundation for the Advancement of Teaching, representing an investigation of the athletic situation in 112 representative colleges and universities throughout the country, has focused attention on the amateur status in college athletics by its findings and recommendations. This is Bulletin 23 on "American College Athletics"; repeated reference will be made to this source throughout this brief.

B. In 1930 the University of Iowa was temporarily ejected from the Western Conference athletic association on charges that it had violated the amateur code.

C. The growing interest in this question caused the Western Conference Debate League to adopt the amateur-professional distinction as the subject for their spring debates in 1931.

IV. Definition of Terms:

A. The present "distinction between amateurism and professionalism" defines an amateur as "one who engages in sport solely for the physical, mental, and social benefits to be derived, and to whom sport is nothing more than an avocation."

224 THE WORKING PRINCIPLES OF ARGUMENT

1. This distinction includes in addition to the above definition a set of rules which attempt to make its application possible. These rules apply specifically to the amateur-professional distinction and are not to be confused with other eligibility rules such as rules governing scholarship and residence requirements for participation in college athletics. The amateur rules are summarized in Section II–B of this Introduction. (See *Carnegie Bulletin*, Number 23, p. 35.)

B. The clause "sports to which admission fees are charged" we take to be a limiting clause and nothing more; *i.e.*, it limits the discussion to intercollegiate sports; primarily, football, baseball, basketball, and track, and to the so-called "minor sports" where admission fees are charged.

1. This clause rules out practically all intramural athletics.

V. Statement of Issues:

A. Do conditions in college and university athletics demand some change in the present amateur status?

B. Is the abolition of the distinction between amateurism and professionalism the desirable change to make?

C. Should this abolition take place in those college and university sports to which admission fees are charged?

VI. Points in Partition:

A. The maintenance of the existing amateur distinction is resulting in a secret and demoralizing evasion of the amateur rules.

B. The enforcement of the amateur rules would cause the abolition of certain practices which are not in and of themselves undesirable.

C. The complete abolition of the distinction between amateurism and professionalism in sports to which admission fees are charged would result in the most desirable situation for college and university athletics.

Discussion

Resolved: That all colleges and universities should abolish the distinction between amateurism and professionalism in sports to which admission fees are charged, for

I. The maintenance of the existing amateur distinction is resulting in a secret and demoralizing evasion of the amateur rules, for

   A. The amateur rules are being flagrantly violated on all sides, for

      1. Athletic scholarships are being awarded in violation of the amateur rules, for

         a. Many colleges and universities are awarding special scholarships which are being given primarily to athletes, for

            (I) The following schools are giving scholarships to athletes from special funds: Columbia University, Hobart, Undergraduate Division of the New York University School of Commerce, Southern Methodist, Stanford, and Ursinus. (*Carnegie Bulletin* Number 23, p. 254.)

            (II) An athletic coach is given a certain number of scholarships to award at New York University. (*Ibid.,* p. 255.)

            (III) Alumni specify who shall receive scholarships from certain funds at Stanford; alumni furnish contributions for 50 such scholarships at Stanford. (*Ibid.,* p. 255.)

            (IV) Colleges and universities using school funds for such scholarships are: Drake; New York University, 75 scholarships; Southern Methodist, 20; Southern California, $40,000; Ursinus, 20, and certain Catholic institutions. (*Ibid.,* p. 255.)

         b. Many schools are awarding honorary scholarships which go mostly to athletes and in the awarding of which athletic ability is openly a qualification, for

            (I) Such schools are: Brown, 1; Des Moines, 15; University of Georgia, 40; Lehigh, 1; Montana, 5; Princeton, 8; Southern California, 2. (*Ibid.,* p. 256.)

         c. Many schools are awarding athletic scholarships which are frankly termed athletic scholarships, for

            (I) Such scholarships exist at: Blue Ridge, 12;

Colgate, 25; Geneva, 35; Gettysburg, 30; Fordham, 40; Lebanon Valley, 16; Muhlenberg; Pennsylvania State College, 75; Syracuse, $14,000; West Virginia Wesleyan, 20; Ursinus, 16. (*Ibid.*, p. 256.)

(II) Such scholarships are given in conjunction with additional aid at: Bucknell, Gettysburg, Muhlenberg, Oglethorpe, Pennsylvania State, Pittsburgh, West Virginia Wesleyan, Boston College, Holy Cross, Notre Dame. (*Ibid.*, p. 257.)

(III) Reeves and Russel report that many schools are awarding athletic scholarships. (See Reeves & Russel, *College Organization and Administration*, pp. 81–85.)

2. Athletes at many institutions are being subsidized through preferential or sinecure jobs in violation of the amateur rules, for

a. At many schools, employment is being secured for athletes by those who correspond with athletic prospects, for

(I) This practice obtains at: Alabama, Amherst, Arizona, Brown, Chicago, Colgate, Columbia, Dartmouth, Denver, Drake, Georgia School of Technology, Idaho, Michigan, Missouri, Montana State College, Northwestern, Oglethorpe, Oklahoma, Oregon Agricultural, Purdue, Queen's, Rutgers, South Dakota, Southern Methodist, Tennessee, Utah, Vermont, Washington State College, University of Washington, Wisconsin. (*Carnegie Bulletin*, Number 23, p. 245.)

b. Many athletic departments or associations give athletes jobs which are mostly sinecures, for

(I) This is done at: Allegheny, Colgate, Harvard, Idaho, Lebanon Valley, Missouri, Montana State College, New York University, Northwestern, Ohio State, Oklahoma, Southern Methodist, Syracuse, Texas, Utah, Wisconsin. (*Ibid.*, p. 247.)

   (II) These jobs include activities such as clerical assistants, caretakers, attendants for locker and equipment rooms, towel-dispensers, gymnasium janitors, gymnasium assistants, concessionaires, field laborers, swimming pool guards, towel-launderers, and waiters at training tables. (*Ibid.*, p. 247.)

   (III) These jobs are in most instances sinecures, for

    (*A*) In many instances the athlete does not render satisfactory service.

    (*B*) In some instances the athlete is not expected to carry out even the duties he is assigned.

    (*C*) The remuneration given is usually far in excess of the value of the services performed. (*Ibid.*, p. 247.)

  c. In some schools the college or university employs athletes in preference to other equally competent students. (*Ibid.*, p. 250.)

  d. Off-campus employers offer athletic sinecures in many places. (*Ibid.*, p. 251.)

 3. Athletes at many institutions receive special subsidies and loans from alumni and other sources in violation of the amateur rules, for

  a. Loans from alumni associations have been given at Arizona, Brown, Georgia School of Technology, Michigan, Washington. (*Ibid.*, p. 253.)

  b. Citizens luncheon clubs have provided several loan funds at Arizona, Colorado, Ohio State, Wyoming. (*Ibid.*, p. 253.)

  c. Such funds are administered at the direction of the athletic organization at Drake, Georgia School of Technology, Ohio Wesleyan, Vermont, Baylor. (*Ibid.*, p. 252.)

  d. Subsidies without scholarships are given at Allegheny, Carnegie Institute of Technology, Centre, Dickinson, Grove City, Lafayette, Lebanon Valley, Northwestern, Pennsylvania, Western Maryland. (*Ibid.*, p. 258.)

  e. Individual alumni often compete with others to

get athletes to attend their Alma Mater by offering money, as at: Dartmouth, Iowa, Pennsylvania, Southern California, Stanford. (*Ibid.*, p. 260.)

 f. Some alumni maintain athletes at preparatory schools before entering them in colleges and universities: Brown, Carnegie Institute of Technology, Dartmouth, Dickinson, Lafayette, New York University, Pittsburgh, Syracuse, Washington and Jefferson. (*Ibid.*, p. 261.)

 h. Fraternities aid athletes by charging low rates for room or board or both in some institutions. (*Ibid.*, p. 262.)

4. Many athletes capitalize on their athletic ability while participating in college and university athletics as amateurs, in violation of the amateur rules, for

 a. College amateurs play summer baseball for money. (*Ibid.*, p. 205.)

 b. College amateurs work as life guards, and athletic directors at summer camps.

5. The study conducted by the Carnegie Foundation found 81 out of the 112 schools investigated, and an estimated ratio of 1 out of every 7 athletes, to be violating the existing amateur rules.

B. These violations of the amateur rules are demoralizing and detrimental in every way to both the athlete and the school, for

1. It is detrimental to the athlete, for

 a. He is forced into hypocrisy and lying, for

  (I) As E. H. Hall, of Harvard, said 25 years ago, "I believe that this rule . . . leads straight to lying." (*School Review*, 13: Dec. 1905, p. 758.)

 b. He is forced to underhandedness and secrecy through fear of exposure. (*Harper's*, Nov. 1930, "Pity the Poor Athlete," Frank Schoonmaker.)

2. It is detrimental to the schools involved, for

 a. "Exposures," such as the recent ones at Iowa and other institutions obviously are unfortunate for these schools.

 b. Schools are forced to employ deceitful and dishonest methods, for

(I) As we have seen, schools from coast to coast openly avow amateur policies and practices, and yet professionalism is carried on in these schools on a wide scale.

(II) Professor E. H. Hall of Harvard states, "I should be willing to see the amount of that act (paying money) increased fourfold, if it would diminish one-quarter the amount of lying about it *which is the main evil*. . . . We might, I say, have possibly more of the paying of money for the support of athletes in colleges if we abolished the money rule, but I am sure we would have vastly less scandal, vastly less lying and deception of all sorts, than we have now." (*School Review*, 13 : Dec. 1905, p. 766.)

(III) Hamilton Holt, President of Rollins College, Florida, has said, ". . . But, if Rollins finds it impossible to secure genuinely amateur competitors, then I submit there is no honorable alternative except to espouse professionalism. What I object to is this disrespect and disregard for law which is demoralizing our colleges, just as it is demoralizing the country at large on other issues. . . . If American colleges will not live up to the amateurism in athletics which they profess, or publicly adopt the professionalism which they practice, I submit that no college that pretends to hold up moral standards before the young may take part in intercollegiate athletics. . . ." ("An Appeal to College Presidents," *Review of Reviews*, May 1927, p. 530.)

(IV) The *New York Telegram* has pointed out that, "One of these days the colleges may be compelled, in self defense, to adopt a program of open professionalism, openly arrived at . . . such a program would at least have the merits of simple honesty, as opposed to the hypocrisy that exists in some academic circles." (*Literary Digest*, Nov. 15, 1930, p. 28.)

II. The enforcement of the amateur rules would cause the abolition of certain practices which are not in and of themselves undesirable, for

Note: (It is the argument of this brief that the real evil in the granting of athletic scholarships, and other assistance to college and university athletes is to be found in the dishonesty and deceit attendant upon violation of the existing amateur rules, rather than in the practices themselves which are held to be entirely justifiable and quite harmless.)

A. There is nothing inherently wrong in the athletic scholarships which the amateur rules attempt to bar, for

  1. Countless scholarships are given students for talents along other lines of university activity, for

      a. The announcement of scholarships in almost every college and university will indicate that this is the case.

      b. Dr. Jacobs, President of Oglethorpe University, states, "I cannot see anything wrong in the giving of a scholarship to an athlete. I do not hesitate to offer a good musician a scholarship to play in our orchestra, and I do not see why we should not do the same thing for an athlete. Any other attitude in the matter is hypocritical." (Associated Press Interview, Jan. 24, 1931.)

  2. Athletics and physical education are definitely a part of the educational program of the college and university.

B. There is nothing inherently wrong in the preferential jobs for athletes which the amateur rules attempt to bar, for

  1. Such jobs merely serve as rewards for productive effort along educational lines as do similar jobs granted to men on college newspapers, orchestras, debating teams, and other organizations.

  2. The athlete puts in a great deal of time practicing for athletic competition which is not demanded of the average student.

  3. Many of the so-called perferential jobs arise out of the athletic program and equipment which would not exist were it not for the athlete.

C. There is nothing inherently wrong in small subsidies and gifts from alumni and other sources which the amateur rules attempt to bar, for
  1. The athlete who lives up to university requirements is at least as deserving of aid as other needy students who do nothing for the school and are at liberty to accept such loans.
  2. There is little evidence to show that these subsidies will be granted in excessive amounts. (See *Carnegie Bulletin* Number 23.)
D. There is nothing inherently wrong in an athlete capitalizing on his athletic ability, for
  1. The fact that there is nothing really wrong in earning money by playing summer baseball has been tacitly admitted by three athletic conferences which have made special rules to permit such playing, for
      a. Summer baseball is now permitted in the Rocky Mountain, Southern, and Missouri Valley Conferences. (*Ibid.*, p. 205.)
      b. See also "Summer Baseball and Amateurism," Editorial, *Michigan Alumnus*, March 30, 1922.
      c. See also "Professionalism in Sports," *Outlook*, Aug. 26, 1925.
  2. The fact that there is nothing really wrong in summer lifeguard work or directing athletics in summer camps is admitted by the Western Conference — which permits such work, but does not permit baseball.
  3. There is nothing inherently wrong in writing athletic articles for magazines or giving boxing lessons to children or any one of countless other things which the college athlete could do easily and legitimately if it were not for the amateur rules.
III. The complete abolition of the distinction between amateurism and professionalism in sports to which admission fees are charged would result in the most desirable situation for college and university athletics, for
  A. The introduction of open professionalism would be much less an evil than either continuing to violate the amateur rules or attempting to enforce them, for
      1. Such abolition would eliminate existing dishonesty and deceit by legalizing practices now carried on

secretly and underhandedly (which practices we
have shown to be entirely justifiable and quite harmless in and of themselves).

    a. Guy M. Wells, editor of "Amateur Sports,"
        Cleveland Plain Dealer, states, "The hue and cry
        comes from people who imagine there is some-
        thing inherently sinful in professionalism. Try-
        ing to take an unfair advantage is the evil. The
        act by which the unfair advantage might have
        been taken is only a violation because prohibited,
        but is not necessarily an evil in itself." (*Literary
        Digest*, July 27, 1929, "Making the Amateur
        Problem Harder to Solve.")

  2. It would legalize certain professional practices which
     we have shown to be altogether justifiable.

B. Possible abuses frequently found in professional athletics
   and professional excesses will be controlled by other
   factors, for

  1. We will still have scholarship rules which can be
     made as strict as we wish, for

    a. Any standard of grades may be required for par-
        ticipation in athletics.

    b. Any amount of college work, measured by
        semester hours or credits, may be required of the
        athlete.

  2. Existing residence restrictions, requiring a student
     to spend a certain time in residence (usually a
     year) before participating in athletics, will still be in
     force.

    a. John H. Haas in 1916 pointed out that refusing
        students the privelege of participating in athletics
        until they had completed a year of residence
        would solve the problem of migrating athletes.
        (*School and Society*, 3: May 1916, pp. 712–714,
        "The Migration of Athletes from One School to
        Another.")

    b. The *Michigan Alumnus* states editorially, "No
        man at heart a professional — which, after all, is
        nothing against one — would pass a whole pre-
        liminary year at the University and endure the
        rigors of scholastic work for the athletic glory to

be gained. And even if someone maintained a
man in college because he played football super-
latively well, he would be a real college man while
he lived up to the scholastic requirements."
(*Michigan Alumnus*, March 30, 1922.)

3. The three-year rule limiting a man's participation
   in athletics of a varsity nature to three years will
   still be in effect.

   a. See *Atlantic Monthly*, 113 : Feb. 1914, pp. 153–60,
   "Athletics and the College."

4. With or without the amateur rules, faculty control
   of athletic funds will insure its careful expenditure.

Conclusion

Therefore, since

I. The maintenance of the existing amateur distinction is
resulting in a secret and demoralizing evasion of the amateur
rules, and

II. The enforcement of the amateur rules would cause the abolition of certain practices which are not in and of themselves
undesirable, and

III. The complete abolition of the distinction between amateurism and professionalism in sports to which admission fees
are charged would result in the most desirable situation for
college and university athletics.

It is to be concluded, That all colleges and universities should
abolish the distinction between amateurism and professionalism
in sports to which admission fees are charged.

3. RULES GOVERNING THE BRIEF. — We suggest the
following rules for brief drawing :

a. General Rules. —

(1) The Brief Should Be Divided into Three Parts, Marked
Respectively the Introduction, the Discussion, and the Conclusion. — In drawing the brief the Introduction, Discussion,
and Conclusion should be treated as units. The various
steps in these sections should be numbered independently.
That is, if there are four main divisions in the introduction,
they should be labeled I, II, III, and IV, respectively ; if

there are three main points in the discussion, they should be labeled I, II, and III, *and not V, VI, and VII*. The main points should constitute separate series in each division of the brief.

(2) Complete Sentences Should Be Used Throughout. — There are two frequent exceptions to this rule. In the introduction, where topical outlining is used, it is often more convenient and just as effective to use statements which do not constitute complete statements. Likewise, in stating statistics, or other similar lists of data in the discussion, it is often necessary to depart from the general rule. It should be understood, however, that when tables of statistics and lists of various kinds are introduced as evidence, they necessarily appear in the smallest subpoints under any given main point. All other points in the discussion must always be stated in complete sentences if the logical sequence of the brief is to be maintained.

(3) A Definite Set of Symbols Should Be Used Consistently throughout the Brief. — We suggest that the following symbols be used : I, II, III, etc. ; *A, B, C*, etc. ; 1, 2, 3, etc. ; *a, b, c*, etc. ; (I), (II), (III), etc. It should be noted in this connection that in using these symbols, the main points in each section of the brief should be indicated by Roman numerals. In no case should the Introduction, Discussion, and Conclusion be marked by these symbols or by any other symbols included in the above system. To do so is to waste a set of symbols and to confuse the brief.

(4) No Heading or Subheading Should Be Marked with More than One Symbol. — The temptation to mark a given statement with two symbols usually arises when the briefdrawer experiences difficulty in finding any main heading which will properly include the various subpoints which he desires to arrange in a coördinate list. Note the following example of this error :

> I. *A.* Free Trade will result in a condition of national economic dependence.
>> *B.* Existing international relations make a condition of economic dependence dangerous.
>> *C.* A Protective Tariff is sound in principle.

One of two things must be done when such a problem arises. Either a main point must be found which logically heads up the list of points, or the list must be broken up and reorganized under headings which will stand as conclusions. In the above case Point *C* is the disturbing element. Discard it or use it in some other connection and the material can readily be briefed as follows:

> I. The removal of the Protective Tariff is dangerous under existing international political conditions, because
>> *A.* Free trade will result in a condition of national economic dependence.
>> *B.* Existing international relations make a condition of economic dependence dangerous.

(5) **All Subpoints Should Be Given a Wider Margin than the Points to Which They Are Subordinated.**

(6) **All Coördinate Lists of Points Should Be Given the Same Margin or Indentation.**

(7) **Each Heading and Subheading Should Contain But a Single Statement.** — While this rule must be interpreted liberally, it is very important nevertheless. It is frequently necessary to use more than a single statement in the explanatory material in the introduction and also in quoting opinion evidence in the discussion. There are even times when more than one sentence is required to express adequately a single idea in some of the other premises of the discussion. The important thing, however, is that every point in the brief should embody one and only one central idea. Because it is tempting to use more than one sentence to express a single premise in argument, and because one sentence is much to be desired, we have phrased this rule as it appears.

b. Rules Governing the Introduction. —

(1) As Many of the Following Steps Should Be Included as Are Necessary to an Understanding of the Discussion. — (1) A statement of the proposition; (2) The origin and history of the question; (3) The immediate cause for discussion; (4) A definition of terms; (5) A statement of irrelevant matter; (6) A statement of admitted matter; (7) A statement of the issues; and (8) A statement of the points in partition.

All of these steps in the introduction should be clear from previous explanations with the possible exception of the statement of the points in partition. In fact the distinction between the partition and the issues frequently proves to be a very troublesome one for beginning students of argument.

The points in partition consist of the main points which are to be taken up in the brief. They are the I, II, III, etc., points in the discussion. Now these points may or may not correspond with the issues. They always differ in that the issues are stated as questions and the points in partition as declarative sentences; and furthermore, they may organize the material quite differently. While the issues are the logically complete and irreducible points upon which the truth or falsity of the proposition turns, the partition simply states the topics which will be handled in the instrument under preparation. If the instrument under preparation, as in the case of the brief, purports to cover all the evidence and argument on one side of the proposition, it is likely that the issues and the points in partition will coincide rather closely, if not perfectly. Even in the case of the complete specimen brief, however, the drawer need not feel obligated to observe this coincidence between the issues and the points in partition unless such a partition proves to be the most effective list of points which can be devised for organizing and outlining the material at hand.

The introduction to every brief should include a statement of the issues in the form of questions and a statement of the points in partition in the form of complete declarative sentences.

In interpreting this first rule governing the introduction, it should be understood that all of the eight introductory steps do not necessarily have to appear in the brief. Students have been known to approach the instructor with the story, " I can't find anything to put in my brief as irrelevant matter " ; or perhaps it will be admitted matter or some other step in the introduction. These students have misinterpreted the purpose of the introduction altogether. Its only object is to prepare the reader of the brief for the discussion that is to follow. Hence, we impose the rule that only those steps should be included which seem necessary to an understanding of the discussion.

(2) Do Not Set Forth Proof of the Proposition in the Introduction. — The introduction to the brief should be an expository and not an argumentative statement. Its purpose is to make way for the support of the proposition and not to set forth that support. It is simply an explanation of the subject preparatory to an argumentative development.

(3) Use Topical Outlining in the Introduction. — Since the introduction is an exposition, topical outlining should be used throughout.

c. Rules Governing the Discussion. —

(1) The Points in Partition Should Appear as the Main Points in the Discussion. — The points in partition should be brought down into the discussion and chains of reasoning introduced to support each heading.

(2) Logical Outlining Should Be Used throughout the Discussion.

(3) The Outlining Should Begin with an Accurate Statement of the Proposition and Be Refined to the Point of Evi-

dence. — This rule is highly important because there is a marked tendency among students of briefing to stop short of evidence in their brief. Evidence should appear in the smaller subpoints under each main heading. While our study of evidence should enable the brief maker to know when he has reached evidence, it is a good rule to raise the question after each point in the discussion, — Why is this true? If the point about which the question is asked is a basic statement of fact or opinion, the point itself will suffice as an answer to the question. If the question is not answered, however, the chain of reasoning needs to be carried further. By applying this rule carefully, every main point and hence the proposition will emanate from a solid foundation in evidence.

(4) All Evidence Should Be Carefully Documented. — There are three methods of documenting evidence in the brief : (1) The exact source can be stated in a footnote with proper reference to the footnote in the context of the brief ; (2) The source may be stated in the margin at the left of the evidence being documented ; (3) The source may be stated in parentheses immediately after the evidence being documented.

All of these methods are good. The important thing is to adopt one method and then use it consistently.

(5) The Points in Each Coördinate Series of Topics Should Be Mutually Exclusive. — This rule, while self explanatory, needs to be emphasized. One of the gravest and most common errors in briefing is to have an overlapping between the various points. As a rule such broad, general terms as undesirable, unnecessary, inadvisable, etc., should be avoided in phrasing headings for the brief. Choose language that is specific and clearly definitive of the particular point you are endeavoring to state, and the danger of confusing two or more points will be greatly reduced.

(6), The Points in Each Coördinate Series of Topics Should Be All-Inclusive. — No matter what point a series of subtopics may be developing, they should constitute a complete, well rounded out development of that point. Perhaps the best way to convey our meaning here would be to say that any subpoint or series of subpoints should constitute a prima facie case for the point to which they are subordinated. Thus, the points marked I, II, and III should constitute a prima facie case for the main proposition. (This is assuming, of course, that these points will be given support.) The points labeled *A*, *B*, and *C* should present a prima facie case for the particular point in the Roman numeral series under which they appear. And the points 1, 2, and 3 should constitute a prima facie case for the point in the capital letter series under which they are listed. Is it not clear that if every series of subpoints presents a prima facie case for the point to which it is subordinated, the brief will include all the significant evidence and argument on one side of the proposition.

(7) Objections to Be Refuted Should Be Dealt with as They Arise. — In drawing up a brief it is frequently desirable to include a refutation of certain points arising on the other side of the question. Such refutation should not be segregated in a separate section of the brief, but should be included in the discussion wherever the point naturally arises.

(8) In Phrasing Refutation, the Heading Should State Clearly the Argument to Be Answered and the Character of the Answer to Be Made. — Wherever refutation is stated in the brief, it should be clearly indicated as such. The best way to do this is to state the precise point to be refuted and to indicate the nature of the answer as in the following illustration:

A. The charge that a Federal Department of Education will result in Federal control of education is false, because

   1. --
   2. --, because
      a. --
      b. --

O'Neill, Laycock, and Scales say on this point,[1]

"Refutation is the name that is given to any attack directed against the proof of an opponent. . . . there must always be more or less of it in any brief, and its effectiveness depends very largely upon the way it is introduced. The writer of a brief, knowing in his own mind what is the position of his opponent which he desires to assail, very naturally falls into the mistake of unconsciously attributing a like knowledge to others, and so goes on to array his answers, without making clear to his audience or readers just what it is he is answering, and *how* he is answering it. This carelessness often proves troublesome; for in order to make refutation achieve its purposes, it is necessary that the attention of an audience be first directed toward the *exact point in controversy*, in order that they may see the comparison of the two sides and so feel the destructive force of the answer."

d. The Rule Governing the Conclusion. —

(1) The Conclusion Should Contain a Summary of the Essential Points of the Discussion. — The function of the conclusion is to set forth the significant points in the brief in a short summary. Ordinarily a statement of the proposition and the main headings in the discussion will suffice. We suggest the following form:

Therefore, since:
   I. The new Ford is the lowest priced car on the market, and
   II. The new Ford can be operated more cheaply than any other car on the market, and
   III. The new Ford has the highest proportional resale and trade-in value, and

[1] O'Neill, J. M., Laycock, Craven, and Scales, R. L., *Argumentation and Debate*, p. 235. The Macmillan Company, 1917.

IV. The new Ford conserves the time and energy of its operator.

It is to be concluded: That the new Ford offers the most economical automotive transportation on the market.

B. The Case Outline. — The case has been defined in a previous chapter as the argument which the persuader plans to take before a specific audience. Hence, the case outline is an outline of the argument which the persuader plans to take before his audience.

1. THE CASE OUTLINE AND BRIEF DISTINGUISHED. — The case outline differs from the brief in the following respects : (1) It is a presentation outline rather than a preparation outline ; (2) The discussion may include either logical or topical outlining or some combination of the two, depending upon the type of support used ; (3) It is more selective than the brief in that only those point are set forth which seem of value for a particular occasion ; (4) The sequence and arrangement are adjusted to persuade a particular audience.

Summing up these points of difference we can readily see that all of them hinge on the fact that the case outline is adapted to take cognizance of the reaction needs and tendencies of a particular audience whereas the brief is a complete, logical survey of proof irrespective of specific reactors. " The case outline is a psychological variable ; the brief, a logical constant."

2. DRAWING THE CASE OUTLINE FROM THE BRIEF. — The process of drawing the case outline from the brief necessitates two steps : (1) Selection ; and (2) Arrangement. After analyzing his audience the persuader must *select* those points from his brief which will most effectively " touch off " their reaction tendencies ; and then he must *arrange* these points in a sequence which will most naturally and easily lead the audience to think or act as the proposition suggests.

The question again arises, can the case outline be prepared without first drawing up a brief?   Let us pause to interpret the position taken earlier in the chapter when it was stated that a brief should constitute a step in the preparation of every comprehensive argument.   Of course, the question is, just what is meant by a comprehensive argument?   A public debate, a formal argumentative address, a legal case, a salesman's canvas, a legislative proposal or bill, all, involve propositions which most certainly should be carefully briefed before any attempt is made to prepare a case outline.   On the other hand, it is frequently a wise economy of time to dispense with a brief in the preparation of short, informal arguments.   We feel that as the student matures in his study of argument he will be able to determine upon his own method of preparation in each particular case.   In the meantime, however, let it be emphasized that no person can count himself accomplished in argument, nor will he attain real effectiveness in argument, until he has mastered the brief and knows how to use it as a basis for drawing the case outline.

3.   THE DIVISIONS OF A CASE OUTLINE. — The case outline like the brief should be divided into three parts, the introduction, discussion, and conclusion.   It might be observed in passing that this rule obtains for all speech outlines, whether argumentative or otherwise.   In Chapter XIII, *Composing Argument*, we shall discuss the different types of introductions, discussions, and conclusions and the rhetorical principles governing their effective composition.   Suffice it to say here that the purely expository introduction, the strictly linear development, and the formal summary, which characterize the brief, are rarely the best rhetorical forms in which to state the finished argument.   The case outline and the argument written or spoken from it, must be composed to attract attention, secure interest, and awaken the desire of the audience; in short, it must be composed to convince or

actuate people who may or may not be most easily influenced by straight confirmatory argument.

4. THE FORMS OF SUPPORT IN A CASE OUTLINE. — It should be thoroughly understood at this point that the case may argue through Confirmation, Explanation, Motivation, or through any combination of these three forms of support. Thus, the case outline must be a form which is capable of being so adjusted as to effectively set forth any one or all of these forms of support.   We have already explained that logical outlining is best suited to the inferences of Confirmation, and that topical outlining is peculiarly adapted to the inferences of Explanation and the implicative system.   It should be added here that there is no special type of outlining for Motivation.   The crux of the motive appeal, as we have seen, is to focus the desire of the reactor on the proposition under discussion.   The language necessary to stir up desire and associate it with the proposition may be outlined either logically or topically.   From this discussion, then, we can see that a case outline might be a logical outline, a topical outline, or some combination of the two, depending upon the support which is to be given the proposition.

Baird, in speaking of " The Rhetorical Outline," has in mind substantially what we are calling the Case Outline.   He has the following to say regarding it :[1]

"The rhetorical outline is a device that aims to set forth completely the processes of exposition and argument contained in a persuasive or informational speech or article. Many speeches, prevailingly argumentative or expository, have a considerable blending of the two elements, with narrative and descriptive passages included. Thus the expositional address or lecture that contains sections of straight argument may be conveniently reduced to a comprehensive outline ; likewise the argument which 'unfolds' and reveals the 'implicative processes'

[1] Baird, A. Craig, *Public Discussion and Debate*, pp. 136–137. Ginn and Company, 1928.

of a 'this-or-nothing' type of logic may be outlined without rejecting whole paragraphs or even distorting utterly the order of development. This rhetorical outline, then, is in reality a combination of the analytical or expository outline, the argumentative brief, and the speaker's outline for delivery."

C. The Speaker's Outline. — Every argumentative speech should be delivered from an outline. This outline may be typewritten on cards and taken to the platform, or it may be memorized by the speaker and notes dispensed with altogether. Whether written or memorized, however, the speaker's outline should consist of such notes as will most readily recall the *ideas* which have been carefully outlined in the case outline and fully worded in the composition. It differs from the case outline in the following respects : (1) It is usually much shorter and more condensed ; (2) It is prepared for the speaker's personal use only ; and (3) It serves to recall ideas during their oral presentation rather than to organize and direct the composition of the case.

The case outline is used during composition when the argument is being stated in language. This composition may be either written or oral, but the process should be undergone before the speech is taken before the audience. The speaker's outline, then, is simply a condensed statement of the case outline, suggesting the ideas that are to be developed and the sequence in which they are to appear.

IV. Organization in Impromptu Argument and Argumentative Conversation

The need for organization is just as great in those forms of argument for which careful written outlines cannot be prepared as in those types which may be so outlined. There is little persuasion in disorganized, rambling speaking of any kind. The individual who would become effective in ready, impromptu argument must learn to organize his thinking and speaking as the argument proceeds. He, too, must have an outline, but that outline of necessity must suggest itself at the time of the presentation and unfold during the course of the argument. We wish to suggest that there is no better way to obtain effectiveness in impromptu argument than through the analytical discipline necessitated by the preparation and delivery of arguments which do permit the deliberate preparation of written outlines.

V. SUMMARY

It has been the purpose of this chapter to explain argumentative outlines. Briefing and outlining is an art. Every student of argument should practice drawing the various types of outlines set forth in this chapter until he has acquired considerable ability in this art. Skill in outlining is indispensable to the arguer and highly valuable in thinking, writing, and speaking of all kinds. No one should leave a course in argument without making every effort to avail himself of the opportunities offered by such a course in the way of training in outlining and organization.

EXERCISES

1. Prepare a short specimen brief on some simple proposition.

2. Prepare a long specimen brief on some proposition of national policy. Avoid the mistakes made in your short specimen.

3. Prepare a short sample of logical outlining on some familiar subject and then restate the argument briefed therein in as many syllogisms as are necessary to state this argument correctly. If the outline does not lend itself to this exercise, revise it until it is possible to reduce it to a series of syllogisms.

4. Prepare a short sample of topical outlining on some familiar subject designed to illustrate instances in which the sub-topics are descriptive parts, narrative parts, and expository parts of the main topics.

5. Choose a proposition and outline an argumentative development of this proposition first logically, and then topically. Be certain to use the same proposition and essentially the same material in each outline. Compare the two outlines. In what respects do they differ?

6. Outline the Explanatory speech in Appendix B, using topical outlining. Are the sub-topics descriptive, narrative, or expository parts of the various main points?

7. Prepare case outlines for argumentative speeches designed to support a proposition by Confirmation, by Explanation, and by Motivation.

CHAPTER XIII

COMPOSING ARGUMENT

Chapter Outline

247

I. SUMMARY OF THE STEPS WHICH SHOULD PRECEDE THE COMPOSITION OF THE CASE

One of the temptations of arguers, especially beginners, is to start the composition of the argument too soon; that is, before certain of the necessary preliminary steps in preparation have been adequately undertaken. In the preparation of a comprehensive argument the following steps should ordinarily precede composition: (1) Phrasing the proposition; (2) Investigating the proposition; (3) Analysis of the proposition; (4) Analysis of the audience; (5) Brief of the affirmative or negative argument; (6) Selection of evidence and the form of support to be used; and (7) Drawing the case outline. Of course, it is to be understood that there are some cases in which certain of these steps may be omitted; certainly in many cases it is unnecessary to undergo as thorough a preparation before composition as a complete consideration of all these points would entail. However, the importance of careful preparation before composition is to be emphasized.

Of the steps mentioned above particular attention should be called to the case outline because it is this outline which the writer should follow in composition. A case outline, roughly speaking, is an organized group of topic sentences which will be amplified and embellished in the various paragraphs of the composition. The case outline should always be the guide and the basis for the entire composition.

II. THE COMPOSITION OF WRITTEN AND ORAL ARGUMENT

The composition of the case, of course, is the last step in the preparation of a written argument. The written argument ready for publication, or any form in which it can be read by others, is the final product in such case. In oral argument, however, even though the case is composed in writing before presentation, there is an additional factor to be considered, viz. delivery. Chapters XIV and XV are devoted to a treatment of this very important phase of our study.

Two interesting questions suggest themselves here: (1) Should oral argument be composed in writing before delivery? and (2) Should there be any significant differences in rhetorical style between the language of argument that is to be read silently by others and argument that is to be delivered orally? The first of these questions is given special attention in Section II, Chapter XV. We may say here, however, that writing is ordinarily a great aid to delivery and in many cases careful written composition should precede oral presentation.

As to the second question, we can say that there are undoubtedly differences between written and oral style in composition. Baird sums up these differences as follows:

"Oral discourse is like conversation — direct, simple, lively. Pedantry and sentimentality are absent. Sentences are short and direct. The chief ideas stand out clearly and boldly, perhaps somewhat mechanically. The general movement is more irregular than in written style, more abrupt, because the speaker substitutes significant gesture for many a word. Imperative and exclamatory sentences are more numerous, because the emotional coloring is more pronounced. Illustrations, examples, swift figures of speech, the use of iteration, and other devices to impress are more necessary than in written discourse." [1]

It should be said that all argument lends itself to oral style and is best composed in oral style even when it is to be read silently. For this reason particular attention must be paid to euphony, to the length of sentences, and to the grouping of thoughts so that the composition can be read aloud easily and forcefully. It is advisable to submit every argumentative composition to the test of oral reading before making

[1] Baird, A. Craig, *Public Discussion and Debate*, p. 302. Ginn and Company, 1928.

the final draft. Read it aloud during the process of composition and after completion.

III. PRINCIPLES OF EFFECTIVE COMPOSITION

There are three fundamental principles of effective composition more or less familiar to every student which we wish to recall briefly in relation to argument. They are unity, coherence, and emphasis.

A. Unity. — By unity is meant one-ness of purpose. An argument is unified if it develops one central idea and if each of its divisions is confined to the development of specific parts of this central idea. The necessity for unity exists in the argument as a whole, in each paragraph, and even in each sentence. Rambling is a vice in writing which is fatal to the composition of strong, dynamic argument. Know what you are talking about in every division of the speech and hew to the line diligently.

B. Coherence. — By coherence in composition is meant the relation between parts; a speech or written argument is coherent when its various parts " hang together " or relate to each other in some readily intelligible manner. The two rhetorical considerations vital to coherent argument are sequence and transitions.

1. SEQUENCE. — Arrange the points in every argument in some sensible sequence. This may be a time order sequence, a sequence of magnitude or importance, a sequence of place, or some other sequence derived from the nature of the material or from the chains of reasoning in a logical outline. The mistake should not be made of simply jumping from one point to another without regard to the order of treatment.

2. TRANSITIONS. — Of equal importance to coherent speaking and writing are the transitions between the various divisions of the composition. A reader or listener must some way or other be made to appreciate movements of thought

from one point to another.   How many times one will be reading along only to realize all of a sudden that sometime, somewhere the writer has shifted from one topic or point in his discussion to another without any indication of such a change.   The reader can retrace his steps and seek out the transition providing he has the patience to do so.   Even this arduous process is out of the question for the listener unless it is possible to interrupt a speaker and inquire into the intricacies of his composition.   Loose, poorly stated transitions, or what is worse, no transitions at all confuse the listener and inevitably result in muddy, incoherent argument. Summaries and partitions, and transitional sentences, as well as the various devices open to the speaker in oral argument such as movement and change in vocal inflection, may be utilized by the arguer to accomplish clear, easy transitions.

C. Emphasis. — By emphasis in composition we mean making one thing stand out over another; it is a matter of lending variety and force to the argument by stressing the more important things.   Very evidently a point may be emphasized in a great number of ways, many of which are open only to the speaker, viz., greater loudness, gesture, etc. Rhetorically, there are two principle types of emphasis: (1) Emphasis in form; and (2) Emphasis in material.

1.   EMPHASIS IN FORM. — By emphasis in form is meant the relative amount of time and space devoted to a given point and the position in the composition which it is accorded.   Thus, a point which is given a five-minute treatment in an eight-minute speech, other things being equal, will be emphasized more than one given three minutes or less time in the same speech; likewise, points placed at the beginning of a speech or at the close of a speech are usually emphasized because of the strategic position which this gives them.   This emphasis in form should be accorded the more important points in an argument.

2. EMPHASIS IN MATERIAL. — Emphasis in material differs from emphasis in form in that the emphatic power is to be found in the very nature of the material itself rather than in the time or place given the topic in the composition. Thus, a point may be emphasized by supporting it with material that is sufficiently interesting and attractive in and of itself to make the point stand out above others less interestingly supported.

IV. SOME SPECIFIC RHETORICAL DEVICES USEFUL IN THE COMPOSITION OF ARGUMENT

Aside from the general principles of effective composition which we have just discussed, there are some specific rhetorical devices which will be found to be helpful in the composition of argument.

A. The Typical Instance. — Typical instances, examples, and illustrations, should constantly be employed in argument. If such instances are *specific* and *concrete*, they will attract the attention of the audience and sustain interest as a constant flow of generalities and abstractions (no matter how profound they may be) never can do. The relating of such instances will make the support of any point much more attractive than it would otherwise be, and at the same time, if corroborated by general data or statistics, will not subtract in any way from the probative force of the argument. We make this last statement because there is a danger in using typical instances of falling into the fallacy of hasty generalization. That is, the speaker will cite a single graphic case and then leap to a conclusion without convincing his audience that his instance is actually *typical* as well as *interesting*. It is good practice to cite a specific, concrete instance, go into it in some detail, make it graphic and realistic ; and then give data of a more general nature which will bear out the instance cited and justify a generalization. If one is arguing for the relief of a drought-stricken area, for instance, how much more persuasive and impelling the argument is which tells of individual suffering and losses than one which simply states that so many thousand people are destitute and in need. Audiences may be stirred by the case of Farmer Jones whose crops have been literally burned up by the intense heat and whose wife and little boy and girl are in actual need, when they will remain quite untouched in the face of an hour of statistics. As we have said, when such specific instances are shown to be actually typical, the argument is at once persuasive and convincing.

B. Figurative Analogy. — Figurative Analogies are valuable for illustrative purposes in the composition of argument, if they are apt and to the point. Chapter VIII developed the literal analogy as one type of inductive confirmation. It might be well to refer to Section VI–B of that chapter at this time, because these two forms should not be confused. Whereas literal analogy compares two things which are in the same general category, figurative analogy compares two things which fall in essentially different categories. Literal analogy has some probative force when properly used, while figurative analogy is illustrative only.

In a recent debate on the advisability of making the St. Lawrence navigable for ocean-going steamships, the affirmative team divided this route into five sectors and pointed out that four of these had already been made navigable, or appropriations had already been made to finance such operations. Their conclusion was, of course, that it would be foolhardy not to complete the fifth sector in lieu of what had already been done for the other four. To illustrate this conclusion they indicated analogically that to fail to complete the project would be like building a new building and then refusing to put on the roof. The analogy here is figurative and such force as it has is to be found in its illustrative power. It simply makes the point clearer and more striking.

Such analogies must be used cautiously in argument, however, lest an opponent turn them against the user. If they are far fetched and loosely drawn, a slight twist of the comparison by a clever opponent will make them appear ridiculous. Shaw says of the use of figurative analogies:

> "No method is more common than this, and yet no method has its path strewn with a greater number of failures. These failures are due to the fact that the speaker does not use analogies that arise spontaneously, but uses rather analogies that he constructs with labor and pulls by the heels into his speech. If analogy is to be striking, it must be spontaneous; its application should be apparent instantly; and its terms should need no explanation." [1]

C. Repetition in Parallel Construction. — Repetition in parallel construction is another rhetorical device useful in argument. It is most frequently used in repeating a group of sentences of like construction in rapid succession. The thoughts expressed by sentences pyramided in this way may be progressive throughout the series, or the same thought may be repeated in different words. In either case the effect is to give power and strength to the language so composed. Such sentences deliver exceedingly well, because the speaker can easily build to a climax by progressively increasing the force of utterance.

The following paragraphs, taken from the conclusion of one of President Hoover's speeches, illustrate this device. Practice reading these lines aloud, and note how readily they lend themselves to forceful delivery.

> "My conception of America is a land where men and women may walk in ordered freedom in the independent conduct of their occupations; where they may enjoy the advantages of wealth,

[1] Shaw, W. C., *The Art of Debate*, p. 299. Allyn and Bacon, 1922.

not concentrated in the hands of a few, but spread through the lives of all; where they may build and safeguard their homes, and give to their children the fullest advantages and opportunities of American life; where every man shall be respected in the faith that his conscience and his heart direct him to follow; where a contented and happy people, secure in their liberties, free from poverty and fear, shall have the leisure and impulse to seek a fuller life."

"Some may ask where all this may lead beyond mere material progress. It leads to a release of the energies of men and women from the dull drudgery of life to a wider vision and a higher hope. It leads to the opportunity for greater and greater service, not alone from man to man in our own land but from our country to the whole world. It leads to an America, healthy in body, healthy in spirit, unfettered, youthful, eager — with a vision searching beyond the farthest horizons, with an open mind sympathetic and generous. It is to these higher ideals and for these purposes that I pledge myself to the Republican party." [1]

D. The Use of Personal Pronouns. — " When a speaker stands before an audience he is in personal relation with them. He should not try to avoid the implications of this relationship. He should talk in terms of *I* and *You* and *We*. Taking thought to put these pronouns into a speech will give it directness and contact — that intimacy of relationship with an audience which is most effective. The nearer public speaking approaches the directness and intimacy of private conversation, the better it is. Of course some speeches can approach nearer to this ideal than others. The point is that each one should come as close to it as circumstances permit, and one of the methods of helping to bring this desirable condition about is precisely this one of using over and over again the personal pronouns, *I, You, We.*" [2]

[1] Speech on "Government Ownership" by Herbert Hoover. Taken from *Contemporary Speeches*, p. 536, J. M. O'Neill and F. K. Riley, The Century Company, 1930.

[2] O'Neill, J. M., and Weaver, A. T., *The Elements of Speech*, p. 289. Longmans, Green and Company, 1926.

Note how Preston Bradley uses personal pronouns in closing his speech on " The Business of Religion and the Religion of Business " :

"That, to me, gave a lesson of life. We are in a stormy period. All about us are evidences of great distortion. You can offset every great ideal of business by a preparation of war. You can offset every gesture of man by a gesture of hate. We are in the midst of great complications and intricate situations. But in the storm we have faith! Faith! The greatest word in the English language is faith! Faith in our ship! Faith in our navigating officer! Faith in our dreams! Faith in humanity! Faith in the potentiality of man! Faith in God! And this faith will bring us out all right in spite of storm and tempest, for the fundamental law of the whole universe is the ultimate, and preëminent triumph of eternal righteousness." [1]

Theodore H. Gordon gives us another illustration of the use of personal pronouns. The following is the closing paragraph of his oration, " Watchdogs."

"Let me put to you a question : Shall we be intimidated by these watchdogs? Shall we permit their growling to hold us off from attacking the problems which confront us today? I plead with you tonight to renounce fear of these Watchdogs, to renounce blind allegiance to the symbols and traditions of the past. We must be done with that deadening fear of change which underlies tolerance. We must infuse into our institutions new life, new hope. If, for us, religion is to become a living dynamic force ; if our economic problems are to come to rational solutions ; if our tradition of nationalism and war is to be replaced by a new and higher tradition of coöperation and peace ; — then you and I must apply our knowledge of the past to the meeting of the present problems. You and I, as college students who have studied the past, must apply the wisdom derived from that study to the creation of our future. We cannot live in the past. We must meet the issues of the present. The conflict between progress and reaction goes on unabated. We cannot stand idly

[1] A sermon by Preston Bradley. Taken from *Contemporary Speeches*, by O'Neill and Riley, pp. 485–486.

by. We must choose our banners and march forward into the future." [1]

E. Short Sentences. — As a general rule short sentences are to be preferred to long sentences in oral discourse. In fact, the short sentence is an outstanding characteristic of oral style. It delivers more readily and is more immediately intelligible to an audience. Speech becomes heavy and ponderous when too many long, involved sentences are used. When long sentences are used, they should be composed in such a way that they can readily be broken up into short, relatively complete, and intelligible thought groups, for purposes of delivery.

Note the use of short sentences and the ease with which the longer sentences can be divided, in the quotation from " Watchdogs " given on the preceding page.

F. The Rhetorical Question. — Baird defines the rhetorical question and distinguishes it from an ordinary interrogation as follows : " The general interrogation creates suspense and so is an easy means of holding attention. It is particularly convenient as a means of introducing new paragraphs. Like all other sentence forms, it must not be worked to death. The rhethorical question is phrased so as to imply a given answer. The question is asked, " Is this not true? " And the suggestion is thus strongly set forth that the idea is true. The rhetorical question is thus a vigorous assertion disguised as an interrogation." [2] The very nature of the rhetorical question is such that its use is likely to prove disastrous unless the audience is certain to answer the question in the way that the speaker desires. For that reason it should be used cautiously lest the wrong idea be conveyed.

We have selected two widely separated paragraphs from a sermon by Bishop Charles Wesley Burns, " Goodwill to-

[1] Taken from *Contemporary Speeches*, p. 394.
[2] Baird, A. Craig, *Public Discussion and Debate*, p. 323.

ward Men "; the first of these illustrates the use of the ordinary or general interrogation to arouse interest and create suspense, and appears early in the speech; the second illustrates the rhetorical question and occurs much later in the speech.

"All are agreed that we have come to a turning point in human destinies. We are passing through the real processes of a new era. We have passed out of the period of astonishment at the world cataclysm into a period of achievement. What is the significance of this crisal hour? Scores of books are written about it. Everyone feels that the 'embattled democracies of the world,' and now the disarming democracies of the world, have brought vast cataclysmic and immeasurable changes. Ramified reconstructions are imminent in society, in commerce, in industry, in organized Christianity. What are those changes? What has happened? What will come out of the social and industrial ferment of the day? What chance has Jesus Christ in the New Day dawning? What is the outlook for peace? Is the world neighborhood being transformed into a World Brotherhood?"

"Dr. McKenzie King, in his great and fundamental treatise on *Industry and Humanity* senses the international unrest and world ferment in a fresh allusion to Mrs. Shelley's *Frankenstein*, written just one hundred years ago. A weird and realistic parable it is indeed, but true to modern life. Are we not chained to the Iron Man of modern life, a 'Frankenstein' more powerful than the genius who created him? Are we not suffering the supreme tragedy of history because of that very genius? Is it not that very materialistic system which has brought about a shattered, broken, and bruised world-heart and has let loose in the world a monster of hate and fear and conflict in industry, in society, in international relationships that strikes terror to the very heart of the race?" [1]

G. Comic Relief or Humor. — Humor judiciously used is effective in most speaking and it has a place in argument. The average argumentative speech by its very nature must be composed in a vein which is predominantly serious, how-

[1] Taken from *Contemporary Speeches*, pp. 471–472.

ever.   For that very reason the injection of a little apt humor at various points is particularly helpful.   It relieves the monotony, injects life into the argument, and tends to establish a stronger bond of fellowship between the speaker and the audience.   In no instance, however, should humor be used as a substitute for good argument; it should be used rather to supplement it and reënforce it.

Comic relief as a rhetorical device may consist of humorous anecdotes, jokes, clever plays on words, and friendly thrusts at an opponent or his arguments.

V. Special Suggestions for Composing the Main Divisions of the Speech

A. Composing the Introduction. — The introduction to an argument ordinarily must serve two functions: (1) Attract the attention of the audience to the subject and arouse interest in the subject; and (2) It must set forth such information as will enable the audience to follow the progress of the argument without difficulty.   Introductions designed primarily to serve the first function may begin the argument with an interesting word picture, a striking quotation, a figure of speech, a challenging question, or any other rhetorical device which is appropriate to the occasion and will serve to attract attention.   It should be emphasized, however, that any such rhetorical device should not only be interesting and attractive in and of itself, but it should relate in some immediate and impelling way to the subject at hand, so that an easy, natural transition can be made to this subject.   Any introduction must be artistically and integrally related to the argument as a whole and not simply " tacked on."

The informative introduction is designed to set forth such information as will enable the audience readily to understand the discussion.   It usually includes a statement of the question, some comment on the origin and history of the question, the immediate cause for discussion, a definition of terms, a statement of admitted and irrelevant matter, an explanation of the issue or issues involved, and a statement of the points in partition. Of course, only as many of these steps need to be included as are necessary to an understanding of the discussion.

A good introduction, however, almost invariably must combine elements of both the types we have mentioned. That is, it must be constructed to gain the attention of the audience and at the same time impart the necessary information. In such case the initial paragraph may be devoted to the business of arousing interest and a second introductory paragraph to the statement of preliminary explanations. It will be found that this sequence is a quite natural one and one that leads up to the discussion with ease and rhetorical grace.

B. Composing the Discussion. — The composition of the discussion will vary greatly with the type of support (Confirmation, Explanation, or Motivation) that predominates in the argument. The same is true of the introduction and conclusion, of course, but these differences are in no other place so significant as they are in the discussion, and for that reason we shall discuss them here.

1. THE COMPOSITION OF CONFIRMATION. — In composing confirmatory arguments, the logical outline should be followed rather carefully. Each step in the argument is indicated by a point in the outline, and each argumentative paragraph in the discussion should contain one such point as a topic sentence. Ordinarily it is wise to begin the paragraph with this topic sentence; it may be stated either in the form of a question which the paragraph is designed to answer, or simply as a terse, attractive statement of the argument to be developed. The development of these topics should consist of the appropriate inductive and deductive types which we have discussed in connection with our study of Confirmation, together with a presentation of the evidence from which the

inferences are being drawn. Any or all of the special rhetorical devices discussed in Section IV of this chapter may be used as needed.

Confirmatory paragraphs of the type we have just described can very effectively be summed up in a periodic sentence. The form of the periodic sentence is such that the various premises of the argument may be restated in the subordinate clauses of the sentence which always appear first, and the conclusion may be drawn in the main clause with which the periodic sentence always closes. The following is an example of a periodic sentence used in this way:

> The dilapidated condition of the buildings, the absence of fences, and last but not least, the difficulty of getting a water supply, prove the impracticality of attempting to rent the ranch at this time.

a. Inductive and Deductive Composition Distinguished. — The type of development where the composer begins with the conclusion and the direction of the reasoning is from this conclusion to the evidence or particular facts bearing it out, is commonly known as deductive composition. This is the type of composition usually employed in Confirmation and the type whose use we have recommended in the preceding section. This process may be just reversed, however, for the entire discussion or for any paragraph in the discussion. That is, the evidence may be set forth first, and the reasoning may then proceed from this evidence to the conclusion. This latter approach is frequently called inductive composition because the composer proceeds from the particular to the general.[1] In such cases the logical outline which is followed in deductive composition is just inverted; this does not alter the reasoning or the evidence, however, but simply reverses

---

[1] The terms *inductive* and *deductive* as used in this connection should not be confused with inductive and deductive argument. They are simply borrowed to describe these types of composition.

the sequence in which the argument is taken up. The following form illustrates an inverted logical outline, and the sequence in inductive composition:

> > > > *a.* ....,
> > > > *b.* ....,
> > > > *c.* ...., therefore
> > > 1. ....,
> > > > *a.* ....,
> > > > *b.* ...., therefore
> > > 2. ...., therefore
> > *A.* ....,
> > > 1. ....,
> > > 2. ...., therefore
> > *B.* ...., therefore
> I. ...., therefore
> *Resolved:* ....

Deductive composition has the advantage of being easier to follow and somewhat easier to present. The arguer can partition what he is going to do in each division of the case and then proceed to do it. The inductive approach conceals the objective because it begins with the evidence and builds toward the conclusion. It has the advantage of climax and suspense, but it is apt to be confusing to an audience unless carefully handled, for the very reason that the audience does not know where the speaker is heading.

2. THE COMPOSITION OF EXPLANATION. — Support by Explanation is somewhat comparable to the inductive composition just described, because it too builds to the conclusion from the various data connected with the proposition. In fact, it is generally wise to withhold the objective in Explanation, aiming to present the case in such a way that the audience will draw the conclusion for itself. Despite this similarity, explanatory composition has certain distinguishing characteristics of its own. The development is descriptive, narrative, and expository, and the organization is topical

rather than logical. It is characterized by a freer and easier style, the loose sentence appearing in abundance, and the whole discourse being generally less didactic and less inclined to weighty, heavy structure than that of Confirmation. If narration predominates, the sequence may well be chronological; if description prevails, some sequence of place will be most effective; and if exposition is used, any sequence dictated by the nature of the subject matter will be adequate.

For further help in the composition of Explanation, we would suggest that the student refer to the discussion of narration, description, and exposition in any standard rhetoric book. The compositional techniques suggested therein, combined with a careful study of the chapter on Explanation in this text, should enable the student to compose this type of argument.

3. THE COMPOSITION OF MOTIVATION. — There is no characteristic compositional technique in Motivation. The objective is of course to stimulate desire and associate desire with the proposition. We are probably safe in saying that the style of Explanation lends itself better to Motivation than that of Confirmation. Certainly, the stimulation of desire is more readily accomplished by vivid description and fascinating narrative than by the more cut-and-dried inferences of Confirmation. The association of desire with the proposition, on the other hand, is effected somewhat better by Confirmation, especially where the association is attempted by open explication.

In explaining the composition of the discussion from the standpoint of the three forms of support, we do not mean to convey the impression that these forms cannot be combined in the same composition. In fact, this is what generally takes place. It is quite common to build an argument with an explanatory introduction, with a discussion that confirms the proposition, and a conclusion which is designed to motivate the acceptance of the proposition. Another usual combination is to arouse desire by an attractive explanation and then follow it with a confirmation of the proposition as a means of satisfying this desire. Still another form is the predominately confirmatory argument which is livened up with explanatory and motivational passages. It is altogether possible to support a proposition or any single topic in an argument with any one or all three of these forms of support. We are anxious to have every reader appreciate the argumentative power of Confirmation, Explanation, and Motivation as separate techniques employed as independent methodologies. At the same time the facility with which they may be combined to compose persuasive argument should not be overlooked.

C. The Composition of the Conclusion. — Like the introduction, the conclusion is concerned with two functions: (1) An informational purpose, *i.e.*, to sum up what has been argued in the discussion; and (2) A persuasive purpose, *i.e.*, to invoke the favorable decision of the audience and to create a good impression in closing. And like the introduction, a good conclusion usually should be designed to accomplish both of these purposes.

The final summary of the case may vary from a single periodic sentence stating the main tenents of the argument, to a formal summary reviewing the entire case in great detail. The comprehensiveness of the summary should, of course, be dictated by the needs of the occasion.

Many times an argument can be closed with a story, a quotation, or with a word picture which will accomplish the purpose of a summary by emphasizing the central idea of the argument and focusing attention there. In many respects this is more effective than a formal summary because it can be made to bring the ends of the speech together with equal facility and at the same time is much more attractive and entertaining.

As we have repeatedly said, the conclusion must seek to clinch a favorable decision and stimulate the audience to activity. Of course, it is aided in this by every other part of the argument, but the " knock out blow " must be struck in the last round. The conclusion in many cases must be dynamic and challenging if the desired objective is going to be gained. The composer will find the short balanced sentence, repetition in parallel construction, the rhetorical question, and language rich in imagery and emotional content, useful devices in composing a plea for action.

EXERCISES

1. Bring to class illustrations of the rhetorical devices discussed in this chapter which you have found in argumentative speeches and debates you have heard or read.

2. Compose in writing an argumentative speech of the Confirmatory type, the Explanatory type, and one designed to support a proposition by Motivation. In each case annotate the speech structurally; that is, note in the margin the precise argumentative types and the rhetorical devices used.

3. Prepare a structural outline of the speech in Appendix B or some other argumentative speech of your own choosing. Let this outline state in detail the argumentative types and rhetorical devices used in this speech from the first paragraph to the last, but make no reference to the actual subject matter of the speech. If a single speech is assigned to the entire class, it will be worth while to go over the structural outlines in class in relation to the argument under analysis.

4. Write an argument of your own following the structural outline prepared in Exercise 3. Use the same argumentative types and rhetorical devices used in the other speech, but a different proposition and totally different subject matter. Make the two arguments identical structurally, but totally different from the standpoint of subject matter and material.

CHAPTER XIV

DELIVERY: A FACTOR IN PERSUASION

I. Certain Non-Rhetorical Forms of Support

Rhetoric may be defined as the art of composition; and the rhetoric of argument is that portion of the art which has to do with the composition of language to the end of convincing and actuating people. Most of our treatment up to this point has been rhetorical. We have analyzed the entire process of building the argument, from the conception of the proposition to the composition of the finished case. While the rhetorician's responsibility ends when the argument is organized, evidenced, and stated in effective, impelling language, the end has not been reached for the speaker. He must present this argument to his fellow men, from the public platform, around the conference table, over the counter, at the club, and in the home. The arguer, then, must be more than a rhetorician; he must be a persuasive speaker as well.

In our discussion of the rhetoric of argument we have analyzed and labeled the materials and forms out of which arguments are built, and we have shown how these materials can be molded into the finished product. To this point, however, we have been dealing with only two dimensions. We have the argument phrased and on paper; it has been reduced to language. The third dimension is brought in when we introduce the speaker, the man, the living organism, who must communicate his thought to other such organisms. It is this third dimension especially which makes of argument a dynamic, living thing, which cannot be analyzed and labeled apart from the personality who gives it utterance. In this Chapter and the following Chapter we purpose first, to analyze these non-rhetorical factors which arise in the presentation of the argument, and secondly, to discuss style and methods in the persuasive use of these factors.

A. What People Argue With. — Before launching into an analytical treatment of delivery as a factor in persuasion, however, let us view a typical argumentative situation to the end of getting the proper perspective on these many factors we have been bringing into our study.

Let us assume a situation in which a man is in the market

for five or ten thousand dollars' worth of life insurance, and he is approached by the representatives of five or six large, reputable companies. To control our hypothetical case somewhat, let us assume further that the offerings of these companies are substantially the same so far as cost and benefits are concerned, and that the prospective customer is interested and open-minded at the outset of each interview. In other words, we are trying to create a situation in which each salesman has a fair and equal opportunity to close the sale. Then let us ask, what factors will determine this sale? First of all the man who knows insurance and knows his company best will have an advantage. A further advantage will undoubtedly lie with the salesman who is most capable in sizing up the prospect's insurance needs and phrasing an argument which will " tie up " his particular offering with these needs. But that isn't all, — the man who has personality, good appearance, physical vigor, vocal control, and the ability to adjust these factors to the personality of the individual before him, will also have an advantage. One of these men will win the argument. Which will it be? Most certainly, should any one of the salesmen combine these abilities in his person in a higher degree than any of his competitors, he would be the man who would make the sale. As to which of these factors would mean the most, we have no experimental data upon which to base a conclusion. All we can say is that these are the things with which people argue, and the equation is certainly not complete which ignores the persuasive power of delivery.

B. Rhetorical and Biological Factors in Argument. — From the case we have assumed above is it not evident that delivery plays a part in argument which is infinitely more significant for the persuader than its function as a mere vehicle of expression? Delivery is not simply a matter of conveying words whose persuasive content and argumentative values are fixed. It is not at all analogous to simply transporting materials from one place to another. New factors and additional values are added to argument by good delivery. If this is not clear, we wish to say that there are many instances in which identical arguments so far as language is concerned have been powerful agencies for controlling the thinking and acting of people when delivered by one person, and weak, ineffectual speeches in the hands of another. For further evidence of additional factors, we have but to recall the many cases in which speakers have delivered winning arguments one night and failed the next with the same argument under almost identical conditions, because they were not attuned to the occasion. We have all heard of cases in which it was alleged that audiences have been swayed by speeches delivered in foreign tongues, where the language content in itself could not possibly have been the persuasive element.

It is to these additional persuasive factors, which arise in oral communication and which are to be distinguished from the ideational, meaning content of the language symbols themselves, to which we wish to devote this chapter. We have referred to these factors as being biological in nature as distinguished from the rhetorical factors which have to do with the composition of language. We have used the term *biological* because these factors are capable of adequate explanation only in terms of those protoplasmic properties which distinguish the animate from the inanimate and which make language possible only for the animate. The following explanation of communication should make this position clear.

II. The Nature of Communication

In Chapter V we discussed the nature of communication in terms of the two types of speech symbols and the five steps in communicating argument, attention, perception, reasoning, judgment, and action. We now wish to amplify and extend our picture of communication so that the persuasive factors arising in oral presentation may be better analyzed and understood. We suggest that the student reread Section II of Chapter V at this time.

A. The Biological Nature of Communication. — All living things are made up of a substance known as protoplasm. This protoplasm is composed of cells, or in other words, the cell is the unit of protoplasm. Protoplasm has undergone two great developments or specializations which are represented in plant and animal life respectively. We are concerned with animal life which may in turn be divided into the protozoa or single celled animals, and the metazoa or many celled animals. There are many types of both protozoa and metazoa, man being the highest type in the latter group.

Protoplasm or living matter has certain properties, and we are particularly concerned with three of these in communication. The three to which we have reference are: (1) Irritability; (2) Extensibility; and (3) Secretion. These qualities are described psychologically as the capacity for stimulation and response. Each protoplasmic cell has these properties of irritability, extensibility, and secretion. Even the single cell animal is sensitive to external stimuli and responds to such stimuli. It can move itself around food and secrete to digest this food. Professor C. L. Meader has said[1] that there are four great impulses or drives behind these life giving activities: food, reproduction, protection, and aggression. Impelled by these drives and possessed of the properties named above (along with certain others) protoplasm has the capacity to change in structure and hence in function as a result of external stimuli.

[1] In a class lecture on "The Psychology of Speech."

In more complex life many different kinds of protoplasm have developed. Certain cells or aggregations of cells have differentiated in structure and because of this differentiation display a resulting specificity of function. Even one celled animals are differentiated in that there are different types of protoplasm within the cell. The more complex animals are differentiated in that they are made up of different types of cells. In these many celled animals certain of the cells develop forms of protoplasm with high capacity for certain cell properties. Some have developed capacity for irritability in a high degree, others for movement, others for secretion, etc. It is by this process of differentiation that the eight tissues of the body have developed. The nervous system, for instance, has developed the capacity of irritability; the muscular system, the property of movement; and the glandular system, the capacity to secrete; etc.

We have said that irritability, extensibility, and secretion were the protoplasmic qualities most intimately connected with communication. Let us see why this is true. To understand this we must realize that as speakers we have only two ways of expressing ourselves, by the movement of muscles (extensibility), and by the secretion of glands (secretion). Posture, movement, gesture, voice — all means of communication are reducible to moving muscles and secreting glands. If this is not quite clear in the matter of voice consider that vocalization is simply an overlaid function [1] which utilizes the organs of breathing and the muscles used in taking food. Realizing further that muscles move and glands secrete only when they are stimulated by nerves (irritability), are we not justified in saying that communication is a function of nerves, muscles, and glands, or in other words a function of irritability, extensibility, and secretion?

[1] See O'Neill and Weaver, *The Elements of Speech*, p. 33. Longmans, Green and Company, 1926.

The fact that in man the organs of breathing and the structures involved in eating and drinking have been utilized in vocalization and in that way adapted to communication should not blind us to the fact that we communicate through many means other than voice. We may communicate by gestures, movements, and postural dispositions of all kinds, — in fact we can and do communicate with anything and everything about us which is capable of stimulating another individual. O'Neill and Weaver define speech as " a code made up of the visible and audible symbols which one person uses to stir up ideas and feelings in other persons without the use of any means other than voice and visible bodily actions." Communication is a broader term than speech, because it is not confined to the *purposeful use* of visible and audible symbols. We may communicate with a red nose, with a sanguine complexion, with tears, and for that matter with our clothes, our type of hair dress, and a good many other factors about us which we either cannot, or at least do not usually, use purposively to control the behavior of our associates.

We are very anxious that our readers understand and appreciate the importance of these non-rhetorical factors entering into argument. As considerations for the student of argument they are not remote and theoretical. On the contrary they are just as immediate, vital, and highly practical as the meaning content of the language used, the sequence of thought, the probative power of the argument, or any other rhetorical consideration. They are factors in the equation of which effective argument is a function.

B. The Two Phases of Communication. — Communication involves two individuals and the two phases of communication to which we refer occur in the communicator and the reactor. A stimulus originating either externally or internally is received by the communicator, conveyed to a nerve center, and a motor response results, causing either muscular or glandular activity. This activity impinges upon the sense organs of the reactor; stimulates him; and he responds, thus setting up communication. It is interesting to note that a complete understanding of the process of communication, thereby, necessitates an understanding of what goes on in the communicator, in the medium between the communicator and the reactor, and in the reactor.

C. The Process of Conditioning. — Many of the stimuli which are effective in eliciting certain responses in an individual were not originally capable of producing those responses. For example, many muscular movements and sounds which can be interpreted by an adult are of course not meaningful in the same sense to an infant. The effectiveness of given stimuli to provoke certain responses is constantly being modified or conditioned by experience. It is in this way that environment plays a rôle in modifying the properties of irritability, extensibility, and secretion.

To understand the process of conditioning it is necessary that we distinguish two types of stimuli, adequate or natural and substitute or indifferent. The infant is brought into the world with a few simple nervous connections whereby a given stimulus will evoke a given response. These early neural connections are known as reflexes (and instincts) and the stimulus in these cases is an adequate or natural stimulus. The substitute stimulus is one which by association with the adequate stimulus comes to have the power to provoke the response which was originally elicited only by the adequate stimulus. Thus, food in the mouth is a natural stimulus for salivary flow. If a red light, for instance, is flashed repeatedly at the same time that food is placed in the mouth, the red light will itself, alone, become as effective as the food in causing a salivary discharge. The red light

in this case becomes a substitute stimulus and the response
becomes a conditioned reflex. [1]

> "All sorts of ordinarily indifferent external agents, not only a
> light, but a sound, a shape, a contact, an odor, indeed anything
> that will influence a sense organ, may be made into an effective
> stimulus." [2]

This principle of conditioning is of great importance
to an understanding of communication, language, and speech,
because most of the stimuli with which we communicate are
substitute stimuli (or symbols) which have acquired their
potency and meaning through association with originally
effective stimuli.

III. THE FACTORS IN PERSUASIVE DELIVERY

With this conception of the nature of communication
before us we are now in a position to analyze those non-
rhetorical factors which are particularly significant in argument. With the understanding that any attempt to classify
these factors is more or less arbitrary and apt to obscure the
whole, we would suggest that the reader constantly refer
back and attempt to " tie up " these factors with the process
of communication as we have explained it. We shall discuss
four factors: external appearances, visible action, vocal
expression, and rhythm and melody.

A. External Appearances. — By external appearances
we mean such physical traits as size (height and weight),
form or proportion, and the color of the hair, skin, and eyes.
The external factor also includes clothes, ornaments, and
other accessories.[3]

These factors without question play a very definite part

---

[1] Illustration taken from Cannon, Walter B., *Bodily Changes in Pain,
Hunger, Fear, and Rage*, Appleton, 1929.

[2] *Ibid.*, p. 259.

[3] Ellis, Robert Sidney, *The Psychology of Individual Differences*, p. 52.

in persuasive communication. Some very interesting studies have been made of the particular effects of different external characteristics, but it will suffice for our purposes to point out that other things being equal, the individual who is impressive in stature, who is well built, who has good color, and who is neatly and appropriately dressed, is the individual who is most persuasive in argument. Or, stating it negatively, an individual who is lacking in these external factors is handicapped in argument to that extent. We do not mean to say that one must be an Apollo in order to sway the multitudes, but we do mean to say *very emphatically* that one who neglects those factors in his personal appearance which he can control, is without question impairing the persuasive force of any argument he may deliver.

B. Visible Action. — A second factor of importance in persuasive delivery is visible action. We shall discuss this under two heads, *facial expression*, and *posture, movement, and gesture*. In each case we are concerned primarily with muscular tonus and muscular movement.

1. FACIAL EXPRESSION. — Allport reduces the large number of possible facial expressions which can be produced by the muscles of the face into six elementary groups: pain-grief, surprise-fear, anger-disgust, pleasure, and various attitudes such as doubt, interrogation, determination, and others.[1] He points out that the studies in identifying facial expressions tend to show that the ability of subjects to recognize different expressions is rather low. This conclusion was arrived at by Professor H. S. Langfeld and others who displayed pictures of different facial expressions to large groups and asked that they be identified. While the identification of isolated pictures seemed to be rather difficult as we have already stated, it was found, however, that facial

[1] Allport, F. H., *Social Psychology*, p. 204. Houghton Mifflin Company, 1924.

expression became highly significant as a contributory stimulus when accompanied by the other factors in a normal speech situation. That is, the expressions acquired their meanings through bodily movements and other stimuli of the whole situation in which they occurred. Thus in the speech situation, facial expression can be looked upon as an important means of stimulation.

The persuader should cultivate an expressive face. A stony, unemotional physiognomy is inimical to effective persuasion. Since argument implies controversy, many speakers chronically assume a frowning, ironical facial expression, which under normal conditions is highly non-persuasive. Let no one be led by this admonition to cultivate the " constant-smile-complex," however; it is fully as bad. The facial muscles should display friendly, sincere determination. Perhaps a word of warning should be given against excessive facial expression. Be moderate in this type of movement as in other types. Exaggerated facial movement is usually an indication of nervousness or affectation.

2. POSTURE, MOVEMENT, AND GESTURE. — The tonus and movement of the larger skeletal muscles are also important in persuasion. In any public address, for instance, it is always interesting to observe how the speaker takes the platform, the posture he assumes, and how he moves and gestures. We are led to say again that in oral argument these factors " say " fully as much and " argue " just as effectively (or just as poorly) as the thoughts expressed in articulate language. Confident, easy movement, and erect, energetic posture are invaluable to the persuader.

Most difficulties in posture, movement, and gesture can be traced to two causes, either bad habits or disturbed muscular tonicity. The first of these causes is rather obvious. The student of argument should observe his own action habits in speech, and submit his presentation to the criticism of a competent teacher of speech. Once attention is directed to specific difficulties, the correction can be given conscious direction until new habits are formed. Generally speaking, there is no better way to secure muscular ease than through directed athletics, dancing, swimming, and other activities of a similar nature, which exercise and coördinate the muscles causing the trouble. Such exercise not only aids in correcting bad muscular habits through the regular habit forming mechanism, but it also builds up and strengthens the muscle tissue.

It should not be thought from the above statement that physical exercises of various kinds will cure or even help all difficulties in posture, movement, and gesture which arise in the speech situation. A much more subtle cause of difficulty is to be found in the state of *muscular tonicity* which obtains in the individual during speech. By muscular tonus we mean " a condition of tension which exists independently of voluntary innervation and greatly affects the readiness of a muscle to respond." [1] When the state of tonicity is low, a muscle is flabby and slow of response. When a state of excessive tonicity exists, the muscles so affected are rigid, jerky, and more or less uncontrollable. We find either one or the other of these extremes to be chronic conditions in many individuals. These are usually referred to as hypo-kinetic and hyper-kinetic types, respectively.

In addition to this difference in the state of muscular tonicity between individuals, we wish to point out further that this condition varies in any person with changes in emotional states. Since speech, public speech in particular, is for many a highly emotional activity, we can readily see the application to posture, movement, and gesture. Many people have difficulty with posture, movement, and gesture because they are frightened, embarrassed, or otherwise emotionally disturbed during speech.

[1] Howell, William H., *Textbook of Physiology*, p. 51.

Professor Walter B. Cannon has conducted a series of experiments which demonstrate rather conclusively that emotional states do evoke noticeable muscular reactions and tensions which evidence a condition of high tonicity. He attributes this condition mainly to an increased secretion of the adrenal glands in times of emotional stress. Dr. Cannon states,

> "The close relation between emotion and muscular action has long been perceived. Every one of the visceral changes which we have seen to be caused by the increased secretion of adrenalin, the cessation of processes in the alimentary canal; the shifting of blood from the abdominal organs to the organs immediately essential to muscular exertion; the increased vigor of the contraction of the heart; the discharge of extra blood corpuscles from the spleen; the deeper respiration; the dilation of the bronchioles; the quick abolition of the effects of muscular fatigue; the mobilizing of sugar in the circulation — these changes are directly serviceable in making the organism more effective in the violent display of muscular energy which fear or rage may involve." [1]

As we have said, presenting an argument orally, especially in public address, constitutes a situation which for many is often accompanied by nervousness and fear. This emotion stirs up all the energizing reactions described by Cannon in the above quotation, but instead of being serviceable as they might be in the case of many situations, the restraints imposed by the occasion cause this great increase in tonicity or "muscular readiness" to evidence itself in muscular rigidities, tense, jerky movements, and other characteristics of nervousness such as trembling hands and pounding knees. The most persistent question the teacher of speech meets is how to conquer such nervousness. The problem is particularly perplexing because the student can do very little by the

[1] Cannon, Walter B., *Bodily Changes in Pain, Hunger, Fear and Rage*, p. 225.

exercise of voluntary control. As Cannon puts it, " It is useless to try to check a racing heart, or to lower high blood pressure, or to renew the activities of an inhibited digestive system by a coldly reasoned demand for different behavior." [1]

The only solution to this problem lies in a careful *reconditioning* of those responses which are making effective action impossible. An audience is not a natural or inherited stimulus for emotional disturbances. This connection has simply been built up by a process of conditioning and it can be broken down only by a process of re-education or re-association. A series of exercises in oral argument, graduated as to difficulty in presentation, will help the student, if each exercise is so planned as to insure success with a reasonable amount of effort. In this way confidence will gradually be built up and with it will usually come physical ease and poise. There is no short cut to the attainment of effective posture, movement, and gesture in argument, but the achievement is certainly worth the effort to anyone who would become competent in the art of persuading others. In short, what we suggest is oral practice in the presence of audiences, class audiences, and otherwise.

C. Vocalization. — The third factor of importance in persuasive delivery is vocal expression. By vocal expression we do not here refer to the meanings of the word symbols which are used, but rather to the qualities of voice apart from these meanings. We shall discuss four characteristics of voice in this section ; force, pitch, time, and quality.

Audible speech is produced by a group of structures the most important of which are the lungs, the trachea, the larynx, the pharynx, the nose, the mouth, and the agencies of articulation, the soft palate, tongue, teeth, and lips. The air, forced out of the lungs in expiration, passes up through the trachea to the larynx. The cricoid or first cartilage of

[1] *Ibid.*, p. 264.

the larynx is in one sense the uppermost tracheal ring.   The vocal cords are a pair of muscular ledges on both sides of the larynx forming a straight slit through which the air passes. The vibration of these vocal cords starts a train of sound waves which pass through the pharyngeal, buccal, and in some cases the nasal cavities.   The relative size and shape of these cavities, the relative hardness or softness of the surfaces exposed, and the size of the openings between these cavities are important factors in determining the speech sounds which emerge at the mouth.   The pure vowels, the diphthongs, the transitionals, and the semivowels are produced in this manner.   Other sounds called the unvoiced consonants are produced without using the vocal cords at all. They are produced by passing the air through small openings or over sharp edges in the mouth.   There is a third class of speech sounds called the voiced consonants which are produced by a combination of the two processes just described.

1. Force. — Vocal force is determined largely by the force with which the air is expelled from the lungs.   In argument there seems to be a tendency to speak with much more force than is necessary or effective for the best results. When force is used discriminatingly, it is one of the speaker's best devices for emphasis.   When it is used constantly in excess of the demands of easy audibility, it becomes monotonous and disturbing.   Cultivate forceful utterance, but learn to control it as means of emphasis and stress.

2. Pitch. — It is well known that a large part of the meaning of speech is to be found in *intonation* and of the factors involved, pitch is probably the most important. Monopitch is bad in speech of any kind, but it is almost fatal in speech which is attempting to win conviction or stimulate activity.   Introspect your own speech habits in this regard, and check your findings against the opinions of others.   What pitch range do you use in speaking?   How much pitch varia-

tion do you have? It is advisable normally to pitch your voice in a middle key, thereby facilitating changes up and down the scale. Many argumentative speakers must also guard themselves against the excessive use of the high pitches which are apt to accompany uncontrolled enthusiasm or excessive force, causing a high, ranting voice.

3. TIME. — The time factor in speech involves the rate of speaking, the use of the pause, and rhythm. There is a marked tendency in argument to speak too rapidly. This difficulty when correlated with high pitch and excessive force, as it frequently is, greatly accentuates the unpleasant effect of the " ranting " quality already mentioned. There is no particular criterion to govern the rate of speaking in most cases other than the reception of the stimuli by the audience. Generally speaking, of course, an individual is safe in talking more rapidly on simple, familiar material than on material which is difficult and unfamiliar to the audience.

No speaker should overlook the opportunities for emphasis and added intelligibility presented by the use of the pause. There are emphatic pauses and there are grammatical pauses. Both lend poise, dignity, and maturity to speech, when effectively used, as well as adding to its understandability.

4. QUALITY. — Quality is a fourth characteristic of voice and is probably least understood by the average person. Physically, quality is explained by the complexity of the sound wave, or by the number, distribution, and relative intensities of the overtones in relation to the fundamental in a complex tone. Students who have difficulty in discerning what is meant by quality and quality changes will find it helpful to note the differences in the sounds produced by two musical instruments, the saxaphone and piano, for instance. Keep force, pitch, and time constant, and the difference which is readily observable is roughly what we mean by quality. Such qualitative differences are evident

in the voices of different persons, and in the voice of any single individual, especially as he experiences emotional changes. This last factor is particularly interesting to the speaker. Anger, sorrow, despair, enthusiasm, in fact, practically all emotional dispositions with dozens of fine shadings are evidenced in the quality of the voice. A persuasive speaker should be able to produce these fine emotional distinctions through qualitative changes.

It is an interesting, and incidentally a highly controversial, question as to whether the speaker must actually experience the emotion which would normally be causative of the vocal quality he is seeking to achieve, if he is going to produce this quality at all perfectly. Scripture says on this point, " Qualitative changes in the voice have powerful emotional effects on the hearer. These emotional changes in vocal action cannot be perfectly reproduced by the speaker voluntarily in the absence of the emotion. It is a familiar principle with orators and singers that to produce the full vocal effect they must first arouse the emotion itself and then allow it to find its natural expression." [1] We are inclined to believe that Scripture's suggestion is good advice for public speakers. We shall discuss the matter of emotional control further in Section IV of this chapter.

D. Rhythm and Melody. — Closely correlated with voice and muscular action in general are two other important stimulating factors which enter into the speech situation. These factors are rhythm and melody.

The term rhythm is commonly used to designate two somewhat different things of interest to the speaker. In one sense it refers to the regular, harmonious beat or cadence as in music or language, and in another meaning it is used to designate the regular recurrence or periodicity of certain fundamental bodily activities where a similar rhythm occurs.

[1] Scripture, E. W., *Elements of Experimental Phonetics*, p. 391.

Physiologists tell us that there are many such body rhythms. Some of the more important of these are the respiratory, cardiac, nutritional, and general metabolic rhythm. While the conclusions regarding most of the body rhythms are as yet undemonstrated in relation to speech, an hypothesis, highly significant to students of argument, is that the process of persuasion finds its explanation, at least in part, in the synchronous reactions or reflexes which are set up in the listener by the physiological rhythms of the speaker. If the persuader can control these fundamental bodily rhythms in his listeners; if he can emphatically induce a quickened respiratory and cardiac rhythm, for instance, it is certain that he can do much in this way to establish the attitudes and emotional dispositions of the audience.

By melody we mean the succession of speech notes or pitches as they occur in utterance. The chief difference between melody in song and melody in speech lies in the fact that the voice in singing proceeds by jumps from one note to another, while in speech it continually slides up and down. Because the pitch is always changing, it is difficult for the ear accurately to detect pitch changes in speech sounds. Perhaps, for this reason, the average person is not aware that we have definite melodies in speech. The term melody also has two rather distinct meanings as applied to speech. We have already spoken of the need of pitch variations in persuasive utterance. We reiterate that statement here because such variation is what most writers have in mind when they speak of melody. The second meaning of the term also has reference to a succession of pitch changes, but more particularly to those melodies which characterize certain classes of people, races of people, and personality types. Knowledge on this subject is decidedly fragmentary and conclusions are precarious. We simply report what seems to be a worthwhile observation. For example, people of downtrodden races, children who have been taught to be seen and not heard by over-strict parents, will many times have an apologetic melody in their voice which is unmistakable. Individuals who have chronically failed and are soured on men and their institutions also seem to have a characteristic speech melody. Likewise there are melodies of arrogance, of conceit and countless other qualities both pleasing and displeasing. That these characteristic melodies play a part in persuasion appears to be certain. They stir up definite reactions in the listener which may dispose him to pity, to distrust, to dislike, to confidence; at least, to some rather definite attitude toward the speaker. It goes without saying that the persuader needs to cultivate a melody which reflects friendly determination, confidence, and assurance, — one which will produce helpful reactions in his listeners.

IV. The Place of Emotion in Delivery

A. The Emotions as Important Conditioners of the Factors in Persuasive Delivery. — Having discussed the factors in persuasive delivery, it is now important to observe that the emotions of the speaker play a significant part in determining and conditioning these factors. Visible action, vocalization, rhythm and melody, and many of the external factors mentioned are affected very definitely by the emotional state of the individual. In fact, the average person if asked to describe an emotion would in all probability describe it in terms of these factors. All emotions manifest themselves to others through these media; *i.e.*, through characteristic facial expressions, muscular dispositions, vocal expressions, and peculiar rhythm and melody patterns. We may say also that the general effect of emotional reactions, in addition to producing these characteristic qualitative changes in the delivery factors, is to " tone them up " and intensify them.

As we have pointed out before, it is known that certain emotions are accompanied by (or perhaps consist of) the secretion of certain endocrine glands into the blood stream, particularly the adrenals. Adrenalin has a definite effect on muscular tissue, causing a general increase in tonicity. This increase in tonicity, in turn, directly affects posture, movement, gesture, and vocalization, all of which are, as we have seen, the direct products of muscular movement. It is known also that both rhythm and melody are affected in a very similar way.

B. Emotional Control. — Realizing the power of the emotions in conditioning and regulating these delivery factors, it follows that emotional control is highly desirable in the speaker if he hopes to be most effective in delivery. The individual who is apparently unable to feel very intensely regarding anything and constantly displays a cold, indifferent, unruffled front is not in our estimation exercising effective emotional control. Neither is the person who is unable to inhibit emotional excesses in his delivery exercising proper control. O'Neill and Weaver list as types of emotional behavior harmful to the speaker, feelings of inferiority, repression, and sentimentalism. Without discussing the " inferiority complex " which is more or less familiar to most people, we wish to say just a word about repression and sentimentalism.

"Repression is a type of emotional behavior in which the outward display of emotion is reduced to a minimum. . . . A feeling develops that emotional behavior is something of which we ought to be ashamed. We get the notion that the great men of the world are intellectual machines, and we desire to be hard, cold, and unemotional as we think they are. This in moderation is a virtue, of course, but carried to excess, it unfits a speaker for his work." [1]

[1] O'Neill and Weaver, *The Elements of Speech*, p. 54.

There is no type of speaking in which emotional repression is more disastrous than in argumentative speaking. Here the speaker has a cause to defend; he is trying to win the beliefs of people and direct their actions. Unless his voice and movement indicate enthusiasm, sincerity, and emotional earnestness for the cause he is arguing, it certainly cannot be hoped that his speech will arouse any very intense feeling for his cause among the members of his audience.

On the other hand there are those speakers who permit themselves to be completely carried away by their emotional reaction. At the present time on the debating teams at the University of Michigan there is a young man, unusually skillful as a debater, who must constantly be cautioned in this regard. In the heat of a debate his tendency is to feel so strongly regarding his cause as to lose the effective control of voice, gesture, and movement. The result in his case is a lot of ranting and dashing around the platform which actually harms rather than helps his cause. This individual has only recently learned to control his emotional responses. He still has strong emotional reactions as a speaker and it is to be hoped that he always will have, but these reactions now display themselves in a reserved, controlled, and yet intense voice and movement; and they occur at those points in his speech which demand such emotional reënforcement.

The problem in emotional behavior in the case of the young man we have just discussed, cannot be described as the "sentimentalism" to which O'Neill and Weaver refer, however. Sentimentalism is emotional excess of a quite different sort. It is the effusive, effervescent, artificial type of emotion which some people seem to like to affect. Such affectations are in no way persuasive, and, in fact, are disgusting to any intelligent audience.

O'Neill and Weaver also list three types of emotional behavior helpful to the speaker, confidence, sympathy, and differentiation. Discussing these very briefly we may say that *confidence* is that air of assurance and self-reliance about an individual which is bred by adequate preparation and properly controlled and regulated emotional activity. " Unless a speaker can somehow give those to whom he speaks an impression that he knows what he is about, that he is reasonably sure of his powers, and that he is comfortable, he has little chance of influencing the audience to do what he wants them to do." [1]

Sympathy is a readiness to notice, understand, and interpret the emotional responses of other people. It is the ability to adjust one's own behavior to the emotional disposition of others. Not only must the speaker be confident then, but he must be sensitive to the emotional attitude of his audience and capable of adjusting his own reactions to them.

A third quality to be sought in emotional behavior is *differentiation*. Monotony is just as deadly in emotional behavior as it is everywhere else. Professor Winans has designated monotony in this connection as " emotional drifting." He says, " By drifting is meant continuing in one mood regardless of the character of the ideas expressed. The effect is as incongruous and monotonous as that produced by a certain fiddler who played always on one string." [2]

We may say then that the individual whose emotional behavior displays confidence ; one who is able to sympathetically and tactfully adjust his emotional reactions to those of his audience ; and the individual who is capable of varying and differentiating his emotional reactions in speech, is the individual who is exerting the proper emotional control. A speaker cannot escape creating impressions with his emotional reactions even though he attempts to avoid such altogether. The nature of communication and delivery is

---

[1] O'Neill and Weaver, *The Elements of Speech*, p. 55.
[2] Winans, James A., *Public Speaking*, p. 107.

such that the very absence of emotional responses (repression) is bound to be distracting and monotonous; it is just as much an abuse as is emotional excess. Only as the arguer realizes that the problem is an inevitable one and takes steps to achieve the proper emotional control can he expect to deliver argument most effectively.

V. Summary

It has been the purpose of this chapter to explain the place of delivery as a factor in persuasion. Very little has been said about types of delivery and methods of delivery. This has been reserved for the next chapter. We consider it important that every person who hopes to control the thinking and acting of other people through speech, understand the important part that delivery plays in persuasion, and of what delivery really consists. To that end we have explained the fundamental nature of communication and analyzed the factors in persuasive delivery before attempting to discuss types and methods.

CHAPTER XV

DELIVERY: TYPES AND METHODS

In Chapter XIV we discussed delivery as a factor in persuasion. With an understanding of the fundamental nature of communication and the factors in persuasive delivery, we are now in a position to study types and methods of delivery. The broad distinction between our two chapters on delivery is to be found in the fact that in Chapter XIV we explained the nature of delivery and pointed out its contributions to persuasion; while in this chapter it is our intention to set forth ways and means of employing the various factors discussed in the preceding chapter.

I. Types of Delivery

There are four types of delivery which may be employed in argument: (1) Reading; (2) Memorizing; (3) Impromptu; and (4) Extemporaneous.

A. Reading. — It is always possible and in some cases advisable to compose an argument in writing and read it from the manuscript. In cases where it is imperative that the argument be absolutely accurate, there is some justification for reading. The advantage of the reading method, of course, lies in the fact that you can compose the language very carefully before delivery and be certain that you will reproduce it exactly in presentation. Business executives, presidents of institutions of various kinds, government officials, and other individuals whose every word is going to be carefully studied and weighed, in many cases deem it wise to read their speeches for this reason. However, it should be understood that for the average individual the occasion is indeed rare on which it is wise to read an argument to an audience. The reading method sacrifices too many of the factors of persuasive delivery to be most effective. It cramps movement and gesture; it often eliminates much of the forceful directness which may be obtained in other types of delivery; and it makes adjustments to meet the needs of the occasion extremely awkward, if not impossible. It should be said that effective debating is practically out of the question where the reading method is employed because it does preclude mutual adaptation and adjustment.

This much may be said in defense of reading, however; so many speeches that are delivered in this way are so miserably read as to bring the method into a general disrepute that is perhaps not altogether deserved. Oral reading demands careful study and practice if it is going to be effectively done. Know the material thoroughly; get it into convenient, readable form; pay particular attention to phrasing and grouping; and delineate exact shadings of meaning and feeling by changes in vocal quality, pitch, time, and force.

B. Memorizing. — Memoriter delivery differs from reading in that the manuscript is discarded and the written speech is reproduced orally from memory. This method has most of the disadvantages of reading. While there is an opportunity for a closer contact with the audience and a greater freedom in movement, there remains the difficulty of adjusting the argument to the occasion, and there is the added difficulty of recalling the language. In fact, the uncertainty of recall and the need for concentration on this point very frequently leads to an utter disregard of meaning and a monotonous rhythm, which so often characterizes memorized delivery. Like the reading method, memorizing is not effective in debating or in any other argument where both sides are represented. The need for refutation and interplay of argument on such occasions places one with a memorized delivery at a tremendous disadvantage. O'Neill, Laycock, and Scales say on this point:

"The most obvious defect of memorizing is the lack of adaptability to circumstances. We have already seen that a large element of debating power lies in the ability to appreciate and grapple with situations; but a speaker who has learned the sentences he is to deliver is powerless if anything unexpected arises, or if his written speech does not happen to fit the occasion. . . . Memorizing also prevents in a great degree, the necessary closeness of contact between speaker and audience. It demands a remarkable degree of elocutionary skill to infuse into committed passages the variety and the spontaneity of extempore speaking. The memoriter speaker all too easily becomes an actor, posing and soliloquizing — an attitude fatal to power in debate, for it destroys the leadership which we have seen is indispensable in the work of persuasion. Then, too, all the inspiration that should come from the reflex action of the audience is lost. The declaimer, instead of being stirred and directed by any manifestation of thought or emotion on the part of his hearers, is liable to be confused by such influences, and is constantly fearful of their appearance. Memorized debating is too likely to be an *exhibition*, not a *communication*." [1]

There are times when some speakers are better off with a memorized argument, but as in the case of reading we feel that these occasions are rare. The circumstances which may justify memorizing are those formal events in which the arguer is the speaker of the day, for example, and there is need for a polished oration with carefully chosen language and smooth flowing delivery. Most argument, however, simply does not lend itself to a set delivery whether it is to be read from the manuscript or from memory.

C. **Impromptu.** — Impromptu speaking is that type of speaking which proceeds without any previous preparation. It is the oral composition of language on the spur of the moment. Needless to say the great majority of the informal arguments as they occur in our homes, on the street corners, at business meetings, etc., are impromptu. Facility in impromptu argument is to be encouraged and sought after by every student of the subject. However, it should be kept in mind that the same test of adequacy which we apply to prepared argument should also be applied to impromptu argument. Impromptu argument must be organized, evidenced, carefully reasoned, and forcefully presented if it is to be effective. Nothing is feebler than the conceited, poorly informed, inexperienced arguer who is constantly bickering on every subject which comes up with apparent indifference as to the adequacy of his argument. Power in impromptu

[1] O'Neill, Laycock, and Scales, *Argumentation and Debate*, p. 432.

argument will come only through practice in prepared argument. " . . . it is undoubtedly true that many veteran speakers can debate a proposition with very brief preparation and from a very few notes; but such powers are begotten of long practice and self cultivation; for a beginner to make such men the models for his own early efforts is foolhardy, and always has unfortunate results. To make such a venture at the start, would be like attempting to learn to swim by jumping into mid-ocean at the first lesson; the well-nigh, certain result is to be lost in a flood of bad habits. From such beginnings are produced the rambling, incoherent, inconclusive speakers that are always inferior or mediocre in debate." [1]

D. Extemporaneous. — A rather careful distinction needs to be made between extemporaneous speaking and impromptu speaking. Whereas impromptu delivery is wholly unpremeditated, extemporaneous delivery involves a very careful and thorough preparation. It is true that the language is composed during delivery in extemporaneous speaking, but the evidence and argument is carefully assembled; and the speech is thoroughly planned and organized before presentation. This difference cannot be emphasized too much. Extemporaneous speaking is not off-hand, unprepared speaking; on the contrary, it demands a very careful and complete preparation.

The extempore delivery is undoubtedly best suited to the presentation of argument. It not only permits the investigation of the subject, the analysis of the proposition and the audience, the planning of the case, the selection of evidence and the form of support — all this before delivery; but it also enables the speaker to adjust his argument as he speaks. As a type of delivery it is flexible, direct, spontaneous, and conversational; or at least it is much more apt to embody

[1] *Ibid.*, p. 435.

these characteristics than any other form.   O'Neill, Laycock, and Scales summarize the advantages of the extempore method as follows:

"The advantages of this extempore method are many and great: (1) The first advantage — and first in order of importance — is the *power of adaptation* — the flexibility — which it gives to the speaker. The debater who depends for his language upon nothing but his ever present power of making up his words as he goes, can at any time omit any of his ideas or arguments that the circumstances make unnecessary; he can put into his proof anything that an unexpected turn of affairs requires; he can, if expedient, adopt a whole new line of demonstration. (2) Furthermore, the extemporizer *can fit himself to the mood of his audience;* if he sees they do not understand a point, he can stop to explain and enforce it upon them; if they seem personally hostile or inattentive, he can resort to persuasion to remedy the situation. At all times, he can hold his position as leader of the assembly both in thought and in feeling. He can reason with his audience. (3) Then, too, extemporizing carries with it *great physical advantages.* 'The voice of the speaker is deeper, stronger, and more flexible, and the effort required to produce it much less. The head being held erect, there is no constriction of the throat, the lungs are fully expanded, and the respiratory muscles are free to perform their functions.' (4) Again, the *inspiration of sympathy from the audience comes with its full power only to the extemporizer.* William Pitt truly said that 'eloquence is not in a man; it is in the assembly.' The response of hearer to speaker may disturb a declaimer, but it gives added strength to the extemporizer, helping him to mount to eloquence with a greater boldness and self confidence."[1]

II. How to Prepare for Extemporaneous Speaking

Since the extempore delivery is best suited to argument and the type which should be generally used and practiced by all students of the subject, we wish to suggest certain methods of preparation. The steps in preparation may be summarized as follows: (1) Assemble material; (2) Prepare

[1] O'Neill, Laycock, and Scales, *Argumentation and Debate*, p. 436.

a case outline; (3) Compose the argument in writing;
(4) Prepare speaker's notes; (5) Think the speech through;
(6) Practice orally. These steps will require some explanation and interpretation. In the first place it should be made
perfectly clear that all these steps need not be taken in the
preparation of every argument. The process we have outlined represents the most complete and thorough preparation
and is recommended for beginners with the extempore
method, and for those who cannot achieve fluency otherwise.
For many it is unnecessary to compose the speech in writing
and for others oral practice may not be essential. Ordinarily,
however, both writing and oral practice are valuable aids
to good extemporization.

The value of writing the speech out lies in the fact that
it compels the speaker to reduce his entire utterance to
effective language. This manuscript when carefully prepared may be read over several times and then laid aside.
It should not be used in practicing the speech nor in delivering
the speech. Nor should efforts be made to recall the exact
language of the composition during delivery. The fact that
it has been written out, however, will contribute greatly
to fluency in extemporization. Words will be at hand,
sentences can be phrased more readily, and the whole development will be familiar and more carefully planned and
hence more readily recalled. Cicero, speaking on the value
of writing as a preparation for speaking has the following to
say:

> "Writing is said to be the best and most excellent modeller
> and teacher of oratory, and not without reason; for if what is
> meditated and considered easily surpasses sudden and extempore
> speech, a constant and diligent habit of writing will surely be of
> more effect than meditation and consideration itself; since all
> the arguments relating to the subject on which we write, whether
> they are suggested by art, or by a certain power of genius and
> understanding, will present themselves and occur to us, while

we examine and contemplate it in the full light of our intellect;
and all the thoughts and words, which are the most expressive
of their kind, must of necessity come under and submit to the
keenest of our judgment while writing; and a fair arrangement
and collocation of words is effected by writing, in a certain
rhythm and measure, not poetical, but oratorical. Such are
the qualities which bring applause and admiration to good
orators; nor will any man ever attain them, unless after long
and great practice in writing, however resolutely he may have
exercised himself in extempore speeches; and he who speaks
after practice in writing brings this advantage with him, that
though he speak at the call of the moment, yet what he says
will bear a resemblance to something written; and if ever, when
he comes to speak, he brings something with him in writing, the
rest of his speech when he departs from what he has written,
will flow on in a similar strain." [1]

Some question the value of oral practice in preparation
for extemporaneous delivery on the grounds that it results
in memorized inflections and rhythms which impair effective
speech. Unquestionably there is this danger. Students who
practice speeches aloud, seated in a comfortable chair with
their feet on a table, and spouting very much like a cheap
phonograph, reproducing the chant of an auctioneer, can
expect only results that are bad. The set-up does not even
approach the real speech situation and detrimental effects
will almost surely follow. On the other hand, let a student
take an outline of the argument he prepares to deliver in
hand, stand up before an imaginary audience, and plead
his cause just as though the real occasion were at hand, and
he is almost certain to do a better job when the real test does
arrive. Cicero again has some helpful advice to offer on
this point:

"I like that method which you are accustomed to practice,
namely, to lay down a case similar to those which are brought on

[1] Cicero's *De Oratore*, J. B. Watson's Translation, Bohn Library, p. 180.
Thomas Bell & Sons, London, 1871.

in the Forum, and to speak upon it, as nearly as possible as if it were a real case. But in such efforts the generality of students exercise only their voice (and not even that skillfully) and try their strength of lungs, and volubility of tongue, and please themselves with a torrent of their own words; in which exercise what they have heard deceives them, that men by speaking succeed in becoming speakers. For it is truly also said, that men by speaking badly make sure of becoming bad speakers. In those exercises, therefore, although it be useful even frequently to speak on the sudden, yet it is more advantageous after taking time to consider, to speak with greater preparation and accuracy." [1]

There is frequently a question about the type of notes (if any) to use in speaking extemporaneously. We have suggested that the speaker prepare a careful, complete plan of the speech. Such a case outline is absolutely indispensable to extempore argument. Then we suggested further that the arguer prepare speaker's notes for use in delivery.[2] These notes should include a brief outline which will serve to recall the plan of the speech while speaking. They may be placed on convenient cards and taken to the platform for reference; or they may be memorized, thus enabling the speaker to deliver the argument as planned, without notes. The use of notes in a comprehensive argument is entirely justified so long as their use is not abused. A speaker's notes should be designed to recall *ideas* and not *words*. Difficulties in extemporization will inevitably arise if the speaker relies on notes to recall the exact language of a prepared speech. In fact, real extemporization ceases when such a plan is followed, and the speaker is really resorting to what might better be described as a poor memoriter delivery.

[1] *Ibid.*, p. 180.
[2] See Chapter XII, "Outlining Argument," Section III, C.

III. Personal Qualities Desirable in Delivery

Having discussed the types of delivery, we are now in a position to examine certain personal qualities desirable in delivery. We shall discuss four such qualities: (1) Sincerity; (2) Fairness; (3) Modesty; and (4) Friendliness.

A. Sincerity. — There is probably no single personal quality more persuasive in argument than sincerity or earnestness. If everything a speaker does or says indicates that he "means it," that he himself is interested and enthusiastic about the cause for which he is arguing, this interest and enthusiasm will almost invariably carry over to the audience.

A few years ago the writer was interested in a man who was preparing to represent his college in a state intercollegiate oratorical contest. He was a big, awkward fellow who didn't look like a very promising prospect. Furthermore, the oration he prepared was hardly of winning caliber. However, this man did have one winning quality, and that was his utter sincerity. On the night of the contest he was just as awkward as usual, and his clothes hung just as poorly as ever, but he did one thing in a way that no other contestant did — he had a real message to deliver and he presented it with such earnestness and enthusiasm that no one could doubt his convictions. In this respect he stood out head and shoulders above his more polished opponents who were uttering carefully prepared words, who were mechanically perfect, but who lacked the rugged power and force which only true sincerity can bring. This man won the contest because he delivered a message which was apparently vital to him. And it should be emphasized that this same quality which won this college oratorical contest has won countless arguments ranging from the most informal street corner discussion to those of the greatest consequence. Some have gone so far as to say, " Enthusiasm in an audience can be aroused only by enthusiasm in the speaker, and earnest conviction is begotten only by belief in the earnestness of him who persuades." The arguer must display a real interest in the cause he is arguing if he expects to stir up much enthusiasm for his cause in the audience.

B. Fairness. — Next to sincerity the personal quality most to be desired in an argumentative speaker is fairness. Every persuader should be enthusiastic for his own proposition, but that enthusiasm should never lead him to say or do anything which will appear to be unfair either to an opponent or to an opposing position. Always state your opponent's position fairly; recognize the strong points in his argument; quote him correctly, and answer what he really said. If an advocate of the other side is not present, be equally careful to recognize the strength of opposing positions, and be entirely fair in every reference to them.

Sarcasm and ridicule (unless very, very tactfully employed) are usually non-persuasive in argument, because they appeal to the average person as being unfair. All too frequently they are used to screen an inability to meet an argument by other methods. Many debaters, for example, resort to sarcasm when they are otherwise unable to refute the argument of an opponent. Nothing is more demoralizing to an arguer and his cause than to have his sarcastic remarks met by a carefully reasoned rejoinder, fairly and forcefully presented, restating and reaffirming the argument under discussion, thereby exposing the weakness of the attack and at the same time bringing into contrast one man's sarcastic attitude and the fair, reasonable attitude of his opponent.

C. Modesty. — Modesty is a third personal quality desirable in argument. People dislike conceit in any one, and most audiences are not only intelligent enough to recognize any evidence of it almost at once, but they are just illogical enough to close their minds to the conceited speaker.

I say they are just illogical enough, because the attitude of the speaker has nothing whatever to do with the probative force of the argument, but it has everything to do with its persuasive power. The conceited speaker simply is not effective in argument. Delivery must display modesty and reserve if it is to be persuasive.

Akin to conceit is affectation. While it is not good advice to all persons to be *natural* in delivering a speech, it is a rather helpful suggestion to most people. Evidence of affectation whether in manner or voice is usually non-persuasive in argument.

D. Friendliness. — Friendliness is a fourth personal quality which is helpful in argument. A speaker should not attempt to fight his audience or his opponent. An argument should not be a fight; it should not even be a battle of words, unless it is possible to have such a thing as a friendly battle. Ill-temper not only stirs up a reaction against the speaker among his listeners, but it seriously impairs his own effectiveness. It should not be thought that we are condemning the arguer who "warms up" to his cause. It is one thing to be sincere, earnest, and enthusiastic; and it is quite another thing to be ill-tempered and pugnacious. The casual, indifferent speaker is just as weak as is the ill-tempered, antagonistic speaker, but it is possible to achieve the greatest sincerity in argument and still remain even-tempered and friendly.

As in the case of meeting sarcasm by a show of utter fairness, there is no better attitude to assume in the face of a hostile or bitter opponent than one of friendliness. It carries the audience and disconcerts an opponent more than would any show of anger on the speaker's part.

In summary of this section on desirable personal qualities in delivery, we wish to urge every student of argument to put forth his best efforts to cultivate these qualities. No one whose personality is weak in these respects can expect to be at his best in argument. You can reason well, evidence your case with facts and opinions which are beyond reproach; in fact, you can do everything that a thorough student of the subject is capable of doing, and yet fail miserably with the average audience, if you are indifferent in delivery, unfair in your attitude, conceited or affected in presentation, or ill-tempered and antagonistic toward the other people involved.

IV. THE CONVERSATIONAL BASIS OF DELIVERY

Aside from the four personal qualities which we have just commended to the arguer, there is one additional quality which should characterize good delivery. That quality is directness, or communicativeness. Directness means talking straight to the audience, but it means much more than that, too. By directness or communicativeness we have reference to that contact between speaker and audience such as exists in everyday conversation. There should be a mutual interchange of reactions in public address just as there is in good conversation. To be sure, the audience will not respond in so many words, but a trained speaker will be sensitive to every detectable reaction in his audience and constantly alert to adjust his presentation to these reactions. It is just as nonsensical and just as fatal to ignore the reactions of the audience in public speaking as it would be to ignore the replies of a friend in conversation In delivering an argument the speaker should be able to lead his audience along with him; he should be able to realize when he has done enough with one point and when another argument needs additional support; he should be able to note signs of restlessness and fatigue and inattention in his audience, and be competent to meet the situation; he should be able to tell when arguments are hitting the mark and when they are not. In conversation the listener can ask for more, question, and contribute as the argument progresses; but in public speech the speaker can be sure that the audience is following the argument only as he develops the ability to converse without these definite and compelling responses which exist in conversation. It is really remarkable how totally oblivious of the reactions of an audience some speakers can be. They simply *talk at*, or deliver themselves before an audience, rather than *talking with* or really communicating with their listeners. These speakers who fail to sense their audiences almost invariably develop habits of speech which are characterized by artificial inflections and monotonous rhythms. They rant at their listeners rather than converse and reason with them.

It is good advice for the student of argument to urge that he make every effort simply to talk with his audience. To be sure, this conversing style of delivery should be animated and forceful, nor does the conversational basis of public speech imply anything else. Far be it from us to discourage force and power in delivery; there are many situations which demand it. The chief implication of the concept we are discussing is the importance for public speech of a lively sense of communication, and the natural inflections and intonations resulting, all of which are characteristic of good conversation.

V. PLATFORM DECORUM IN DELIVERY

A. Taking the Platform. — The first problem in platform decorum, and one which many beginning speakers meet very poorly, is taking the platform. The initial impressions of a speaker are formed as he takes the platform and faces the audience preparatory to beginning his remarks. Every effort should be made to make this first impression a good one. Many beginners rush to the platform, while others saunter up with an air of complete indifference. Either of these approaches is, of course, poor. The speaker should take the platform confidently and deliberately, face the audience quietly for a moment, and then begin speaking. If the chairman is to be addressed, this should be done just as the speaker arises from his seat (if he is on the platform) at the time of introduction. The audience and any other special groups or individuals should be addressed after stepping to the front of the platform.

Another mistake frequently made is that of beginning the argument before it should properly be begun ; nervousness, and perhaps in some cases eagerness to get it over with, prompt some speakers to start speaking before they have reached the rostrum, and before they have paused to face the audience. Such a hurried beginning is not only indicative of uneasiness, but it gives the speaker a bad start which is apt to bother him throughout the speech.

B. Posture, Movement, and Gesture. — Having taken the platform, the next problems are how to stand and how to move about. If there is a speaker's stand of some kind, it is generally advisable to take a position slightly behind and a little to one side of this stand. In this way any notes can be placed on the table within convenient reach of one hand and at the same time the body and the other hand are free of the stand and ready for action. The speaker should take a comfortable, yet erect, dignified posture, with his weight on the balls of his feet, and equally divided between the feet. It will be found convenient as a general rule to stand with one foot just slightly ahead of the other. This position not only enables one to make effective changes in posture by shifting the weight, but it is the most convenient position from which to move. A little practice will demonstrate these advantages.

The head, the face, the arms, and the hands are the agents of gesture. Movements of these agents must be spontaneous, coördinated, and reserved if they are to constitute effective gesture. For the beginner in argument the problem is usually one of breaking down inhibitions which check all movement. As soon as this is done there usually follows a stage of excessive gestures of the embryonic type — little nudges and hand movements which are never completely executed. And finally there comes a time, if the speaker keeps at it, when smooth, coördinated gestures, indicative of power and reserve, can be made without conscious direction and the awkwardness which conscious attention to gesture almost invariably brings.

Needless to say, these visible speech symbols play an important part in oral argument and when used in moderation, can be made to contribute greatly to its persuasive power.

C. Mannerisms. — One other point which we should like to discuss in connection with platform decorum is mannerisms. Almost every speaker at some time or other in his career has cultivated some little habit such as turning a ring on his finger, playing with a watch chain, or jingling money or keys in his pocket. Such habits as these are known as mannerisms; they may become both distracting and annoying to an audience and should be guarded against.

It is a problem for many speakers to know what to do with their hands while speaking in public. The best thing that can be done is to let them hang easily at one's side when not engaged in gesture or handling notes. The very worst thing that can be done is constantly to toy with some article, or one's wearing apparel, or otherwise call attention to these unruly members.

VI. Voice in Delivery

Voice as a factor in delivery has been pretty well discussed in the preceding chapter. (See Section III, C.) There we pointed out the mechanism of voice production and articulation very briefly, and discussed vocal force, pitch, quality, and the time factor in vocalization. Needless to say, the control of these factors to insure ready intelligibility and the maximum meaning content in speech is unquestionably one of the most important problems of the speaker.

Enunciation and pronunciation are other problems which must be given attention in this connection. Enunciation is largely a matter of consonants. Whereas vowels are open, unstopped sounds formed by shaping the vocal tube differently, consonants are formed by stoppages and constricted apertures at various points above the vocal folds. Unless these occlusions are complete in the stopped consonants (voiced: b, d, j, g; unvoiced: p, t, ch, k) the resulting sound is muffled and distinguished with difficulty. These sounds should be enunciated in such a way as to make them clean-cut and staccato. The fricative consonants (voiced: v, z, th, "then," zh, "azure"; unvoiced: f, s, th, "thin," sh) are also apt to cause trouble. In fact, Fletcher points out " that for intensities commonly used in conversation the sounds v, f, and th (thin) count for more than half of the mistakes in the recognition of the fundamental speech sounds . . . and the sound z which is readily recognized at normal intensity becomes very difficult at weak intensity." [1] Since the typical intensity values of these sounds are among the lowest of all the fundamental speech sounds, the difficulty of distinguishing them and the need for care in production are evident. Fletcher makes the very interesting observation that the

[1] Fletcher, Harvey, *Speech and Hearing*, p. 276. D. Van Nostrand Company, 1929.

most powerful sound ɔ : (awl) is 680 times as intense or loud as the faintest sound th (thin), which is one of the fricative consonants about which we have been speaking.[1] The weaker sounds will be the first to be misunderstood since the ear fails to hear their essential characteristics first. Perhaps we should add that the vowels and semi-vowels are as a whole considerably louder than the consonants.[2]

It is a good rule in pronunciation to conform as nearly as possible to that of the cultured class in the community or section in which you live. While this rule applies to sectional accents such as eastern, southern, midwestern, etc., it should be understood that correct pronunciation, as indicated by Webster's International Dictionary and other acceptable authorities, should be followed. Most certainly, slovenly pronunciation, characterized by pronouncing the final " ng " as "en" and other such crudities should be avoided. Professor Russell points out the tendency of Americans to substitute the vowel ə (the or idea) for any of our other vowels (except i "ee") when they occur in unaccented syllables. In fact, because of this substitution ə is far and away the most frequent English vowel. The operation of this phonetic law is as inevitable as it is interesting for several reasons which we shall not go into here.[3] The tendency to prolong this sound, however, and the further tendency to vocalize on this vowel between words, gives the impression of a constant refrain of ə (the or idea) to one's speech. This is a very common habit which can and should be corrected.

VII. Transitions and Delivery

The problem of making effective transitions from one point in argument to another is just as much a matter of delivery

[1] Fletcher, Harvey, *Speech and Hearing*, p. 72.   [2] *Ibid.*, p. 74.
[3] Russell, G. Oscar, *Speech and Voice*, p. 126. The Macmillan Company, 1931.

as it is of composition.   As we mentioned in Chapter XIII, The Composition of the Case, transitions are not only very important in argumentative speaking, but they seem to be just about as hard to achieve as they are significant.   An audience simply must be given to know when a speaker is leaving one thought and taking up another.   Rhetorical devices useful in effecting transitions, as we have already seen, are the partition, summary, and transitional sentences. The speaker can do fully as much, however, by pauses, vocal changes, and movement in transitions.   Every arguer should be accomplished and versatile in the use of these various methods of leading his listeners from one step in his case to another.

VIII. EFFECTING CLIMAXES THROUGH DELIVERY

We wish to call attention to the need for climax in argument; here again fully as much can be accomplished by delivery as by the rhetorical devices set forth in Chapter XIII. Vocal force, pitch, quality, and timing, coördinated with proper posture, movement, and gesture can achieve climaxes ranging from the strong emotional appeals of great oratorical arguments to the emphasis of a climactic sentence in a given paragraph of any argumentative speech.   Generally speaking, every sentence, every paragraph, every section of the speech, as well as the argument as a whole, should have its climax.   We simply wish to call attention to the possibilities of delivery as a means of achieving these climaxes.

CHAPTER XVI

REFUTATION

I. The Nature of Refutation

A. Refutation Defined. — All of argument may be classified broadly as being either constructive or refutatory. Constructive argument consists of arguments which are advanced
to build up or support a case for or against the proposition,
independent of opposing positions. Refutation, on the other
hand, consists of the destruction of opposing arguments.
" With regard to any given proposition, there are always two
contrary beliefs that a person may hold : he may believe that
the proposition is true or that it is not true. Consequently,
if we can induce him to reject the opposite of what we uphold,
we are thereby preparing him to accept our own views. Refutatory argument pure and simple is rarely, if ever, sufficient ; for belief is always essentially positive in nature, so
that to destroy without building up will not usually serve our
purpose. Refutation, therefore, is properly auxiliary and
supplementary to positive argument." [1]

B. Refutation and Rebuttal Distinguished. — The terms
refutation and rebuttal are frequently used synonymously ;
they are not quite that, however. Whereas refutation consists of the destruction of opposing arguments and nothing
more, rebuttal consists of the destruction of opposing arguments plus efforts to defend, or reëstablish a given constructive position. " Rebuttal is like refutation in that both aim
to destroy rival arguments ; but rebuttal is both an offensive
and a defensive practice. Rebuttal not only sweeps away
opposition but furnishes further substantiation for one's own
constructive argument." [2]

C. The Place of Refutation in Argument. — We shall consider the place of refutation in argument from the standpoint

[1] O'Neill, Laycock, and Scales, *Argumentation and Debate*, p. 345. The
Macmillan Company, 1917.

[2] Baird, A. Craig, *Public Discussion and Debate*, p. 254. Ginn and Company, 1928.

of those arguments in which both sides are represented and those arguments in which only one side is represented.

1. IN ARGUMENTS WHERE BOTH SIDES ARE REPRESENTED. — Refutation and rebuttal are most significant as might well be imagined in arguments where both sides are represented, such as debates, public discussion, and informal argumentative controversies. Here there is constant need to refute opposing arguments and to adjust one's own case to the developing position of an opponent. In any argument, debate or otherwise, it is ridiculous to project constructive arguments if the very foundations upon which they must rest have been undermined by the destructive work of an opponent. These basic contentions must be reëstablished before constructive argument can be carried forward. When opposing argument is being hurled at one's constructive position, weakening certain points and destroying others, it is essential that the more damaging of these arguments, at least, be met before construction is continued. To do anything else is almost surely to result in defeat.

We wish especially to emphasize this interrelation of constructive and refutatory argument in those arguments where both sides are represented. Ways and means of presenting refutation in connection with constructive argument are discussed in connection with debating in Chapter XVIII. It might be well to read Section VI of that chapter in this connection.

2. IN ARGUMENTS WHERE ONLY ONE SIDE IS REPRESENTED. — Even in arguments where only one side is represented, such as argumentative orations, lectures, and most written arguments, there is need for some refutation. To be sure it does not play the important part that it does in those cases where the advocate of the other side is present, but it does enter in nevertheless. This is especially true where the audience is hostile or undecided. As we have seen in an

earlier chapter, the causes of this hostility or indecision must be removed before much constructive progress can be made. Ordinarily, this can best be accomplished by a refutation of the argument upon which the objection is based. Such refutation should be worked into the argument where it naturally arises, with special care being exercised not to confuse one's organization by so doing.

D. The Forms of Support in Refutation. — We have developed three kinds of argument or three methods of supporting propositions in argument, Confirmation, Explanation, and Motivation. We wish now to say that whether the argument is constructive or destructive, the same types of reasoning may be employed. In other words, an opposing argument may be attacked by proving that it is not true through a confirmatory refutation; by explaining the data connected with the argument in such a way as to imply its falsity; or by causing the audience to desire its rejection. The only difference between constructive and refutatory argument in this respect is that one employs these forms to support or build a case for or against the proposition, while the other employs the same forms to destroy opposing argument.

II. Openings for Refutation

There are three important openings for attacking opposing argument and every arguer should be alert to detect them. They are: (1) Mere assertion; (2) Unreliable evidence; and (3) Weak argument or reasoning. While these openings are undoubtedly clear from previous explanations, we wish to say just a word or two about them here. Every proposition in argument, whether it be the main resolution, or some point in the case, must be supported by *evidence* and *reasoning*. Argument consists of *reasoning* from *evidence* to conclusions. In Confirmation this reasoning is either inductive or deductive; in Explanation the inferences are those of implication; and in Motivation, they vary with the nature of the association which is attempted between the desire of the audience and the proposition under discussion. In any case, however, since every conclusion must be supported by evidence and reasoning, isn't it clear that any refutation of a conclusion must constitute: (1) An attack of the evidence which has been adduced in support of the conclusion, or (2) An attack of the reasoning which has been undertaken to sustain the conclusion, or (3) A demonstration that the conclusion is nothing more than an unsupported assertion, which is equivalent to saying, of course, that no evidence or reasoning has been advanced.

III. General Methods of Refutation

In general, an opposing argument may be refuted in three ways: (1) By showing the argument to be irrelevant; (2) By admitting the argument and justifying this admission; or (3) By attacking the argument directly. In case a direct attack seems advisable, the arguer should then consider the openings discussed in the preceding section. As we have pointed out, mere assertion, unreliable evidence, or weak reasoning constitute the openings for such an attack.

Any one of the methods, demonstrations of irrelevancy, admissions, or direct attacks, will dispose of an opposing argument adequately if properly executed. There are times, of course, when one or more of these methods cannot be executed properly in the refutation of an argument. For example, it is clear that in many cases an opposing argument may be both relevant and vital to the case. In such instances a direct attack is the only method of refutation open to the arguer. In other instances an opposing argument may be entirely relevant, unusually sound, and yet one that can be admitted without destroying one's constructive position.

Again one may be confronted with a sound argument which it would be embarrassing to either admit or deny. If this contention can be shown to be irrelevant to the discussion and beside the real point at issue, the argument may be disposed of in that way without necessitating a stand either for or against the point involved.

By arguing hypothetically it is possible to first show an opposing argument to be irrelevant; second, to admit the argument, and show how this admission does not damage one's case; and third, to attack the soundness of the argument, assuming for the sake of the discussion that it is relevant and vital. This method of refutation, while logically unnecessary, and sometimes confusing unless skillfully handled, is devastating in its thoroughness and completeness.

IV. Special Suggestions for the Refutation of Confirmation

In general, a proposition supported by Confirmation may be refuted by attacking the evidence or reasoning set forth in its behalf, or by demonstrations of irrelevancy and admissions. In giving some special suggestions for refuting Confirmation, it will be necessary to deal only with the direct attack, because it is only here that there are any significant variations.

A. The Importance of the Reliability of Evidence. — Since the persuasive power of Confirmation lies primarily in its probative force, an attack of the evidence upon which such argument rests is striking at its very roots. Destroy the evidence and the whole case falls. The adequacy of opposing evidence should, therefore, be submitted to all the tests discussed in Chapter VII, especially those of logical adequacy, and every weakness should be exposed.

B. Testing Induction and Deduction. — Opposing arguments employing support by Confirmation should be care-

314 THE WORKING PRINCIPLES OF ARGUMENT

fully scrutinized to determine the exact confirmatory type that is being attempted. If inductions are being drawn, the tests of generalization and analogy discussed in Chapter VIII should be applied, and any weaknesses in the argument pointed out; if deduction is being used, the tests of antecedent probability and sign should be invoked as they apply. Furthermore, the deductive inferences will appear either as enthymemes or syllogisms. In either case, a searching test of the soundness of the reasoning can be obtained by stating the argument in syllogistic form and applying the appropriate syllogistic rules. Not infrequently, the subtle errors in reasoning which are revealed by this process, may be pointed out with telling effect.

C. The Exposition of Logical Fallacies. — A fallacy may be defined as any defect in proof that destroys its validity. We shall discuss fallacies in connection with Confirmation just briefly, — "in connection with Confirmation," because, of the three forms of support, its effectiveness depends most upon its probative force, and "just briefly," because most of the fallacies are simply violations of the rules already discussed in connection with induction and deduction in Chapters VIII and IX.

1. A CLASSIFICATION OF FALLACIES. — The following list of fallacies can be studied profitably. The *Fallacies of Confirmation* and the *Fallacies of the Syllogism* should be studied in connection with Chapters VIII and IX. We would suggest a review of those chapters at this point.

> I. Fallacies of Confirmation.
>> *A.* Fallacies of Generalization.
>>> 1. Insufficient number of instances.
>>> 2. Instances not typical.
>>> 3. Negative Instances.
>>> 4. Relationship of causation or classification faulty.
>> *B.* Fallacies of Analogy.
>>> 5. Compared cases differ in essential respects.

      6. Negative instances.

      7. Analogy is single (not cumulative).

  C. Fallacies of Antecedent Probability : Cause to Effect.

      8. Cause-effect connection incomplete.

      9. Preventing cause has operated.

      10. Part cause.

      11. Known cause inadequate.

  D. Fallacies of Antecedent Probability : Substance to Attribute.

      12. Substance wrongly identified.

      13. Attributes not inherent in substance.

  E. Fallacies of Sign : Effect to Cause.

      14. Alleged cause inadequate.

      15. Effect uncertain sign of cause.

      16. Effect-cause connection incomplete.

  F. Fallacies of Sign : Attribute to Substance.

      17. Attribute wrongly identified.

      18. Attribute uncertain sign of substance.

II. Fallacies of the Syllogism.

  A. Fallacies of the Categorical Syllogism.

      19. Four terms.

      20. Undistributed middle.

      21. Illicit major or minor.

      22. Negative premises.

  B. Fallacies of the Disjunctive Syllogism.

      23. Incomplete disjunction.

      24. Members of disjunction overlapping.

  C. Fallacies of the Hypothetical Syllogism.

      25. Denying the antecedent.

      26. Affirming the consequent.

III. Special Fallacies.

  A. Fallacies of Begging the Question.

      27. Non-evident premise.

      28. Argument in a circle.

  B. Fallacies of Argument beside the Point.

      29. Discussion of personalities.

      30. Appeal to passion or prejudice.

      31. Appeal to tradition and custom.

      32. An appeal to ignorance.

  C. Fallacies of Equivocation.
    33. Equivocation in quantity (composition and division).
    34. Equivocation in quality.
  D. Fallacies of *Non-sequitur*.
    35. *Post hoc ergo propter hoc*.
    36. Simple *non-sequitur*.

 2. A Discussion of Certain Special Fallacies. — We wish at this point to discuss the group of fallacies we have labeled " special fallacies " in the above classification. This group contains those fallacies of interest to the student of argument which cannot readily be classified otherwise. These special fallacies or material fallacies as they are sometimes called have been variously classified by writers in this field, but it has seemed best here to distinguish four types, begging the question, ignoring the question, equivocation, and non-sequitur.

 a. Fallacies of Begging the Question. — Fallacies of begging the question consist in assuming the truth of some proposition which is the same as, or equivalent to, the conclusion to be proved, and thence inferring the truth of the conclusion. The most common forms are : (1) Non-evident premise, and (2) Arguing in a circle.

 Non-evident premise is the fallacy of assuming as true a premise requiring proof when that proof is not given. Every premise in argument requiring proof is at the same time a conclusion. It is a *conclusion* of the particular evidence and reasoning adduced in its support, and a *premise* in that it is used as a basis for drawing a further conclusion. Thus, if any premise requiring proof is set forth as an unsupported assertion, it is a case of assuming the truth of a proposition which is the same as the conclusion, and therefore an instance of begging the question.

 Arguing in a circle is a question begging fallacy " which

consists in taking two propositions and using them each in turn to prove the other — as in trying to prove that a train is on time because it agrees with your watch, and then proving that your watch is correct because it agrees with the train." [1]

b. *Fallacies of Argument beside the Point.* — Fallacies of argument beside the point, or ignoring the question as they are sometimes called, consist in mistaking the conclusion to be proved, or endeavoring to prove something which has no important bearing on the point at issue. There are four common fallacies of this type: (1) Discussion of personalities; (2) Appeal to passion or prejudice; (3) Appeal to tradition and custom; and (4) An appeal to ignorance.

It is frequently a practice in argument, especially where both sides are represented, to attack the sincerity, honesty, or some other personal trait of an opponent, concluding therefrom that his argument is not sound. The fallacy of discussing personalities in this way, of course, lies in the assumption that a conclusion based on what may be perfectly good evidence and reasoning, is unsound because the person pronouncing the conclusion has certain undesirable personal characteristics.

Another instance of ignoring the question is argument which attempts to sustain a conclusion by arousing the passion or prejudices of an audience in its favor. It usually occurs where the arguer is either unable or too lazy mentally to go through the more laborious process of proving his point. It must be admitted that this fallacy is in many respects quite similar to support by Motivation, wherein the desires of the audience are stirred up and associated with the proposition. This observation should not be especially disturbing, however, because we have pointed out repeatedly that Motivation seldom has probative force. In other words, an argu-

[1] O'Neill, Laycock, and Scales, *Argumentation and Debate*, p. 190. The Macmillan Company, 1916.

ment that is logically fallacious may at times be quite persuasive.

Another rather subtle fallacy which also bears some resemblance to Motivation is an appeal to tradition and custom. It is the fallacy of ignoring the real point at issue, and arguing that we should not think or do what the proposition suggests because it has never been thought or done before, or that we should accept the proposition because it represents the customary and traditional viewpoint. The fallacy, of course, lies in the assumption that a conclusion is right or wrong irrespective of the evidence and reasoning advanced simply because it either does or does not represent common practice and custom. It may be persuasive at times to make such an appeal, but it is none the less fallacious, logically considered.

The last fallacy in this group is an appeal to ignorance or argument to the effect that a proposition is true because it cannot be disproved, or false because it cannot be proved. The fallacy lies in the assumption that ignorance concerning a matter has anything to do with its truth or falsity.

c. Fallacies of Equivocation. — Fallacies of equivocation are caused by the equivocal or ambiguous use of terms. These fallacies are of two kinds: (1) Those of quantity; and (2) Those of quality.

Equivocation in quantity usually consists in using a term *collectively* in the minor premise of an argument and *distributively* in the major premise, or using it *distributively* in the minor premise and *collectively* in the major premise. The two fallacies resulting therefrom are commonly known as *composition* and *division* respectively. These two fallacies may be illustrated as follows:

> All the angles of a triangle are less than two right angles.
> A, B, and C are all the angles of a triangle.
> Therefore: A, B, and C are less than two right angles.

In this example of the fallacy of composition, the middle term, *the angles of a triangle*, is used in the major premise to mean that *each* angle is less than two right angles, or in other words, it is used distributively. The same term is then used collectively in the minor premise to mean *all* the angles taken together. " This same fallacy is committed when we argue that what is true of the various states in the union is true of the United States as a nation, or what is true of members of a class or of the college, taken as individuals, is true of the class as a class or of the college as an institution." [1]

An example of the fallacy of division follows:

All the angles of a triangle are equal to two right angles.
A is an angle of a triangle.
Therefore: *A* is equal to two right angles.

Here the term, *angles of a triangle*, is used collectively in the major premise to mean that *all* the angles taken together are equal to two right angles, while in the minor premise it is used distributively to mean *each* angle.

Equivocation in quality consists in using a term to denote certain attributes in one premise and to denote different attributes in another premise in the same argument or in the conclusion of the argument. For example, it is common to equivocate in this way on the term *state*. The word *state* is often used to refer to certain political units of a country, as the states of the United States. It is also used to mean the sovereign power of the government without regard to any political unit. To use the term in both senses in the same argument as though but one term were being used, results in the fallacy. It is really a species of the fallacy of *four terms* discussed in connection with the categorical syllogism. It is a very subtle case of four terms, however, because the language of the argument reveals only three terms, and the

---

[1] O'Neill, Laycock, and Scales, *Argumentation and Debate*, p. 183.

fourth term can be discovered only by a careful inquiry into the meanings or attributes assigned to the term causing the equivocation. To use the same term with two different meanings is the equivalent of using two terms.

d. Fallacies of Non-sequitur. — Non-sequitur, meaning " it does not follow," consists simply in asserting a conclusion that does not follow from the premises, because the conclusion has in it new matter that is not covered by the premises.

The most common form of this fallacy is known as *post hoc ergo propter hoc,* or " *after this, therefore on account of this.*" The fallacy consists in assuming that because one occurrence precedes another in time, the one is the cause of the other. To be sure, causes precede effects, but it does not follow that because one event precedes another that there is necessarily any causal relation between the two. O'Neill, Laycock, and Scales give the following illustrations of this fallacy :

"Many of the common superstitions of ancient and modern times illustrate this fallacy. For instance, thirteen people sit at table together, and within a few months one of the number is accidentally drowned; immediately someone argues that the death is the effect of the thirteen sitting at meat together."

"Again, it has been argued that, because the number of crimes perpetrated by negroes in the Southern States has increased since educational opportunities were first offered to the negro, therefore the growth of crime is directly due to the growth of education. It certainly is not sufficient for the arguer to base his contention simply on the fact that the one thing has followed the other, and few thoughtful men will be inclined to accept the conclusion thus drawn. Until something more is done to show a definite causal connection, we may safely call this a post hoc fallacy."

"The most common form of this fallacy, perhaps, is that used by the political arguer. It runs something like this : 'Such and such a political party came into power at such a time, and for a number of years thereafter the country suffered from financial depression ; therefore the policies and administration of this political party are the cause of the unfortunate state of affairs.'

Now, the statement may or may not be true, but the argument in the above form certainly contains a fallacy. To show that this fallacy does exist, and that the conclusion is not worthy of acceptance, it is necessary only to point out the fact that any one of a half dozen other causes might, at least as readily, have produced the same result." [1]

Simple *non-sequitur*, the last fallacy in our list, arises when the conclusion covers new matter with no attempt made to show a cause and effect connection. " Jones is a good husband and father, so he ought to be elected mayor." " All men are rational. Socrates is a man. Therefore Socrates is noble." This fallacy is much more apparent than *post hoc ergo propter hoc* and therefore not as difficult to expose.

D. Meeting Confirmation by Explanation or Motivation. — Our suggestions for refuting Confirmation up to this point have more or less assumed that constructive Confirmation should be attacked by refutatory Confirmation. Under most circumstances this is probably advisable, but it is true nevertheless that explanatory argument and argument designed to motivate can also be used to refute Confirmation. Such refutation in the case of Explanation would be a matter of correcting, rearranging, and adding to the data presented by one's opponent, and then presenting it with a new emphasis and color in the form of an implicative system designed to imply the desired conclusion. In the case of Motivation, it would be a matter of enlisting the desire of the listener in the cause in such a way as to make him desire to believe or act in opposition to the point being refuted. The point to be emphasized here is that these forms of support are employed in refutation just as they are in construction. The proposition for support in refutation is simply a denial of the conclusion this refutation is designed to meet, and as such, it can be supported by any one of the forms we have studied.

[1] O'Neill, Laycock, and Scales, *Argumentation and Debate*, pp. 194–195.

V. Special Suggestions for the Refutation of Explanation

A. The Reliability of Evidence Again Important. — As in the case of Confirmation, evidence plays an important part in Explanation. It is, of course, the presentation of evidence and its collocation in an impelling description, narration, or exposition, upon which Explanation relies for the implication of the proposition. If the evidence can be shown to be logically inadequate or otherwise rendered unacceptable, it is very likely that the desired implication will not result. Sometimes an Explanation can be effectively refuted by supplying additional evidence which has either inadvertently or designedly been omitted. Of course, in so doing the arguer offering the additional information must be certain that it will not fit into the system he is trying to refute and thereby corroborate and strengthen the opposing argument rather than weaken it.

B. Applying the Rules Governing the Implicative System. — A second attack which can be directed against an explanatory argument is to counter with a reëxplanation, painting a different picture, relating another narrative, or setting forth a new exposition. This refutation in many cases can employ the same evidence that has been presented in support of the point being refuted, and simply set it forth in new relationships, or in a new *system*. More often, however, this method is combined with an effort to correct opposing evidence and to submit additional evidence as discussed in the preceding section.

In preparing a reëxplanation, the arguer must first know the weaknesses of the system which has been presented to support the point being refuted. These weaknesses can best be detected by reducing the opposing argument to a " This or Nothing " disjunction, and applying the rules applicable thereto. If it is found that the disjunction is not *all inclusive*, present an explanation which will imply some alternative proposition rather than the one sought by the opposition; if it is discovered that the " This " and the " Nothing " are not *mutually exclusive*, prepare a refutatory explanation which will bring to light and emphasize the objections causing this discrepancy; and finally, if it is found that the opposition to the proposition or the " This " is such that the audience is disposed to accept the " Nothing " in preference to the opposing proposition, explain the situation in such a way as to encourage this acceptance. In other words, we are stating here as we stated in Chapter X that the implicative system in order to be effective in argument must confront the audience with a " This or Nothing " disjunction, and furthermore that the members of this disjunction must be all inclusive, mutually exclusive, and be so presented as to insure the choice of the " This " rather than the " Nothing." The disjunction, and hence the argument, may be successfully refuted by breaking it down in respect to any one of the rules we have discussed in this connection.

C. **Meeting Explanation by Confirmation or Motivation.** — An explanatory argument may also be refuted by either Confirmation or Motivation. Let us say for example that an opponent has presented a very attractive explanation which has scored heavily with the audience, and you feel that the implication is entirely unjustified by the actual facts, that the conclusion is basically false. It might be worthwhile in such case, especially if the audience is open-minded on the subject and fairly intellectual in its reactions, to attempt to state the confirmatory inferences which the audience logically must make in order to imply the conclusion you are trying to refute. Having done this, expose the weaknesses and fallacies in these inferences by applying the appropriate confirmatory rules. It is a matter of bringing to light and

submitting to careful scrutiny inferences which would otherwise merely be implied.

As in the case of Confirmation, it is frequently possible in
refuting Explanation to destroy, or at least nullify as far as
practical results are concerned, the carefully reasoned conclusion of an opponent by causing the audience to desire to
oppose this conclusion, through a rebuttal employing support
by Motivation.

VI. SPECIAL SUGGESTIONS FOR THE REFUTATION OF MOTIVATION

A. The Reliability of Evidence Less Important. — In
refuting Motivation the exposure of a weakness in evidence
is ordinarily much less effective than in the other forms of
support, because the mind convinced by its own wish, or the
individual acting because of strong desire, is not disposed
to examine evidence very critically. Any discrepancies in
evidence will usually be rationalized quite glibly or else
simply ignored and " pooh-poohed."

B. Destroying or Diverting Desire. — Much more effective as a means of attacking Motivation is an argument designed to destroy, or what is probably more expedient, to
divert desire. Generally speaking, this can be accomplished
in one of three ways: (1) The obstacle, apparent or real,
which is causing the desire may be removed or greatly minimized; (2) The association between the desire and the proposition may be broken down by showing that acceptance of
the proposition will not satisfactorily meet the desire; or
(3) Another desire, counter to the one associated with the
proposition being refuted, and based on stronger, more impelling motives, may be substituted. This last process has
been referred to in previous chapters as re-motivation.

C. Meeting Motivation by Confirmation or Explanation.
— As in the case of refuting Motivation by exposing weak-

nesses in evidence, it is frequently difficult to attack a position which has been fortified with strong motives, by an argument whose only claim to persuasive power lies in its logical
adequacy.   However, either Confirmatory or Explanatory
argument, if designed specifically to attack the logical justification of the desire which has been incited, or designed to
point out the practical difficulties in the way of satisfying
this desire through the proposition being refuted, may in
some cases, refute Motivation quite as satisfactorily as an
attempt to meet it by refutatory Motivation.

VII. SPECIAL RHETORICAL DEVICES USEFUL IN REFUTATION

Earlier in the chapter we discussed three general methods
of refutation, demonstrations of irrelevancy, admissions,
and direct attacks.   We have taken considerable time to discuss the direct attack in relation to the three forms of support,
Confirmation, Explanation, and Motivation.   We purpose
now to discuss four special methods of refutation : (1) Reductio ad absurdum; (2) The dilemma; (3) The method of
residues; and (4) Turning the tables.[1]

A. Reductio ad Absurdum. — One of the most commonly
used methods of refutation is that of reducing an argument
to an absurdity, or, as it is named, the *reductio ad absurdum*.
The refuter adopts for the moment the line of argument of
his opponent; then, by carrying it out to its logical conclusion, shows that it results in an absurdity.   For example,
" When a lawyer asserted in court that a corporation can
make no oral contract because it has no tongue, the judge
exposed the fallacy by saying, simply, ' Then, according to
your own argument, a corporation could not make a written
contract because it has no hand.' "[2]

[1] The discussion of these devices is reprinted from O'Neill, Laycock,
and Scales, *Argumentation and Debate*, pp. 356–365.

[2] Foster, W. T., *Argumentation and Debating*, p. 177.   Houghton Mifflin
Company, 1908.

Cicero uses this method in the following:

"Nor, if Publius Crassus was both an orator and a lawyer, is the knowledge of the civil law for that reason included in the power of speaking. For if any man, who, while excelling in any art or science, has acquired another, shall hold that his additional knowledge is a part of that in which he previously excelled, we may, by such a mode of argument, pretend that to play well at tennis is a part of the knowledge of civil law, because Publius Mucius was skilled in both." [1]

Macaulay makes striking use of this device:

"Many politicians of our time are in the habit of laying it down as a self-evident proposition, that no people ought to be free till they are fit to use their freedom. The maxim is worthy of the fool in the old story, who resolved not to go into the water until he had learned to swim. If men are to wait for liberty until they become wise and good in slavery, they may indeed wait forever." [2]

This method is effective because of its simplicity and directness; it also has in it an element of ridicule that is persuasive against an opponent. William Ellery Channing, in a reply to Henry Clay on the slavery question, used this method as follows:

"But this property, we are told, is not to be questioned on account of its long duration. 'Two hundred years of legislation have sanctioned and *sanctified* negro slaves as property.' Nothing but respect for the speaker could repress criticism on this unhappy phraseology. We will trust it escaped him without thought. But to confine ourselves to the argument from duration; how obvious the reply! Is injustice changed into justice by the practice of ages? Is my victim made a righteous prey because I have bowed him to the earth till he cannot rise? For more than two hundred years heretics were burned, and not by mobs, not by Lynch law, but by the decrees of councils, at the instigation of theologians, and with the sanction of the laws and religions of nations; and was this a reason for keeping up the fires, that

[1] Quoted by Foster, *Argumentation and Debating*, p. 177.
[2] Quoted by Foster, *ibid.*, p. 178.

they had burned two hundred years? In the Eastern world, successive despots, not for two hundred years, but for twice two thousand, have claimed the right of life and death over millions, and, with no law but their own will, have beheaded, bowstrung, starved, tortured unhappy men without number who have incurred their wrath; and does the lapse of so many centuries sanctify murder and ferocious power?"

Again:

"But the great argument remains. It is said that this property must not be questioned, because it is established by law. 'That *is* property which the law declares *to be* property.'[1] Thus human law is made supreme, decisive, in a question of morals. Thus the idea of an eternal, immutable justice is set at naught. Thus the great rule of human life is made to be the ordinance of interested men. But there *is* a higher tribunal, a throne of equal justice, immovable by the conspiracy of all human legislatures. 'That is property which the law declares to be property.' Then the laws have only to declare you, or me, or Mr. Clay, to be property, and we become chattels and are bound to bear the yoke! Does not even man's moral nature repel this doctrine too intuitively to leave time or need for argument?"[2]

B. The Dilemma is one of the oldest of all known rhetorical forms. As a method of refutation, it consists in reducing an issue to an alternative, and then showing that both members of the alternative are untenable. These two members are called the "horns of the dilemma." The refuter says in substance: "Now, with respect to this point at issue, there are two and only two possibilities, viz., A and B. But A is not true, and B is not true; consequently your contention fails." In order to make the dilemma conclusive, obviously two things are necessary: (1) The horns of the dilemma must include all the possibilities in the case, i.e., *the alternative must be exact.* (2) *Both members of the alternative must be destroyed.* James Wilson, speaking in the convention for the province

[1] The italics are by Mr. Clay.
[2] *The Works of William E. Channing, D.D.*, Vol. V, pp. 48–49.

of Pennsylvania, in vindication of the colonies, January, 1775, used the dilemma as follows:

"In the first place, then, I say that the persons who allege that those employed to alter the charter and constitution of Massachusetts Bay act by virtue of a commission from his majesty for that purpose, speak improperly, and contrary to the truth of the case. I say they do not act by virtue of such commission; I say it is impossible they can act by virtue of such a commission. What is called a commission either contains particular directions for the purpose mentioned, or it contains no such particular directions. In either case can those, who act for that purpose, act by virtue of a commission? In one case, what is called a commission is void; it has no legal existence; it can communicate no authority. In the other case, it extends not to the purpose mentioned. The latter point is too plain to be insisted on: I (will) prove the former." [1]

Jeremiah S. Black, in defense of the right of trial by jury, thus attacked the contention of his opponents, which was that the law of nations was binding in the trial of the cause in question:

"Our friends on the other side are quite conscious that when they deny the binding obligation of the Constitution they must put some other system of law in its place. Their brief gives us notice that, while the Constitution, and the acts of Congress, and *Magna Charta*, and the common law, and all the rules of natural justice shall remain under foot, they will try American citizens according to *the law of nations!* But the law of nations takes no notice of the subject. If that system did contain a special provision that a government might hang one of its own citizens without a judge or jury, it would still be competent for the American people to say, as they have said, that no such thing should ever be done here. That is my answer to the law of nations." [2]

1. MORE THAN TWO HORNS. — Sometimes the possibilities with respect to the point in issue cannot be reduced to two.

---

[1] *Eloquence of the United States*, Vol. V, p. 56.   E. and H. Clark.
[2] *Great Speeches by Great Lawyers*, p. 507.

There may be a choice offered of any one of three or more possible conditions, or courses of action. In such a case, to state the issue in the form of a dilemma, presenting a single alternative, would not be an exact disjunction, and so would be fallacious; to be truthful it is always necessary to state *all* the possibilities of choice, whatever their number. When more than two possibilities are to be considered, the method is, properly speaking, not a dilemma; but the *modus operandi* is similar. Webster, in his argument in the case of the Providence Railroad Co. *vs.* City of Boston, made a division into three possibilities. Mr. Webster is here contending against the proposition that a certain street or piece of land is a public highway:

"If this street, or land, or whatever it may be, has become and now is a public highway, it must have become so in one of three ways, and to these points I particularly call your honors' attention.

"1st. It must either have become a highway by having been regularly laid out according to usage and law; or

"2d. By *dedication* as such by those having the power to dedicate it, and acceptance and adoption so far as they are required; or

"3d. As a highway by long user, without the existence of proof of any original laying out, or dedication.

"It is not pretended by any one that the land in question is a highway, upon the last of these grounds. I shall therefore confine myself to the consideration of the other two questions; namely, 'Was there ever a formal and regular laying out of a street here? or was there ever a regular and sufficient dedication and acceptance?' " [1]

2. IF THE DISJUNCTION OF THE DILEMMA IS FAULTY an opening is left for an opponent which may result in great discomfiture to the author of the defective dilemma.

" Thus Lincoln, in his speech on the Dred Scott Decision,

[1] *Works of Daniel Webster*, Vol. VI, p. 186.

refused to accept either of the horns of the dilemma presented by Douglas.   Lincoln said of Douglas :

"He finds the Republicans insisting that the Declaration of Independence includes all men, black as well as white, and forthwith he boldly denies that it includes negroes at all, and proceeds to argue gravely that all who contend it does, do so only because they want to vote, to eat, and sleep, and marry with negroes. He will have it that they cannot be consistent else. Now I protest against the counterfeit logic which concludes that because I do not want a black woman for a slave, I must necessarily want her for a wife. I need not have her for either. I can just leave her alone." [1]

C. The Method of Residues, like that of the dilemma, is founded upon a division of the point in question into parts. The difference is that in the dilemma all the parts are destroyed, whereas, in the method of residues, one of the parts is left standing. By the method of residues, the matter in dispute is divided into two or more sections, which include all the possibilities in the case ; then all but one of these are demolished, the one left standing being the aspect of the issue which the refuter wishes to establish.   " There are," says the refuter, " three possibilities, A, B, and C.   But A and B are false, consequently the presumption is that C is true."   This method is not, strictly speaking, a method of refuting.   It is rather a method of using refutation : the ultimate purpose of the speaker or writer is not destructive, but constructive ; he destroys some of the parts into which he divides the question, in order that he may establish the remaining part.   He uses refutation to accomplish his end ; but the end itself is constructive proof.

1. DIVISION MUST BE EXHAUSTIVE. — *The first requisite in using the method of residues is, that the division of the whole into parts shall be exhaustive.*   The strength of the method depends entirely upon the assumption that all the possibilities

[1] Foster, *Argumentation and Debating*, pp. 182–183.

in the case are destroyed save one. If, then, the disputant omits, in his division, to mention one of the possibilities, he has proved nothing, for it still remains uncertain which possibility is true, — the one he seeks to establish or the one he failed to mention. Again, in order to make the work complete, it is necessary that the residuary part be enforced by positive demonstration. The refuting of all but one of the possibilities leaves a presumption that the remaining possibility is true; but there may well be a suspicion that even this last part too is false, or that there is some fallacy in the division. Consequently, to be at all convincing the residuary part must be enforced by positive proof.

An excellent example of the use of the method of residues is that found in Thomas H. Huxley's Lectures on Evolution, delivered in New York in 1876. Professor Huxley was here endeavoring to establish the theory of evolution, as the true theory respecting past history of the universe. In his first lecture he divided the question into three possible hypotheses as follows:

"So far as I know, there are only three hypotheses which ever have been entertained, or which well can be entertained, respecting the past history of Nature. I will, in the first place, state the hypotheses, and then I will consider what evidence bearing upon them is in our possession, and by what light of criticism that evidence is to be interpreted.

"Upon the first hypothesis, the assumption is, that phenomena of Nature similar to those exhibited by the present world have always existed; in other words, that the universe has existed from all eternity in what may be broadly termed its present condition.

"The second hypothesis is, that the present state of things has had only a limited duration; and that, at some period in the past, a condition of the world, essentially similar to that which we now know, came into existence, without any precedent condition from which it could have naturally proceeded. The assumption that successive states of Nature have arisen, each without any relation of natural causation to an antecedent state, is a mere modification of this second hypothesis.

"The third hypothesis also assumes that the present state of things has had but a limited duration; but it supposes that this state has been evolved by a natural process from an antecedent state, and that from another, and so on; and, on this hypothesis, the attempt to assign any limit to the series of past changes is, usually, given up." [1]

He then proceeded, in his series of lectures, to overthrow the first two hypotheses, leaving the third — the theory of evolution — standing as the residuary part, and finally he supported this theory by positive proof of its probability.

Burke, in his speech on *Conciliation with America*,[2] used the method of residues. He began:

"Sir, if I were capable of engaging you to an equal attention, I would state, that as far as I am capable of discerning, there are but three ways of proceeding relative to this stubborn spirit which prevails in your Colonies, and disturbs your government. These are: — to change that spirit, as inconvenient, by removing the causes; to prosecute it as criminal; or, to comply with it as necessary. I would not be guilty of an imperfect enumeration; I can think of but these three. Another has indeed been started, that of giving up the Colonies; but it met so slight a reception that I do not think myself obliged to dwell a great while upon it. It is nothing but a little sally of anger, like the forwardness of peevish children, who, when they cannot get all they would have, are resolved to take nothing."

He then considered the first two ways at length and proved them impracticable, and concluded:

"If then the removal of the causes of this spirit of American liberty be, for the greater part, or rather entirely impracticable; if the ideas of criminal process be inapplicable, or if applicable are in the highest degree inexpedient, what way yet remains? No way is open, but the third and last, to comply with the

[1] *Popular Science Monthly*, Vol. X, p. 44.
[2] Cook's edition, pp. 30–31.

American spirit as necessary; or, if you please, to submit to it as a necessary evil." [1]

D. " **Turning the Tables** " is simply showing that something presented by your opponent really supports your case and not his. It is " stealing his thunder." To turn the argument of an opponent against him is not often possible. But circumstances sometimes give the opportunity. A piece of testimony may be used by a writer, when he has not fully considered all the interpretations that may be put upon it. It not infrequently happens that evidence, or an argument, is introduced to give support to some particular point, and, in its bearing on that phase of the question, the evidence may be favorable to the speaker or writer who introduces it; but as the discussion proceeds, it may turn out that, with respect to some other phase of the question, the evidence or the argument may be interpreted in another way, adversely to its inventor. The effect of such an unexpected turn of affairs is obvious; the opponent is " hoist with his own petard." The very manner of introducing the proof adds to its effectiveness. Webster, in the Girard Will Case, used this method in attacking one of the proofs of the defendants:

"The arguments of my learned friend, may it please your honors, in relation to the Jewish laws as tolerated by the statutes, go to maintain my very proposition; that is, that no school for the instruction of youth in any system which is in any way derogatory to the Christian religion, or for the teaching of doctrines that are in any way contrary to the Christian religion is, or ever was, regarded as a charity by the courts. It is true that the statutes of Toleration regarded a devise for the maintenance of poor Jewish children, to give them food and raiment and lodging, as a charity. But a devise for the teaching of the Jewish religion to poor children, that should come into the Court of Chancery, would not be regarded as a charity, or entitled to any peculiar privileges from the court." [2]

[1] *Ibid.*, pp. 38–39.
[2] *The Works of Daniel Webster*, Vol. VI, p. 166.

Lincoln " turned the tables " admirably in his speech at Cooper Union in February, 1860.

"Some of you delight to flaunt in our faces the warning against sectional parties given by Washington in his *Farewell Address*. Less than eight years before Washington gave that warning he had, as President of the United States, approved and signed an act of Congress enforcing the prohibition of slavery in the North-western Territory, which act embodied the policy of the government, upon that subject, up to and at the very moment he penned that warning; and about one year after he penned it, he wrote Lafayette that he considered that prohibition a wise measure, expressing in the same connection his hope that we should at some time have a confederacy of free states.

"Bearing this in mind and seeing that sectionalism has since arisen upon this same subject, is that warning a weapon in your hands against us or in our hands against you? Could Washington himself speak, would he cast the blame of that sectionalism upon us who sustain his policy, or upon you who repudiate it? We respect that warning of Washington and we commend it to you, together with his example pointing to the right application of it." [1]

[1] Quoted by Foster, *Argumentation and Debating*, p. 189.

CHAPTER XVII

THE FIELDS OF ARGUMENT

It is the purpose of this chapter to discuss the fields of argument and consider some of the more important specializations in these fields.

I. WRITTEN ARGUMENT

All argument can be divided very broadly into written and oral argument. Written argument is an extensive field in itself, including many of the articles and editorials appearing in newspapers, magazines, and other periodical literature. Not a few books are predominantly argumentative, as are many scholarly papers and theses. The same is true of both business and personal letters. Then there is the whole field of advertising and sales literature of all descriptions. We have pointed out in earlier chapters that much of oral argument is preceded by written composition, and this too must be included here.

Written argument is indeed an important field in our study, but important as it is, the working principles applicable in the composition of written argument do not differ in any fundamental way from those applying in oral argument, except that in oral argument we have delivery as an additional consideration. Of course a news story has its own particular form, as does a letter or an advertisement, and most other written argument. While these forms require special investigation and study, the principles of argument are essentially the same no matter where they are applied, and it is with these principles that we are concerned.

We have said that written argument is best composed in oral style and we wish to repeat that statement in this connection. Whether an argument is to be presented in writing or delivered orally, it should be composed in such a way as to lend itself readily to vocalization.

II. Oral Argument

Oral argument is to be differentiated from written argument primarily on the basis of its mode of communication. We have discussed the persuasive factors in the speaker-reactor relationship which do not obtain in the writer-reactor relationship. We now wish to consider the four important fields in oral argument, conversation, public address, public discussion, and debate.

A. Conversation. — Perhaps the most important field of oral argument, from the standpoint of quantity at least, is argumentative conversation. The study and application of the principles set forth in this book should enable one to engage in both formal and informal conversation in a more persuasive and a generally more acceptable manner than he would otherwise be able to do.

B. Public Address. — It is very difficult to distinguish carefully between conversation and public speaking, because as Professor Winans puts it, ". . . there is practically nothing true of public speaking that may not be true at times of conversation, or nothing true of conversation that may not be true of public speaking." [1] O'Neill and Weaver state on this point:

"Good public speaking is, therefore, as close to private speaking as the circumstances under which it is given will permit. But often the circumstances under which one is speaking make it necessary that the variation from private conversation be considerable. It is impossible to speak to twelve thousand people adequately and use the same voice, the same language, or the same action, which would be adequate in presenting the same material to one or two people in private conversation. In public speaking, therefore, vocalization, language, and action vary as much as demanded by the exigencies of the occasion on which we are speaking. We should not change them for the sake of changing them. A safe rule to follow is to have one's speaking on every occasion as close in every way to one's best conversation as circumstances will allow. There seem to be no qualities which belong to either private speaking or public speaking exclusively." [2]

Training in argument is invaluable to anyone who would be effective in public address, not only because much of public speaking is argumentative in nature, but because all speaking can profit at times by an intelligent application of certain of the working principles of argument.

C. Public Discussion. — Perhaps the best way to define what we mean by public discussion is to distinguish between it and debate. Whereas debate is a more or less formal argument on a set proposition and the affirmative and negative

[1] Winans, James A., *Public Speaking*, p. 24. The Century Company, 1924.

[2] O'Neill, J. M., and Weaver, A. T., *The Elements of Speech*, p. 346. Longmans, Green and Company, 1926.

sides are definitely represented by advocates who argue the question before a group of listeners, public discussion is the type of argument which takes place in the committee room, around the conference table, in deliberative assemblies, and in gatherings of all kinds where a chairman presides and parliamentary procedure or at least some semblance of it is observed.   In public discussion all present are privileged to participate in the discussion of the subject under consideration, and the object of the discussion is to *arrive at* a proposition which seems to represent the consensus of opinion.   It is less formal than a debate, the arguments are less definitely pro and con, and the discussion aims to end in the formulation of a proposition rather than *beginning with* a definite resolution as is the case in debate.   It perhaps should be pointed out also that public discussion may be either expository or argumentative.   In expository discussion the members of the group are reporting, explaining, expounding, telling what the situation is in regard to some subject being discussed.   In argumentative discussion the members of the group are making decisions, passing motions, going on record in favor of or against certain resolutions, and deciding to do or not to do various things.   The object of argumentative discussion is always a judgment or a proposition representing the opinion of the group.   It is this type of public discussion with which we are concerned.

In large discussion groups of any type it is imperative that parliamentary rules be invoked and rigidly enforced if much progress is going to be made.   Even in smaller groups such as committees of three or four persons it is highly desirable to observe certain parliamentary rules.   The field of public discussion is such an important one for the student of argument, and is tied up so intimately with parliamentary procedure, that it is strongly recommended that students of the subject secure some handbook of parliamentary law and make a careful study of the rules of procedure.[1] It is impossible for a speaker, no matter how effective he may be in argument, to make his argument count most effectively in public discussion, unless he knows the rules governing such discussion. We are including here some of the more important parliamentary considerations, but these can be very profitably supplemented as we have suggested.

"*Parliamentary law* consists of a system of common rules and practices for the government of deliberative assemblies. To this same body of rules and practices the name *rules of order* is often applied. The rules included are the ones that are employed in assemblies generally. In individual assemblies there are often special rules which arise as motions and which are not embodied in the *constitution* or *by-laws* of an organization. These special rules are known as *standing rules*. The record of standing rules is found in the written minutes of the organization; the rules of order are usually those contained in some manual of parliamentary law; while the constitution and by-laws are usually the written instruments of an organization."

"In so far as there is an ultimate authority for parliamentary law, it will be found in the practices common to deliberative assemblies generally. General usage is the ultimate authority, and this usage has been the slow evolution of centuries. It has been added to now and then by legal-minded philosophers, and 'infiltrated with the common sense of the many,' so that while even yet it is not a perfect system, it is well adapted to the needs of ordinary deliberative assemblies."

"Parliamentary law may vary in the details of its rules, but underlying it all there are found four invariable foundation principles or corner stones, upon which every portion of the superstructure rests. They are (1) justice and courtesy to all, (2) one thing at a time, (3) the rule of the majority, (4) the rights of the minority." [2]

The following table of motions represent those used in most deliberative assemblies:

[1] See *Handbook of Parliamentary Law*, by F. M. Gregg. Ginn and Company, 1910.   [2] *Ibid.*, pp. 51–52.

TABLE OF PARLIAMENTARY MOTIONS

MOTIONS	NEED A SECOND?	AMEND-ABLE?	DEBAT-ABLE?	VOTE RE-QUIRED	MAY INTER-RUPT A SPEAKER
I. Principal Motion					
1. Any main question or any independent matter of business before the meeting	yes	yes	yes	maj.	no
II. Subsidiary Motions					
2. To amend	yes	yes	yes	maj.	no
3. To postpone indefinitely	yes	no	yes	maj.	no
4. To refer to a committee	yes	yes	yes	maj.	no
5. To postpone to a certain time	yes	yes	yes	maj.	no
6. Previous question	yes	no	no	$\frac{2}{3}$	no
7. To lay on (or take from) the table	yes	no	no	maj.	no
III. Incidental Motions					
8. To suspend a rule	yes	no	no	$\frac{2}{3}$	no
9. To withdraw a motion	yes	no	no	maj.	no
10. Question of consideration	no	no	no	$\frac{2}{3}$	yes
11. A point of order	no	no	no	Chair [a]	yes
12. Appeal from decision of chair	yes	no	no	maj.	yes
IV. Privileged Motions					
13. To make a matter of business a "special order" for a given time.	no	no	no	$\frac{2}{3}$	yes
14. Questions of rights and privileges	no	no	no	Chair [a]	yes
15. To adjourn (unqualified)	yes	no	no	maj.	no
16. To fix time for next meeting.	yes	yes	no	maj.	no

[a] Require only decision of Chair; no vote unless appealed.

The sixteen motions listed in this table are divided into four groups and are arranged in the order of their precedence from the weakest to the strongest. Principal motions are characterized by the fact that they are never in order when there is any other question or business before the assembly. Subsidiary motions are applied to other motions for the purpose of modifying, or disposing of them, or of cutting off debate on them. It is important to note that these subsidiary motions are so arranged in the table that each one takes precedence over those preceding it in the list and yields to those following it. Incidental motions are motions that arise out of other motions and come up in an incidental way. The order in which these five appear is not significant, as these motions rarely come in contact with each other. Privileged motions arise independently of other motions and concern themselves with the needs and rights of the assembly, and therefore are of the very highest rank. They take precedence over all other motions, if made following them, though they yield to certain incidental motions arising out of them, and in some cases to subsidiary motions applied to them.[1]

Every motion we have listed has a definite purpose and is designed to meet a rather specific situation. To facilitate the use of the chart we have submitted, therefore, we are listing these same motions below with their object or objects.[2]

Objects of Motions

1. Main motion — to bring original business before the assembly.
2. To amend — to modify a question that is before the assembly.
3. To postpone indefinitely — (1) to dispose of a question for the session without voting on it directly; (2) it is

[1] Quoted with some changes from Gregg, *Handbook of Parliamentary Law*, pp. 71–72.   [2] Taken from Gregg.

used by the opponents of a question to determine their strength.

4. To refer to a committee — to secure the advantage of action by a smaller group, or of greater freedom in debate in dealing with a question.

5. To postpone to a certain time — to defer action on a question to a certain time.

6. Previous question — to suppress debate and bring the assembly to a vote.

7. To lay on the table — (1) to postpone a subject so that it may be taken up at another time during the same session; (2) to stop debate and suppress a question for the session, providing a majority cannot be secured to take the question again from the table.

8. To suspend a rule — to make temporarily possible an action contrary to the standing rules or rules of order of an organization.

9. To withdraw a motion — to expedite business in case of a changed opinion by the maker of the motion.

10. Question of Consideration — an objection to the consideration of a question to enable the assembly to avoid irrelevant, unprofitable, or contentious questions.

11. A point of order — to correct a breach of order or an error in procedure.

12. Appeal from decision of chair — (1) to invoke a rule which the chairman has ignored or misinterpreted; (2) to appeal to the assembly to overrule the chairman on any rule where an opinion or a judgment may be exercised.

13. Special order — to set a specific time to consider a certain matter of business when all other things will be set aside.

14. Questions of rights and privileges — to secure to the assembly or any of its members some right with respect to safety, comfort, dignity, reputation, or freedom from disturbance.

15. To adjourn — to bring a meeting to a close.

16. To fix a time for the next meeting — to fix a time or place for reassembling.

D. Debate. — A debate may be defined as " a joint argument on a given proposition between two opposing sides, one of which, the affirmative, affirms the proposition, and the other of which, the negative, denies it." [1] The reader is referred to Chapter XVIII for a discussion of debate.

III. Some Fields of Specialization in Argument

There are certain more or less well defined fields of specialization in argument. They are legislative argument, campaign argument, judicial argument, and sales argument. It is interesting to observe that legislative argument usually appears as public discussion; campaign argument, as public address; judicial argument, as debate; and sales argument, as conversation. A brief discussion of these fields will be helpful.

A. Legislative Argument. — " Legislative speeches are speeches that are delivered to definitely organized legislative bodies, such as the United States Senate or House of Representatives, the State legislature, a city council, a college faculty meeting, the board of directors of a corporation, or a college class, meeting for the purpose of transacting business. In fact, legislative speeches are those given in any meeting in which those present have membership standing, in which only certain people are privileged to participate, or which is operated under the rules of parliamentary procedure. Such bodies are really legislatures, and speeches delivered to such meetings for the purpose of getting action in regard to what should or should not be done, are legislative speeches." [2]

It can be seen that legislative argument from its very nature is typically a form of public discussion. It is commonly practiced under strict parliamentary procedure. Practice in public discussion under parliamentary rules, therefore, affords excellent training in legislative argument.

B. Campaign Argument. — " The campaign speech differs from the legislative speech in that it is given to a general

---

[1] O'Neill and Weaver, *The Elements of Speech*, p. 392.
[2] *Ibid.*, p. 447.

audience rather than to the members of a formal organization. The general audience listening to the campaign speech are not subject to rules and regulations of parliamentary procedure; nor do they enjoy personal privileges of one kind or another, such as are to be found in legislative assemblies. Of course, legislative speeches and campaign speeches are much alike. It is even possible for a man to deliver the same speech in the United States Senate and before a general meeting of citizens, and yet even so the situation is not precisely the same. In the Senate the speaker has certain privileges and immunities which he does not have before the general audience. In the Senate also he may be subject to interruptions, questions of privilege from other members, decisions of the house in regard to the order of business which will interfere with his speech. In the campaign speech he is without parliamentary restrictions and privileges.

" By *campaign* is not meant, of course, merely political campaign. The following all call for campaign speaking: propaganda speeches before general audiences in favor of prohibition enforcement or the repeal of the eighteenth amendment; the raising of funds for any cause; the promotion of a movement to secure a new national reservation; tuberculosis prevention; and, in fact, any speech outside a definitely organized assembly, the purpose of which is to influence the belief or action of a general audience in regard to future policies." [1]

It can be seen that the nature of campaign argument is such that it is generally presented in the form of a public address.

C. Judicial Argument. — By judicial argument we have reference primarily to courtroom argument, the presentation of the cases and the pleas in legal trials. In addition to this, however, judicial argument includes the written opinions of

[1] O'Neill and Weaver, *The Elements of Speech*, p. 448.

judges which are usually defended by a statement of a predominately argumentative nature. Counsels are frequently called upon to present similar opinions to their clients. Perhaps the most interesting observation for the student of argument, however, is the fact that a courtroom trial is a form of debate, meeting every requirement of our definition of a debate. It is a joint argument on a given issue between two opposing sides, one of which, the plaintiff, affirms the issue, and the other of which, the defendant, denies it. It should be mentioned in this connection also that the legal brief which outlines a legal case is very similar to the brief used in general argumentation as discussed in Chapter XII.

D. Sales Argument. — Sales argument is another field of interest to many students of argument. While salesmanship like law is a special study in and of itself, and should be given specific study and investigation, every salesman can profit greatly by a knowledge of the principles of argument. The application to salesmanship of the principles we have discussed in this text is evidenced rather strikingly in the following quotation from *The Principles of Salesmanship* by Whitehead. This quotation is taken from his chapter on " The Preparation of the Selling Talk."

"To build up a logical argument that will make the most powerful appeal, the nature of the offer, whether of goods or of service, must first be analyzed. This analysis will reveal those special features — often called 'talking points' or 'points of contact' — which can be elaborated so as to appeal to as many and as varied buying motives as possible. Everything salable has these talking points, otherwise it is so obviously inferior a product that it is unworthy of a salesman's attention. These various talking points have to be woven into a fluent sales talk which is readily adaptable to any situation and to any type of buyer.

"Nothing impresses a prospective buyer more than for a salesman to state his case in crisp and logical phraseology and meet every objection courteously and decisively. On the other hand, little does so much to create distrust as inability either to explain the merits of an offer logically and readily or to meet an objection when raised.

"The salesman who takes his work earnestly and seriously will never trust to a fluent and ready tongue for the construction of his argument. Many a glib talker who admires his own verbosity only irritates the buyer because he fails to present his argument *clearly*, *persuasively*, and *logically*. Clear, persuasive, and logical argument requires it to be put down in black and white and closely studied. . . .

"A sales talk does not consist of a mere description of what the salesman has to offer the customer or what the thing offered will do for the customer. A convincing argument is a composite appeal to the buying motive which is strongest in a particular case; to the temperament of the customer; and to the general attitude of the customer toward the salesman. This argument, as explained in the preceding chapter, is to be so modified that insensibly it attracts attention, rouses interest, and from interest leads to desire and action." [1]

Sales argument may be defined rather tersely as that argument which is designed to sell goods or services. It is ordinarily presented in *conversation* with customers.

[1] Whitehead, Harold, *The Principles of Salesmanship*, pp. 44 and 54. The Ronald Press Company, 1923.

CHAPTER XVIII

THE FIELDS OF ARGUMENT: DEBATE

I. Debate Defined

We have already defined a debate as a joint argument on a given proposition between two opposing sides, one of which, the affirmative, affirms the proposition, and the other of which, the negative, denies it. In general there are two kinds of debates: (1) Those of the courtroom, the political campaign, the legislature, the business meeting, — all the *actual debates of life*, including those which take place on the street corner and around the dinner table; and (2) Those *contest debates* held between teams in debating clubs and literary societies, or teams representing schools and colleges, — debates designed primarily to provide practice and training in debating.

II. The Functions of Contest Debating

A special consideration of contest debating seems advisable because of the magnitude of this activity and because of the many misconceptions regarding its educational functions.

Contest debating has had an interesting development in

this country.   Beginning with the debates between college and university literary societies before the days of intersectional football games and great stadia, it was an activity of first importance on the average college campus.   The interest in the activity spread beyond the college walls and was practiced by debating societies and literary organizations of various kinds, especially in small communities and rural centers.   With the advent of intercollegiate athletics and their rapid growth, however, debating suffered a serious setback as an important activity in colleges and universities. Attention was diverted from it, and even the debates in the country school houses and town halls dropped off when the moving pictures and improved methods of transportation made other entertainment available.   In recent years, however, there has been a new and rapid development in contest debating.   Debating, like athletics, has invaded the sphere of interscholastic and intercollegiate competition.   While intercollegiate debating dates back to some very early contests between Harvard, Yale, and some of the other old universities, this development on a large scale has occurred in relatively recent years.   Today colleges and universities all over the country are grouped together in debating leagues of various kinds.   College debating teams make debating tours in which they compete with other colleges, many of these trips being interstate in scope, and some even international.   Secondary schools have also taken up the activity on an interscholastic basis.   They too have organized their debating activities in competitive leagues, many of them being statewide in their scope, and terminating in state championships.   In the Michigan High School Debating League in the year 1930–1931, 275 high schools of the state conducted over 700 debates.   These debates were participated in by more than 1800 high school students and were heard by more than 150,000 people of the state.   An audience of 5000 persons assembled in the University of Michigan auditorium to hear the final state championship debate.

There are some who are beginning to fear lest this inter-scholastic and intercollegiate competition in debating will be overdone and perhaps is being overdone, just as there are many who believe that such competition has been over-emphasized in the field of athletics. Certainly those con-cerned need to consider this possibility carefully and make every effort to avoid the reaction against debating which over-emphasis is sure to bring. Just what its place should be in the educational system can be determined only by a care-ful consideration and evaluation of the educational oppor-tunities which it presents.

A. Three Important Objectives. — The more important objectives of contest debating are three in number : (1) To develop skill in argument ; (2) To develop ability in public speaking ; and (3) To develop competence in the investiga-tion and analysis of public questions.

An argument between two opposing speakers or groups of speakers such as is found in a debate affords excellent train-ing in argument. The presence of opposition stimulates the participants to greater endeavor and compels them to con-sider both sides of the question. The real issues are much more apt to develop where both sides are represented by care-fully prepared advocates such as appear in a debate, and much more consideration is usually given to the logical ade-quacy of evidence and the soundness of reasoning. The rules of debate, furthermore, promote the observance of certain dignities and decorum which keep the controversy within bounds and insure both sides a fair hearing.

Good debating demands an extemporaneous presentation and for that reason affords excellent training in extempo-raneous public speaking. The debater learns to think on his feet, adapt his case to that of an opponent, and in general adjust himself to the situation at hand. Debating develops a self-reliant, ready type of speaker who is competent to meet situations as they arise.

Ability in the investigation and analysis of public questions is no small advantage of contest debating. Rarely in other situations do high school and undergraduate college students study a public question with the zeal, enthusiasm, and thoroughness exhibited by debaters preparing for a debate. No one can debate a proposition effectively until he knows the evidence bearing on it and the significant arguments pro and con. The activity encourages not only the analytical study of the subjects selected for debate, but develops habits of reading and thoughtful consideration which are applied as well to other public questions of the day.

B. A Consideration of the Chief Objection. — The oldest and most persistent objection to contest debating is the contention that it makes students argue against their convictions and thereby develops intellectual dishonesty. The criticism is that the debater is encouraged to look for arguments rather than truth.

Those who voice this objection apparently do not realize that the only responsibility of a debater is to set up the best possible case for the proposition he is supporting in view of the evidence bearing on the question. His convictions are in no way at stake. It is the object of contest debating to develop the ability to take the available evidence and argument on a given side of a given proposition and present the best possible case for that side. Equipped with such training the contest debater, it is believed, can then argue his convictions in the debates of life and make truth prevail as he sees it with much greater force and power than had he never been so trained. It is the debater's task to build sound, persuasive argument and contest debating is designed to cultivate that ability. Whether or not a debater argues his convictions in life's debates is an ethical consideration which should not be confused with rhetorical competence.

The assumption of the objection to debating we have been discussing is that the truth is known in advance of the debate. We wish to suggest that debate may be one means at least of determining just what the truth is. The question is this: Is John Jones more likely to find the truth and acquire the ability to defend it against opposition by beginning with some ready made, preconceived opinion in the matter and sticking to it through thick and thin, or by studying both sides of the question, preparing the strongest possible cases on the affirmative and negative, and then engaging in debate in which he can weigh the relative strength of these cases? We feel that the latter is most emphatically the safer and surer way to discover the truth and formulate convictions of merit.

C. Contest Debating as a Preparation for Other Debating. — We wish to emphasize the point that contest debating should be looked upon as a preparation for the debates of life, — the debates of the courtroom, the legislature, and the countless less formal arguments in which people engage every day of their lives. As such a preparation it is believed to be one of the most valuable exercises in which students can take part. Every class in argument should avail itself of the opportunities for training presented by debate, especially since these contests can be conducted in so many different and interesting ways.

III. Types of Contest Debates

A. The Usual Debate. — In the usual contest debate each side is represented by three speakers and the debate is divided into two sections known as the constructive period and the rebuttal period. The affirmative opens the constructive argument and the sides alternate until every speaker has

appeared.   The negative then opens the rebuttal argument
and again the sides alternate until every speaker has had an
opportunity to speak.   The constructive speeches are usually
each ten or twelve minutes in length and the rebuttals each
five minutes in length.   The winner of the debate is decided
by a judge or board of judges who state which team in their
opinion has done the better debating.   In the case of a board
of judges each judge votes separately and the team receiving
the larger number of votes wins.

B.   Variations in Number and Arrangement of Speakers. —
There are a number of interesting variations in the standard
debate.

1. TWO MEMBERS ON A TEAM. — A very usual deviation
from the standard debate is that in which each side is represented by two speakers.   The chief advantage of this form
lies in the fact that it takes less time and for that reason is
apt to be somewhat more attractive to audiences.   The
greatest disadvantage is that it gives fewer people an opportunity to participate in the debate.

2. THE TWO-MAN DEBATE. — A convenient form of debate for class work is that in which only two persons participate, the affirmative opening with an eight- or ten-minute
speech, the negative responding with a twelve- or fifteen-
minute rejoinder, and the affirmative closing with a four- or
five-minute rebuttal.   This type has the advantage of being
short and not requiring team work.   The latter is an advantage in class debates where it is often difficult for students
to get together to prepare their cases.

3. THE ONE-REBUTTAL DEBATE. — The one-rebuttal
debate presents a third interesting variation in the number
and arrangement of speakers.   In this form of debate each
side is represented by three speakers and each speaker is
given an opportunity in constructive argument, but only
the first speaker on each side gives a rebuttal speech.   A

convenient time arrangement for such a debate is eight-minute constructive arguments and six-minute rebuttals. In this way the debate takes only sixty minutes rather than ninety or one hundred two minutes as in the standard debate. Not only is the time shortened without reducing the number of speakers, but it has been found also that this form has the tendency to stimulate more adjustment and adaptation on the part of the debaters during the constructive period. Since altogether too many debaters, especially beginners, are tempted to prepare set, memorized constructive speeches when they know they will have a rebuttal opportunity, the one-rebuttal debate has been found to reduce this practice, and thereby result in better debating. It is certain that the team with memorized constructive speeches is at a much greater disadvantage in the one-rebuttal type of debate than it is in the debate where each speaker gives a rebuttal. This form is especially recommended for secondary school debates.

C. Other Variations. — There are several other variations in the usual debate form with which students of argument should be familiar.

1. THE NO-DECISION DEBATE. — It is felt by some that there is apt to be too much emphasis placed on the winning of debates and that more profitable contests take place where no decision is given. While there is no great objection to no-decision debating, if interest can be maintained without a decision, at the same time there does not appear to be any good reason why a decision need to produce anything but helpful results. It constitutes an excellent and altogether natural method of motivating the contest so far as the debaters are concerned, and it adds greatly to the interest of the audience. If the decision is properly given, it of course rewards the team which has done the better debating. We fail to see how such a reward should operate to produce anything but better debating. A decision to be most

helpful should always be accompanied by a competent criticism of the debate.

2. THE OPEN-FORUM DEBATE. — The open-forum debate has in recent years become a very common form. It consists of any of the other types we have discussed plus a discussion after the debate in which the audience takes part. The chairman of the debate presides, and members of the audience are urged to ask questions of either side. Some very spirited and interesting discussions frequently result. The open-forum debate is usually a no-decision contest.

3. THE CROSS-QUESTION PLAN. — The cross-question or so-called " Oregon " plan of debate is distinguished by the following arrangement of speeches. There are usually only two speakers on a team but three may be used.

" 1. The first affirmative speaker presents the entire affirmative case. Length of speech twenty minutes.

2. The second negative speaker presents the entire negative case in an equal time.

3. The first affirmative speaker (or in three-man teams the second speaker) comes to the platform and for ten minutes is cross-questioned by the second negative speaker. Answers must be short and definite and the chairman acts as arbiter of any objections raised by either questioner or questioned.

4. The first negative speaker (or second negative) returns to the platform for similar cross questioning by the second affirmative speaker.

5. The second negative (or third in three-man teams) gives ten-minute rebuttal and summarizing speech.

6. The second (or third) affirmative performs similar duties for his case in a ten-minute final speech." [1]

The cross-question debate like the open-forum debate is usually a no-decision contest. It makes a very interesting and worthwhile debate.

[1] O'Neill, J. M., and Cortright, R. L., *Debate and Oral Discussion*, p. 55. The Century Company, 1931.

4. THE SPLIT-TEAM DEBATE. — The split-team debate is a deviation from the usual debate in that the competing schools or societies exchange one man. That is, one man from school X will debate with two men from school Y, and one representative from school Y will debate with two men from school X. This form of debate has little merit unless one considers it advantageous to reduce the competition between the schools or societies concerned. It is bound to make team-work very difficult if not impossible, and is not generally conducive to serious effort.

5. THREE-TEAM DEBATES. — O'Neill and Cortright report the following instance of a three-team debate :

"In 1929, Washington University, St. Louis University, and the University of Missouri met in a three-cornered debate on the prohibition question. Two-man teams were used. One team advocated modification. A second demanded more money for enforcement. The third upheld the present system, the status quo." [1]

This novel form of debate lends itself rather well to the discussion of propositions in which three well defined positions present themselves. Those three positions will usually be (1) A defense of the status quo, (2) A defense of the plan embodied in the proposition, and (3) An outstanding alternative plan or a counter proposition.

6. IMPROMPTU OR SHORT-NOTICE DEBATES. — An impromptu or short-notice debate as the name suggests is one in which the debate is given after a very short period of preparation. Such debates have been conducted with the purpose in mind of stimulating more extemporaneous speaking and making set, memorized speeches impossible. Sometimes the debaters are asked to prepare themselves on some general subject, and then a specific proposition embodying some phase of this general subject is chosen a few hours before the

[1] O'Neill, J. M., and Cortright, R. L., *Debate and Oral Discussion*, p. 57.

debate. This latter method is certainly more defensible than that of trying to debate a proposition on short notice where the dabaters have not even had the opportunity to do some general reading on the subject. In either case, however, the debating will almost surely be superficial and poorly done. As O'Neill and Cortright put it, " A very large part of the valuable training coming from debate work lies in the careful search for evidence, thorough preparation of the case, and, finally, the careful adaptation to the audience. The short notice debate places a premium on lack of preparedness and forces a debate of superficial information where the clever talker who can say little but say it well makes the best impression. There is too much of such uninformed so-called debating in real life that is nothing more than superficiality, shallow-minded arguments, high sounding words, and mere talk. We may be guilty of enough of that without deliberately practicing it."[1]

IV. The Affirmative Case

The affirmative case in a debate should always be, in plan, a prima facie case. It should present evidence and reasoning which if unanswered will logically win the argument. It should be based on a sound interpretation of the proposition and organized as simply and clearly as possible. Affirmative teams should be cautioned against assuming any more of a burden of proof than the proposition requires. Under ordinary circumstances it is good advice to take as conservative a position as the proposition will permit, and then concentrate the support of that position upon as few arguments as will constitute a prima facie case. Radical affirmative cases or cases based upon an unusual or strained interpretation of the question, with the support scattered over a great variety of points, are seldom effective.

[1] *Ibid.*, p. 58.

V. The Negative Case

The negative case should constitute a vital objection to the proposition.   As in the case of the affirmative, it is generally advisable to take as conservative a position as the circumstances will permit and to concentrate the attack on a few decisive arguments.   Radical departures from the status quo are difficult to defend except in certain unusual instances, and the force of the negative case is invariably lost when the attack is spread over a great variety of arguments.   Concentration upon a few simple, direct arguments is almost always the best course to follow.

Negative cases are of four kinds: (1) Pure Refutation; (2) Defense of the Status Quo; (3) Adjustment or Repairs; and (4) A Counter Proposition.

A. Pure Refutation. — Since the burden of proof is on the affirmative, if the negative can successfully refute the arguments of the affirmative it need do nothing else to win the debate, at least so far as the logic of the situation is concerned. Thus it is possible for the negative to take no constructive position and devote its entire time to attacking the affirmative's evidence and reasoning.   If it prevents the affirmative from constructing its prima facie case, the negative attack has succeeded.   This is usually safe only when the affirmative has a very weak case.

B. Defense of the Status Quo. — An out and out defense of the status quo is frequently a strong case for the negative, if the present situation is at all defensible.   Such a defense may usually be coupled with a direct attack on the practicability and feasibility of the affirmative suggestion.   Even in those instances in which the present situation is not entirely defensible, it is good debating if at all possible to minimize the evils pointed out by the affirmative, thereby removing a great deal of the force of the affirmative argument.

C. Adjustment or Repairs. — In this type of case the negative admits that there are some things that are not quite
satisfactory in regard to the present situation. Rather than
defending the status quo outright, they propose certain
reforms, changes, or repairs which in their estimation will
remedy the difficulties in the present situation without
resorting to the affirmative proposal which is a more radical
departure from the status quo. This is a very usual negative
case and ordinarily a strong position to take. It admits that
the present situation is not perfect, argues that the evils are
not inherent, and contends that they can be removed by
minor changes and reforms involving much less effort and
expense than the change proposed by the affirmative.

D. Counter Proposition. — The most radical case possible
for a negative is that of a counter proposition. This is admitting that there is a situation which demands remedy,
admitting a cause for action, but advocating a different
remedy. The counter proposition is the most daring and
radical case. There are two principles that must always be
lived up to in this case: (a) *The counter proposition must be
stated with perfect clearness.* The negative has to take the
burden of proof on this proposition, and for safety and clearness the proposition must be carefully worded and stated.
(b) *A counter proposition must be counter.* It must be inconsistent with the proposition of the affirmative. If the
affirmative can say, " We have no objection to the theory
proposed by the negative, but it does not answer our case,"
then the counter proposition is useless. It must, in order to
be any good, be antagonistic to that which the affirmative
case is advocating. It is an " affirmative defense " in legal
phrase, and must effectively negative the affirmative, as the
" affirmative defense " of insanity is a complete negative in
a murder trial. Here the defense takes the burden of proof
and has to prove insanity, while the prosecution takes the

viewpoint of the presumption of sanity, and becomes for the time a negative. This situation must be paralleled in general argumentation when we are using a counter proposition.

It is the duty of the negative *to clash* with the affirmative, therefore if the counter proposition is such that the affirmative can accept it the negative is responsible for the failure to meet. It is not enough that the counter proposition be different; it must be *vitally inconsistent* with the affirmative plan.

VI. Rebuttal

A. Suggestions for Preparation. — Good rebuttal requires careful preparation. There are some debaters who conceive of rebuttal as being a purely impromptu effort which requires no attention before the debate takes place. This position is wholly indefensible. It is just as important that rebuttal receive consideration before the debate as it is that constructive argument be planned. To be sure it cannot be planned in exactly the same way, but it can profitably be considered nevertheless. A debating team ought to consider all the more important arguments which their opponents may present, and decide upon a line of attack for each of these which will be consistent with their own constructive position. These rebuttal points may be outlined on cards if it seems advisable. Such preparation is not " canning " rebuttal. " Canned rebuttal " is that rebuttal which is prepared before hand, usually memorized, and delivered in the debate no matter what the opposition may say. This practice of course results in the very worst kind of debating and should never be followed.

B. How to Use Rebuttal in a Debate. — In the usual debate, as we have said, there is a series of speeches known as the *constructive* speeches which is followed by another series known as the *rebuttals*. These labels are in many respects unfortunate, because they imply that the first series of

speeches must be merely constructive in nature and the
rebuttals, refutatory in nature.   It is true that refutation
should be given in the rebuttals, but it is rarely if ever
advisable to confine the so-called constructive speeches to
constructive argument.   As we have said in a previous connection, every speech in a debate after the first affirmative
speech should ordinarily include some rebuttal.   The proof
in most debate cases is cumulative; that is, the premise of
the second speaker depends upon that proved by the first
speaker, and the argument of the third speaker cannot
progress logically unless the first two arguments remain
standing.   How often in a debate we have the ridiculous
situation of a second or third constructive speaker going
ahead with an argument without any attempt whatsoever
to reëstablish a premise of a colleague which is vital to the
case and which has been badly damaged by an opponent.
Even though refutation is unnecessary in order logically to
proceed with the constructive case, it is excellent debating to
refute one or two opposing arguments before continuing the
constructive development.   Make every effort to take the
" sting " out of an opposing argument as soon after it has
been presented as possible, especially if it has seemed to score
against you.

While we are urging the importance of refutation and
adjustment during the constructive period, there are two
precautions which should be observed in connection with
this practice: (1) Constructive responsibilities must not be
neglected; and (2) Organization and coherent development
must not be sacrificed.   Affirmative teams especially can
easily spend so much time in refutation during the constructive period that they fail adequately to present their own
prima facie constructive case.   The same precaution applies
to the negative team whose plan of attack includes some
constructive case.

The danger of sacrificing organization and coherent development presents itself to both teams when rebuttal is attempted in the constructive period. Cleancut, well organized cases are apt to become muddy and incoherent unless the refutation is skillfully handled. If the refutation is germane to the constructive point under discussion, then weave the rebuttal into the development where the adaptation can best be made. On the other hand, if the refutation does not apply directly to the constructive point under discussion, it is advisable definitely to separate the two in order to avoid confusion. Take up the rebuttal first and then turn to construction.

The point to be emphasized is this: From the remarks of every speaker in the constructive period of the debate, whether these remarks are primarily refutatory or primarily constructive in nature, one or more definite arguments should emerge. Furthermore, these arguments should be related to the case as a whole in some clear and helpful way. Random refutation and hit and miss rebuttal is never effective. There should be evidence of planned progression in every debate case, even if it consists entirely of refutation.

Some advice on the matter of handling rebuttal in the rebuttal section of the debate will be apropos at this point. There should always be some guiding plan in rebuttal. While this plan should never be so rigid as to deny the freedom necessary to meet important arguments as they arise, and handle unforeseen situations promptly, such a plan should exist nevertheless, especially where there are two or more persons on a team giving rebuttals.

How should the various rebuttal points be distributed among the speakers? This and other similar questions can profitably be considered before the debate takes place. One method of organizing rebuttal is that in which a " man to man " defense is employed. That is, the first speaker refutes what is said by the first speaker on the other side, the second speaker handles the second speaker, and so on. Another much more effective plan of rebuttal organization is the " zone " defense or that in which each speaker is assigned a certain portion of the case to defend or a certain portion of the argument to attack.   For example, one person might be made primarily responsible for the need argument, another primarily responsible for the affirmative plan, another primarily responsible for alternative plans, etc.   This method usually works very well if certain precautions are observed.   First of all, it should be made very clear that there is no single plan applicable to all situations.   The assignment of rebuttal responsibilities will vary with almost every proposition.   Secondly, every speaker, regardless of his special rebuttal responsibility, should be prepared to rally to the defense of his colleagues, and be prepared to meet pressing, damaging arguments as they arise.

The last rebuttal speaker on each side should devote at least a part of his time to a summary of the debate.   Similar summaries are sometimes helpful in the last constructive speeches.   These summaries may be done in several ways. One method is to summarize just what has been said against each main argument advanced by the opposing side, and then climax the statement with a terse review of one's own case. Another method is to state what appears to be the ultimate issues in the debate, and then compare the significant arguments advanced on these issues by both sides, concluding in this case also with a short summary of one's own position.

VII. Conduct in a Debate

" Any one who is going to take part in debates, either in contest debates or in the debates of real life, should be familiar with the ordinary conventions of debating in order to obey them easily, courteously, and unobtrusively, just as he should obey the conventions of any polite function." [1]

A. The Presiding Officer. — A debate is usually presided over by some official who announces the speakers and in general takes charge of the debate from the platform. In decision debates, the presiding officer announces the decision of the judges except in those cases where the judge or judges give the decision orally. He should never discuss the question for debate before the debaters have spoken. In general it is wise for him to refrain from saying anything at all about the question other than to announce what it is to be. Probably a few general remarks about the importance of the question would do no harm, but it is dangerous for the presiding officer to go beyond such a statement. The chairman's function is to start the debate off, see that it progresses smoothly, and bring the meeting to a close.

In introducing the speakers the chairman should announce the debater and remain standing until he has been recognized. If the debater's table is on the platform, the debater should rise at the table, address the chairman, and then proceed to the front of the platform. If the debater is not seated on the platform, he should walk to the platform when introduced, pause momentarily when he has reached the platform, address the chairman, and then go on up to the front of the platform.

B. Salutation. — When the speaker has reached the front of the platform or the speaker's stand, he should pause briefly and then address the audience. The salutation " Ladies and Gentlemen " is preferable to any other if the debate is held before a mixed audience, and in other cases simply " Ladies " or " Gentlemen " is adequate. In some instances where the debate is held before a society, club, or

[1] O'Neill, J. M., and Weaver, A. T., *The Elements of Speech*, p. 407. Longmans, Green and Company, 1926.

some other special group, it may be well to address the members of this group as " Members of the Rotary Club " or with some similar salutation. It is neither necessary nor in best form to address the judges or one's opponents separately in addressing the audience. There may be occasions when it is advisable to speak to the opposing team during the course of the debate, but such instances are rare. It is a good rule to address all remarks to the audience and proceed on the assumption that both the judges and the opposing team are included therein.

In the case of a debate in which one team is entertaining another as in the case of most intercollegiate debates, there are certain courtesies which should ordinarily be observed. The first speaker on the entertaining team may express a few words of welcome and the first speaker on the visiting team may respond by expressing the pleasure of renewing forensic relations with X College, or by making some other appropriate remark of this nature. Such comments, however, should always be simple, brief, genuine, and unaffected.

C. Judge or Critic. — The judge or critic of the debate should be seated in the audience and be provided with satisfactory facilities for note taking. If the decision and critique are to be given orally by the judge in the presence of the audience, he should be informed of that fact before the debate, and introduced for that purpose by the presiding officer at the close of the debate. If the judge is not to appear before the audience, an usher should call for his ballot and convey it to the presiding officer who may then announce the decision.

D. Audience. — A good audience adds tremendously to any debate and debates should be arranged with this factor in mind. In recent years there has been a very interesting tendency for debaters to go to their audiences when their audiences refuse to come to them. That is, debates are scheduled as special programs for civic clubs, school assemblies, college convocations, and other such groups. This practice is an excellent one since it furnishes worthwhile occasions for a number of debates and at the same time removes the necessity of scheduling an excessive number of home debates with the consequent danger of flagging interest on the part of home audiences.

There are several forms of debate which enable the audience to take an active part. This is especially true of the open-forum debate and those contests in which an audience decision is given. Such debates usually make the occasion somewhat more interesting for the audience, and if not overdone, are very much worthwhile.

In regard to the debater's attitude toward the audience in any debate, O'Neill and Weaver state,

"A speaker in a contest debate should talk to an audience precisely as though the audience were going to settle the question upon which he is debating, and were going to vote for or against it at the close of the debate. He should conduct himself, in other words, as though the debate were a real debate in which a question were being settled. This is the whole duty of the debater, as far as the audience is concerned, and represents the attitude of the debater toward the proposition and the occasion at its very best." [1]

E. Opponents. — The attitude of debaters toward their opponents should be fair, courteous, considerate, and honest. Any evidence of hostility, unfairness, or dishonesty is not only bad form, but invariably turns an audience against a debater. Such conduct is inexcusable from every point of view.

F. Timekeepers. — The timekeepers in a debate should ordinarily be seated in the audience and far enough forward so that their signals can readily be perceived by the speaker with a minimum of confusion and distraction. It is custom-

[1] O'Neill, J. M., and Weaver, A. T., *The Elements of Speech*, p. 409.

ary to have representatives from the two competing teams act as timekeepers, although on some occasions this function is performed by the presiding officer.

One convenient system of timing is that in which time cards are used. If a ten minute speech is given, for instance, the timekeepers will display ten cards during the course of the speech, changing them at one minute intervals, with each card indicating the number of minutes remaining to speak. The usual procedure is to begin with a card marked " 10 "; display this until one minute has elapsed; and then display a similar card marked " 9 "; and so on every minute until the time is up. In that way the speaker can always know at a glance just how much time he has left. When the time is up the timekeepers usually stand, and remain standing until the speaker concludes. Of course, a bell or a tap may be used to inform the speaker that his time is up.

When time cards are not used, it is generally advisable to give a warning one or two minutes before the speech is to close in addition to the final signal. The number and time of the warnings should be thoroughly understood by the debaters and the timekeepers so that no misunderstandings will arise during the debate. For the same reason it is important that time signals be given in such a way that the speaker will be certain to notice them.

G. Properties. — The properties in a debate should include tables and chairs for the competing teams, a chair for the presiding officer, and a speaker's stand. The two tables should be provided with a pitcher of water and the required number of glasses. The affirmative team should be seated on the right side of the platform and the negative team on the left. Thus, an affirmative speaker will have his opponents on his left as he speaks, and a negative speaker will have them on his right.

Another property which sometimes is used in debate is a

chart. As a general rule, however, charts add little if any-thing to the effectiveness of a debating team, and furthermore they are usually open to damaging refutation by an opponent. Their use should be discouraged except in those cases where there is a peculiar need for a graphic or a diagrammatic repre-sentation of an argument. Whenever a chart is used by a debater, however, it should always be left before the audience until the debate is over. Under no circumstances should a speaker put up a chart for his own use and then take it down when he is through with it. The opposing team should be permitted to use the chart, and if it is taken down they not only have a right, but should ask the presiding officer to have the chart put back before the audience.

VIII. How to Criticize a Debate

A. Criticism and Judging. — The criticism of a debate and the judge's decision in a debate should not be confused. It is possible to have a criticism without a decision, and a deci-sion without a criticism. In interscholastic debating at least, criticisms are rarely given unless a decision is given also, and even then it is unusual to have a criticism except in those cases where a single critic judge gives the decision. All in all, the most satisfactory arrangement seems to be one in which a single critic judge is employed, the decision being read to the audience by the presiding officer, and the judge giving his criticism to the debaters and other interested parties at a special session after the debate. It is a very usual and altogether acceptable practice, however, for a critic judge to give both his decision and critique in the presence of the audience.

A competent, thoroughgoing criticism contributes greatly to the educational opportunities presented by a debate. After a debate in the classroom or on the contest platform, criticism should be given by someone who is well qualified to criticize this activity. This should be done whether or not a decision is given, and regardless of the nature of the decision.

B. Types of Votes. — There are three kinds of decisions which can be given in debates. These types should be thoroughly understood by all parties concerned, because only in this way can anyone know what the decision actually means.

1. THE LEGISLATIVE VOTE. — The legislative vote is one in which the judge bases the decision upon the merits of the question. In other words, if he votes for the affirmative, it means that he believes in the affirmative side of the question, and if he votes for the negative, it means simply that he believes in the negative side of the question. Very evidently this type of vote is not well adapted to the decision of contest debates. In such contests the interest lies primarily in the merits of the debate rather than in the judge's opinion regarding the merits of the question. In *no case should a judge or board of judges give a legislative vote in a contest debate.* This type of vote has its place in legislative assemblies where business is being transacted and actions taken. Here the vote should be on the merits of the question, but there is little to be gained from such a vote in a contest debate, where the decision should of course go to the side which has done the better debating.

It should be pointed out, however, that a legislative vote is usually used in a contest debate in which the *audience* is given an opportunity to vote. This is an entirely different situation; the members of the average audience do not pretend to be competent critics of a debate, nor are they competent to give a critic's vote. If there is to be an expression of opinion from the audience, by all means make it a legislative vote and use the so-called shift-of-opinion ballot. The audience in such case is given an opportunity to express its belief on the proposition before and after the debate, and the various shifts of opinion are then recorded. The sample shift-of-opinion ballot on p. 371 will be interesting in this connection : [1]

"For two years before our use of the present ballot began in 1924, we experimented with various forms and wordings. Our attempt was to get: first, a form simple to vote; and second, one that would encourage the registering of opinions on the question discussed and discourage, in so far as possible, the voting of preferences as to teams. For the latter purpose, the form requires that the chairman state the subject to the audience as an interrogative and ask the audience to vote their answer to this question both before and at the close of the formal discussion. It helps to get people to vote on the subject if they are not voting on a resolution and if the mention of teams and of sides is studiously avoided when the listeners are asked to use their ballots. For the same reason we have eliminated from the ballot the word 'debate,' using instead 'discussion.' " [2]

Professor Woodward states regarding the shift-of-opinion ballot :

"Such balloting does something to make audiences think on the question, to arouse an expectation of learning and an interest in learning something worth knowing. I am sure that it tends to make the debater feel that he has an opportunity to be an instructor in the expanding field of adult education. Debating then becomes to him a more serious and significant task in playing the student part of his rôle. . . . The change in audience opinion may be used as a debate decision. In most cases it is so used when the Reserve students debate. But there is no need whatsoever that this be done. Whether the audience vote is used as a decision or not, the analysis of results is generally studied with interest by the debaters." [3]

---

[1] The sample shift-of-opinion ballot given here is that used by Western Reserve University. It was presented and discussed in a paper read by Howard S. Woodward at the Speech Conference of the Michigan School Masters' Club held in Ann Arbor, April 25, 1930. See *Journal of the Michigan School Masters' Club*, 1930, pp. 302–313.

[2] *Ibid.*

[3] *Ibid.*, p. 310.

SHIFT–OF–OPINION BALLOT

TO THE AUDIENCE

The idea to be discussed will be found on the program, stated in question form, — or the chairman will so state it.

Will you express

YOUR PERSONAL OPINION ON THIS QUESTION by marking this ballot both *before the discussion* and again *after the discussion.* Your coöperation will be much appreciated.

This form is filled by a
□ man □ woman, whose age is..................

BEFORE THE DISCUSSION

□ YES (This expresses my belief on the question).

□ —— I am undecided.
□ NO (This expresses my belief on the question).

THE REASONS FOR MY OPINION ARE:

Date ....
Place ....

If the speakers and the audience both desire it, opportunity will be given before adjournment for the asking of questions that are pertinent to the discussion.

AFTER THE DISCUSSION
(Mark one place)

I have heard the entire discussion, and now
□ YES (I believe more strongly than I did before in answering "yes").

□ YES (This expresses my present belief on the question).
□ —— I am undecided.
□ NO (This expresses my present belief on the question).

□ NO (I believe more strongly than I did before in answering "no").

THE REASONS FOR MY OPINION ARE:

Comments on the Discussion

1st Affirmative........................

1st Negative..........................

2nd Affirmative.......................

2nd Negative..........................

3rd Affirmative.......................

3rd Negative..........................

While the shift-of-opinion ballot will unquestionably yield some interesting data, and serve to stimulate the interest of the audience, the advisability of basing a decision on the results is at least open to question. Certainly if a decision is rendered to that team which has been the more successful in shifting opinion, the exact basis upon which the decision is given should always be announced. Such a decision is not comparable with a critic decision and only confusion and misinformation can result unless the distinction is clearly understood by all parties concerned.

2. THE JURYMAN'S VOTE. — The juryman's vote is one in which the decision is based solely upon the evidence submitted. When a judge gives a decision of this kind, it means that in his opinion the weight of evidence lies with the side to whom he awards the decision. Since effective debating includes much more than the accumulation and marshaling of evidence, a decision based solely on the weight of evidence is obviously inadequate for contest debates. To be sure, the presentation of evidence is an important part of debating and should be considered in a critic decision, but a vote based solely on this criterion might not be awarded to the team which has done the better debating, everything considered.

O'Neill and Weaver state regarding the juryman's vote:

There are a number of reasons why the juryman's vote is wholly improper in contest debating.

"1. The questions debated are rarely the sort of questions which are the subjects of jury votes in a court room. Jurymen vote on *questions of fact*, on which it is usually possible to lay aside any knowledge or prejudice which one may have. It is comparatively easy to find men who have little knowledge or prejudice in regard to questions such as are usually submitted to juries.

"The questions that are debated in contest debates are practically always *questions of policy*, and practically always questions upon which any mature and intelligent person has knowledge and opinions. Any assumption, therefore, to the effect that the judge of debate has neither knowledge nor opinion on the question debated is a false and unwarranted assumption.

"2. A jury trial on a specific question of fact may last from one day to a number of weeks or even months. A contest debate on a great question of policy begins and ends within the limits of one evening. It is absolutely impossible to produce an exhaustive argument either for or against such questions in the time limits allowed. In the juryman's vote the jury is under oath to vote for the negative unless the affirmative proves its case beyond a reasonable doubt. The law courts are not engaged in making decisions between two contestants on a well-balanced proposition. They are interested in settling disputes and awarding justice. In a civil case, unless the affirmative can prove his case, he should not be allowed to collect from the negative the money he is suing for. In a criminal case, unless the affirmative can prove its contention and establish the guilt of the alleged criminal, the accused person should not be punished. In the courts, therefore, both civil and criminal, unless the affirmative can prove its case, all the negative has to do is to point out to the jury the fact that the affirmative has not proved its case, and the jury must vote for the negative.

"If we apply the juryman's vote in the same way to a contest debate, the time limits make it practically necessary for the judge to vote for the negative team. It is obviously very much easier for a negative team to point out that a case has not been established by the affirmative, than it is for an affirmative to establish its case. Any attempt to use the juryman's vote in a contest debate gives an almost conclusive advantage to the negative team." [1]

3. THE CRITIC'S VOTE. — A critic's vote is one in which the decision is made upon the merits of the debating. When a judge casts a vote of this kind, it means that in his opinion the better debating has been done by the team to whom he awards the decision. It does not necessarily mean that he

[1] O'Neill, J. M., and Weaver, A. T., *The Elements of Speech*, pp. 416–417. Longmans, Green and Company, 1926.

believes in that side of the question, nor does it necessarily mean that the weight of evidence lies with the side in whose favor the vote is cast. It simply means that in the estimation of the judge the team which receives his vote has done a better job of debating than has the opposing team.

Since the purpose of contest debating is to teach those taking part how to conduct themselves in the actual debates of life, to teach the debaters how to do well those things which constitute good debating, most certainly the decision ought to go to that team which excels in those things. Who can better say which team has done the better debating than a competent critic of that activity?

Both the debaters and the judge ought to know what constitutes good debating, and when a judge gives a critic decision he ought to be able to point out the strong points and weak points of both teams in respect to acceptable debating standards. He should also be able to explain his decision in respect to such standards. If the debaters have a wrong conception of debating, who is better able to set them right than a competent critic? Is it not clear that the critic vote is the one that best insures the educational advantages that are supposed to come from debating. It places the emphasis precisely where it should be placed, — on the ability of the debaters to debate well.

C. The Criticism Blank. — The following criticism blank is suggested for the use of critics and for debaters working in classes or in clubs or in societies in preparation for debate.[1]

"This blank should be typewritten or printed on a full-sized sheet (8 × 11) of substantial paper or light cardboard. It should be easy to handle and write on. The spaces should be ample to allow for markings or brief notes. The critic should take this

[1] This blank together with the explanation of its use is reprinted from *The Elements of Speech*, pp. 418-419.

blank to the debate with him. He should also be furnished with paper for running notes and comments if he cares to make them. He should not write on the blank while a debater is speaking. At the close of each speech, the critic should make, in the column for that particular speech, whatever remarks he cares to make. Using plus or minus signs is usually sufficient. If he has no

CRITICISM BLANK FOR A CRITIC OF DEBATE

POINTS TO BE CONSIDERED IN CRITICISM	AFFIRMATIVE				NEGATIVE			
	1	2	3	Team	1	2	3	Team
1. Analysis, or Interpretation of the proposition (Plan of case)								
2. Knowledge, information, evidence								
3. Reasoning, inferences, based on evidence								
4. Ability in extemporizing								
5. Conduct or deportment								
6. Ability in rebuttal								
7. Use of English								
8. Clearness of speech — Easy to hear? Pronunciation, enunciation, etc.								
9. Power, or effectiveness, in public speaking								

Note. — The critic may fill in grades or percentages for each speaker or for each team as a whole; or he may use +, V, and — to indicate his general opinion on each point, either for individuals or teams, using the V for "neutral" or "no particular impression." The critic shall decide for himself the relative weight to be given to each of the points mentioned.

DECISION

On the basis of the criticism indicated by the above markings on these nine points, and considering nothing else, it is my decision that, on the whole, the better debating was done by

The .... team.

(Signed) ....

Critic.

impression to record on a given point, he may simply check it to indicate a neutral attitude.

"If a critic uses plus and minus signs, he may use two or three plus signs for particularly good work or two or three minus signs for particularly poor work. Instead of plus and minus markings a critic may use percentages, or any system which he chooses.

"The purpose of the blank is simply to call to mind each of the points in which excellence contributes to good debating, in order that the critic may record, at the close of a speech, a definite impression, if he has one, on each point. This list is offered as the whole list of points which ought to be considered; in other words, no critic should base a decision in any way upon any points not listed on this blank. He should consider all of these points and use them in coming to his decision. He should consider nothing else."

APPENDIX A

AMATEURISM VERSUS PROFESSIONALISM IN COLLEGE SPORTS

NORTHWESTERN UNIVERSITY
versus
UNIVERSITY OF MICHIGAN
Stenographic Report of a Debate [1]

CHAIRMAN
Mr. Royal L. Garff

My ideas of being Chairman are much the same as those of an old Swede who lived in a Western town from which I came. He was invited to introduce a particularly noted speaker one night, and he got up and said, "Ladies and Gentlemen: I am here this evening to introduce Mr. Reed, who will speak to you. Now I have done it; now he will do it." But this being a debate, there are a few more things that need to be done.

The teams debating this evening are from the University of Michigan and Northwestern University. These teams are ancient rivals — in fact, they debated each other years ago before the formation of this present Western Conference Debating League. It was then called the Central Debating League, and was the oldest triangular league in the Middle West. The teams belonging to it then were the University of Michigan, the University of Chicago, and Northwestern University. So, this evening, we are really renewing an ancient, traditional rivalry. These teams have seen battle before, and they are waiting to engage in this contest tonight with a good deal of eagerness. It is with pleasure that we welcome the University of Michigan with us tonight.

[1] Reprinted from *The University Debater's Annual*, 1931, by permission of the H. W. Wilson Company.

As you came in the door, you were given a ballot. If you will notice it, you will find that there is a place on the left-hand side of the ballot which says, "I believe in the affirmative of the resolution to be debated," "Am undecided," and "I believe in the negative." If you will fill out that ballot now, then, of course, your prejudices won't have any chance to work.   Then, after the debate, on the other side of the ballot you will find spaces there, which may be marked for any change of opinion which may have taken place as a result of the debate.   Students who are in beginning public-speaking classes, will each of you kindly put your names on the ballots, and the name of the instructor under whom you are studying.

The proposition to be debated this evening is: *"Resolved:* That all colleges and universities should abolish the distinction between amateurism and professionalism in sports to which admission fees are charged."

The debaters representing the University of Michigan are: Lawrence Hartwig, Victor Rabinowitz, and Nathan Levy. Those representing Northwestern University are: J. Stillwell Conner, John A. Blackmore, and Richard Peterson.

Each speaker is allowed twelve minutes for a constructive speech. At the end of ten minutes one time-keeper will arise; and at the end of twelve minutes both of them will arise, signifying that it is time for the speaker to finish his speech.

The first speaker this evening, opening the case for Northwestern University, is J. Stillwell Conner.

First Affirmative
J. Stillwell Conner, Northwestern

Mr. Chairman, Ladies, and Gentlemen: First of all, I want to welcome the three gentlemen from Michigan tonight. We of Northwestern are always glad to meet representatives of Michigan in any sport.   It used to be that Chicago was our traditional rival; but now that Chicago has gone strictly academic, we have shifted our pugnacity to other schools, and Michigan stands in the forefront of our new competitors.

I am sorry that we had to have one of our Easter snows come a bit early to welcome the gentlemen, because I presume that they intended to have a little entertainment afterward.

Tonight we are going to talk about entertainment. Perhaps many of you remember that once upon a time the most popular American entertainer was the glorified American girl; but now there is a new entertainer, none other than the glorified American college boy, who may be seen in action on almost any day in the college year, either making a touchdown, sliding into third base, or dribbling down under the basket. Wherever he goes, there follow in his wake cheering crowds, blaring bands, and heaps of gold.

But how different is the lot of these two popular entertainers. The girl, after finishing her performance, with her blond head held high, trips lightly through the front door of the bank to cash her check. The boy slinks down the alley to the back door to get his hand-out. Why this difference? The answer to this question lies in the fact that there exist on paper certain rules which attempt to carry out the traditional distinction in sports between the amateur and the professional — namely, that an amateur plays solely for the love of the game, while a professional plays for money.

Suppose we look at some of these paper rules to see the practical application of this abstract principle.

The Western Conference, of which the institutions in this debating league are members, bars from competition, on the grounds of professionalism, any athlete who is guilty of one or more of these four acts:

Playing under an assumed name.

Playing on a team any member of which receives compensation for his services.

Receiving any remuneration whatsoever from the university under whose colors he plays.

Earning or winning, either with his athletic or gymnastic skill, a monetary reward.

The Michigan I. A. A. adds, "No student shall be eligible to compete who has ever played in any game in a professional league which is under national jurisdiction."

The Rocky Mountain Conference further gilds the lily by adding "or who has ever played on any team which is on the black list of the National Commission."

The Pacific Coast I. A. C. brands as professional:

First, any athlete who writes on sports in which he is participating, for any newspaper, periodical, or journal other than those of his own institution.

Or, second, any athlete who is employed by the athletic association or the student body for more than fifty cents an hour, or who is allowed to earn more than fifty dollars a month. Here is the sharpest distinction. It is worth exactly one cent, hourly or monthly, as you please — fifty cents an amateur, fifty-one cents a professional.

But the most comprehensive attempt to make the amateur-professionalism distinction clear is made by the Intercollegiate Association of the Amateur Athletes of America, of which forty prominent institutions, chiefly in the East, are members. This association sets forth rules similar to those quoted, and then adds this pearl: "An athlete loses his amateur status if he eats at a training table without paying for his meal, or if he competes with or against ineligible persons." Here forgetting to pay the cashier, or failing to check up on all the players in the game, may change a pure-minded amateur into a low-down professional.

Thus you see that even in the minds of the American colleges and universities themselves, amateurism is not an inherent quality. It varies with locality, and in many cases a professional in one conference would be a recognized amateur in another. Thus, you can see that these ostensible, out-worn distinctions are, at best, a sorry structure on which to build so important an edifice as American intercollegiate sport — this glorification of the American boy.

But let us now see what are the actual conditions existing in college sports — the actual, which is seen to be the sordid — the cellar, or dungeon, of this structure. A systematic exploration of these depths has been made by investigators from the Carnegie Foundation. Their findings have been published in a series of official reports. These Carnegie investigators reveal that eighty-one out of the one hundred twelve institutions they visited did subsidize and recruit their athletes. At Drake, Gettysburg, and

Oberlin a member of the administrative staff conducted the subsidizing and recruiting. At California, New York University, and Pennsylvania the coach took care of the matter himself. At the institution which our opponents have the pleasure to attend, it was found that the coach, the athletic director, and an alumni officer united to extend and form relations with athletes.

The subsidies given at the various institutions vary widely. At the University of Southern California $40,000 was given in scholarships to athletes; at New York University seventy-five scholarships were given to worthy young sportsmen; while at Stanford only fifty athletes were favored with free tuition. Some of the more naïve institutions, such as Boston College, Holy Cross, and Notre Dame, preferred simply to assure their prospects that they would be cared for. This usually meant full college expenses. At some institutions slush funds were found existing from $25,000 to $50,000, so the Carnegie investigators revealed. At Carnegie Tech $13,000 was found; at Lafayette, $3,000; at tiny Grove City, $8,000; and elsewhere similar slush funds were in evidence. All these sums, my friends, were used for what? To buy, help, and support pseudo-amateur athletes.

But the Carnegie investigators did not reveal everything; for who could look into the check-book of every alumnus? One rather striking example of their leniency, or perhaps it was their nearsightedness, is Iowa. When *Bulletin 23* was published, Iowa was accused of one thing — harboring athletes who had been hired by off-campus employers. Three months later Iowa was kicked out of the Big Ten. For what? Because it was found that fourteen of her foremost athletes had been subsidized from a general university slush fund, which seems to have escaped the rigid inspection of the Carnegie investigators. The findings of this obviously biased authority — the Carnegie Foundation — avowedly dedicated to maintaining the amateur-professional distinction, must lead us inevitably to one conclusion, that in the majority of the institutions the amateur-professional distinction exists only on paper. And we can logically be expected to agree with President Faunce of Brown University, when he says, "The present system is nothing more than a systematic prevarication."

I should like to ask the gentlemen of the Negative a question. How do they account for the fact that 70 per cent of the typical educational institutions visited by the Carnegie Foundation did subsidize and recruit, when these amateur-professional distinctions emphatically forbid such action as being dishonest and hypocritical? There is but one answer: These distinctions discourage honesty and truthfulness.

The situation at these colleges might be likened to a father who says to his son, "Honesty and truthfulness are magnificent virtues. I want you to follow them that you may become a worth-while citizen. Now, here is $50 that I stole yesterday. Go out to Leo's and get drunk. But if your mother asks you where you got the money, tell her Uncle Bill gave it to you for being such an honest boy." Every American college and university has dedicated itself to further in its sons honesty, truthfulness, and other desirable social qualities; and yet 70 per cent of these institutions turn about and give their athletes room and board, tuition, a worthless job, or a permanent loan, to engage in amateur sports under their colors. What is the logical result of such hypocrisy? Is it not the lessening of the college student's appreciation of the value of honesty and truthfulness? Can the professional athlete who has gotten away with playing pseudo-amateur football for three years be expected to look upon honesty as a necessity? No; he will look upon it as most people look upon Santa Claus — to be displayed on every street corner, but not to be taken too seriously.

As an editorial in the *Christian Century* puts it, "Whether or not the colleges hire their athletes is of little importance, but that they should lie about it is important. All colleges have agreed to conduct their athletics on a strictly amateur basis. Righteousness and religion would be just as well satisfied with honest professionalism, but they cannot stomach dishonest professionalism." This forthright declaration sounds the fundamental note of our contention — honesty is more important than amateurism! It is to further honesty and truthfulness and to eliminate hypocrisy that we make our proposal that this distinction between amateurism and professionalism, sometimes so petty as one cent, be abolished in sports to which admission fees are charged.

CHAIRMAN GARFF: The first speaker for the Negative tonight, from the University of Michigan, is Lawrence Hartwig.

FIRST NEGATIVE
Lawrence Hartwig, Michigan

MR. CHAIRMAN, LADIES, AND GENTLEMEN: Speaking for the negative team, I can assure you that it is a pleasure for us to continue our forensic relations with Northwestern University; and although the snowstorm did hinder somewhat our progress in coming to this city, I am sure it will not further hinder our having a good time here.

Let us examine for a few minutes the speech of the first speaker of the Affirmative. A large part of his talk was devoted to portraying a bad picture of violations under the existing amateur-professional rule; but let me point out to you, in the first place, that the gentlemen of the opposition may be just a bit inclined to overdraw the picture tonight. The Negative, understand, is not contending that the rule is not being violated, because every rule, Ladies and Gentlemen, is violated. Despite any of the borderline cases which the opposition may cite, they cannot overlook the large field which does exist between amateurism and professionalism.

They have asked us, "Why is it that 70 per cent of the schools examined by the Carnegie Foundation were found to have violated the distinction in some respect?" and it is my purpose in the next few minutes to point out to you just exactly what is the nature of those violations.

In the first place, the violations of the eighty-one schools, which were pointed out to you by the last speaker, were not violations of the amateur rule in its entirety; in fact, they were mere violations of some minor aspect of it — some athlete who, under the rule, should have gotten fifty cents, perhaps got fifty-one cents.

Benny Friedman, at Michigan, wrote articles for a magazine; and for that reason Friedman was placed in the list of professional students. And then, too, it is significant to note that of the one hundred and twelve schools examined by the Carnegie Foundation, twenty-eight of those schools, Ladies and Gentlemen, were enforcing the rule to the very letter, indicating clearly that all of the schools could enforce the rule, because in that list were included such important institutions as Yale and Oberlin.

Now, the Affirmative must show you that conditions are getting continually worse; whereas if they had examined the Carnegie report more thoroughly, they would have found that the Carnegie investigators, after finding the conditions which have been thrown up to you by the last speaker, Ladies and Gentlemen, and after examining all of these conditions, came to the conclusion in their report that conditions are becoming better, so that on page 225 we read that "with all due allowance for the tendency to magnify the past in comparison with the present, there can be little doubt that the evils of soliciting and subsidizing athletes have diminished over the last twenty-five, twenty, or even fifteen years." Ladies and Gentlemen, that is the report which was quoted to you by the last speaker; that is the situation as they found it.

Now, they cited to you the Carnegie report; and, incidentally, Ladies and Gentlemen, despite what the opposition has said about the "biased authority," it is the most authoritative information of conditions that we have. They cited to you cases of violations from this very report. After this thorough investigation, after finding the various violations of the rule, what was their conclusion? Did they conclude, as the Affirmative is advocating tonight, that the distinction should be abolished? No. Their conclusion was, Ladies and Gentlemen, that the abolition of the distinction would be a counsel of defeat, and that the correction lies in an intelligent application of the rule; and that is what the Negative is advocating tonight. Their conclusion was as follows: "The proposal that the amateur convention in college sport be abolished is a counsel of defeat. Such a step is far from justified by present conditions. The abolition of the amateur code, assuming for the moment that it could be abolished, not only would destroy the best that is now gained from college sport, but would bring with it a new set of evils that would be infinitely worse than any that now obtain." And that is the conclusion of the authoritative investigation which has been quoted to you by the Affirmative.

My colleagues will go on to show you that in the face of these violations the rule can be and is being maintained.

Now, let us go a step further. Let us examine the conditions which have arisen as a result of the publication of the Carnegie report. The report was published in 1929. One year has passed since that investigation; and what has been the result? Fifteen universities and colleges and three conferences have taken definite steps to reform the existing evil. As a result of the publication of this report — and, understand, the report said that conditions were getting better — and since the publication of that report, fifteen universities and colleges have bettered their conditions. In an article in *World's Work*, December, 1930, John Tunis writes: "If *Bulletin 23* (the bulletin which has been quoted) did nothing more than quicken the pulse of American intercollegiate athletics and give those interested something to ponder over, the report would have served its purpose abundantly well. There is reason to believe, however, that it has done more than this, that many of its recommendations have been taken to heart by the authorities of the universities, that some reforms have been commenced, and that others may follow in due course; for many reforms have unquestionably been instituted that are directly traceable to the effect of the first report." And so, we notice that since the publication of this first report, definite reforms have been instituted in the following institutions: Lehigh, Pennsylvania State College, Ohio Wesleyan, Harvard, Princeton, West Virginia, Drake University, Grove City College, Oregon Agricultural, Washington and Jefferson, University of Nebraska, Texas College, Allegheny College, the University of Minnesota, Butler University, and the University of Wisconsin. And the Carnegie Foundation, Ladies and Gentlemen, is engaged, at the present time, in investigating the improvements which are being made in the present situation, and is in the process of compiling a bulletin, which will be published in the near future, to show how conditions are becoming better. Now, keep that in mind, Ladies and Gentlemen, in considering the question of whether or not there is a need for the abolition which the Affirmative is advocating tonight.

Although we admit that the rule is being violated in some of its aspects and there is a need for correction, the major consideration tonight is this: what would result if we took away entirely the distinction between amateurism and professionalism? What would happen if we abolished the one check which we have upon the practices which were cited to you by the preceding speaker?

It is our first constructive contention that if we abolish the distinction, the result would completely demoralize intercollegiate athletics — in the first place, because the abolition of that distinction would result in an unprecedented traffic in athletes. We admit that there is subsidizing, recruiting, and proselyting under the present rule, as cited to you by the previous speaker. How much worse would those practices be if we had no rule! It is our contention that, in the face of present conditions, if there were no rule in force, the universities and colleges of the United States would engage in commercialism, in an intense rivalry that would be without limit. We could picture, for instance, the financial resources of Michigan competing with the financial resources of Northwestern in attempting to secure the best teams that money can buy. Both schools would recruit and subsidize and proselyte, and they would have no rules and no limits, understand, to the extent to which they could go, with the result that it would be extremely detrimental to the institutions themselves and to the individuals who were put upon the auction block in this intense rivalry. And when we consider that the boys who are bargained back and forth in such a commercialistic system are in an impressionable age, when we consider that they are high-school graduates, we can see that the result of these tactics would have a very detrimental effect upon the individual as well. And so, the abolition of the distinction would cause a great traffic in athletes. But further, it would destroy the democracy of the playing field; it would destroy the equality of opportunity which is now presented the amateur under the present rule.

Amateurism, Ladies and Gentlemen, is that rule which protects the natural rights of the many as against the privileges of the few. If we take away the rule, we will place the amateur in competition with the professional, and the amateur, who regards sport as an avocation, against the professionalized man, who regards it as a vocation. Certainly the individual who regards sport as merely play would be placed at a disadvantage when forced to compete with a man who makes sport his life's business. So we see that, in the second place, the abolition of the distinction would create a situation whereby paid competition would create a disadvantageous situation as between the amateur and the professional.

It is our further contention that the objectives of intercollegiate athletics cannot be obtained under professional régime. Now, what are the objectives of amateurism? Page 35 of the Carnegie report says: "An amateur sportsman is one who engages in sport solely for the pleasure, physical, mental, and social benefits he derives therefrom; and to whom sport is nothing more than an avocation." These, Ladies and Gentlemen, are the objectives of amateurism. If we admit professionalism into intercollegiate athletics, it is our contention that these objectives could not be fully realized, because the professional, as the last speaker stated, has his outlook besmirched and perverted by the ultimate idea of capitalizing upon his ability. So, while the amateur does not have monetary gain as the ultimate goal of what he is achieving, the professional does; and inasmuch as the ideals of amateurism, the aims of amateurism, which I have pointed out to you, can be more fully realized when we have a distinction between amateurism and professionalism, and whereas the professional has his outlook beclouded by the ultimate aim of securing money, of capitalizing upon his efforts, it is our contention that the objectives of amateurism could not be fully obtained if we admit the professional into intercollegiate athletics.

I have shown you, then, Ladies and Gentlemen, that the abolition of this distinction would completely demoralize intercollegiate athletics. Thank you.

CHAIRMAN GARFF: The Affirmative will now continue its constructive case, Mr. John A. Blackmore being the next speaker.

SECOND AFFIRMATIVE
John A. Blackmore, Northwestern

MR. CHAIRMAN, LADIES, AND GENTLEMEN: Indeed, I was impressed with the words of the gentleman who has just left the platform. I believe the words that ring in my ears most clearly are those that he quoted from the Carnegie report with regard to the twenty-eight schools, I believe it is, who are now lily white, who are pure, and who are enforcing the rules to the limit.

Now, Ladies and Gentlemen, we will admit that the keen eye of the Carnegie observers did not find any difficulties in those institutions; but we further showed you that over in Iowa where they did their best, they were unable to find any such thing as a slush fund. And, Ladies and Gentlemen, can you deny that that is the most serious of difficulties — a great slush fund through which these men borrow money to an extent that we know absolutely nothing about? The fact remaining is this: that there were 70 per cent of the schools who were found to be subsidizing. And our contention is not so much that everyone subsidizes, but that it is an actual inherent quality in the system of athletics as we have it today. The gentleman read to you from the Carnegie report and told you that conditions are bettering themselves. But our fundamental contention would have been established if he had only read just a few lines further in that same paragraph, where we learn that "on the other hand, letters, accounts, and other records indicate that this improvement has been one of degree, but not of kind." In other words, there is no change of kind; in other words, these difficulties are inherent in the system. Regardless of whether slowly they are improving in one school, on this or that, still they are inherent.

Ladies and Gentlemen, this is just exactly the quality that we are objecting to today. We say that honesty is more to be preferred than pseudo-amateurism; and as long as it is one of kind, it is inherent in this system. We learn that there are no changes of kind; so we see, Ladies and Gentlemen, that we have struck the vital issue so far in this debate when we speak of honesty. The gentleman admits that there are difficulties in the system today, but that we do not need a radical change, that they will take care of themselves. Yet they are inherent, and we have this report to prove it.

Now, Ladies and Gentlemen, we would also have you know that the Carnegie Foundation has been an institution which has continually made it their goal to establish and to maintain this relationship, to maintain this distinction between professionalism and amateurism. Certainly they are a biased authority; but yet we have these facts from them.

Now, Ladies and Gentlemen, it is obvious that the present system of athletics forces the modern university into an inescapable dilemma. On the one hand, if the university is to subsidize in secret and display a pseudo-amateurism in public, then they are fostering nothing short of criminal dishonesty and hypocrisy; on the other hand, if they wish to retain the unpaid athlete, this unrewarded man, and still commercialize him to the extent of hundreds of thousands of dollars, then they offer nothing more nor less than the exploitation of the youth of today.

The fact that the college is forced into the first of these evils, hypocrisy, was demonstrated by my colleague. It shall be my purpose to point out to you under the second alternative of this dilemma, the unfairness that the present system has forced upon the college of today. We submit, therefore, secondly, that in games to which admission fees are charged it is the just right of the college athlete to receive remuneration, at least to the extent of educational expenses, and that anything short of this concession is open exploitation.

Now, we realize this fact more clearly when we view the returns that the university gains through athletics. From 1905 down to the present, trustees of American universities have built, or have allowed to be built, twenty stadia, with an average seating capacity of 50,000. In football, Notre Dame, when away from home, demands 60 per cent of the gate receipts — on the average. Yale University, through their Athletic Commission, announced to us that in 1929, just in October and November alone, their football profits were nearly $1,000,000 — $1,000,000 for two months of football. The University of Georgia invades a New York ball park to play New York University, and demands and receives a $50,000 guarantee — Ladies and Gentlemen, $50,000, the nominal fee paid a Southern institution of learning for sending twenty young amateurs, boys who play for the love of the game, to New York for one afternoon. In short, who can find a business more spectacularly profitable than this little game of football? But profitable for

whom? That is the question. For the men who earn the money?
Of course, we are assured that all this money is turned over to other
athletics incapable of self-support. Well, let us just grant this fact.
We then see that we are confronted with a further difficulty, and
the question is this : Are these other sports in which you and I are
engaged — intramurals — worthy of being considered essential
to college curricula? Are they worthy? If you say No, then
Yale University misspends half a million dollars a year. If you
say Yes — and most of us will, for they are important — then it
seems that this university owes to those certain undergraduates
who earn for it by their ardent efforts those hundreds of thousands
of dollars, some special consideration — at least as much as is paid
to other participants in college activities.

Now the *a fortiori* weight of this argument is redoubled when
we consider that in few other fields of college activities does the
participant go unrewarded. If a man has journalistic talent, he
may work on the school newspaper to help defray expenses. Band
members may play in professional dance orchestras, yet they are
not ineligible to play in the band. Public speaking contestants
receive prizes — and far more! Why, a debating team visiting us
from a well-known university in the East just last week tells us that
each of those three men has had his tuition and incidental fees paid
by the university since his freshman year, because of his ability
in debate. Yet the athlete alone, my friends, is asked to go without
remuneration for his natural talents. Why, Ladies and Gentlemen,
should this man be without the same privileges that are given to
other people in other lines?

Now, we see that not only is a man exploited while he is in the
university, but during the summer, during his vacation time, he is
given not the chance that he should be given. We see that even
during vacation time he is so limited by obnoxious, petty laws and
rulings that his chances of making any returns even during vacation
time are practically nil, that they are few and far between. If a
man has played football during his college year and wishes to teach
swimming during the summer, if he does so, he is called a "professional" and can no longer play college football. If he teaches
swimming in the summer, he can never play college football again.

Ladies and Gentlemen, I ask you, can you see the slightest correlation between these two activities? He is exploited in school, and still he must suffer through the petty and obnoxious rulings during the summer.

Now, just to make this thing a bit more concrete, our own "Red" Woodworth in this University, one of our star football players, as you all know, goes out and gives the University the best he has in the line of football for two whole seasons; and then last summer, when out of school, he shows his ability in another line by winning several speed-boat races in open competition. Yet he was forced to refuse some thousands of dollars as prizes, which rightfully belonged to him — prizes for these contests.

But still, this limitation would not be so intolerable were it not for its flagrant inconsistency with other similar cases. Jack Riley, another of our football stars here at school, and besides a wrestling champion, finds no difficulty in capitalizing his ability of holding the job of lifesaver out here at one of these beach resorts nearby; yet it is interesting to note that if this young man were to have given as much as one swimming lesson, perhaps to some fair damsel — notice I said swimming lesson — he would no longer be eligible to play amateur football, nor even take part in amateur wrestling.

Now, Ladies and Gentlemen, we ask, why this distinction? Certainly you will admit that if there is any preference shown, this latter case shows the greatest capitalization of amateur ability.

Let us consider for just a moment the returns for the athlete, now that we have seen what the university gains through athletics — hundreds of thousands of dollars. If you know the hours that must be spent on the football field, if you know the place football must hold in the mind of the man who is playing for those four months in a year, you will realize it takes a sacrifice in studies. More than this, he gambles with injuries at odds which we could hardly consider fair. Out of three thousand football players observed by the Carnegie Foundation, 17 per cent sustained injury in one year. In other words, if you play football for three years you have less than a fifty-fifty chance of escaping unscathed — a reckless gamble with injury, besides a sacrifice in studies.

But now let us cross the ledger and seek to determine the benefits for the athlete. What about physical conditioning? It can be gained through tennis and swimming — and far better conditioning than that obtained through football or basketball, the sports through which we gain all the profits. As a matter of fact, the overdevelopment in these sports during the playing seasons, if not continued, is likely to degenerate into a serious physical condition, to say nothing of the resultant flabbiness. That fact is well known. And is there anyone who can deny that a track or basketball star is considered a very poor life insurance risk? Certainly there is little to be gained in the physical line. How about sportsmanship, where the sportsman is required to be a puppet in the hands of the coach, the ringmaster? Is he to be considered as one receiving lessons in good sportsmanship? How about fame? It is ephemeral! Is this due reward? Here today, gone tomorrow! What is more fleeting than the fame of an athlete? Where are the snows of yesteryear, and who knows the All-Americans of 1920?

Certainly, my friends, you will come with us in believing that the athlete receives nothing in comparison to what the university reaps from this field of athletics. He sows his natural talents; his Alma Mater reaps a harvest of gold! Is this fair?

CHAIRMAN GARFF: The case of the Negative will be continued by Victor Rabinowitz.

SECOND NEGATIVE
Victor Rabinowitz, Michigan

MR. CHAIRMAN, LADIES, AND GENTLEMEN: I might remark that teaching fair damsels to swim has its own reward.

The gentlemen of the opposition have made a great deal of to-do over the fact that the Carnegie Foundation is biased. They say that the Carnegie Foundation is determined to keep the amateur-professional distinction. Why, of course the Carnegie Foundation is biased; the Carnegie Foundation is determined to keep the amateur-professional distinction. But why? Because the Carnegie Foundation is dedicated to the advancement of teaching, to the advancement of education, and because the Carnegie Foundation sees that the abolition of the distinction, as suggested by the gentlemen of the opposition, will not help the advancement of teaching or the advancement of education. That is why the Carnegie Foundation is biased, because it sees very good and very powerful reasons for opposing the proposition of the gentlemen of the opposition.

The gentlemen of the opposition also said that the Carnegie Foundation does not see everything, and that is why they did not see things at Yale and other institutions where no subsidizing exists. They gave as an instance the University of Iowa, where the Carnegie Foundation could not discover the slush fund. On page 254 of the Carnegie report, the report tells about this University of Iowa general scholarship fund, in which a disproportionate award appears to have been made to athletes. That was the University of Iowa slush fund that the Big Ten Conference discovered.

The gentlemen of the opposition have said a great deal about hypocrisy, how the amateur-professional law leads to hypocrisy. Every law leads to hypocrisy. Every law is being violated. Does that mean we should throw up our hands in disgust and say, "Oh, well, we won't bother to enforce this law because it leads to dishonesty"? Every law is being violated. Every law leads to hypocrisy and dishonesty. That is no excuse for withdrawing the law.

The gentlemen of the opposition have said a great deal about the injustice to the athlete because of the fact that he isn't being paid and that other people are — debaters and journalists. We might point out that the purpose of an educational institution is educational; the purpose of a college is to give a good education to its students. The purpose is not to provide a living for any man who can play football well. Debating, musical ability, and journalism are all educational pursuits; playing football isn't. The only thing that a college owes to its athletes is good physical condition. They get this good physical condition. The university owes no man a living from his athletic ability. The gentlemen of the opposition have said, "Well, let's give him his tuition; let's give him a little bit of what he earns for the university. You are exploiting his ability. Why not pay him, at least his tuition?"

I would like to read a quotation from an interview with Coach Yost of the University of Michigan. This interview was given two days ago. He says, "To me, it is a question of what is best for the boy. Giving a scholarship or permitting an alumnus to establish funds is purely paying the boy. Once started, where are you going to draw the line?" Coach Kipke, coach of the football team, said in an interview on the same day, "Nobody knows what subsidizing would grow to once you permit any form of it. The best athlete is the one who does not think the school owes him a living. As far as the boy goes, he gets the idea that he is a 'big shot,' and when he gets out in life he naturally thinks that the world owes him his living. It is the worst thing in the world for the boy." That is what the gentlemen of the opposition are offering to you — reward to the boy for playing football. They have made a great deal of the fact that Yale erects great intramural buildings, due to the money it gets out of intercollegiate athletics. Yale does not subsidize its athletes, according to the Carnegie report, which was, perhaps, a little bit more thorough than the gentlemen of the opposition give it credit for.

The first speaker for the Negative pointed out that professionalism in intercollegiate athletics would demoralize intercollegiate athletics. I would like to go on to point out the effect of professionalism on the university entirely apart from athletics, on the university as an educational institution. Now, the first objective of a university — perhaps not the only objective, but certainly the first — is an intellectual one. What is the effect of professionalism on the intellectual objectives of a university? In the first place, it would give an entirely disproportionate emphasis to athletics. The gentlemen of the opposition told you a great deal about overemphasis as it exists today. They told you about the huge football stadia that exist all over this country. Conditions, they said, are pretty bad — that is, the condition, according to the gentlemen of the opposition, as it exists today. What do the gentlemen of the opposition plan to do to remedy this condition? They plan to remove one of the laws that holds the present conditions down to where they are, one of the rules that does not make conditions even worse than they are.

I would like to read a quotation from the Carnegie report. It says, page 307, "It is the undergraduates who have suffered most and will continue most to suffer from commercialism and its results.

(These huge football stadia that the gentlemen of the opposition are speaking about.) More than any other force it has tended to distort the values of college life and to increase its emphasis upon the material and the monetary." Why, the very word "professionalism" means an increased emphasis upon the material and the monetary.

The Carnegie Foundation report, on page 310, one of the last paragraphs in the report, says, "Commercialism in college athletics must be destroyed." The gentlemen of the opposition are picking a strange way to destroy commercialism — by making everything commercial, by permitting professionalism in college athletics.

The second effect of the abolition of the distinction on the intellectual objectives of a university is that it would lower academic standards. The gentlemen of the opposition told you that the rule was being violated in a good many institutions today. Let us see what the effect of this violation is on the academic standards of those universities. The report here has a number of illustrations of letters from coaches to members of the faculty asking them to please reëxamine a student and, if possible, to pass him in the course. The report draws the following conclusion : "The presence of a man whose prime interest in college is dependent upon payment for his athletic services delays and reduces academic instruction to his intellectual level and speed, both in the classroom and in every other phase of college work. It invokes concessions at entrance and at every point at which an academic requirement is set. It leads in the direction of special privilege in tests and examinations, the relaxation of standards of grading in class and in written work, the granting of special opportunities to repair academic standing when it is injured by the close attention to athletic practice that subsidies entail, and much excusing from the obligation to meet academic appointments promptly and sincerely. It disunifies the student body, and soon brings other undergraduates to feel that efforts to fulfill the intellectual purposes of the institution avail nothing, if men are to be supported merely for the sake of winning games." The passage concludes with this very significant remark : "No other force so completely vitiates the intellectual aims of an institution and each of its members."

This, Ladies and Gentlemen, is the situation as it exists today in those institutions where the amateur rule is being violated in some of its aspects. What do the gentlemen of the opposition plan to do to remedy this situation? They plan to make everything professional. Where professionalism exists today in its present limited form, we find that there is pressure brought upon members of the faculty to "please pass star athletes." Is it not fairly obvious that when we pay all of our athletes, more and more pressure will be brought to bear upon members of the faculty? Perhaps most of our members of the faculty will not succumb to this increased pressure, but there will always be some who, as now, will succumb to this pressure, and lower academic standards to meet the athlete.

A second objective is the socializing objective. The Carnegie report points out several instances where athletes, notably at Harvard, Penn State, and Pennsylvania, have become a separate class, where the athletes are in one class and the rest of the student body is in another. The gentlemen of the opposition to remedy this condition will pay athletes. You will have, on the one hand, men who are coming to college for education; and, on the other hand, men who are coming to college to make a living by playing football.

In closing, I would like to point out that my colleagues and I have drawn a number of conclusions. I would like to say that these conclusions are not wild flights into the future; they are not wild guesses as to what may or may not happen sometime when we may or may not abolish the distinction. Every statement my colleague and I have made this evening is based on conditions as they exist today where the amateur rule is being violated. Does it not seem plain that conditions will be worse when the amateur rule is removed entirely?

CHAIRMAN GARFF: The constructive case of the Affirmative will be concluded by Richard Peterson.

THIRD AFFIRMATIVE
Richard Peterson, Northwestern

MR. CHAIRMAN, LADIES, AND GENTLEMEN: The last speaker of the Negative has endeavored to fasten a particular contention on us, which he would like very much to see us advocate, but which we refuse to advocate. He says that our stand all through this is to have everything professional — to abandon all rules and regulations, and make everything professional. We refuse to take that stand, in spite of the assertions of the Negative.

I will explain to you just exactly our stand on this matter. The proposition has two parts: first, the abolition of the distinction; and, second, limiting that abolition to those sports in which admission fees are charged. If we put our whole proposition into effect, here is just exactly what you would have: You would have a division of the educational institutions of today into two fundamental parts. First would be a school retaining gate receipts and abolishing the distinction in those sports; and the other would be a school which abolishes gate receipts and therefore retains the distinction.

Considering this school which abolishes the gate receipts and retains this distinction, we find that professionalism very naturally does not exist. Such a school has been recently proposed by Nicholas Murray Butler, President of Columbia University, and by President Day of Union College. In such a school, once you remove the gate receipts you remove the urge to pay. A little ditty will explain the idea:

> Where no money is made,
> No athletes will be paid.

Now, our negative team has contended that in our proposal, first, there would be a disproportionate emphasis laid on sports. The only way that you can remove a disproportionate emphasis, according to them, is to maintain this amateur ideal. The only way you can really maintain that amateur ideal which they hold up so high is to abolish these gate receipts in those particular schools, because if you remove those gate receipts you do not have to have the winning team to get these immense piles of gold, and you don't have to pay the player to get these winning teams. And you see that in such a school only, and in the affirmative proposal only, could you remove a disproportionate emphasis on these sports.

Their second contention was that it would lower the standards.

You can easily see that the standards can be best maintained in a school which abolishes these gate receipts, even according to the negative contention tonight. In the second place, the result of putting our proposal into practice would mean that at least we would have equality of teams. You notice back there awhile they said that one of the principal faults here with our proposal is you would have professionals playing against amateurs. That is just exactly what you have today. When the University of Chicago plays almost any other university, it is a case of amateur playing against professional. That is one of the reasons they don't win. The object of practically all of our present restrictions is to secure an equality of team. Frederick Ran Eagles, a figure of national significance in this controversy, says, "The problem of justice in games and sports may be restated positively as one of securing approximate equality between colleges playing competing teams." Thus, you can see that in those schools which abolish the gate receipts it would mean that in these schools amateurs would not unwittingly compete against professionals. Furthermore, in those schools there would be a chance for the believers in the amateur tradition actually to try out their ideals; perhaps — who knows? — even the ideals of the Negative might stand a chance in this future school. They certainly don't in the present school. The more important result in such a school is this: you would have the temptation of dishonesty removed. In other words, you would not be tempting the American college boy. If Adam had not had an apple, he would not have eaten the apple, and he would not have fallen. As a more concrete illustration of that, why put more pitfalls in the path of American youth and college youth? Why, there are plenty of pitfalls already, too many of them already, in a coeducational institution like this.

Seriously, you can see the immense weight of that fact, that the temptation of dishonesty and crookedness and hypocrisy would be removed in those schools abolishing gate receipts. We would be led back to the fundamental contention that honesty is more important than pseudo-amateurism. So you can see that since the desired emphasis, and only that amount, could be placed on sports in colleges, since standards would not be lowered, since there would be a chance for the believers in amateur traditions to try out their ideals, and since this temptation of dishonesty would be removed in colleges, our plan would work out beneficially if put into effect in such a college.

Now, let's consider the other type of college, the type of institution which desires to retain gate receipts and abolish the distinction in those colleges. A little line there will explain the idea : "Wherever there are gate receipts, there are no amateurs." That is best explained by analogy. A long time ago American college and university presidents realized they could not obtain the necessary funds for their institutions merely by sitting back in the office and dictating amateur form-letters ; they were forced to become professional solicitors. "Wherever there are gate receipts, there are no amateurs."

What is the result of putting that plan into effect, abolishing the distinction in those institutions? First of all, we see that the fundamental requirements of the eligibility rules could be enforced. We would have the intelligent application of eligibility rules that the Negative is advocating tonight. Furthermore, you see that all the present confusion in the present system is caused not by the scholarship requirement, the residence requirement of the athlete, but the particular one rule, out of roughly sixty that we have — this amateur rule requiring that distinction. If you remove that source of the trouble, then at last you will be able to get down to the real fundamental functions of this eligibility code, you will remove that trouble, and you can raise the standards of these colleges, because you have admitted the part that causes the trouble and causes any standards to be lowered.

Now, at present we are paying attention to this minor aspect of the eligibility code ; we are paying attention to the scratch on our hand, — whether "Red" Woodworth took the $5,000 he won in the motor-boat races. We are worrying over a bump on the head — whether Albie Booth paid for his meals at Yale. We are worrying about a corn on the toe, — whether an all-American from Southern California got fifty or fifty-one cents an hour for winding the electric clock.

Seriously now, paying attention to all these minor ideas we are forgetting the vital function — in other words, the scholastic requirements of the eligibility rules — and they can best be brought into accord by abolishing this troublesome distinction.

What would be the second good result of our proposal? The fact that the present danger of exposure to danger would be eliminated. What is the condition we have at present? We have some young chap coming to college from high school. Perhaps, like most of us, he has a little bit of trouble meeting the financial requirements; he has to work for part of his money. Perhaps he is fortunate to get upon the football team. He sees most of the other fellows receiving money for playing football, and he would seem like a "sissy" if he turned down the money and said, "I am a pure-minded amateur; I will take no more of your filthy lucre." As if any man on the Northwestern team would say that! That is a very real danger, because if he does go ahead in this sport it means that at any time the fact might come out that sometime on the Pacific Coast he received more than $50 a month; and therefore he is brought into disgrace and dishonor. That is a very real chance. It is a chance that Bradley of Iowa ran and lost. It is a chance that Jim Bausch, of Kansas, took and lost; and Jim Bausch suffered national disgrace because the fact came out that he accepted $70 a month for not selling life insurance.

Seriously, now, you can see this is a real danger; and it is a danger existing in 70 per cent of our colleges and universities. This danger would be obviated, removed, if you would abolish those distinctions.

What would be the third result? The fact that once more sports in our colleges would be restored to an honest, just, and truthful basis. Our opponents have charged that our system of professionalism would have a bad effect upon the student body. Consider the effect today of the present system. You see how it is impossible not to hurt the general morale of the campus when they realize that all this dishonesty and crookedness and hypocrisy is at present existing in their athletes, men to whom they look up. To abolish this distinction would immeasurably benefit the athlete. Once more he could hold up his head and look the world in the eye, because at least the world did realize that amateurism is not as important as his honesty.

So you see that the results are beneficial, because of the fact that the fundamental requirements of eligibility could be observed, because of the fact that the danger of exposure would be removed, and because of the fact that once more we would have sport on an honest, just, and truthful basis.

Now, let's just briefly summarize the case that the Affirmative has presented tonight. We have built up our presentation upon three fundamental contentions: first, that the present system is hypocritical — hypocrisy exists, dishonesty, crookedness, and moral turpitude, because in 70 per cent of the colleges, according to the Carnegie report, of which our opponents seem to have so high an opinion, these colleges are indulging in crookedness and dishonest subsidy today; in the second place, that the present system is unfair, that the athlete is not treated fairly. Instead of receiving his just due, he receives over-physical development resulting in permanent injuries. This is obviously unfair. Furthermore, we base our contention on the fact that if you put this proposal which we advocate into practice, if you actually had it adopted at present in both these types of schools — the type who retain the gate receipts and the type who abolish the gate receipts — this proposal would work out to give us beneficial results.

CHAIRMAN GARFF: The constructive case of the Affirmative is now concluded.

Nathan Levy will bring the constructive negative case to a conclusion.

THIRD NEGATIVE
Nathan Levy, Michigan

MR. CHAIRMAN, LADIES, AND GENTLEMEN: I suppose in order to get rid of the pitfalls that the gentlemen of the opposition pointed out we should abolish coeducation.

You know, the gentlemen of the opposition have taken this stand, or they have refused to take this stand. The gentlemen on the opposition pointed out to you that my colleagues spent twenty-four minutes telling you of the excess that is going to result if we abolish the amateur-professional distinction. The gentlemen of the opposition have come to this conclusion: We refuse to stand on that argument. Well, now, the mere fact that the gentlemen of the opposition don't get up and advocate excess is not any proof of the fact that the excess is not going to result; the mere fact that the gentlemen of the opposition refuse to argue that point with us is no proof of the fact that that excess will not result. The gentlemen of the opposition are doing something like this: "We find that there are evils existing at the present time. Well, we are going to do away with those evils, and we present to you this plan." They give you the plan. They say, "Oh, well, the mere fact that worse things could happen from our plan does not worry us a bit. You have evils all the time."

They have not pointed out, they have not accepted, they have not refuted, and they have not even considered the excess that is going to result from handing the control of all athletics to the professional, with the professional idea as the main idea. The gentlemen of the opposition have not said one word concerning the results of the abolition of the amateur-professional distinction.

Then, the gentlemen of the opposition have taken a peculiar stand in their last speech. The gentlemen of the opposition have said that the proposition can be interpreted this way: First of all, either abolish the amateur-professional distinction and allow all professionals; or, by the last clause in the proposition, abolish all gate receipts and maintain the amateur-professional distinction.

In the first place, we had conceived the last clause, "in all sports to which admission fees are charged," to be a descriptive clause and to include within such all sports to which admission fees are charged, so that the statement of the proposition, *"Resolved: That all colleges and universities should abolish the distinction between amateurism and professionalism,"* would apply to those sports — football, basketball, track, swimming, hockey, or any sports — to which admission fees are charged. So it is only under protest that we accept the interpretation that the gentlemen of the opposition have put on the proposition; and having accepted that interpretation under protest, we want to point out to the gentlemen of the opposition that this distinction is not complete, that they cannot take this proposition — even if that clause can be interpreted the way they would like to have it interpreted — and make the distinction "either/or," because there is a third alternative. We believe that the third alternative is the reasonable alternative; we believe that the third method of attack and approach is the sanest and the most reasonable of all approaches; and that is, maintain the amateur-professional distinction and maintain gate receipts — simple, clear and absolutely cannot be read out of the proposition by any interpretation that is put upon it.

But supposing for the moment we accept the interpretation put on the proposition by the gentlemen of the opposition. First of all, they say, "Let's abolish the amateur-professional distinction and have all universities be professional." Well, then, they go on to the second one, "Let's abolish gate receipts and maintain the amateur-professional distinction." After having ragged us quite a bit about being people who stand up for the spirit of amateurism and who want Simon-pure, lily-white athletes, the gentlemen of the opposition, by that very stand, tacitly admit that the amateur-professional distinction is a reasonable and worth-while distinction.

Then, let's go back to the first. The gentlemen of the opposition would abolish gate receipts and allow professionalism to come in, and yet the gentlemen of the opposition have not for one minute taken up with you the excesses that we have pointed out. The gentlemen of the opposition have not taken up with you the fact that the abolition of the amateur-professional distinction and the introduction of professionalism into intercollegiate athletics will demoralize both the objectives of intercollegiate athletics, and, secondly, would demoralize the objectives of the educational institution and of the socializing agency as we conceive the university to be.

But there is something else that is of tremendous importance when we consider the proposition that the gentlemen of the opposition advance. The gentlemen of the opposition gave you a couple of little rhyme phrases. I am sorry I did not get the rhymes, or I would repeat them back to you. The sense of the rhyme is:

> Where there is money taken in at the gate,
> You can't have any amateurs,
> Because they are all going to be paid;
> And where there isn't any money taken in at the gate,
> They can all be amateurs.

First, off-hand, that might sound rather reasonable. Yet if the gentlemen of the opposition would merely look at the facts, they would find that the opposite is true, and that the thing they have said is true, whichever way the authorities want it to be.

Now, then, we claim that there is no causal connection between gate receipts and the professionalization of amateurs — the paying, the subsidizing, the recruiting, and the proselyting of amateur sportsmen. Now, then, how do we get that way? Simply this: Well, Yale and Illinois have as much tradition to uphold, and as much, if not more, gate receipts, than any other university in the entire United States; and yet Yale and Illinois and twenty-six other universities, plus fifteen more since the report has been issued, are actually, wholly, and completely amateur, enforcing the rule in its full vigor. Then, on the other hand, if we look over the history of the amateur-professional distinction we find this to be true: The first instance of professionalism in the United States in the 1850's took place in rowing, the sport rowing, to which no admission fee was charged. For thirty years England fought professionalism in rowing on the Thames between their universities, and no admission fee was charged. In the United States, between 1890 and 1905, the period in which the violation of the amateur-professional distinction was most violent, widespread, and flagrant, there were no, or very few, gate receipts; and if there were any gate receipts they did not come in until after 1900, leaving a ten-year period of flagrant violation of the amateur-professional rule — recruiting, subsidizing, proselyting, and all of that — without any gate receipts. Then, at the present time, as I have pointed out, we have these twenty-eight universities, plus the other fifteen, which, without gate receipts, are absolutely, wholly, and solely amateurs.

Now, then, let's take up portions of the case that the gentlemen of the opposition have presented. You know, they considered with you the case of Mr. Riley and the case of Mr. Woodworth, and that is what we want to accuse the gentlemen of the opposition of at the present time. The gentlemen of the opposition have taken up for you only borderline cases. How do I know they have taken up borderline cases? I quote to you the examples they have given.

They took the case in which the difference was between fifty and fifty-one cents. Well, now, if any law is to be made to maintain a distinction, that law must be arbitrary at some one point. No law can be made to maintain a distinction without being along the line of arbitrary law.

Now, this is the way it goes. Here is the line. This arm is a line. On this side is amateurism, and on this side is professionalism. The gentlemen of the opposition have taken cases right along this line, and have pointed out to you that they think perhaps an injustice is being done; and then they have said "abolish the line." The gentlemen of the opposition, in order to take care of the few cases along here, want to accept into colleges and universities this entire field of professionalism that exists over there; and the gentlemen of the opposition have talked to you about amateurism this side of the line as if it were nothing at all but perhaps the air that exists at that side of the line. It is something more. It is the protecting bar against the excess that the gentlemen of the opposition will allow to come into the educational system of the United States, whether or not they advocate it, if they abolish the amateur-professional distinction.

Now, then, with regard to these men who get paid fifty-one and fifty cents. We believe that the gentlemen of the opposition are perfectly aware — although they did not point out to you — that practically every amateur conference, practically every amateur rule, allows a certain amount of reinstatement of athletes into the amateur class. You do not have to abolish the distinction to apply a rule intelligently. We believe that the rule can be enforced; and we believe that, in addition to being enforced, it should be applied with intelligence. Now, then, the gentlemen of the opposition did not point out to you that at the present time there is in all amateur conventions the possibility of an athlete being reinstated if he becomes a professional through pure technicality — that is, the cases they were telling you about — or through ignorance — that is, like teaching the young girl to swim and accepting $5 for no good reason at all — or if they are made professionals through the actions of a second party; or if in the mind of those authorities administering the law, the distinction, circumstances, and conditions and the mind of the individual were such as to make him not wholly and solely a professional, but an amateur.

The gentlemen of the opposition have taken the peculiar stand that the university owes a man a living because he can play football. It doesn't owe him any living at all. He doesn't have to play football. He doesn't have to run the risk of injury which doesn't give him a fifty-fifty chance. He doesn't have to over-train. He doesn't have to eat at the training table. He doesn't have to do any of these things. It is for him to choose and to decide. The university owes a man an education; beyond that, it owes him nothing at all. Once the universities are burdened with this idea of professionalism they will not be able, because of the excess that will result, to fulfill the objectives for which the universities are really founded. They will not be able, in other words, to teach well, to maintain educational standards; and they will not be able to allow the students to gain from intercollegiate athletics the things that the universities want students to gain from those athletics.

In conclusion, if the gentlemen of the opposition will consider for you the fact that borderline cases are to be found in every law and that intelligent application can take care of most, if not all, borderline cases, the gentlemen of the opposition will find that the amateur-professional distinction should not be abolished.

CHAIRMAN GARFF: We are ready to begin the rebuttals for this debate now. The Negative are going to open the rebuttal speeches, Mr. Lawrence Hartwig being the first rebuttal speaker for the Negative, speaking for the University of Michigan.

FIRST NEGATIVE REBUTTAL
Lawrence Hartwig, Michigan

MR. CHAIRMAN, LADIES, AND GENTLEMEN: Let us take up in detail the case of our opponents tonight. The first speaker attempted to show you that the present amateur-professional distinction is hypocritical. He pointed out that there were certain violations of the rule, that these violations were hypocritical and dishonest, and that not only was the dishonesty detrimental to the

individual, but detrimental also to the university. We, on the
other hand, pointed out that any violation of a rule must necessarily
be hypocritical or dishonest, but that that does not necessarily
prove that the rule is bad. We also showed you that despite the
violations of the present rule conditions are getting better. We
cited the Carnegie report to indicate that conditions are getting
better. We pointed out that since the publication of that report
sixteen universities and colleges and three conferences have bettered
themselves in regard to violations in the amateur-professional
distinction. That, Ladies and Gentlemen, is the first thing that
the Affirmative must substantiate tonight before they can propose
any new case. Before they can propose an abolition of the status
quo they must absolutely, conclusively beyond any shadow of a
doubt, point out to you a need. They must prove to you, Ladies
and Gentlemen, that a need for this abolition exists, whereas we
have showed you that conditions are continually becoming better,
that these conditions are self-corrected, that they are not in themselves inherently bad. That, in substance, was the speech of the
first speaker of the Affirmative.

The second speaker of the Affirmative pointed out to you that
the university owes the athlete a living. He said that the universities are gaining much money at the expense of the poor athlete,
and that 70 per cent of the athletes are injured. He pointed out
the dangers of the athletic heart and what not. He showed that
the poor amateur cannot get any monetary gain because of his
service to the college. On the other hand, he pointed out that the
universities and the colleges are attaining great reward at the expense
of the poor athlete. My colleagues came back and showed you
that the university does not owe the athlete a living, rather that
the objectives of the university are intellectual and social. If we
removed the distinction between amateurism and professionalism,
the evils would be far greater than the evils which exist under the
present situation.

We quoted to you Coach Kipke of the University of Michigan.
He said, "We do not know where to draw the line once we abolish
the distinction. Once we abolish the distinction the situation will
become so bad that it will be out of control."

Then the third speaker, assuming that his colleague established a definite need for the abolition of the distinction, pointed out a disjunctive case. He analyzed the proposition, "*Resolved:* That all colleges and universities should abolish the distinction between amateurism and professionalism in sports to which admission fees are charged," as follows : In the first place, he says, "Let us abolish gate receipts and retain the distinction," or "Let us retain gate receipts and abolish the distinction."

My colleague, the third speaker, pointed out that we accept that interpretation of the proposition under protest, that on those sports to which admission fees are paid the distinction should be abolished — in football, basketball, and other sports to which admission is paid. Then my colleague, the third speaker, pointed out to members of the Affirmative that even though we accept their interpretation, we find there is a third alternative, that amateurism is compatible with gate receipts. Then he pointed out to you that there is absolutely no causal connection between amateurism and professionalism.

Let us examine the case of the twenty-eight universities and colleges which today, under the amateur rule, are maintaining the letter of that rule. Yale and Harvard are two of the schools, for instance, which have maintained the distinction ; and yet those colleges and universities have gate receipts which are as large as those of any university or college which has been found to violate the rule. He pointed out to you that between 1890 and 1900, when professionalism in this country was at its highest point, gate receipts were at the lowest point ; and that whereas today gate receipts to athletic intercollegiate contests are enormous compared with previous times, professionalism, Ladies and Gentlemen, has declined.

CHAIRMAN GARFF : The first rebuttal speaker for the Affirmative is Richard Peterson.

FIRST AFFIRMATIVE REBUTTAL
Richard Peterson, Northwestern

MR. CHAIRMAN, LADIES, AND GENTLEMEN : We have heard a lot just in the last few minutes about the causal connection between gate receipts and amateurism. They tend to have you believe it is merely a casual connection, and not a causal connection. Let us investigate the present condition and see just exactly how this comes about. Take a logical order of reasoning. At present, as our second affirmative speaker pointed out, the universities and colleges have dedicated themselves to obtaining huge gate receipts in order to pay for their stadia and the other expenses. In order to receive good, huge gate receipts you must have winning teams. In order to get winning teams at the present time you must have paid players. Here is certainly direct, logical causal relationship. If we didn't have to pay the players, why would we? The university does not get any particular kick or pleasure out of giving the player any money. They do it because they have to, and yet our opponents assert that Yale and Illinois are Simon pure and lily white, and that they don't give any money. What is their authority for that fact? The fact that the Carnegie Foundation placed them on the white list and said they weren't bad. Now, the Carnegie Foundation does not find all the facts. For instance, in the Iowa case they investigated and found only that there was a scholarship fund and that a few students had employment with townspeople. What they did not discover was the slush fund — dollars and cents by the authorities to the students — and that which they didn't discover became the reason why Iowa was ejected from the Big Ten, although later reinstated.

As to these borderline cases referred to so much, it seems to be the fundamental contention of the Negative that we are considering only those cases at the borderline. They hold up this arm as a line between professionalism and amateurism, and say we consider only these cases on the borderline. Why do we? Because according to the Carnegie report 70 per cent of the cases are at the borderline. The Negative are wandering over there by the piano with the other fifteen; we are getting right down with the majority. That is why we are considering the borderline — because of the fact that most of the cases are there.

Then they charge that the mere violation of the law is not sufficient reason for its repeal. Of course not. We don't charge that. Every law is violated to a certain extent; but when a law causes frequent and numerous violations, and the violations as a whole work far more harm than would occur if the law did not exist, then we hold, and every legal authority in this world will hold with us, that such a law should be repealed. Only such casuists as Carnegie investigators and Wickersham reporters refuse to accept the conclusion to which their facts inevitably lead. We wonder why!

Let us consider the fundamental issues in this debate. They have narrowed down to just two or three. First, there is a need for a change. We have pointed this out by the fact that there is a hypocrisy under the present system. The Negative has not attempted to deny that this hypocrisy exists; they merely say that it isn't important. You can judge that for yourselves. Our second contention is that there is a need for a change, and a need that can be met only in the way we propose, because of the fact that there is an unfairness in the present situation. They merely say that the university does not owe them a living. We do not contend that they do. They charged, too, as the third issue of the debate that we did not consider the results. I think they misquoted me there. We advocate that schools be divided into two different classes: first, those retaining the gate receipts and abolishing the distinction in those sports; and those which abolish the gate receipts and therefore do not abolish the distinction. You see, the proposition is talking about only those sports which have admission fees. If you don't charge admission fees, you are dealing with an entirely different class of sports.

We took up all the different results at considerable length in pointing out just exactly how this system would work out, that it would mean that the standards would not be low, that the quality of pure sports for sport's sake would at last be realized. It would mean that you would have these fundamental requirements brought into existence, that you would have a restoration to an honest, truthful basis as to the competitive bidding idea.

Don't let yourselves be confused. There must be some rule somewhere. There must be a mutual rule. The question is, is that rule reasonable? At present the rule is not reasonable. It is down at nothing. We advocate making this rule reasonable, at a reasonable standard of what they earn; and, therefore, you can see that you ought to abolish the distinction and make this rule reasonable.

CHAIRMAN GARFF: The second rebuttal speaker for the Negative is Victor Rabinowitz.

SECOND NEGATIVE REBUTTAL
Victor Rabinowitz, Michigan

LADIES AND GENTLEMEN: The preceding speaker for the opposition attempted to reëstablish this connection between gate receipts and amateurism. I think that my colleague proved that there is no connection between gate receipts and amateurism. You have professionalism, or at least you had professionalism, in sports in which there are no gate receipts; on the other hand, you have gate receipts in sports at colleges at which there is no professionalism. Does not that break down the connection?

The causes of professionalism are not gate receipts. The causes of professionalism are an inordinate desire to win games, an intensified, improperly perhaps, amount of college rivalry. This does not depend on gate receipts. Colleges in England were anxious to win the annual Oxford-Cambridge crew race; therefore they had professionalism — not because there were gate receipts. The colleges in our early days in America were anxious to win their football games. They had professionalism regardless of the fact that there were no gate receipts. Professionalism does not come from gate receipts. Professionalism comes from a desire to win, regardless of what may cause that desire.

The gentlemen of the opposition have said that a law should be abolished if it causes frequent violations, and if the law itself causes greater harm than the abolition of the law. In the first place, this first point — "causes frequent violations" — as we have said, merely proves that the law should be enforced more strictly. If there are a good many violations, that means that we should have fewer violations and the law should be enforced, not abolished. Of course, if you abolish the law, you will have no violations; but that is hardly a very rational way of going about it. We can make everybody honest in that way by merely repealing all our laws.

They said, also, that the maintenance of the law causes greater harm than its abolition would. Well, we maintain — and the gentlemen of the opposition have not taken us up on this yet, in spite of the fact that the debate is almost over — that professionalism would cause much greater evils than any that may possibly exist today. We want honesty, too; we want truth. But we refuse to abolish a rule just because a few individuals are hypocritical about it, when the entire university is going to suffer from its abolition. My colleague and I both pointed this out in great detail in our constructive speeches, that the abolition of the rule will cause traffic in athletes it will cause the destruction of the objectives of amateurism, it will cause a lowering of academic standards, and it will cause a still greater emphasis upon football. The gentlemen of the opposition have not disputed any of these points; they have merely said that it causes some unfairness now. Intelligent application of that rule, as the third speaker for the Negative pointed out, can do away with most of those unfair practices that may exist at the present time. We refuse to abolish the rule merely because a few people are being treated unfairly, when you consider the fact that the entire university will be treated very unfairly if the rule is abolished.

The gentlemen of the opposition have said that we ought to give an athlete what he has actually earned, not a living, but what he has actually earned. It has been estimated that Albie Booth this last season at Yale University earned for Yale University a total of $50,000 a game. That means for eight games $400,000. Of course, some of those games are smaller than others. Suppose we reduce it to a smaller figure, — $250,000, — a quarter of a million. Will the gentlemen of the opposition dare to stand up here and tell you that we should pay Albie Booth a quarter of a million dollars, the amount that he earned, for playing football for Yale, for going to Yale and getting an education? That is what he actually earned. The gentlemen of the opposition will hardly do this. This is certainly excess.

CHAIRMAN GARFF: You will notice a feature of our program tonight is a critic decision. Those of you who will stay a little longer will hear an interesting criticism of the debate. The next speaker for the Affirmative is Mr. Conner.

SECOND AFFIRMATIVE REBUTTAL
J. Stillwell Conner, Northwestern

Albie Booth would be paid a quarter of a million dollars if the affirmative proposal would be accepted, so say the Negative. We want to point out that we do not mean to give an amateur such exorbitant sums. But if Albie Booth brings in a quarter of a million dollars, is Albie Booth to pay his own tuition; or is his mother (and I understand he does come from a poor family) to work hard to send him to school, and is Yale to exploit Albie Booth to such an extent that they will not even give him, say for instance, tuition, when a debater gets tuition or a man on the editorial staff gets tuition? We do not, and I want to point this out emphatically, intend to give an athlete as much as he earns, because he would not earn it if he did not play for the institution. If Albie Booth were to go out by himself and give an exhibition in Yale Stadium, he would not earn that much; but he most certainly does deserve tuition and the same consideration that other people who engage in activities deserve and get.

I pointed out in my constructive speech that under the present system there is hypocrisy, and the Negative do not take this into consideration to any great extent. It is their contention that an educational institution is fundamentally existent for one purpose — education. Do they mean to say that the maintaining of ideals, of honesty and truthfulness, is not as fundamental as getting an education? We maintain that these are the fundamental reasons for an institution, inspiring the undergraduate to ideals of honesty, truthfulness, and the other desirable social qualities.

It has become a fundamental issue in this debate whether or not amateurism is connected up with gate receipts, whether or not there could be professionalism where there are no gate receipts. Then they point out that in the past there were no gate receipts and there was no subsidizing. Under our plan if a school wants to subsidize, why should it go into the amateur class? It has nothing to gain. Why not subsidize honestly and truthfully and admit it, and not be subject, for instance, to exposure? So you see that while under the present distinction where a school is not in one of these two classes, professionalism might be connected up where there are no gate receipts, under our system there would be absolutely no sense for such procedure.

They say that under our system professionalism would cause greater evils than the present situation. Under the present system 70 per cent of the schools are hypocritical. The schools are either exploiting the youth, or they are lying; and they are deterring and undermining the fundamental roots of ideals and virtues in the undergraduate. Under our system we would have truthfulness, we would have uprightness, and we would have honesty above pseudo-amateurism. The Negative have pointed out that there is an ideal, and that this ideal is amateurism. They consider it fundamentally and inherently good. How do they account for the fact that this amateurism varies so much that it contradicts itself? We admit there are variations in any law. We admit that you can break a law and that you still should not do away with that law. But do our laws contradict each other? Do our laws fundamentally contradict each other? No. And yet, in the Michigan I. A. A. an amateur is any man who has never played on any team which is under the jurisdiction of a National Commission, whether that team be professional or amateur; and yet in this Western Conference such an amateur would be a professional.

Ladies and Gentlemen, it is the fundamental contention of the Affirmative that honesty is more important than amateurism, that anything that is inherently good cannot vary so much that it contradicts itself, such as the present distinctions do. I thank you.

CHAIRMAN GARFF: Nathan Levy will conclude the debate for the Negative.

THIRD NEGATIVE REBUTTAL
Nathan Levy, Michigan

LADIES AND GENTLEMEN: Concluding, the preceding speaker for the opposition has pointed out to you that amateurism varies so much that it contradicts itself. Well, now, what conclusion do you draw from that? That argument is not a conclusion for the abolition of the present distinction. It is an argument for a distinct codification of the rules. The conclusion they always draw is the abolition of the amateur-professional distinction, whether or not the argument goes to that conclusion. Let me remind you, gentlemen of the opposition, that in laws other than the amateur-professional law there are differences that contradict themselves from state to state; and if the gentlemen of the opposition realize what is in some states called a "felony" and which is in other states called a "misdemeanor," they will know exactly what it is that we mean by pointing out to you that there must be certain rules sometimes to match the needs of the locality. So long as the definition of the amateur is the same, allow the authorities to use their discretion to determine whether or not this slight, technical, borderline case involves a violation of the spirit of amateurism.

Now, the gentlemen of the opposition have talked to you about honesty and truthfulness. We have pointed out to you that we are as much in favor of honesty and truthfulness as the gentlemen of the opposition are, and that is honest and true. The gentlemen of the opposition forget this fact: that the mere existence of dishonesty and hypocrisy does not prove that the rule should be abolished. It might prove that the rule is a very good rule and should be even better enforced. That is what we believe with regard to the amateur-professional rule. The gentlemen of the opposition have talked to you about honesty and hypocrisy until I suppose that you believe that each one of these eighty-one institutions is nothing more or less than a breeding ground of dishonesty and hypocrisy; yet the matter of fact is, from the Carnegie report — the source that the gentlemen of the opposition have used — that among these institutions there was no institution that was helter-skelter violating every single provision of the amateur convention. These institutions were violating the amateur convention in one or two, or perhaps three, of its component parts with regard to one or two, or perhaps ten or maybe seventy-five, out of thousands of athletes competing for that school; and so the amount of dishonesty and the amount of hypocrisy that the gentlemen of the opposition have talked so much about is not so great when we consider the fact. And then, when we consider further the facts that the situation is actually cleaning up, when we consider that in less than two years fifteen of the institutions which were violating the amateur convention threw out these violations and have now become, as the gentlemen express it, Simon pure and lily white, we can see that the rule is being better enforced. We can see, in addition to that, that the Big Six, the Southern Conference, and the Southwestern Athletic Conference have actually begun to take this problem into consideration and to study the schools, to drive out the violations, and with that to drive out the hypocrisy.

We want to summarize our case just like this: The gentlemen of the opposition said that 70 per cent of the violations were on this line, and that 15 per cent were over there by the piano. What the gentlemen of the opposition are going to do when they abolish the amateur-professional distinction is to tear down the 70 per cent and bring it down to 1 per cent, and bring the vast field of professional practice over into intercollegiate athletics and then have the real evils of professionalism that the gentlemen of the opposition themselves recognize as existing.

The gentlemen of the opposition do not want to pay Albie Booth what he earns, if he earned it. They don't want to pay him a quarter of a million dollars. No. They want to pay him maybe his tuition. If they pay him maybe his tuition, then maybe they will pay him a little subsidy; maybe they will get him a job winding an electric clock. All of those things, they say, will be correct and all right. Well, the point is this: The job winding the electric clock will start out as a $20-a-week job. Mind you, there is no limit. Another school has a similar job. They will offer $25 or $30. It opens up the whole way to professional practice absolutely, and to unreasonableness; not to reasonableness, which the gentlemen of the opposition have not maintained on the platform before you.

The gentlemen of the opposition have not discussed excess. They have not discussed with you the results of the excess. They have considered only the individual, and have not taken into consideration the institution and all of those other individuals who do not play in intercollegiate games.

For these reasons we believe that the distinction between amateurism and professionalism should not be abolished. Thank you.

CHAIRMAN GARFF: The debate for this evening will be concluded by Mr. Blackmore.

THIRD AFFIRMATIVE REBUTTAL
John A. Blackmore, Northwestern

MR. CHAIRMAN, LADIES, AND GENTLEMEN: In just these few remaining moments, may I try to briefly summarize this case, as we proposed to do tonight, to see exactly what the Negative has offered in opposition to the proposal which we have made to you. Let's lay the cards on the table and see how the situation is made.

First of all, the first speaker of the Affirmative addressed you with the proposition that the present system is hypocritical. We would like to know, first of all, what the gentlemen of the opposition have told us. They say, "We believe in honesty and truthfulness. We believe in honesty. There are violations of many laws. Therefore, are we going to abolish laws altogether?" I say, my friends, that when a law is such that the violations are to the extent of 70 per cent, that it is just a promiscuous affair, that it is happening here and there, that it is just a matter of our catching them at it, there certainly must be something wrong with it. They give you no reason for holding the ideal, yet say simply that because they break the rule, we must keep it. It is not analogous with other laws. Now, we would like to know why this one is not. Let us see if we can find out. As far as that first issue is concerned — "hypocritical" — they absolutely admit the fact that there is hypocrisy in the present system. They say so and compare it to other laws.

Secondly, we find they do disagree on the fact of unfairness. I believe there is one thing where the gentlemen are so negative that they not only deny our argument, but one gentleman denied himself. First of all, he said that the university does not owe a man anything more than an education, owes him no living whatsoever. He says then again, at the conclusion of his speech, that "We refuse to abolish the rule because there are a few men who are not treated fairly, when there is a great student body in comparison." Now, my friends, is that not a direct inconsistency? He tells us that there is no unfairness to the athlete because he

418 THE WORKING PRINCIPLES OF ARGUMENT

deserves nothing more than an education; but yet he tells us that since he is treated unfairly, there is no reason for abolishing it. Let me call your attention to Princeton University, where out of a total of 332 men there were eight who, in addition to being scholars, were athletes, and were given scholarships. These men had been chosen on the basis of the Rhodes Scholarship, in open competition. After having been reprimanded, President Hibben tells us that he has revoked those scholarships. Now Princeton is lily white and Simon pure. Do they deny and forget the fact that those same men brought in $375,000 in the preceding autumn?

We only say, Ladies and Gentlemen, that these men deserve some special consideration, and if not such, at least as much, as is given to students in other activities. Thus, we say, there will not be competitive bidding; we will not have that difficulty, my friends. It is simply a matter of giving them the just deserts that they deserve, as we do people in other activities. Thus we will break down the distinction. I will remind you of one fact, that there is very little to be broken down except the little sham that is covering the hypocrisy. For we are professionals today — we are professional always — but we simply say to the public that we are not. Listen, my friends; we would like to break away this sham. We would like to present to the world, as much as possible, present to all people, honesty. Present yourself honest. My friends, that is all we want to give today. We have to break down the bars of hypocrisy; then we will have a breaking up of the distinction, whereas today it is really broken, but not granted.

As far as the results are concerned, they claim it would demoralize athletics. I would like to know if it would demoralize athletics to bring in the quality of honesty. Today they are dishonest. Now, certainly it would give a moral stimulus. In the second place, they tell us that it would have an effect upon the academic work in the university. We told you, my friends, that there is only one little clause that would be abolished. It is simply that they must admit their professionalism — that is, in the professional school. On the other hand, this amateur school may go on and give the desired emphasis it cares to to athletics.

My friends, listen. Other men receive their recompense for

debating, for journalism, for musical ability, and the like. We say, "Break down this distinction! It is unfair!" Unless our opponents have shown you that they can have the present system without hypocrisy; unless they have shown you that it is absolutely fair, Ladies and Gentlemen, fair to the athlete, to commercialize the game of football and not give him his just returns; unless they have shown you that the proposal this evening would bring into this situation undesirable results to outweigh its good effects; and, Ladies and Gentlemen, unless they have shown you these things, they have not shown that you should reject the affirmative proposal this evening.

CHAIRMAN GARFF: The coeds have been referred to rather facetiously tonight several times. Maybe after listening to this debate you may subscribe to the following limerick:

> A man convinced against his will
> Is of the same opinion still;
> A woman convinced against her will
> Is not convinced, nor is she still.

We have among us tonight a very fine gentleman who has been much in demand in judging debates. He has not been very conspicuous so far, but has been listening keenly to what has been going on. He has had a great deal of experience in the field of debate, and is well qualified to judge this contest. I take very great pleasure tonight in introducing the critic judge, Professor Mitchell from Lawrence College. Professor Mitchell.

CRITIC JUDGE
Professor Rexford S. Mitchell

LADIES AND GENTLEMEN: I was told some time ago of a lawsuit which was being tried before a justice of the peace. When the attorney for the plaintiff had just about concluded his argument, the justice said, "Counsel, it will not be necessary for you to proceed further." He said, "You have convinced me. I have made up my mind. I have my decision ready."

Of course, the attorney for the defense was immediately on his feet protesting, and said, "Your Honor, certainly you are going to hear what the defendant has to say."

The justice said, "No, I have made up my mind."

"But," the attorney said, "I insist that you hear the viewpoint of the defendant."

The justice said, "Well, I have my mind all made up; and if I listen to you, it might confuse me. So I guess I won't do it."

Whenever I am a judge in a debate as closely contested as this one is, and the argument waxes warmer and warmer, I wish that like the justice, I could halt the discussion before I am entirely confused; but since the rules of debate don't permit the judge that arbitrary power, we will have to do the best we can after having heard all that both sides have to say.

I want to say right now that I have enjoyed a great deal this splendid discussion of this interesting question. It is a question that I have never before heard discussed in formal debate.

I think you understand what I am asked to do this evening, and you want me to get to that. I am not asked to decide who is right about the matter of abolishing this distinction, but rather to tell you which of the two teams I think has done the better and more effective debating this evening. Of course, I realize that the debate ought to be judged as a whole, but I think perhaps I can make my decision more clear by resorting to the four conventional divisions in debate, those of analysis, constructive argument, delivery, and refutation.

Let's consider the matter of analysis just briefly. What is the purpose of analysis? It seems to me it is somewhat analogous to the opening statement in a lawsuit. The attorneys in the opening statement attempt to inform the judge and the jury with regard to the nature of the case, the issues involved, and just what they expect to show; and it seems to me that is about what we expect of debaters in analysis. The Affirmative, however, in this debate did not make it clear what the question meant to them from the start. I think we want to know right at the start just what the question means. It seems to me the men on the Affirmative were probably aware that the question was open to two interpretations, and that probably the place for presenting their interpretation was the first speech, and not the third. I think, however, that the Negative handled the matter well and that the Affirmative was probably wrong in the matter of the interpretation. I haven't had much time to think about it because it wasn't discussed, and I had other things to think about. Moreover, I feel that it is not necessary to decide the matter, since the Negative adopting the affirmative interpretation under protest, rather successfully handled the situation.

Now in constructive argument, after they have outlined their contentions we expect the debaters to go on through the use of authority and logical argument — in other words, evidence — and establish those contentions which they have laid out; and we expect them to do that, of course, in an organized, orderly fashion. We expect the argument and the speeches to be closely knit and easily followed. At the close of the constructive argument it seemed to me there were two major issues that had developed. First, it seemed to me that the question of whether the present situation was a cause for concern was an issue. I think it was the third speaker of the Affirmative who called it the "need" issue. It seemed to me involved under that were the questions of whether the present system is hypocritical, whether it leads to exploitation, whether the violations are minor borderline cases, and whether the conditions are actually improving. It seemed to me the other major issue was whether the abolition of this distinction would make matters better or worse. Outstanding among the minor issues perhaps under that was the matter of whether it lowered standards and whether there was a causal relation between gate receipts and amateurism.

At the close of the constructive speeches then, we had those two questions in mind as a result of the argument; and we had the evidence presented by both sides. It seemed to me, weighing that evidence — I don't want to take time to explain in detail just why; I know that you don't want to listen to so long a discussion — that the weight of argument at the close of the constructive speeches was with the Negative.

In the matter of delivery, I think, in view of the fact that this is a speech contest after all, that that ought to be a vital factor. I should like to say, first, that I think that both teams did some very effective speaking. All through the debate I compared the two teams on the basis of what I thought was effective speaking. I think considering the teams as a whole I should award a slight margin to the Negative.

Then there is the matter of refutation. I am going to deal with that as briefly as I can. It seems to me we want the debaters to do about four things in refutation. We have had these two major issues put before us and all these minor issues and the evidence presented by both sides in the constructive speeches. In the rebuttal it seems to me we want them first, to center their attention around the major issues that have developed. It is going to be a lot easier for us to settle these questions if they do center the argument around these major issues which have developed. In the second place we want them to point out the fallacies and the weaknesses in the evidence the other side has presented. In the third place we want them in what we call counter-refutation, to point out in what ways the attack on their evidence is not sound. And lastly, it seems to me, we want them to weigh what is left on each of these issues, so that we can decide what we think about them.

I thought there was a slight tendency on the part of some of the speakers to select several minor issues and to treat them as unrelated issues, without recognizing that every one of those minor issues was a part of one of the two major issues which had developed. It seemed to me it would have been much easier for us to think the thing through with them if they had organized it on a somewhat different basis. In other words, my thought is that perhaps they were unable at times to see the forest because of the trees.

I felt that at the close of the rebuttal the weight of argument was still with the Negative and you can tell by what I have said how I am going to vote. I want to say in conclusion that I have always made it a practice in judging a debate just as a final check to ask myself, "Now, if you could have either one of these two teams to represent your institution, which one would you take?" Now, of course, I should like to say that I would be tickled to death to have both of them. I think they are two splendid teams, and I should be glad to have them represent our institution; but I think, on the whole, the Negative has done slightly the better work this evening. Much as I hate to disappoint a Northwestern audience, I am casting my vote for the Negative.

APPENDIX B

DEONTOLOGY, OR THE MORAL OBLIGATION OF MEDICINE[1]

By MALCOLM L. HARRIS

Delivered by the President of the American Medical Association at the eightieth annual session of the Association, Portland, Oregon, July 9, 1929.

It is difficult to state just when medicine first assumed a definite status in human affairs, but its origin may be traced to the primal sympathy of man with man. Sympathy is the quality of being affected by the state of another with feelings corresponding in kind. Sympathy is one of the most effective of the emotions and, like all emotions, is an antecedent of desire. Emotion is an attribute of mankind and in a primitive form is found even in animal life. With the advent of the emotions of sympathy and pity, the heart of man was inspired with a desire to relieve human suffering and pain. Desire has an object in view which is the end to be attained; desire, therefore, may be said to be the impulse, the motivating power, or the spark that starts action.

In the mind of primitive man, emotions and desires were quite simple in their nature and were concerned almost entirely with the necessity of self-preservation; they lacked, therefore, the more complex and highly intellectual character of modern civilization and the present advanced state of knowledge.

Having little or no knowledge of the phenomena of nature with which he was constantly surrounded, man sought an explanation in the supernatural. All objects were supposed to be peopled with invisible spirits, with a controlling influence for good or for ill

[1] Reprinted from *Contemporary Speeches*, O'Neill, J. M., and Riley, F. K., by permission of the Century Company.

which had to be invoked or propitiated. It was thought that all nature was filled with a mysterious force which inhabited persons as well as things. To this mysterious force was assigned the nature of an invisible spirit, and a distinction was made between the spirits that exerted a benign and those that exerted a malign influence. The subtle force that emanated from the benign spirit brought health and happiness and success and was called "mana," while the malign force emanating from the evil spirits was destructive to health, life, and property, and was called "miasma."

The influence of the good spirits, the benign mysterious force or mana, was invoked either by supplication or by various forms of sorcery, while attempts were made to propitiate or conciliate the malign force, or miasma, by incantations and the utterance of magical words for enchantment or exorcism. In order that the tribe or group should be successful in the hunt or war or in the daily affairs of life, it was necessary that it be in touch with the good force or mana and at the same time shun the miasma, and this was supposed to be accomplished by having in the tribe one or more members who kept themselves so absolutely aseptic and pure that they could have access to mana without danger. These men became priests, and priests and physicians were often one.

As disease was supposed to be due to miasma, or to the possession of the body by an evil spirit or demon, these priests sought to exorcise the disease by magical incantations. In this way medicine and religion may be said to come in contact or to have had a common origin. Gradually these mysterious forces were deified, and innumerable gods arose possessed of supernatural powers, each tribe often having its own particular god or gods.

Medicine and religion now parted company. Those who followed medicine devoted themselves to the study of disease and the relief of human suffering, while those who followed religion devoted themselves to ritualistic forms of worship of their various gods. The priests by the development of an emotional culture instilled into the benighted minds of the people the belief that they were able to invoke or propitiate the gods, and this emotional culture became the greatest force in maintaining unity in the tribe or nation.

Medicine had a much more difficult task before it in the relief of pain, suffering and disease. In an age when every object in nature, every incident in life, seemed full of deified presences, medicine was dominated by a belief in a pantheon of gods, both great and small, who were held responsible for all things mysterious.

Since no knowledge of the fundamental sciences on which an intelligent conception of disease must ever rest was in existence, it is not surprising that the resources of the physician were limited to magic, sorcery and incantations to drive out the evil spirits that had taken possession of the body, or by supplications to invoke the help of the good gods in special diseases.

Knowledge in its essence consists of conditioned reflexes and was of slow acquisition by man. Without a knowledge of human anatomy and physiology, medicine could make but little progress. The study of human anatomy was greatly hindered by a fear of that mysterious force which was called miasma and which was destructive to health and life. "This was a subtle force that radiated from certain objects and persons bringing disease, death, bad luck and drought to all whom it touched. It was directed against all things and people associated with death such as the corpses of men and animals and blood" (Denison). This superstition was so powerful that, even after all these centuries of supposed enlightenment, there are people who faint at the sight of blood and who fear to touch a dead body.

Even at a later age, religious prejudice placed a ban on the dissection of the human body; dissection was often prohibited by law, so that only a few who were undismayed by religious fear surreptitiously dared to touch a human corpse for the purpose of studying anatomy.

How imperfect and untrained were the powers of observation of these early physicians is well shown by their fanciful and fantastic drawings of anatomy as they supposed it to be. The liver from its great size, its richness in blood, and its location in the center of the body was regarded as the most important organ. It was thought to be the seat of life, of the mind and even of the soul. As the seat of life, or soul, the liver became the divine element in the sacrificial offerings and was studied with great care, its markings and lobes playing an important part in divination.

Closely following on the art of divination came a belief in the supposed influence of the heavenly bodies on man's welfare, and astronomy and astrology were eagerly studied both by physicians and by priests. The mysterious forces that ruled the sun, moon, and planets were the same that controlled the affairs, the disposition and the fate of man. The reading of the horoscope was practiced not alone by quacks and charlatans but also by philosophers and priests.

Under the influence of the remarkably constructive imagination of the Greek philosophers, who were often physicians as well, astrology degenerated into superstition, a superstition that has persisted even to the present day. In Greece, medicine became still further separated from religion and the priests, and a closer relation was established between medicine and philosophy; in fact, many of the great philosophers were physicians. The great impression that Greece made on medicine was due to the philosopher-physicians. It was not so much the wonderful discoveries in medicine they made as it was the introduction of philosophical reasoning and vivid imagination that led to constructive thinking. It was one of these great philosopher-physicians, Empedocles, who introduced the theory of the four elements, fire, air, earth, and water, of which in varying quantities all bodies were supposed to be composed. It was the existence of these four elements in due equilibrium in the body that constituted health, while disease consisted in a disturbance of this relation.

Following this theory of the four elements was that of the four essential qualities of heat and cold, moisture and dryness, which formed the basis of the humoral theory of disease, which dominated medicine for many centuries. Notwithstanding the fact that these theories were erroneous, they marked a great step forward since in them is found an attempt to analyze matter and to attribute the cause of disease to other than the mysterious influence of malign deities or evil spirits. The Greeks were the first to transcend mysticism, superstition, and ritual and to grasp the conception of medicine as an art based on accurate observation and to recognize that diseases are only a part of the processes of nature.

Greek medicine as expounded by Hippocrates and later by Galen ruled the practice of the art for hundreds of years, but during this time, owing to a lack of knowledge of the fundamental sciences on which sound practice must always rest, little progress was made. Although Galen gave public lectures on anatomy, he lamented the fact that religious prejudice had prevented him from ever having dissected a human body, his anatomy having been learned largely from dissections of pigs and apes.

With the fall of Rome came the darkest page in the history of civilization. The European world became obsessed by a religious fervor that diverted men's thoughts from all things related to the physical or material body and caused them to be concerned with death, judgment, heaven and hell, and the salvation of the soul.

This period of religious prejudice and intolerance, which lasted for nearly a thousand years, left a trail of blood following in the wake of the numerous crusades and was marked by deeds of man's inhumanity to man done in the name of Christianity. Medicine, as practically all other sciences, languished during these dark ages and made almost no progress. The land was overrun by traveling quacks and charlatans, who preyed on the credulity and ignorance of the people. What was left of real medicine fell into the hands of the monks, who kept the flickering light burning.

It is a curious and remarkable fact that, while Christianity was forging its way from the West to the East, the vast riches of the Greek literature probably would have been lost to the world had it not been for the barbarian hordes of Arabia. The Arabs, spurred on by a firm belief in the power of their great god Allah, started out to conquer the world. Egypt was the first to fall before them. Here they found in the great libraries of Alexandria the marvelous writings of the Greeks. Inspired by a desire for knowledge, they translated many of the works of the Greek philosophers and physicians into Arabic, and the libraries of Alexandria were burned.

Before the Arabs were stopped in their mad rush they had conquered all of northern Africa, Greece, Spain, and Sicily.

In the thirteenth and fourteenth centuries the little spark of medical knowledge that had survived the dark ages was fanned into a flame in southern Italy, and there arose a great medical school that became famous. With the advent of this school may be dated the renaissance of medicine.

With the increase in the knowledge of anatomy, physiology, and chemistry that came from the Arabs, medicine made slow progress, but for several centuries the real cause of disease remained a mystery until the epoch-making works of Pasteur, Lister, and Koch were given to the world. From this time on medicine assumed the dignity of a real science and it made more progress during the following twenty-five or thirty years than it had made in as many centuries next preceding.

The purpose of this brief and sketchy review of the history of the evolution of medicine is to bring to mind anew the great struggle it had to undertake before it could emerge from the darkness of ignorance into the light of modern science. It survived the magic and incantation of the sorcerers, the ritualism of the priests, the prejudices, intolerance and tabus of religion, the superstitions of the astrologists and the divinators, the fraudulent representations of the quacks and charlatans, and last but not least the almost innumerable pathies, isms, and cults that sprang up to prey on the people.

The arch of the science of medicine may now be completed. The first stone of the arch is anatomy, beginning in Alexandria and carried forward by the Arabs and Italians. The second is chemistry, born in Egypt and nourished by the Arabs. The third is physiology, beginning with the pneuma of Galen, the spiritus of the Latins, which lingered long until the knowledge of anatomy and chemistry led to an understanding of function. Fourth may be mentioned pathology, starting with the humoral pathology of the Greeks and ending with the cellular pathology of Virchow. The last, or keystone, of the arch is bacteriology, developed by the genius of Pasteur, Lister, and Koch. On this solid arch of the science of medicine is builded the art of practice.

The practice of medicine may be said to consist of the making of a diagnosis and the proposal or execution of measures or means for the prevention, relief or cure of the suffering, ailment or deformity of another, either physical or mental. Any method or system of practice not based on this solid foundation of science cannot be otherwise than fallacious.

Medicine has played a most important rôle in the evolution of civilization. As marvelous and important as have been the discoveries and inventions of the physical sciences, the common inconveniences that would result from their loss would be small indeed compared with those which would result from the loss of modern medical science. Civilization never could have advanced to its present state of development had it not been for medical science, and if the world were to be deprived of the benefit and protection of medical science the great cities would be depopulated by disease and pestilence, and civilization would be set back hundreds of years.

Civilization of man in years is as but yesterday, while his instincts and emotions have dwelt with him for untold ages. While education has enabled man to subjugate his instincts and beliefs to reason, there are still those who are governed and controlled by superstition and primitive instincts.

Superstition is a belief founded on irrational feelings. These feelings exhibit the elements of fear and of reverence for the occult and the supernatural. All superstitions are founded on ignorance and are characterized by beliefs in omens, signs, and charms, or false religious rites, or an undue proneness to accept the improbable and absurd claims of medical healers. Medical healers of one kind or another have flourished from the earliest times down to the present day: exorcisers of devils and demons, priests and saints with their ritualistic formulas, sorcerers with their magical incantations, mesmerists and hypnotists, the king's touch, quacks and charlatans of all kinds, and last but not least faith healers, such as Dowie, Eddy, and Coué. "The strength of all such healers lies in the faith of their disciples; so long as confidence is supreme, treatment brings peace and security even though death results" (Haggard). Many of the so-called systems of medicine have bloomed and flourished for a day only to fade before the inexorable truths of medical science. As fast as one fad has had its day, another arises to take its place. All of them, however, have the same basic principle, that of faith, the same as existed centuries ago in the magic or ritualistic formulas of the ancient priests.

The influence of the mind on the bodily activities is not to be denied or ignored, but the danger consists of relying on it in the presence of actual disease which it cannot benefit and which, if not properly treated, may result disastrously to the patient. The practice of medicine, therefore, should be in the hands only of those who are qualified by having a comprehensive knowledge of the fundamental sciences.

Attention has already been called to the important rôle that medicine has played in making possible man's present state of civilization. That it was rather slow in making itself felt is due to the fact that man's primitive instincts and desires had to be satisfied first, and that these had to be developed and elaborated before sufficient knowledge could be acquired to permit scientific medicine to come into being.

The commercial world is now recognizing the great value of medicine in the industries and to human welfare. Commercial, industrial and agricultural pursuits cannot thrive and maintain progress without the continued support of medicine. Man has not yet reached a state of material development that will permit him to harness the forces of nature and bid them to do his will. Man power and brain function are still necessary to human existence, and the essential factor in the maintenance of these is health. The great commanders of industry, the great leaders of nations, have come to realize more than ever before that progress and prosperity depend on the health of the people and that health can be secured and maintained only by the active coöperation of the medical profession. It is a realization of this general truth that induced industries to install medical departments to care for injured and sick employees. Not only is the provision of such a medical service by the industries a humane act, but it has been the means of adding millions of dollars to the industries and to the employees by rehabilitating the injured and by preventing or diminishing time lost on account of illness.

As contributing to the health and happiness of mankind, medicine occupies preëminently the first rank. It practically has banished from the intelligent world such dread diseases as the plague, typhoid, smallpox, cholera, yellow fever, and tetanus; it has reduced the mortality from tuberculosis 60 per cent; it has cut the death rate in children under 5 years of age in two several times and has added fully ten years or more to the average life expectancy. All these have been accepted by the people with an equanimity amounting almost to indifference. Little thought is given to the thousands of men whose lives have been spent and, indeed, often sacrificed in toil and labor endeavoring to wrest from nature the great truths that have made these living conditions possible.

Has it ever occurred to the people that not a single truth has been added to the science of medicine by the hordes of quacks and charlatans, by the faith healers, by the magic venders, by the drugless practitioners and cultists, who by an advertising propaganda have spread broadcast tales of their marvelous knowledge and skill? It is not difficult to understand how uneducated and unintelligent persons with primitive beliefs and superstitions in the mysterious and occult can be led astray by such claims, but it is quite a curious psychologic phenomenon when those who are otherwise intelligent become obsessed by an unreasonable credulity in matters concerning their health.

In attempting to find a solution for this curious phenomenon, one is forced into a discussion of the subject of civilization. Civilization is a term in common use but difficult to define accurately in words. It is a stage in the evolution of man characterized by the development of his intellectual and cultural faculties. There is no sharp line of demarcation, however, between the savage and civilized man, as the change is a gradual one. In the progressive evolution of man, not all of his faculties have developed at a uniform rate. Therefore, practically all stages of civilization are found existing at the same time, the minds of a few representing the highest point of development while that of the masses scale down to the lowest. It is those in whom the primitive instincts and emotions and desires are not yet subjugated by reason who forsake scientific medicine for the mysteries of the cultists and the innumerable varieties of faith healers.

The intellectual, reasoning, cultural, ethical, and emotional faculties do not all develop uniformly even in the same individual, and it is this variation in the growth of the faculties that creates character and individuality. One may be highly intellectual and cultured and yet be deficient in his reasoning powers or in his ethical and emotional senses.

Medicine is the first profession in the world to formulate and adopt principles of ethics as a guide to rules of conduct. These principles have withstood the vicissitudes of a changing world for thousands of years. They are as sound in principle today as they were in the beginning, and they have been a constant and ever-present inspiration to the profession. These principles were dictated in a spirit of humanity for the benefit and protection of the sick and suffering who placed themselves in the care of physicians.

The medical profession has been chided of late by the commercial world for its adherence to its principles of ethics. It is meet to mention, however, that the ethical and ideal faculties of the commercial world have been held in check by the superdevelopment of the faculty of cupidity, which seems to justify the means to the end. It is chiefly the press that has raised its voice the loudest against the principle of medical ethics that places a tabu on advertising by the physician. It is readily admitted that the lifting of the ban against advertising by the physician would result in a great financial gain to the press, but at the expense of demoralizing the profession and removing the most powerful barrier that now protects the public against the quack, the charlatan, and the faker.

Ethics is concerned with the principles that help to determine rules of conduct. Medical ethics has for its purpose the protection of the people and the creation of an idealism in the profession. Divested of all excess verbiage, it means that the conduct of physicians at all times shall be honest, honorable, fair and just to all concerned, the patient, the public, the profession and to one another. The terms "honorable," "fair" and "just" do not admit of exact reasoning but must be judged by the consensus of prevailing public opinion based on a knowledge of all the factors involved.

Attention has already been directed to the value of medicine as an essential factor in the development of the present state of civilization. The economic value of medical service to the individual may not be discussed briefly. By economics is meant the science that investigates the production, distribution, and consumption of wealth, or the material means of satisfying human desires. The terms "wealth" and "value" are frequently used in connection with economics; therefore one should have a clear conception of their meaning. The simplest conception of wealth perhaps is the power of one commodity to command other commodities in exchange, while value refers to the ratio of exchange. Commodities tend to exchange in proportion to the cost of production or the toil and labor that enters in. This all applies to concrete commodities; but medical service is not a commodity in the sense here used and therefore it has no intrinsic value. Its value is dependent on its utility or its fitness to satisfy human needs or desires. There is a difference between a need and a desire. The former may be a necessity for continued existence while the latter may but contribute to one's pleasure or comfort. There are degrees, therefore, of value, depending on the character and the necessity of the services rendered.

There is another factor, however, which must always be taken into consideration in placing a value on medical service, and that is the question of ethics. Ethics has decreed that medicine is a humane profession and that the physician must deal justly and fairly and equitably with all. The governing factor, then, in the determination of the value of medical service or the fees charged by the physician must be the economic status of the patient.

This leads to the final point of my theme, which is the subject of deontology, or the science of moral obligation and duty. I have endeavored to show not only that the knowledge given to the world by medical science has been instrumental in enabling civilization to reach its present state of development, but also that without a continuance of this knowledge civilization would crumble and the world be set back hundreds of years. The medical profession alone is in possession of this knowledge, and the qualified physician alone is competent to care for the sick. The practice of medicine, therefore, is a natural monopoly in the hands of the profession. Every monopoly, whether it is a natural or an artificial one, has a distinct obligation to the public to make its services available to all the people. The obligation of the profession in this respect is absolute since there is none other to whom it can be delegated. As the profession is an essential factor in the maintenance, progress and prosperity of the social organization, society owes an obligation and duty to it to enable it to progress and prosper in like manner. The moral obligation, therefore, becomes a reciprocal one.

Medicine differs from all other lines of human endeavor in that it deals with life and health, with human suffering and ills, which give to it a humanitarian purpose that has been the most cohesive force binding the profession together in a united group, and this cohesive force has its origin in the emotions. Emotions are fundamental attributes of the human mind; but if the unity of a group depends on the permanent action of an emotion, some means must be created that will cause the minds of its members to react to the emotion in the definite manner desired. The means to this end are found in the principles of ethics and the noble purposes adopted and proclaimed by the American Medical Association. These constitute an emotional culture which should enter into and form a part of every physician's life. The American Medical Association is the one organization that every physician who lives and honors his profession should be united with, and its ethical principles should be emotionalized as the only means of giving reality to its ideas and its ideals.

INDEX